13th April '61

RETURN TO LIBRARY

DAILY EXPRESS.

THE SUPREME COMMAND
1914–1918

VOLUME TWO

The Author at his desk in 2 Whitehall Gardens

LORD HANKEY

THE SUPREME COMMAND

1914-1918

The weight of this sad time we must obey,
Speak what we feel, not what we ought to say.
The oldest hath borne most; we, that are young,
Shall never see so much, nor live so long.

SHAKESPEARE, *King Lear*, Act v, sc. 3

VOLUME TWO

WITHDRAWN
☐ DESELECTED
☐ LOST
☐ DAMAGED
☐ MISSING (INV.)
☐ OTHER

London
GEORGE ALLEN AND UNWIN LIMITED

D
546
H43
v. 2

FIRST PUBLISHED IN 1961

This book is copyright under the Berne Convention. Apart from any fair dealing for the purpose of private study, research criticism or review, as permitted under the Copyright Act, 1956, no portion may be reproduced by any process without written permission. Inquiries should be addressed to the publisher.

George Allen and Unwin Ltd., 1961

PRINTED IN GREAT BRITAIN
in 12 on 13 point Fournier type
BY UNWIN BROTHERS LIMITED
WOKING AND LONDON

WARD CHIPMAN LIBRARY
U.N.B. IN SAINT JOHN

CONTENTS

ILLUSTRATIONS

P*

THE WAR COMMITTEE

CHAPTER XLI

REORGANIZATION OF THE
SUPREME COMMAND

'For armies can signify but little abroad unless there be counsel and wise management at home.' (CICERO, *Offices*, c. 22.)

By general agreement the new War Committee, which exercised in the main, though not exclusively, the functions of the Supreme Command from November 1915, until the fall of the first Coalition Government in December 1916, was a marked improvement upon its predecessors. In the first place it was at the outset much smaller than the Dardanelles Committee or the earlier War Council, though not so small as Asquith had wished. He announced the new organization in the House of Commons on November 2nd, and some extracts from his speech deserve attention:

I am told there is great anxiety in some quarters, as to what is called the higher direction of the war. . . . Some people seem to think that a Cabinet of twenty-one members is incompetent to conduct the affairs of a great Empire in times of emergency like this. Mr Pitt, when he carried on the great war against France, had, I think, a Cabinet of seven or nine, but the exiguity in size of that Cabinet did not prevent him from committing great blunders, or from suffering from many strokes of ill-fortune. For myself, I do not think there is any numerical specific against either want of foresight or want of good luck. . . . I do not propose to change the size of the Cabinet; but, of course, there is a great deal to be said in time of war for having one, or it may be more—at any rate one—comparatively small body of men who will deal with the daily exigencies of the State. . . . I do not think any Prime Minister has ever, to a greater degree than I have done, delegated work, which in normal conditions is done by the Cabinet as a whole, to committees and smaller bodies. . . .

In particular, we have had since a very early period of the war a body fluctuating in number from time to time, and which has varied in name. Sometimes it has been called a 'War Council', sometimes a 'War Committee'. Sometimes it has gone by other designations. It is a body to which either general questions of State or questions of strategy in particular areas and arenas have, by the consent of the Cabinet, been referred. I have come to the conclusion . . . that it is desirable to maintain that system, but to limit still further the number of the body to whom what I may call the strategic

conduct of the war is from time to time referred. I think . . . that the Committee, or by whatever name it may be called, should be a body of not less than three, and perhaps not more than five in number, but with this important proviso that, whether it be three or five, it should, of course, have power to summon to its deliberations and to its assistance the particular Minister concerned with the particular Department whose special knowledge is needed, or is desirable, for the determination of each issue as it arises. I think further . . . that the relations between any such body and the Cabinet should be of an elastic kind. At the same time, it should be understood that the Cabinet, which, as a body, has the ultimate responsibility for questions of policy, shall be kept, not only constantly informed of the decisions and actions of the Committee, but in all questions which involve a change, or a new departure in policy, should be consulted before decisive action is taken. It is only on these lines that you can successfully conduct a war like this.

I entirely agree with those who say that it is very undesirable, and leads to delay and often to confusion, that decisions which have to be taken, very often at short notice, should not become effective until they are referred to the Cabinet as a whole. That is perfectly true. I think that a Committee such as I have indicated ought to be clothed with power to take such decisions, and to act upon them. On the other hand, I am very jealous of the maintenance of collective Cabinet responsibility for large changes and new departures in policy; but I believe that in practice it will be found perfectly capable of working the two things together. . . . I attach very great importance, first of all, to a more complete and intimate co-ordination between the staffs of the Allied Powers. . . . We should also have a more intimate and regular interchange by some form of combination with the staffs, not only of the War Office and the Admiralty, but with those who conduct our diplomatic affairs. It is impossible to carry on these things in watertight compartments. You must have co-ordination of contact—close, constant, practical, continuing.[1]

On the same occasion, Carson, who had lately resigned from the Cabinet, made a very notable contribution to the debate, in which with trenchant criticism he picked out the weak points of the new War Committee and forecast the lines on which, some fourteen months later, the Supreme Command was to be shaped. Note the following passages:

What is wanted for carrying on a war is a small number—the smaller the better—of competent men sitting, not once a week, but from day to day, with the best expert advisers they can get, working out the problems that arise in the course of the war. You want the best military staff you can get, and so far as I could see when I went to the Cabinet and up till very recently

---

[1] *Parliamentary Debates* 1915, Commons, Vol. LXXV, col. 520 *sq.*

there was no staff at all, or at least I never saw their productions. It is quite true that during the last few weeks I was there there was a staff who furnished us with certain information, but in my opinion the staff should not be a scratch lot. .... The whole question is one of concentrating responsibility, and if you have three or five men, I care not which, who are to be accountable to the Cabinet, or for whom the Cabinet is taking responsibility, you will only be back on the same system. It is quite clear that, if you are a member of a Cabinet, either of two things must happen: either you must be satisfied to be a nonentity and endorse whatever is put before you, or you must get exactly the same information and go through exactly the same reasoning and sifting that your Committee of three or five have done. .... I would much prefer to see the right hon. Gentleman exercise the right he has of cutting his Cabinet down even to five or six from twenty-two, placing upon those five or six the whole burden of responsibility, and then the country would know that there was no divided responsibility, or anything of the kind. ....

I do not believe in a Committee of the Cabinet, then a Cabinet, and then an Inner Cabinet. The Committee decides something. The Cabinet knows nothing about it. Sometimes it says ditto, and sometimes it may have a discursive talk over why this or that was done. Then, all of a sudden, you see in the paper, even after your Committee and after your Cabinet, that the offer of some important territory has been made to some foreign Power for a particular purpose. You wonder where on earth the offer came from, and you find, I suppose, that it is a process evolved from the Inner Cabinet. I press upon the right hon. Gentleman once more to consider whether when he is making this change he should not make it in the direction I have indicated and concentrate the responsibility upon the best small Cabinet he can choose.[1]

For the next thirteen months the Supreme Command was carried on on the principles enunciated by Asquith. On the very next day (November 3rd) the new War Committee met for the first time, and was attended only by the Prime Minister, Kitchener and Balfour. No secretary was present, but (as in the case of the first meeting of the Dardanelles Committee) the decisions were communicated to me for record and action immediately after, namely, that Kitchener should proceed to the East to examine the whole situation in that region.[2] Thereafter I was present at all the War Committee's meetings and was usually allowed to take with me an assistant secretary (Swinton or Dally Jones), as it was essential to have an understudy, and at times the meetings were so frequent as to be almost beyond the capacity of one man to keep pace with. After the first meeting of the new War Committee the usual process of rapid growth set in. Before the second meeting

---

[1] *Parliamentary Debates, ibid.,* col. 533, 534.   [2] *vide Macedonia,* I, p. 45.

Grey and Lloyd George had become regular members, bringing the number up to five, which Asquith had announced as the maximum. Within ten days the Committee was again enlarged by the addition of Bonar Law and McKenna. It was not until long after that I learned the reason of this increase to the numbers, which is given in the following extract from my diary for October 7, 1920:

... Bonar Law also told me yesterday how when Asquith was forming his War Committee in the autumn of 1915, he overheard him telling McKenna on the front Government bench of the House of its composition and his own name was not included. Meanwhile the Unionist Whips had got hold of it and were making a row with the Liberal Whips, with the result that a little later in the afternoon Bonar received a message from Asquith asking him to see him. When he arrived Asquith said he had sent for him to ask him to join the War Committee! Bonar then told him what he had heard on the bench.

On November 11th, Asquith informed the House that, during the temporary absence of Kitchener, the Committee was to consist of five members—the Prime Minister, the First Lord, the Minister of Munitions, the Secretary of State for the Colonies and the Chancellor of the Exchequer. If Kitchener and Grey, who was always present, are added, the number of Ministers in normal times was seven, or if we include the First Sea Lord and Chief of the Imperial General Staff, who always attended regularly after the first meeting (whether as members or expert assessors was never laid down) the real number was nine, and later on other Ministers became to all intents and purposes regular attendants, notably Curzon as Chairman of the Shipping Control Board, and Austen Chamberlain as Secretary of State for India, and later as Chairman of the Man-Power Board in addition. The principle of restricted numbers was not adhered to for very long.

The period of the Dardanelles Committee had been to a great extent transitional, and the War Committee inherited the reforms that had already been accomplished. Even Carson had had to admit, even if grudgingly, that the General Staff had been reorganized. There was already a much improved service of information, both on the military and diplomatic side, and on all important matters with which the Committee had to deal regular appreciations were submitted by the staffs of the departments.

The new Committee met very frequently, at first not daily, as might have been desirable if the members had had the time, but every two or three days. Between November 3rd and the end of the year the Com-

mittee met twenty times, in spite of the fact that during that period there were several international conferences, which took most of its members to France, and that time had to be provided for Cabinet meetings. Complete records were kept in manuscript, and all the appropriate documents were appended to the Minutes, so far as they were obtainable. One development of great importance was inaugurated by Asquith. Copies of the conclusions of the War Committee were henceforward circulated to all members of the Cabinet, except in matters of exceptional secrecy, when they were communicated verbally. If a member of the Cabinet disagreed with any conclusion, it was open to him to raise the matter at the Cabinet, and occasionally the Cabinet reversed or modified the conclusions of their War Committee. This was a wise provision on the whole, as it deprived members of the Cabinet of any sense of grievance, but the privilege was occasionally abused. The War Committee met so regularly, and could so easily be summoned at short notice in emergency, that all excuse for any 'Inner Cabinet', disappeared, and for a long time these irregular informal group meetings of Ministers ceased. Thus, not only did the War Committee provide a greatly improved organization for exercise of the Supreme Command, but even the lumbering Cabinet system was deprived of some of its most glaring defects. Nevertheless the greatest weakness of the new system was this existence, side by side with the War Committee, of the old-time Cabinet, working to no agenda, and keeping no records. For, while the Cabinet knew exactly what the War Committee was doing, the converse did not apply. Ministers, being members of both bodies, of course possessed a general knowledge of what the Cabinet had decided, but this knowledge was often of a vague and contradictory kind. The previous decisions were not on record for the secretary to produce at the psychological moment in the discussion, as were those of the War Committee. At a very early stage of the Committee's career, the defects of the system were to make themselves felt in a painful way, and to bring us to the verge of a great disaster. And later on, as the growing needs of the war tended to absorb more and more of the resources of the nation; as the naval and military operations became inextricably intermingled with what in less exacting times were civilian matters; as, in consequence, the War Committee's range of activity became insensibly widened in scope, the inconvenience of the system of dual responsibility made itself more and more felt—until a reformer came and swept it away.

Another serious defect was that, with the sole exception of the Prime

Minister, all the members of the War Committee were administering great Departments of State. The frequent meetings of the Committee and the Cabinet took up so much of their time that Ministers found it difficult to devote sufficient time and attention to their departmental and Parliamentary work. In the long run this told on nerves and tempers and was an important contributory cause of the eventual breakdown of the system.

Although the War Committee was smaller than the Dardanelles Committee, the personnel had not changed very materially. The principal actors sustained the same parts as before. The most important absentee was Churchill who, shortly after the announcement of the new Committee, had resigned office; he eventually decided to take up military duty and was given command of a battalion in France.

Soon after the inauguration of the War Committee Kitchener disappeared for a time from its deliberations on a visit to the Dardanelles. Probably some members of the Committee hoped that he would never sit with them again in the position of War Secretary, for he had many critics among his colleagues. During the crisis which brought the War Committee into being, the feeling against the great Field-Marshal had been very strong. He was as incomprehensible to his colleagues as they were to him. They claimed that he was not a good administrator. Above all, they were convinced that he never told them all the facts, a belief which was not without some foundation. When Kitchener went to visit the Dardanelles there was an idea in Asquith's mind, and I think in Kitchener's own mind, that he might remain there as Commander-in-Chief of all the military forces outside France. During his absence Asquith took charge of the War Office, and he had in mind to hold the post, not as a mere *locum tenens*, but sufficiently long to carry out a drastic reorganization. During Kitchener's absence, other plans were canvassed for his future; 'when the cat's away the mice will play' but, when he came home on December 1st, he settled the matter quietly and effectively by asking Robertson to be Chief of the Imperial General Staff. Robertson[1] replied by formulating conditions; the War Committee was to be the supreme authority but no military operations were to be discussed without the General Staff having the first word even on suggestions made by members of the Committee; all operational orders were to be signed and issued by its Chief on the authority of the War Committee and not of the Army Council. Eventually he and Kitchener came to terms as part of a general rearrangement of the higher military

[1] Robertson, I, p. 168.

commands and, in fact, they worked in perfect harmony until Kitchener's death.

French, wearied by his immense exertions and responsibilities, and less suited to the present phase of trench warfare than to a war of movement, left the command of the Expeditionary Force with a peerage and was appointed Field-Marshal Commanding-in-Chief Home Forces. Haig took his place as Commander-in-Chief in France. Kiggell left his post as sub-Chief of the General Staff at the War Office to become Haig's Chief of Staff. Archibald Murray who during his brief sojourn at the War Office had done admirable work in reorganizing the General Staff—a sort of John the Baptist to Robertson—was given the chief command in Egypt. The importance of this command was shortly after considerably increased, but at the moment Murray was entitled to feel badly treated though he accepted the situation like the good soldier and loyal man he was. Henry Wilson, who had been liaison officer at French headquarters, might have become Chief of the Imperial General Staff then, instead of later, but for the mistrust he had awakened at the time of 'the Curragh incident' just before the war; he had to content himself with the command of an Army Corps.

Robertson took up his appointment on December 23rd. He was a self-made man, and in the profession where of all others this was at that time most difficult. He had risen from the ranks. Before the war he had been head of the Army Staff College and Director of Military Operations. It was in this latter capacity that I first came across him. It was just after I became Secretary to the Committee of Imperial Defence, and it was at a meeting of the Home Ports Defence Committee, of which I was *ex officio* chairman, and he the senior military member. He was sitting on my left, the senior naval member being on my right. It was Robertson's first attendance at the Committee. Almost immediately he sat down he turned round in his chair, half left, and took no part in the proceedings, showing thereby how much he disapproved of so humble a person as myself being in the chair! I determined not to quarrel, and conducted the business without taking any notice. Before the next meeting I paid him a visit, and, without referring to his attitude at the previous meeting, asked his advice as a senior officer and more experienced man on how to approach the questions on the Agenda. From that day onwards we remained good friends, and during the war, even in circumstances of great delicacy, we remained on the best of terms and kept in the closest touch. As Quartermaster-General of the British Expeditionary Force in the early days of the war Robertson had proved

his sound military qualities, and, when Archibald Murray's health temporarily failed, French took him as chief of his staff. As a strategist he was sound but rather lacking in imagination. His critics said that he based himself entirely on the text-books, from which nothing would induce him to depart by a hair's-breadth. To people of vivid imagination and inspiration, like Lloyd George, his principles seemed to be platitudes. Nevertheless, at the time with which we are dealing it was principles and common sense rather than inspiration that were needed. In speech he was slow and deliberate. He never uttered an opinion which he had not thought out. He would address international conferences in correct French (carefully written out as a rule) and with an English accent. He would nearly always meet the brainwaves of the nimble-minded French politicians with a negative, so that eventually they gave him the nickname of '*General Non Non*'. Robertson was a great organizer, and, building on Murray's foundations, soon had the General Staff on a high level of efficiency. The structure was supported on two great pillars—Macdonogh, the Director of Military Intelligence, who was probably the best intelligence officer in Europe, and Maurice, the Director of Military Operations, a highly cultured and scientific soldier, who had been with Robertson in France, and was well equipped to supplement his work. Very soon Robertson obtained a complete control of the strategy in all theatres. But perhaps his greatest quality, transcending his great powers of work, his mastery of principle, his organizing capacity, and his judgment of men, was 'character'. His was a dominating personality. He knew what he wanted, and he nearly always got his way. It was this which made him a tower of strength to the War Committee. It was this which enabled him to retain his post in difficult times for more than two years, when he had to give place to a more nimble and versatile mind.

Robertson's appointment decided for years the main strategy of the war. He might have to make concessions now and again to French military opinion, which from now onwards strongly supported the Salonica expedition. But he contested it point by point. For him there was only one theatre of war that counted, and that was the Western Front. Taking him all in all he was within his limitations a rugged, dogged, able and likeable man.

CHAPTER XLII

DEVELOPMENTS IN THE
ALLIED SUPREME COMMAND

'It hath been an opinion that the French are wiser than
they seem . . .' (BACON, *Essays*, 'Of seeming wise'.)

WE left the Salonica expedition at a point where, as the result of a visit
by Joffre to London, the British Government had given a somewhat
grudging consent to his proposal that the British forces at Salonica
should hold the base at Salonica itself and the lines of communications
as far as Krivolak, while the French forces were to be responsible in the
more dangerous sector beyond that point for the attempt (in which our
military authorities did not believe) to reopen a line of communications
with the Serbian Army, which was facing the Germans and Austrians
in front and the Bulgarians in rear. It is important, however, to keep in
mind that this consent had been subject to the important condition that,
if communication with the Serbian Army could not be opened and
maintained, the Allied forces should be withdrawn. The British
Government had incurred an obligation to send its half-share of
150,000 men to the Balkans, the French sending an equal number. The
French had been very much more prompt than we in sending their
quota. As early as September 5th they had decided to send four divisions to the Dardanelles in addition to one already there; and when the
Salonica expedition was decided on, they merely had to divert some of
these divisions to the new but adjacent theatre of war. By mid-November the French claimed to have already some 72,000 men in the Balkan
theatre, while our force was limited to two divisions, the 10th from the
Dardanelles which had begun to land at Salonica on October 5th, and
the 22nd from France which was beginning to arrive. The 28th from
France was at Alexandria awaiting transport and the 26th was at sea *en
route* to Alexandria.

The position at Salonica was still one of great uncertainty. On
October 5th Venizelos had resigned, and thereafter no reliance could be
placed on the Greek Government which at once became suspicious and
sullen. There were at the time no less than two complete Greek divisions at Salonica with two more not far away. Until the Greek Government could be induced to declare itself the position, with the Allied

forces strung out up the line towards Serbia and with a large and potentially hostile force living in their base, was to say the least precarious. The whole situation was fraught with confusion and misunderstanding.

The advent of a new French Government was eminently favourable for some development in the Allied Supreme Command. Briand and Galliéni were known to be strong partisans of something of the kind. In the British Cabinet also the same view was held. More prescient than most, Kitchener had urged some move in this direction as early as January 1915. Lloyd George was a strong advocate of closer relations with the French Government. Robertson, I had noted, was also of the same mind:

November 1st. After lunch Robertson called to try and induce me to push the idea of closer arrangements for concerting war plans and policy with the French, which I promised to do.

Finally the state of affairs in the Balkans was crying out for a more thorough understanding between the two countries. Consequently when on November 2nd, Asquith told the House of Commons: 'I attach very great importance first of all to a more intimate co-ordination between the Staffs of the Allied Powers', he was speaking the mind, not only of the Cabinet, but of the best military opinion, and was proposing something that was vitally necessary for the effective conduct of the war. Clearly the first thing to be done was to arrange a conference to clear the situation in the Balkans, advantage of which might be taken to try to establish some closer and more permanent system of liaison.

One step in the right direction was taken even before a conference could be arranged. Millerand had established a direct personal relationship with Kitchener by means of a liaison officer. His choice had fallen on a young officer of Spahis, Captain Doumayrou, who had proved an admirable selection. He soon won the confidence of Kitchener and of all with whom he came in contact. Young, handsome, debonair, intelligent, understanding, quick in the uptake, discreet, trustworthy, a master of the English language, it would be difficult to imagine a person better adapted to interpret one nation to the other. He was continually on the move between the two capitals, and his dapper figure in its khaki uniform, with his long row of polished medals, was everywhere welcome. Usually a change of Government in France leads to a *bouleversement* among the personal entourage of Ministers, but Briand, with his penetrating, quick mind, had the wisdom to see what a valuable man

Doumayrou had become, and promoted him to act as liaison officer, not merely between the two War Ministers, but between the two Prime Ministers, an arrangement in which Asquith acquiesced. Doumayrou's normal communication with Asquith was to be conducted through myself. He became a *habitué* in my office, where he was very popular, and he and I struck up a friendship which lasted until long after his breakdown in health a year later. It is impossible to over-estimate the value of the quiet, unostentatious service he rendered in the difficult negotiations between the two Governments during the next twelve months.

Oddly enough the occasion for the much needed conference arose immediately out of a telegram which Kitchener had sent from the Dardanelles:

November 13th. . . . After we had got home I received a copy of another telegram from Kitchener again urging his Alexandretta scheme and demanding immediate answer. As the Prime Minister had gone into the country for the week-end I felt very uncomfortable. At 9.30 p.m. therefore I went first to the War Office, where I spoke to Murray on the telephone, and then on to Balfour. After a long talk we decided that there ought at once to be a Staff Conference between the British and French naval and military staffs. The situation is a most difficult one for the Government. First, they sent Monro to the Dardanelles, as a sort of Pope, whose word was to be final. When he recommended evacuation they refused to accept his opinion and sent Kitchener, as a sort of super-Pope, who not only knows the East better than any living man, but has created the new armies and ought to know where best to use them, more especially as he has been practically in control of the war for a long time. What does he do? He apparently recommends evacuation (though this is not quite clear) and advises a new landing at Alexandretta, which our own General Staff, Joffre, and the French General Staff and Government condemn utterly. The Government may be had either way, if anything goes wrong. Most difficult. Home about midnight.[1]

November 14th. No Sabbath calm today. At 10.15 a.m. I was at the War Office to see Murray; 10.45 a.m. Balfour, whom I met in the passage of his house in a nightgown. He said 'I am really not in a costume for serious talk, so I will first get into bed.' At 11.15 a.m., as result of previous conversations, rang up McKenna at 'Munstead' (Lady Jekyll's place, where he and the Prime Minister are staying) and got the Prime Minister's permission to summon a Staff Conference for Monday. At 11.45 a.m. went to Foreign Office and drafted a telegram with the clerk on duty. At 12.15 saw Grey at his private house and got his agreement to the telegram. Then (sending the

----

[1] We were spending the winter in furnished rooms near the Marble Arch.

telegram by a messenger to Foreign Office), motored to lunch at 'Munstead' near Godalming in a fine War Office car in crisp sparkling sunshine. After lunch had a short talk with the Prime Minister and McKenna and drafted telegrams to Kitchener asking his views as to the need for evacuation apart from his new plan, and to Paris, asking for a Ministerial Conference to follow the Staff Conference. At 3.45 p.m. reached London; got off telegrams at War Office and Foreign Office, and so home to tea about 5 p.m.

During the next two days the War Committee definitely decided that our representatives at the Paris Conference should not support Kitchener's Alexandretta plan.

November 16th. Started in evening for Paris with Prime Minister, Grey, Balfour, Lloyd George, Jackson, Callwell, George Clerk, Arthur Lee, Robertson, Bonham Carter, Bartolomé, and Doumayrou. Crossed in a fast light draught destroyer in order to ride over mines. On arriving at Boulogne we tied up alongside the hospital ship *Anglia*, and walked across her on to the wharf. A few hours later she was blown up by a mine on the very track we had taken. We had a fine special train in France in which we dined. The four Cabinet Ministers sat together and were very jovial and cheery, much to Doumayrou's delight, as he said we must succeed with such cheerful people in charge of the war. At Paris we were met by Briand and all went to the Hotel Crillon, arriving soon after midnight.

At the conference the Alexandretta proposal was dismissed almost in a word and the greater part of the day was devoted to Salonica. Our people questioned whether the attempt was really worth pursuing. They pointed out that the situation had definitely altered for the worse owing to the suspicious attitude of Greece, which put our whole force in danger. The military representatives in particular pointed out that the object of the Allies was to beat the Germans. We could not do that at Salonica and ought consequently to keep our numbers in the Balkans down to the irreducible minimum. In any event 150,000 men were not likely to prove sufficient to settle a campaign in that region. If we sent so many we should become involved to an extent that would compel us to send more, which we could not afford without detriment to our position in the main theatre.

The French were rather reproachful at our slowness in carrying out our part of the bargain. If we had been more prompt, they hinted, the situation would have been better. We could not leave Serbia in the lurch. We could not afford to let Salonica fall into the hands of the enemy, to become another focus of submarine and naval activity, and so

forth. They had the better of the argument, and eventually we agreed to renew the undertaking given to Joffre; to divert the 26th Division, then at sea, from Alexandria to Salonica; to expedite the transport of the 28th Division from Alexandria to the same port; to undertake no new operation in the Eastern Mediterranean, and to await Kitchener's appreciation on the Dardanelles.

That evening the Prime Minister and his Cabinet colleagues met the French Cabinet under Poincaré's presidency at the Elysée, and, besides confirming the conclusions of the conference which Doumayrou and I had drafted at the British Embassy, approved in principle a sort of embryo constitution for future conferences and invited Asquith to work it out in detail. I put in hand the British draft of the new constitution immediately after our return and, after approval by the War Committee, it was sent to Briand by the hand of Doumayrou. After a considerable interchange of views through the same channel it was adopted and initialled by both Prime Ministers at a later conference in January 1916.

As finally approved the scheme provided for a Standing Committee of an advisory character. Its conclusions were to be subject to the approval of the Governments concerned. Its composition was to be as elastic as possible. It was to consist of the Prime Ministers of any of the Allies and of such other members of Governments and Staffs as were required for the discussion of the subjects brought before it. Whenever possible its meetings were to be preceded by an interchange of views between the naval and military staffs and other departments of the Governments interested. Conclusions were to be formulated after each meeting. Each Government was to nominate a Secretary-Liaison Officer, whose function was to act as joint secretary, and to ensure permanent contact between the respective Governments. Except for the fact that Asquith's original draft had provided for a permanent Secretariat the foregoing scheme was almost identical with the plan proposed by the British Government, which was a deliberate adaptation to international intercourse of the principles on which the Committee of Imperial Defence is founded. The deletion of the permanent Secretariat, however, on which Briand insisted, was a blot on the new organization, which might otherwise, at this early stage of the war, have achieved the position occupied later by the Supreme War Council in unifying the efforts of the Allies. Doumayrou and I, who were nominated as the Secretary-Liaison Officers, did our best, but, of course, we could not take the place of a permanent bureau. Moreover Doumayrou

was handicapped by the Quai d'Orsay, who not unnaturally rather resented this intrusion into a domain which they regarded as their own. With the Foreign Office I had no such difficulty. I was working every day in close touch with them. I always shared with George Clerk the secretarial work of these conferences and was on the best of terms with him. I regarded myself in these matters practically as an agent of the Foreign Office, and they seemed glad to have the advantage of my knowledge of the war as a whole. Nevertheless this step, even though it did not achieve all that it might have done, was a distinct advance in the direction of co-ordination of the Allied Supreme Command. Moreover, there were no more conferences without records or conclusions such as had occurred in the past.

Before turning to the death throes of the Dardanelles expedition, we must witness the final agony of the birth of the Salonica expedition. Soon after the Paris Conference it became clear that the small French spearhead of the Allied Army in this region was unable to make junction with the retreating Serbian Army. The conditions were therefore fulfilled in which, under the reservation made to Joffre on October 29th, we were entitled to demand the withdrawal of the whole Allied force. The situation was indeed about as threatening as it could be. The enemy had overrun Serbia. Nish had fallen on November 5th; the Babuna Pass and Prilep on the 16th. Meanwhile the Austro-German Army had forced its way into the south-west of Serbia and had taken Novi-Bazar and Pristina (November 23rd). On December 2nd the French force had begun its retreat and Krivolak was evacuated. The Serbians had already abandoned all hope of making contact with the French and on November 30th had begun to retire through Albania. The French force under Sarrail, almost surrounded by enemies, was in a precarious position. Dependent on a single line of railway, which furnished almost the only means of extricating its artillery, its communications for some thirty miles were within striking distance of the enemy. Our own 10th Division was not in much better plight. By the valley of the Struma the Bulgarians, had they the available force, had open to them a direct line of advance on Salonica, which was guarded only by the Greeks, whose attitude was dubious, and who held all the more important tactical positions around Salonica. Kitchener, on his way back from the Dardanelles, had, at the request of the Government, visited King Constantine, but without producing any effect. Such troops as we had at Salonica were almost without artillery and not yet mobile.

December 2nd. In the meantime the position in Serbia and Salonica is more serious than ever. Our people want to get out altogether and to insist that the Greeks shall hold their own territory. The French, however, flatly decline to come out and continually refuse our repeated requests that they shall hold a conference. We sent them a very stiff telegram yesterday and a still stiffer one today. Kitchener, whom I saw this afternoon, told me he had given the French Military Attaché a strong hint that nothing would move us on this, that the Cabinet and the military authorities were unanimous in their insistence that we must come out, owing to the menacing attitude of the Greeks, and he seems to have hinted that we might have to withdraw troops from France. He acted the whole scene to me in a most amusing manner.

On December 3rd the Cabinet decided to insist on a conference, which actually took place on the following day at Calais. We were represented by the Prime Minister, Kitchener, Balfour, Murray, Oliver, with George Clerk and myself as secretaries; the French by Briand, Galliéni, Lacaze, Joffre and some other generals, including Graziani the Chief of Staff at the French War Office. Asquith and his colleagues insisted strongly on the need for withdrawal. Not only had the original policy completely failed, but the Allied forces at Salonica were in a position of no small danger. The French replied by pointing out the greater dangers which would be run by abandoning Salonica. Greece would inevitably go over to the enemy. Salonica would become a base for German and Austrian submarines. Russia, who had concentrated some 400,000 men in the south to show her interest in the Balkans, would be greatly discouraged. Roumania would be forced into the enemy's camp. All hope of Italian intervention in the Balkans through Albania would be lost. The attempt to reconstitute the Serbian Army at Corfu for service in the Balkans would be rendered abortive. In fact Serbia, abandoned by her Allies might even treat for peace. In any event the evacuation of Salonica would take time. For heaven's sake do not take a decision yet! That was the gist of the French argument. Asquith and his colleagues, however, held firm. At the end of the conference Asquith read a considered statement, which had been prepared during an adjournment, to the effect that the question of extended operations was one for further examination by the Allies, but that, in the opinion of our military advisers, to hold on at Salonica with 150,000 men was from a military point of view to court disaster. They insisted, therefore, on preparations being made for a withdrawal. To secure a safe retreat the Greeks must be told that military necessity compelled the Allies to occupy and defend such tactical positions as they required, though such

measures must not be regarded as infringing the independence and sovereign rights of Greece. The French had no option but to accept this statement, though they made it clear that the responsibility was ours.[1] Asquith's statement was telegraphed to Paris, in order to make sure that there could be no misunderstanding.

It was a strained and difficult conference. On our return journey we had a truly terrible crossing to Dover in the black darkness of a December night in a full gale from the south-west. Our destroyer was drifted far to the eastward and we suddenly found ourselves close to the Goodwins. Balfour lay prostrate aft in the captain's cabin. Kitchener and Asquith remained in the chart house on the bridge with their feet on the table, as the deck was awash within the coamings, with no light but that of their cigars, since all lights were masked in view of the danger of attack. Neither of them was in the smallest degree incommoded by the weather. Over my own sufferings on the open bridge outside, swept by huge seas and overcome by *mal de mer*, I will draw a veil! This was the occasion of the story which has often been told of Balfour. After we had landed and were settling down in the train, someone remarked that at least we had escaped the enemy's minefields, on which a mournful voice from the corner ejaculated—'a mine was the one thing I was praying for!'

Next day (December 5th), however, we learned that the French had gone back on the whole arrangement. The War Committee met all day. Albert Thomas, the French Minister of Munitions, ostensibly in London on munitions business, became very active. Eventually it was decided to await the result of a very important conference of the Allied Generals and Staffs, which was being held at Joffre's headquarters at Chantilly. At this conference the Italians and Russians supported the French view in favour of holding on at Salonica.[2] On December 8th came a telegram from the Czar expressing disappointment at the result of the Calais Conference. It was clear that the French had mobilized every military and diplomatic resource to negative the conclusions of that conference, so that on the Salonica question we were isolated and outwitted. The War Committee then came to the conclusion that we must not quarrel with the French at any rate, and Kitchener and Grey were on December 8th sent over to Paris to patch up an arrangement. On December 10th they conferred with the French Government. They found French opinion profoundly disturbed, but they succeeded in establishing a better atmosphere. They discussed the measures to extri-

[1] *vide Macedonia*, I, p. 63. [2] *Ibid.*, pp. 49 *sq.*

cate Sarrail's force and the Allies in general from their immediate difficulties at Salonica, but they avoided the vexed question of evacuation. The future was left for subsequent decision.

In the event there was some hard fighting in this theatre and both the French and British sustained heavy casualties, but none of the disasters, which seemed so imminent, actually occurred. After all, considerable reinforcements were beginning to arrive at Salonica—the 28th Division on November 25th; the 27th on December 4th; the 26th on January 8th, making a total of four British and four French divisions, which, even though not yet fully mobile, could probably have held Salonica against any attack which could be brought to bear. If put in at the Dardanelles, which was seriously considered at the beginning of December, these divisions might possibly have settled the business. But it would have been very risky to make the attempt so late in the year when the weather might break at any moment, and the General Staff were much opposed to the idea. This month, however, in spite of our many mistakes, our luck was in, not only at Salonica, but also at the Dardanelles, from whence as many divisions were about to be released as anyone could wish. It may be that, as the quotation at the head of this chapter suggests, the French were wiser than they seemed.

CHAPTER XLIII

THE EVACUATION OF
THE GALLIPOLI PENINSULA

' "Honourable retreats," says Lord Bacon, "are no ways
inferior to brave charges, as having less of fortune, more
of discipline, and as much valour." ' (NAPIER, *War in the
Peninsula*, Book IV, c. 6.)

BY far the most important of the many difficult problems which the new
War Committee had to face was the future policy at the Dardanelles.
Monro had been appointed on October 15th, to relieve Hamilton as
Commander-in-Chief at the Dardanelles. He came to see me before
starting:

October 20th. In morning had long talk with Monro, just appointed to
succeed Hamilton at Dardanelles. He is a cheery old fellow with an odd trick
of slapping you on the arm and ejaculating 'Ja!' Rather a sound old bird, I
thought, but not very quick.

His Chief of Staff, Lynden Bell, came on the 22nd, and my comment
was 'Very good officer and nice fellow'. I implored him to insist on
'proper drafts'. On October 27th Monro arrived at Mudros, and on the
following day he assumed command. On October 31st, after what must
have been a perfunctory inspection, he sent home by telegram a very
full appreciation advising evacuation. It had, of course, always been
certain from the first that events would take this course. It was inconceivable that officers like Monro and his Chief of Staff, who had served
all the war on the Western Front,[1] would report differently. For practical purposes the Government might just as well have taken the decision
themselves, though politically it was convenient to fortify themselves
with an expert opinion.

Nevertheless Kitchener could not make up his mind to accept
Monro's report. On November 1st he asked for the views of the corps
commanders on the Gallipoli Peninsula to be sent by telegram. Byng
and Davies (both Western Front men) shared Monro's view.
Birdwood, in whom Kitchener always felt the most implicit confidence,
gave a contrary opinion.[2]

[1] Monro went to France in August 1914 in command of the 2nd Division and had remained
there ever since.
[2] *Gallipoli*, II, p. 408.

On October 28th a new factor had been introduced by the arrival in London of Roger Keyes, de Robeck's Chief of Staff. Ostensibly he had come on leave, but the real object of his visit was to persuade the Government to sanction a renewal of the naval attack on the Dardanelles. On November 2nd Kitchener saw Keyes, and, as I noted, was 'immensely attracted' by his scheme; Balfour was also 'warming to the idea'.

It was in these circumstances that the new War Committee met on November 3rd and decided to send Kitchener to the Dardanelles; their decision was confirmed by the Cabinet on the following day. By November 3rd Kitchener's views had hardened against evacuation, and on that date he sent a personal telegram to Birdwood telling him of his forthcoming visit; warning him that the Admiralty were leaning towards Keyes's project for a renewed naval attack, asking him to explore the possibility of a fresh landing at the Bulair Isthmus with a view to helping the Navy after they had effected the passage of the Straits; and ending with the following significant passage:

I absolutely refuse to sign order for evacuation, which I think would be greatest disaster and would condemn a large percentage of our men to death or imprisonment. Monro will be appointed to the command of the Salonica force.[1]

At a midnight interview with Keyes on November 3rd, however, Kitchener learned that he considered it hopeless to land at Bulair. Keyes, according to the official historian, 'firmly believed' that the attempt to rush the Straits might yet be sanctioned after a meeting in Balfour's room with Kitchener. This was in the afternoon of November 4th, and an hour later what the official historian calls 'a final meeting of Ministers'—this 'final meeting' was unofficial and unrecorded—apparently decided that the attempt could be sanctioned only in co-operation with a new attack by the Army. For that no fresh troops were available, so Kitchener telegraphed Birdwood cancelling his previous day's message.

November 3rd. In afternoon Kitchener asked me to accompany him. Saw Prime Minister to ask his permission, and he said I was to get ready to go immediately but that he reserved his final decision until tomorrow. Saw Balfour and asked his opinion whether I should go; his opinion was that I ought to go on the clear understanding that I was to return within a week of my arrival at the Dardanelles. . . .

[1] *Gallipoli,* II, p. 409.

November 4th. After all I did not go to the East with Kitchener. In the morning the Prime Minister and Kitchener wrangled over my body, and, as the Prime Minister told me, had a row about it. At 2 p.m. I received a telephone message to say that I was not to go to the East, but was to go with Kitchener as far as Paris to a conference with Galliéni. Adeline had been to Limpsfield to fetch my gear, and turned up to lunch, delighted to find I was not going. I was flattered at being asked by Kitchener, but not sorry not to have to go, as I felt much doubt whether we could do any good. In the evening the Prime Minister sent for me to say that I was not to go to Paris, and that he wanted me to help him to reorganize the system (or lack of system!) for running the war. He wanted me to have a room in the War Office, of which he intended to take charge. I then went to see Archibald Murray, to make sure that I should stand all right with him. Saw Kitchener to say goodbye. He called me a deserter—but added that he knew I would have come if the Prime Minister had not wanted me.

The Prime Minister's plan that I should have a room in the War Office made no appeal to me, and did not take effect. It all depended upon the assumption that Kitchener would leave the War Office, on which I had my doubts. Meanwhile, I was very careful not to commit myself to the false step of merging my small office in a vast organization like the War Office, where it would have lost its individuality and all the advantages of a central co-ordinating department, respected by all, envied by none, at everyone's disposal within its own sphere of activity. From that time onward, however, I had a standing appointment to see the Prime Minister at some time in the forenoon of every day.

Kitchener left London late on November 4th. In Paris he found the French Government opposed to the evacuation of Gallipoli, which prompted him to send his telegram to Birdwood. On November 9th he arrived at Mudros, where his views underwent a change. On November 15th, after many conferences with the naval and military authorities and after a personal inspection of the positions on the Peninsula, he telegraphed a long appreciation[1] in which he indicated the view that the position at Gallipoli was less important than hitherto, and that 'if another position in the neighbourhood of Alexandretta were occupied, where Turkish movements eastward would be effectively stopped, the realization of the German objective against Egypt and the East would be prevented'. He stated that 'careful and secret preparations for the evacuation of the Peninsula are being made' and expressed a hope that losses might be less than hitherto expected, i.e. less than Monro's esti-

---

[1] *Gallipoli*, II, pp. 415 *sq*.

mate of 30–40 per cent in personnel and material. He also telegraphed that de Robeck would like to hold on to Cape Helles, if Suvla and Anzac were evacuated.

On November 19th after the Paris Conference, Asquith telegraphed that the Government had decided against the Alexandretta project and asked Kitchener to give his considered opinion on the evacuation of the Peninsula in whole or in part. On November 22nd Kitchener replied that, as German assistance to the Turks was now practically available— the adherence of Bulgaria to the Central Powers and the defeat of Serbia opened a direct line of railway communication from Germany to Constantinople—our position would become untenable and evacuation seemed inevitable. While Suvla and Anzac should be evacuated, he advised that Cape Helles should be held for the present, as its retention would enable the Navy to maintain the advantages already gained, threaten the seizure of the Straits, and facilitate the evacuation of Suvla and Anzac. Next day (November 23rd) the War Committee reached the following conclusion, which is quoted textually in the report of the Dardanelles Commission:

Having regard to the opinion expressed by Kitchener in his telegram dated November 22nd, and by the General Staff in their Memorandum dated November 22nd, the War Committee feel bound to advise the evacuation of the Gallipoli Peninsula on military grounds, notwithstanding the grave political disadvantages which may result from the decision. They have carefully examined the naval considerations in favour of the retention of Cape Helles as stated in a note by the Chief of the Admiralty War Staff, printed with the General Staff Memorandum. They are of opinion, however, that the naval advantages to be gained by this course are not commensurate with the military disadvantages involved.

It might have been supposed that, once this difficult conclusion had been reached by the War Committee after exhaustive inquiry, and on such unanimous military advice, orders would at once have been given for the evacuation both of the Suvla–Anzac and Cape Helles positions, more particularly in view of the time which had already been lost in reaching it. Not so. The Cabinet must needs have its say. At this point indeed the disadvantages of dual control in the Supreme Command made itself felt as never before or after.

It is true that at this juncture a new factor was introduced, which may have had the same effect on the minds of Cabinet Ministers as it did on my own thoughts. As the report of the Dardanelles Commission

Q

narrates, Bonar Law was the principal protagonist in the Cabinet for evacuation and Curzon against it. I myself was most reluctant to express any personal opinion. The highest naval and military authorities had concerted their advice, and, incidentally, had consulted me at every stage. The last thing I desired was to do anything to weaken their authority—especially in the case of the new and reorganized General Staff, which was beginning to establish its position. My instincts, it is true, were all against evacuation, but I found it difficult to meet the hard facts of the situation.

I was, however, not allowed to keep my opinions to myself:

November 22nd. War Committee at 11.30 to consider a telegram from Kitchener *re* future of operations in the Gallipoli Peninsula. In accordance with Lord K.'s advice it was decided to evacuate the Gallipoli Peninsula. The final decision however was left to the Cabinet. Personally I felt desperately depressed at this decision. I believe it to be an entirely wrong one. Since Churchill left the Cabinet and the War Council we have lacked courage more than ever. Still, in view of the advice of Lord K. and the other generals, which corresponded to that of the General Staff, it is doubtful if any civilian Cabinet would have decided otherwise. Saw Stamfordham in the evening to communicate the above decision (i.e. for the King's information, which was at that time part of my duty).

November 24th. Cabinet for some unaccountable reason postponed a decision *re* the Gallipoli Peninsula until Friday. Very bad news from Mesopotamia, where Nixon's force, though partially successful, failed to drive the Turks out of their position at Ctesiphon. This about crowns our situation in the East. The Salonica expedition was always doomed to failure, if not to disaster. The impending decision *re* Gallipoli means we cannot tell what. And this last reverse in the one part of the world where success was anticipated with some confidence is the last straw. Combined, these three misadventures will destroy the last vestige of our prestige, upon which our eastern Empire depends; it will ruin our hopes among the Arabs, in Persia and probably in China; it will place our position in India, and possibly in Egypt, in jeopardy. But still Robertson insists that we can beat the Germans in France. The darkest hour is not yet, but will soon come. Will it precede the dawn of better things?

November 26th. Cabinet seem to have had a fairly hectic meeting about the Dardanelles, and eventually postponed decision until de Robeck's return. Curzon circulated a Memo.[1] before the meeting in favour of holding on, of which he gave me a copy It was one of the most able papers I have ever read. . . . Dined with Hamilton to meet the French General d'Amade, who told us how disastrous would be the effect on Russia of withdrawal

[1] A summary of this is in Ronaldshay's *Life of Lord Curzon*, III, p. 184.

from the Dardanelles. He is actually on his way back from Russia. Sir Ian very pleased at Curzon's attitude over the Dardanelles question.

November 27th. Prime Minister at 11.30. Afterwards called at Curzon's house by appointment to discuss Dardanelles question with him. He was very pleased with what I told him and listened intently, but had a disconcerting trick of taking notes every time I opened my mouth. He told me that he had often heard the Prime Minister and other Cabinet Ministers speak in the highest terms of my judgment, and implored me to write a paper on the Dardanelles question. I replied that it was difficult as it brought me into conflict with high military authorities like the General Staff, and I could not write a paper on this subject without taking a controversial line. He rejoined that this was such a critical occasion that all such considerations ought to be brushed aside, and said he intended to demand from the Prime Minister to order me to express my views. After one and a half hours I left and went off with Adeline to lunch and afterwards to see the old church of St. Bartholomew the Great in the city. Returning to the office on the way home I found a letter from the Prime Minister directing me to write a Memo. on the Dardanelles, and I sat up until midnight doing so.

The Memo. was completed on Sunday (November 28th) and circulated next day. There were festivities at this time in connection with the wedding of Violet Asquith to Maurice Bonham Carter, but, as I record in my diary 'the shadow of this horrible decision about the Dardanelles was ever present'.

My own Memorandum took the form of an appreciation of the war position in all its aspects. So far as the Dardanelles was concerned my views are summarized in the Official History:[1]

Colonel Hankey pointed out that the evacuation of the Peninsula would enable Germany to obtain her ambition of increasing our difficulties in the East without any effort at all on her part. The cessation of strategic pressure against the Turkish capital would free the whole Turkish Army to attack Mesopotamia, the Caucasus or Egypt; and Britain and Russia, on the outside of the circle, would have to be strong everywhere to resist these possible attacks. Lord Kitchener was already asking for fourteen divisions to defend Egypt; four divisions and more would be required to hold our gains in Mesopotamia; Russia would have to reinforce her Caucasian front. Persia was already asking for more Russian troops to defend her territories, and was even hinting that, in case of refusal, she might have to join the Turks. More troops might be needed for the defence of India; and there was even a fear that Russia might sign a separate peace. Colonel Hankey urged that the arguments in favour of holding on in Gallipoli were overwhelming, *pro-*

[1] *Gallipoli*, II, p. 431.

vided that it could be done.[1] 'It so happens', his paper concluded, 'that good divisions are about to be set free from Salonica, and the main plea of this paper is that the question may be considered from the point of view of their possible use to save the position on the Gallipoli Peninsula, and, if possible, to take the offensive.'

The result was to divide the Cabinet more than ever and to delay the final decision—the last thing I wanted.

December 1st. Met Stamfordham at 10 Downing Street. He told me that he did not think the Cabinet could decide on evacuation with my Memo. in front of them. It is a terrible responsibility to have to advise on such a question. I cannot help feeling that disaster may face us either way, and only recommend holding on as the least of two disasters.

Kitchener was now back and de Robeck had reached London.

December 2nd. Meeting of Dardanelles Committee at 11 a.m. to cross-examine de Robeck about the situation at the Dardanelles. Followed immediately by a meeting of the Cabinet. At the latter I gather that my Memo. was the main topic of conversation. I met the Lord Chancellor and F. E. Smith coming out of the Cabinet room. The former said that my paper had divided the Cabinet, and the latter said that it was a perfectly splendid paper. Meanwhile the evidence is accumulating (Lord K. and de Robeck) that Suvla cannot be held without a push. The decision of the Cabinet was to inquire how soon an offensive could be undertaken at Suvla with four divisions from Salonica. . . . I lunched with Balfour, Lansdowne being also present. He congratulated me most warmly on my Memorandum and said he fully agreed in it.

Henry Jackson and Oliver, according to a note in my diary, both shared my view that, if troops were released from Salonica, another effort should be made at the Dardanelles. On December 3rd I had a long talk with Kitchener, who, as I noted, 'wants to attack at Suvla if he can'. After the French Government had 'ratted' on their agreement at Calais to evacuate Salonica, it became clear that no troops would be available from that theatre—unless we were prepared to leave the French in the lurch, which would have brought down Briand's Government. The risks of so serious a quarrel with our Allies were too grave to be run, especially on an issue on which opinion in the Cabinet itself was divided.

On December 7th, therefore, the Cabinet decided to evacuate Suvla

[1] The Official Historian's italics; he added in a note here that 'Col. Hankey added that only the General Staff were competent to advise on the practicability of this'.

and Anzac, retaining Cape Helles for the present. Thus, for one reason or another, a fortnight elapsed between the recommendation of the War Committee in favour of evacuation of our positions on the Gallipoli Peninsula and the decision of the Cabinet, which applied only to Suvla and Anzac, and, as we shall see, nearly three weeks more were allowed to elapse before the decision to evacuate Cape Helles was taken (on December 27th). In the meantime the weather had been the subject of grave preoccupation to all responsible and it was an intense relief when on December 20th the evacuation of Suvla and Anzac was completed virtually without loss. That very night, the weather broke.

Meanwhile Wemyss, who had taken over the command from de Robeck, had asked permission to renew the naval attack on the Straits. The War Committee had discussed this matter very fully with de Robeck and the Admiralty vetoed the new proposal. On December 20th Monro telegraphed advising the evacuation of Cape Helles. Wemyss and Keyes agreed. As the original decision to retain Cape Helles, as a kind of Gibraltar, had been taken mainly on naval grounds, the War Committee on December 23rd advised that it should be evacuated—confirming their earlier conclusion reached exactly a month before. Again the dangers of a dual control in the Supreme Command made themselves felt. A debate in Parliament on the adjournment was taking place on December 23rd and 24th, and it was not convenient for the Cabinet to meet. It was not until the afternoon of December 27th, notwithstanding the immense urgency of the question, that the Cabinet decided to confirm the War Committee's decision, and orders were issued for evacuation. Thanks to the admirable arrangements of Birdwood and his staff, this evacuation too, was successfully accomplished almost without loss on January 8, 1916.

So far as concerns the local command, the Gallipoli evacuation will ever stand out as one of the great retreats of history; an honourable retreat which sheds lustre on all concerned, and one to which the quotation at the head of this chapter well applies. But from the standpoint of the Supreme Command it is a deplorable story of vacillation, delay and divided counsels.

After the defection of the Bulgarians on October 14th, there was no excuse for further delay. All the elements required for a decision were available. There was no need to send out Monro, whose advice was a foregone conclusion. But when the Cabinet did send the General out, they ought to have been prepared to abide by his advice. Kitchener's visit was unnecessary and only made for further delay at a time when

delay was getting daily more dangerous. Once Kitchener's advice was received the War Committee acted with promptitude. They assembled at once and reached their decision—distasteful as it was to some—in a single meeting. It was our old friend, the Cabinet of pre-war type, with its twenty-one members and its incredibly unbusinesslike procedure which, with all the facts before it, *took a fortnight* to make up its mind to evacuate only Anzac and Suvla, regardless of the advice of the War Committee and of the terrible danger of a midwinter evacuation. Again, after the receipt of Monro's telegram of December 20th, the War Committee took its decision without unreasonable delay, but a whole week elapsed from the receipt of the telegram, before the Cabinet was able to make up its mind on a matter on which it had been advised by its own War Committee more than a month before. All this delay while the sands were running out!

If the War Committee, composed of members of the Cabinet most immediately concerned and with a personnel skilfully blended to reflect every shade of opinion in the Cabinet, could reach a decision promptly when opinions differed fundamentally, why was this impossible in the Cabinet? If Asquith could do well with his War Committee why was he not equally successful with his Cabinet? Apart from the faults of the old system so often touched on here, the Cabinet, as Bonar Law's Memorandum clearly showed,[1] was unwilling to trust implicitly the strong War Committee it had itself created. Ministers who were left out must needs assert themselves. Decisions taken in the smaller body which was far better equipped with information and expert advice, had to be fought out again in the larger. On matters of major policy debate among the nine must needs be repeated among the twenty-one. Finally the exasperating delays must be attributed to the fact that the first Coalition Cabinet was not homogeneous. It was a mechanical mixture not a chemical compound. With all his patience and sagacity Asquith could not make the ponderous machine work sufficiently smoothly and rapidly to serve the purpose of a Supreme Command in time of war; probably no one else could have made it work at all.

The results of the evacuation are well known. Within a few months the Turks were rioting all over the East, capturing our besieged Army at Kut (April 29th), attacking our vital communications through the Suez Canal (July) and penetrating far into Persia; in August they even sent a corps to help the Germans in Galicia while the Allies, with armies even larger in the aggregate than had been employed on the Peninsula,

[1] *vide supra*, p. 460.

were everywhere on the defensive. Nevertheless, in the teeth of the formidable consensus of military opinion in favour of evacuation, the Supreme Command could not have taken a different decision. If the Dardanelles was a failure as a strategical offensive, it may justly be considered as a splendid example of the offensive-defensive. The heroic sacrifice and loss—about 110,000 casualties, equal only to about those of three weeks' heavy fighting on the Western Front—was not in vain.[1]

[1] Ludendorff (I, p. 174), at least, did not think the enterprise foolish.

CHAPTER XLIV

THE BEGINNING OF
THE WAR OF ATTRITION

'It has been well said: "Man is based on Hope; he has
properly no other possession but Hope; this habitation of
his is named the Place of Hope".' (CARLYLE, *French
Revolution*, Book II, c. 3.)

LIKE Pilgrim relieved of his burden, the nation, freed from the incubus
of the Dardanelles, entered on the year 1916 on a note of hope. The
new armies were rapidly putting on final touches and preparing to take
the field. Many divisions had already been in action and behaved
creditably. Others were fully prepared to outshine them. All over the
country new munitions factories were sprouting up like mushrooms.
Before the year was half spent what seemed an inexhaustible supply of
heavy guns, light guns, machine-guns and munitions of all kinds would
be pouring into the various theatres of war. The Dominions were not
behindhand. From Australia, New Zealand and Canada men were still
coming in an unceasing stream to replace the wastage of war. The
Union of South Africa had long since conquered German South West
Africa, and ere long would send its contingent to France, besides taking
the main share in the campaign in German East Africa. And let us not
forget Newfoundland with its seamen and its naval battalion at the
Dardanelles. At last the British Empire was to play a part on land
commensurate with that which it has already played on the sea. India
had taken her share magnificently in every theatre of war from the
outset.

The conduct of the Supreme Command in the matter of the decision
to withdraw from the Gallipoli Peninsula has been criticized as dilatory.
No such criticism can be levelled in the all-important matter of the military policy for the year 1916. At the beginning of December 1915,
Asquith had called on Archibald Murray to prepare a complete review
of the military situation in all theatres. This was circulated on December
15th, and Robertson on relieving Murray expressed his concurrence in
the views of his predecessor, and supplemented them with some brief
remarks of his own in the form of a series of draft conclusions or resolutions, to which he invited the War Committee to adhere. Thus on
December 28th, the day following the Cabinet's decision to evacuate

Cape Helles, when the War Committee met to consider the military policy to be adopted during the year 1916 they had before them the unanimous advice of the new and of the old Chiefs of the Imperial General Staff. This advice amounted to an uncompromising assertion of the Western Front theory. So far as possible the British forces were to be concentrated on the Western Front. Risks were, if necessary, to be run elsewhere in order to facilitate this concentration in the decisive theatre. The general plan envisaged simply a simultaneous and sustained offensive on the three main fronts; elsewhere the Allies were to act on the defensive. Subject to some minor but not unimportant reservations, the plan was to all intents and purposes accepted in principle in the course of a single meeting.

Why did the War Committee assent so readily to this policy? Have we not been told that throughout the summer and autumn of 1915 its members had become more and more disillusioned about the policy of hammering against these impregnable defences in France and Flanders? Were the lessons of the previous year and its failures entirely overlooked? Did not the German lines still stretch from Switzerland to the sea unbroken and stronger than ever? Was not this a decision to attack the enemy at his strongest point? In taking it were not the Supreme Command consigning hundreds of thousands of men to destruction under the most adverse conditions which held out no reasonable prospect of success? Was not the risk seen that our man-power would be shattered as French man-power was already being shattered on these impregnable lines? In short were we not simply playing the enemy's game? And what about the Eastern Empire and the prestige upon which it depends? How were we to thwart German ambitions in the East by a purely passive attitude there, particularly if we were to fail in the West, as in all probability would be the case?

None of these considerations were overlooked; they were ever present and were the cause of much misgiving. But there were new factors in the problem. The generals and all ranks of the Army were by this time reported by the military authorities to have learned the lessons of this new form of siege warfare. Great confidence was felt in Haig and Robertson and, above all, by the time the attack was to be begun, the armies were to be equipped with the means of surmounting the difficulties. It was believed that with heavy guns, howitzers, trench mortars and high explosives, concentrated in unlimited quantities, the armies could blast their way through any system of trenches and barbed wire by the simple process of laying them flat and killing, stunning or

Q*

demoralizing the defenders. This time the advantage of numbers would be decisively with the Allies. By concerting the attacks in point of time on all the fronts the enemy would be prevented from utilizing his wonderful railway system to transfer his divisions from one front to another, as he had done in the previous year. He would be riveted to three main fronts and would have nothing to spare for adventures in the East, except so far as he could induce the Bulgarians and Turks to do the work for him in these regions. What alternative theatre could be suggested? Mesopotamia? No decisive result was obtainable there. Egypt? In order to take the offensive we should have to cross the desert of Sinai, and, when we had crossed it, we could inflict no vital blow even on Turkey much less on Germany the central *réduit* of our enemies. Salonica? The Allies went there in the teeth of all British naval and military opinion to try to save the Serbian Army. The plan had failed as we knew it must. What could we do there now? We should merely bring ourselves into active opposition with the Bulgarian Army and nation. Why open up a new theatre against an enemy whom perhaps we never need fight there at all? Why not fight on the Italian Front? But there the terrain available for manœuvre was so restricted that the Italians had scarcely room to deploy their armies and were held up by a quarter of a million Austrians. We could not waste our forces there. Trust to economic pressure to bring victory at long last? That economic pressure is a powerful weapon was admitted but it worked very slow; it was not by itself decisive but the handmaid of military pressure. The Germans were a staunch, devoted race and would endure for a long time so long as they did not suffer military defeat. Could France afford to contemplate the possibility of an eventual peace negotiation at which the German delegates sat at the table with Northern France and Belgium still in their occupation, while we had no other asset in our hands than some unprofitable German colonies and the threat of sustained economic pressure? France and Belgium would regard such a suggestion as black treachery! So ran the debate on the policy for 1916.

The policy which the War Committee were asked to adopt, was based on the recommendations of the Chantilly Military Conference (December 6th to 8th). The representatives of the Allied Armies had been unanimous *inter alia* that a decision could be won only on the Russian, Franco-British, or Italian fronts; that the decision must be sought by simultaneous offensives on these fronts; and that in the secondary theatres of war the minimum possible forces ought to be

employed. So far, then, the War Committee were confronted with a rare and remarkable unanimity of military opinion. Whatever misgivings they might feel—and some felt them acutely—the civilian members of the War Committee had no alternative but to give their consent. Moreover, as we have seen, the 'Eastern Fronters' had no other plan. Nevertheless their anxiety on the subject is reflected in the form which their assent took, for, while affirming that, from the point of view of the British Empire, France and Flanders were the main theatres of war, and, while deciding that every effort must be made to concentrate there in the spring the maximum strength for correlated operations of all the Allies, the War Committee expressly laid down that this must not be construed as an authority for undertaking the offensive.

These reservations give the impression that the War Committee still retained in their power the possibility of preventing the attacks on the Western Front on which so much doubt was felt, and that the main offensive could, if necessary, be diverted to some other theatre. In fact, however, any such change of plan would have been very difficult and perhaps impossible except at the cost of very long delay, owing to the time required to concentrate the enormous quantities of war material required for an attack. Once authority was given to concentrate our maximum strength on the Western Front it was inevitable that the generals would lose no time in setting to work. Very soon our available resources would be irretrievably committed to and locked up in that theatre. When the French, Italians and Russians were all attacking on their respective fronts it would have been morally impossible for the British Supreme Command to refuse the co-operation of the forces at their disposal in accordance with the plans of the Allied generals.

By the decisions of December 28th, tentative and cautious as they were intended to be, we were in fact committed irrevocably to a great offensive on the Western Front during 1916. Robertson must have come away from the meeting of December 28th well satisfied. He had obtained the adoption of his main principle that the Western Front was the main theatre of war and he had been authorized to prepare for a great offensive there. He had also secured the application of the principle of a defensive role to the Egyptian and Mesopotamia campaigns. Moreover, he had the satisfaction of knowing that the British War Committee were now in line with the Allied military authorities on their military policy. It is true that the decision merely to 'prepare' did not enable him to fix a date for the offensive. At Chantilly March had

been recommended for a beginning on the ground that a succession of great military offensives would be required in order to obtain a decision and it would be necessary to take advantage of the first favourable weather of the spring. Our own military advisers were doubtful whether they could be ready before May. Lloyd George considered even this too optimistic and that the Ministry of Munitions would not be able to maintain the supply of munitions and other war material on the requisite scale before June. It was realized, however, that we might have to start before we were completely prepared in order to conform to the general plan. The actual date was left for later decision, but the question was settled for us by the enemy. On February 21, 1916, the German massed batteries opened at Verdun a bombardment unprecedented in intensity, as it was destined to be unprecedented in duration. The initiative for the year 1916 was with the enemy. The war of attrition had begun.

CHAPTER XLV

NATIONAL MILITARY SERVICE

'Lead forth my armed Saints
By thousands and by millions ranged for fight;'
(MILTON, *Paradise Lost*, VI, 47.)

'But considering all wars of late years in Europe as
contests of revenue, rather than of arms...' (FOX,
Speech on Traitorous Correspondence Bill, 1793,
Parliamentary Debates, vol. xxx, col. 585.)

PROBABLY it was not generally realized by the War Committee that
the decision of December 28th, to prepare for a great offensive in
France, was bringing us straight into a war of attrition (*guerre d'usure*).
It was recognized, however, that a big offensive must entail very heavy
casualties, and that consideration must be given to the means by which
the necessary recruits were to be obtained. The raising of this problem
at once produced a political crisis. The question of compulsory military
service had already been smouldering for some time, and to some
extent the fumes had been poisoning the atmosphere in which the
Supreme Command worked. As Bonar Law remarked to me one day,
when I had shown him some draft conclusions about East Africa: 'We
have bigger things than East Africa to quarrel about.' In January the
controversy burst suddenly into full flame.

On the day (December 28th) on which the policy for 1916 was
determined, the Cabinet decided on a modest instalment of compulsory
service, limited to men of military age who had not attested under the
Derby scheme and who could not give a satisfactory reason for exemption. This at once precipitated a crisis and certain members of the
Cabinet seemed likely to resign. Obviously this was most undesirable.
It might well have caused a split in the nation, have weakened the will
to win, and must have encouraged the enemy.

Next day (December 29th), Lloyd George gave a dinner to
Robertson; present also were Reading and myself. It was not a very
exhilarating repast. The conversation was largely on the questions of
munitions and finance. It was impossible not to feel that Lloyd George
and Robertson were temperamentally rather far apart, and neither
showed at his best. Nevertheless useful results followed. Robertson
drove me home in his car and urged me, not for the first time, to try to

get the question of finance raised at the War Committee. This set me thinking furiously. I knew that McKenna, the Chancellor of the Exchequer, desired nothing more than to have his arrangements co-ordinated with the demands of the General Staff for man-power. And here was the Chief of Staff practically asking that his arrangements should be co-ordinated with those of the Treasury. The opportunity must not be missed. However far apart they might be, if both desired a settlement, it could probably be achieved. Early next morning (December 30th) I went to McKenna's house and saw him in his dressing-gown. We talked for an hour and he agreed to see Robertson. With Asquith's approval a meeting was arranged for that very morning with satisfactory results, as they agreed to discuss the question on the basis of maintaining the British part of the Empire's Army in France at a strength of fifty-four divisions. Next day (December 31st) the subject was discussed by the Cabinet both morning and afternoon, with the result that a committee composed of the Prime Minister, McKenna a Liberal and Austen Chamberlain a Conservative was set up to co-ordinate the military and financial effort.

The Cabinet crisis was for the moment averted. I received the warm thanks of the Prime Minister for my efforts, and to this day I have a cigarette case which Mrs Asquith gave me to commemorate the occasion.

The next day (New Year's Day, 1916) I was sent for at very short notice to act as secretary to the new Military-Finance Committee. It was a Saturday and I had not expected that they would begin work until the Monday, nor had I received any warning that I was to be the secretary. When I arrived at 10 Downing Street, I found the Committee already at work and beginning to take evidence on the financial side of the inquiry. It was a very important and responsible task, for on the issue depended not only the co-ordination of our military and civil effort, but the existence of the Coalition Government. It was fairly clear that, if agreement could not be achieved, many of the Liberal members of the Cabinet would resign. This would have caused great confusion. No one but Asquith was clearly marked as yet for Prime Minister. If a Conservative Minister had tried to form a Government he would not have been able to rely on a majority in Parliament. The crisis which had just been temporarily terminated would have broken out anew, and might even have resulted in a General Election. This would have been an immeasurable disadvantage if fought on such an issue as the proper employment of our man-power, involving the question of

compulsory military service, and at a time when many of the voters were at the front.

The inquiry continued without intermission for a month, during which the Committee met nearly every day and sometimes twice a day. The struggle eventually became one between the War Office and the Board of Trade, the former wanting the men for the Army and the latter insisting (but in a most reasonable spirit) that they could not be spared from industry without imperilling our ability to maintain our sea-power, and to continue the huge supplies of munitions and war material on which our Allies, no less than our own armies, depended. I was incessantly engaged in abstruse calculations with the various officials concerned. Eventually the military authorities became convinced that the great offensive operation would require a longer time to prepare than had first been anticipated, which would shorten the actual fighting season, and this enabled them to accept a lower estimate of casualties, so that they were able to make some reduction in their original demands. The President and officials of the Board of Trade also made a tremendous effort of conciliation and eventually saw their way to a revision of their original estimates and agreed to release a larger number of men. In this way a gap of some 200,000 men was bridged, and on February 2nd agreement was reached to the intense relief of all concerned.

My own efforts in this affair, for what they were worth, seem to have been appreciated. First I received a present of half a dozen pheasants from the King at Sandringham, a very welcome addition to the family larder in war-time; next I received an insistent invitation to spend the week-end at 'The Wharf', the Prime Minister's place on the river; then came an invitation from Reading, the intimate friend of the Prime Minister, to lunch alone at the Courts of Justice, when he said many nice things about my share in the business. On January 24th I was sent for to 10 Downing Street, on 'a matter of immediate urgency'. I found there Doumayrou, who was very mysterious and refused to speak until he saw Asquith, for whom he had a private message from Briand. We waited until the Cabinet was over and then went together to Asquith. I was anticipating that some ugly and embarrassing issue was to be raised, but Doumayrou, in the most delightful way, told Asquith that Briand desired him to hand me the order of Officer of the Legion of Honour, which took me completely by surprise. An even greater surprise awaited me on February 4th, when I received from Asquith a letter couched in most flattering terms informing me that the King, on

his recommendation, had decided to give me the KCB. A day or two later the King invested me privately with this order, accompanied by words that I can never forget.

About this time also I took my first spell of leave since the beginning of the war, but my week at Eastbourne was interrupted by summonses to Town to attend meetings of the War Committee, and by the arrival every morning of a huge bag of official papers, for in war those working with the Supreme Command cannot afford to lose touch for a single moment with the course of events or they may miss some vital piece of information.

The man-power crisis, however, though temporarily allayed, was by no means at an end. The efforts of the Cabinet Committee had resulted in authority being given to the Army Council to aim at a policy of maintaining sixty-two divisions in the field abroad by the end of June with three months' reserves, as well as five complete divisions without reserves for home defence. It had always been doubtful, however, whether, even if the necessary numbers of recruits were forthcoming, the recruiting machine could obtain the men sufficiently rapidly. As this point as well as other points were obscure the Committee arranged to meet again in April to review the whole recruiting situation.

This fresh review, which occupied the first half of April, led to an even sharper crisis in the Cabinet, and in Parliament. As had been feared the military recruiting machine had not been able to produce the number of men that the military authorities required. In December 1915 only 55,152 recruits had been enlisted; in January and February respectively no more than 65,965 and 98,629. On the other hand, great pressure was being exerted by Jellicoe and other high naval authorities for more destroyers and other vessels, and the slow progress on the construction of warships was shown to be due mainly to the withdrawal of labour from the shipyards and the industries on which they depended. The Port and Transit Committee also was reporting a very serious and growing congestion in our ports, which was also mainly due to the recruitment of labour; while in the financial field Ribot, the French Finance Minister, had met Asquith in Paris on his return from a visit to Rome, and had demanded an immediate further loan of £60,000,000. Both sides of the controversy, therefore, were able to reinforce their case with fresh arguments.

On this occasion the crisis was very prolonged. The Prime Minister had promised to make a statement to Parliament before Easter. More than once it was postponed. On April 19th the Prime Minister had to take the extreme course of informing the House of Commons that the Cabinet was split on the subject. This announcement created a deplorable impression. It was listened to with consternation by a number of officer members who had returned from France on short leave to take part in the debate, and who were gravely embarrassed and inconvenienced by this postponement. In these circumstances it was decided on April 20th to ask the two Houses of Parliament to meet in secret session, when the subject could be discussed with a freedom which was impossible in the usual open session, the accounts of which would, of course, be rigorously scrutinized by the enemy's intelligence department.

I spent the greater part of the Easter holiday in collecting and compiling material for the Prime Minister's speech in secret session.

April 24th. Up to Town early to complete notes for Prime Minister's speech. Saw Robertson and Macready the Adjutant-General. The latter admitted to me that his department was in a very unsatisfactory state and that he could not rely on his figures. Robertson told me that Kut is bound to fall. At 2 p.m. I started off in a fine War Office car to 'The Wharf', lunching *al fresco* in the car. I arrived at 4 p.m. and spent three hours with the P.M. . . . There was a conclave to decide whether it would be best for him to spend the night at 'The Wharf' or to motor to Town that night. Finally it was left to me to decide—in fact the whole party treated me as though I were a 'trainer' charged with the duty of bringing 'the Bantam' into the ring in the pink of condition. I decided, knowing his habits, to go up that night, so he and I started at 10.30 p.m. to motor to Town. He was very chatty and jolly and I thoroughly enjoyed the ride. Bonham Carter followed in the car I had brought down. We arrived at 12.30 a.m. and I went to spend the night at the Bonham Carters'. Just as I was going to sleep, about 1.15 a.m. 'Bongie' came in to say they had telephoned that a Zeppelin raid was expected. For a moment I rather regretted bringing the P.M. up, but was sleepy, and with a 'damn the Zepps' I turned over to sleep. . . . I omitted to mention that on arrival in Town we got the first news of the Dublin outbreak. Asquith merely said 'well, that's something' and went off to bed.

Next day (Tuesday, April 25th) Asquith made his speech in the famous Secret Session and announced, as transpired in the sequel, that the Government had decided on the following relatively minor proposals:

1. The prolongation until the end of the war of the service of time-expired men whose period of service under the then law could be extended for one year only.

2. To empower the military authority to transfer men enlisted for Territorial battalions to any unit where they were needed.

3. To render an exempted man liable to military service immediately on the expiry of his certificate of exemption.

4. To bring under the terms of the Military Service Act all youths under 18 on the previous August 15th as they reach that age.

5. As the numbers required to discharge our military obligations would not be available for service at the time required, immediate efforts were to be made to obtain the numbers by voluntary enlistment among unattested married men. If by May 27th 50,000 recruits had not been secured, the Government would ask Parliament for compulsory powers, and if any week after May 27th the numbers of recruits should fall below 15,000 the same course would be taken, any surplus over 15,000 in any week being carried over to the next week. This plan to be carried on until 200,000 unattested men had been obtained.

Meanwhile the situation was to be kept under constant observation. This policy, however, was rejected by the House of Commons. When introduced in the form of a Bill, two days after the Secret Session, the criticism was so great that the embarrassed Prime Minister had to ask leave to withdraw the proposal.

Whatever might be the merits of the controversy, it was by this time clear that Parliament would be content with nothing short of compulsion, and on April 29th the Cabinet adopted the principle of National Military Service. Asquith introduced the Bill on May 2nd. I heard him make the speech. He did not much like the job and was not at his best. The House was astonishingly cold. The fact was that the people who wanted compulsory service did not want Asquith, and those who wanted Asquith did not want compulsory service. Nevertheless Asquith faced the situation with his usual courage. He repeated a statement he had made in the previous November that his own attitude had always been to treat compulsory service merely as a matter of expediency. If it was to be applied successfully it must be with something in the nature of general agreement. Just as he alone had been able to ensure national unity in August 1914, so it was again he, a Liberal Prime Minister, who alone was likely to be able to induce his countrymen to adopt such a measure as compulsory service, which was associated in men's minds with the Conservative Party. The Bill passed its second reading the same day without a division and became law on May 25th.

Those who fought the battle for voluntary service have come in for much abuse from their opponents. This is unjust. They were just as sincere as their adversaries, just as anxious to win the war, and just as confident in their beliefs. They did not think that the war could be won by hurling vast bodies of men on the enemy's barbed wire and trenches. According to their view the huge demands for men could only be justi-fied on the assumption that the offensive could succeed and this they were certain was impossible. The line could be held with a far smaller expenditure of man-power. In these circumstances they believed that the proper course was to conserve our strength and not to run any risks over our sea-power, economic strength or financial resources on which the whole of the Allies depended. Their general idea was that the side which could last longest would win the war and secure the best results in the peace. Where they were completely wrong was in their belief that the country would not put up with compulsion. Public opinion, with that 'horse-sense' which is often right when the astutest politicians go astray, was prepared to put up with anything which it thought would win the war. The Military Service Bill was welcomed by public opinion, and everyone was glad to see an end put to this distracting controversy.[1]

[1] The following figures provide the best epitaph for the voluntary system:

Raised under the voluntary system in the first eighteen months of the war ..	2,532,684
Raised under the compulsory system in the last thirty-three months of the war	2,438,218
TOTAL	4,970,902

In other words, more than half the man-power for military service during the war was raised by the voluntary system.

CHAPTER XLVI

PEACE KITES

'Also he sent forth a dove from him, to see if the waters
were abated from off the face of the ground; But the dove
found no rest for the sole of her foot, and she returned
unto him into the ark, for the waters were on the face of
the whole earth.' (*Genesis* viii. 8, 9.)

DURING the spring of 1916 there began a certain amount of back-chat
on the subject of the possibility of peace. Naturally it was very private
and unofficial. Nevertheless one began to meet it in the most unexpected quarters. This arose, as had happened once before, from a
visit by House.

In the autumn a Presidential Election was due in the United States;
Woodrow Wilson intended to stand for a second term. What would be
more likely to bring about a favourable result than a successful intervention by the President in the cause of peace? So House, the prudent,
cautious House, the President's intimate friend and trusted counsellor,
was sent over to explore the situation. Such, at any rate, appeared to us
to be the motive of his visit.

The 'Colonel' arrived in England early in January 1916. Naturally he
had to deal mainly with Grey, but he saw a great deal of other Ministers
and was much liked. I only met him once during this visit, though
afterwards I got to know him very intimately. My first impressions had
not been very favourable; fortunately they turned out to be wrong.

January 18th. . . . Dined with St. Loe Strachey (of *Spectator*) to meet
House who, Balfour tells me, is over here on a peace mission, or at least to
probe the ground. No doubt Wilson wants to get kudos for the Presidential
elections next November by posing as a peacemaker. The other guests were
the Archbishop of Canterbury, Stamfordham, and Hall, Director of Naval
Intelligence. A very dull dinner; all teetotallers except Hall and myself. They
brought round champagne, and I was the only person who took it (nasty
sour stuff too!), Hall drinking whisky and soda. House was a very quiet and
rather depressed individual. Anyone less like one's idea of an American party
'boss' I cannot conceive. He posed as tremendously pro-ally and as hating
his forthcoming trip to Berlin beyond anything, but I did not feel quite sure
of him. . . . I also wrangled a good deal about the desirability of taking
reprisals against German submarines by putting prisoners on board our

ships, but they all (except Hall) held up their hands in pious horror! I think Hall's impressions were the same as mine. . . .

Altogether it was not exactly a hilarious evening!

House returned from Germany early in February 1916. His reports were not encouraging:

February 12th. . . . Called at Balfour's house by appointment at 6 p.m. and remained one and a half hours, discussing naval and general situation. It appears that House, who has returned from Berlin, thinks that both the German Navy and Army are stronger than we calculate, and thinks they may outlast the Allies, notwithstanding their economic difficulties. He says they launch a submarine every three days and that they have plenty of men for the army for another year's hard fighting. Balfour a bit depressed, I thought. I told him that the Germans had probably deliberately stuffed the u.s. naval and military attaché's with exaggerated accounts of their strength in order to create an impression on House, and through him on us. House appears to contemplate the possibility of American offers of mediation, the object being, if Germany rejects them, for America to enter on the side of the Allies. Personally I am sceptical. . . . I do not believe that President Wilson cares about peace or intervention so much as about returning to office next November.

March 11th. . . . Lunched at Carlton with Montagu, who told me that following our talk at lunch last Monday he had urged that Robertson should be told of House's proposal, that we should tell the u.s.a. our peace terms, which President Wilson should then invite Germany to accept, threatening that if they would not do so the u.s.a. would join the Allies. My view was that Robertson ought to know of this, and that he ought to be asked whether in his opinion we could defeat the Germans this summer or not, and to be warned that after the summer economic pressure would probably compel a reduction in our maximum effort. If Robertson was sanguine of success, then the Government would be justified in going ahead, but otherwise in my view they ought to test House's suggestion in order either (1) to discuss peace before we passed our zenith, or (2) to get the u.s.a. behind us, in which case we could go on for ever.

March 14th. . . . From the King I went to Robertson to warn him that the House question was coming up, and that the decision would largely depend upon what he and Jackson thought about the prospects of the war. Robertson thanked me for coming. . . .

March 15th. . . . Today I was shown the House papers. H. when in England on his return from Berlin had a conference with Grey of which a record was made. The purport of it was that, if the Allies would state their peace terms to President Wilson, the latter would invite Germany to a conference to discuss them. If Germany stuck out for impossible terms the u.s.

would *probably* then join the Allies. The papers included a telegram from House to Grey stating Wilson's concurrence in the record, so far as he was in a position to speak for the u.s., but insisting on the word 'probably'.[1]

March 16th. In the morning I went to see the Prime Minister who was still in bed with a nasty attack of bronchitis. He was in good spirits, and surrounded by pots of exquisite flowers which Mrs Asquith had put there. Apart from Bonham Carter I was the only person who saw him. He decided to postpone tomorrow's War Committee until Monday. We talked of House and he asked me to see Grey and ask him to talk to Robertson informally. The Prime Minister himself affects to regard the whole thing as humbug, and a mere manœuvre of American politics. . . . In the afternoon I had a talk with Grey about House, and he told me the whole story. He spoke of the heavy responsibility which this laid on him. If he took no notice of it, and the war went wrong, he would have missed a great opportunity either to get a decent peace or to bring in America. If, however, we were likely to be completely victorious it would be better to ignore it. A middle course was to postpone action, but this would probably be to miss our opportunity. Much depended on the anticipations of the naval and military authorities in regard to the course of the war. He therefore wished to bring it before the War Committee. Briand had had a similar communication from House, and was likely to mention it when they met at the forthcoming conference in Paris. . . . Grey told me he had reliable information of Tirpitz's downfall.

March 20th. . . . Saw Grey in afternoon about House's proposals. Also saw Robertson.

March 21st. Meeting of War Committee. At outset discussed House's proposals, everyone being excluded except members of Cabinet, Jackson, Robertson and myself. Decided not to adopt them at present. Lunched 10 Downing Street. Whole afternoon drafting conclusions, on which I saw Robertson in evening.

Although the War Committee decided to leave the matter alone for the present, the idea of peace began to get into the minds of the Supreme Command, and about this time (March 24th) the Prime Minister held a meeting of a 'Reconstruction' Committee, which met and discussed the possibility of a 'Peace Book', which should be drawn up on the analogy of the 'War Book' to facilitate the passage of the nation, when the time came, from war to peace.

Meanwhile House had to return to America with a report that for the present there was 'nothing doing'.

---

[1] Grey's Memorandum summing up the conversations is in House, II, pp. 200–202.

CHAPTER XLVII

ITALY

Virtu contro al Furore
Prendera l'arme e fia il combatter corto:
Che l'antico valore.
Negli italice cuor non e ancor morto. (PETRARCH).

(Virtue against fury shall advance the fight,
And it i'th' combat soon shall put to flight;
For the old Roman valour is not dead,
Nor in th' Italians' breasts extinguished.
                    (Translation by Edward Daire, 1640.)

AT the end of March 1916, just before the opening of the second inquiry into man-power, there was something approaching a lull in the usual overwhelming pressure of business, and the Prime Minister decided to pay a visit to Rome. Italy had declared war on Austria-Hungary on May 23, 1915, but was not as yet at war with Germany. The Italians, perhaps, felt a little out in the cold. They had not been invited to the numerous conferences between the French and our-selves; there was no definite liaison between the three countries; and from every point of view it was felt desirable to tighten up our relations. With this object in view Cadorna[1] had visited London in the last half of March, where I met him at lunch at 10 Downing Street. Advantage was to be taken of an Allied conference in Paris, at which the Italians were to be present, for the Prime Minister to continue his journey as far as Rome and afterwards to accept Cadorna's invitation to visit the Italian Army.

Some of Asquith's friends were profoundly suspicious that an attempt would be made in his absence to stampede the Cabinet and the War Committee and Parliament prematurely into compulsory military service. In fact, towards the end of the Paris Conference the Prime Minister received a telegram from one of his anti-conscription col-leagues to the effect that the conscriptionists were on the warpath. At that moment, too, our military authorities were hesitating a little about the proposed offensive on the Western Front. At a meeting held during the Paris Conference Kitchener and Robertson demanded the return of

[1] Cadorna's title was Chief of the General Staff, the King of Italy being titular Commander-in-Chief of the armies in the field.

one British division at once from Salonica and of others later on with a view to their taking part in the Western offensive. The French, as before, took the proposal very badly and at the last moment drew the Russians into the discussion, which was to have been *à deux*. Kitchener and Robertson were much annoyed and told the French that, after we had recently taken over a large stretch of the French line on the Western Front, we could not take the offensive without the Salonica divisions. After the meeting they declared privately that without these divisions they would not undertake an offensive in the generally accepted sense, involving heavy losses. Anyhow, for the moment it was clear that the big offensive was rather 'in the air', that the man-power problem was easier, and that the situation could not be exploited by hot-headed people in Asquith's absence.

Of the conference which preceded our Italian trip there is very little to be said. A certain amount of useful work in arranging to supply the Russians and Italians with war material was done at a sub-committee. The main conference, however, was too large for serious work, as it was attended by numerous representatives of all the Allies—Britain, France, Italy, Japan, Russia, and Serbia. There was a great deal of talk and froth and a Press communiqué designed to show the *solidarité* of the Allies, and not much beside.

Before proceeding to Rome we gave the Italian representatives at the conference a day's start. That day was spent by Asquith and myself in a visit to the battlefields of the Marne and Ourcq, and on the morrow (March 30th) we started for Rome in the luxurious special train of the President of the Republic, lent for the occasion. The party consisted only of Asquith, Bonham Carter, O'Beirne, and myself. Never before or since have I so much regretted my ignorance of 'bridge', which compelled the others to play 'dummy' until we were joined in Italy by the Military Attaché. The visit is described in a few notes made at the time:

March 31st. Arrived Rome about 3 p.m. Official reception at station by the Ministry. Great popular demonstration as we drove through the streets. The Prime Minister and Bonham Carter stayed at the Embassy, O'Beirne and I at Grand Hotel, where, as guests of the Italian Government, we had each a magnificent suite of apartments on the first floor. I was rather alarmed to find that a full colonel on the Staff and a captain had been attached to me during my stay, but it proved to be more or less an empty form of compliment and they did not bother me. The head of the British mission with the Italian Army, Radcliffe, a most admirable British representative, was of great assistance to me. At 5 o'clock I accompanied the Prime Minister with the

Ambassador, Rennell Rodd, and O'Beirne to visit in succession the Queen of Italy, the Duke of Genoa, who acts as Regent in the King's absence at the front, and the Queen Mother. Both the ladies most delightful and simple. The Duke not so interesting, though intelligent. We were all much taken with the Queen, a handsome vigorous Montenegrin girl. She had been under fire at the front and had thoroughly enjoyed it, and did not appear the least bit perturbed at the idea of an air raid on Rome. She said she would fetch out her rifle and take pot shots at them!

Dinner at the Consulta (Ministry of Foreign Affairs). I sat between the Minister of Public Works and an elderly duke. The former told me that at Venice and Ancona the dockers were out of employment through the closing of the port and that the trade union at Genoa would not permit them to work there. Memo. Why not recruit these dockers for employment in our docks at home, which are so much congested? The Prime Minister made a good speech in French.

April 1st. My birthday. Spent a good deal of the morning in the delightful garden at the Embassy. Then did some sightseeing. A motor car, placed at my disposal by the military authorities, came in most useful. . . . The Prime Minister visited the Pope in the morning with O'Beirne, who is a Roman Catholic. O'Beirne tells me that the Pope made some suggestion of the desirability of an early peace, but the Prime Minister pursed up his mouth and said words to the effect that we should continue to the end.

Civil reception at Campodoglio (Quirinal) in afternoon. Badly organized affair. The Prime Minister made an admirable speech in English, but the Sindaco led off too soon; it was all done at the same end of the room as people were entering by, there was no platform, with the result that those who had succeeded in getting in hung about round the doorways, blocking out the crowds on the stairs, while the Prime Minister and the Sindaco spoke to a comparatively small circle. . . .

April 2nd (Sunday). A nice quiet morning in the Embassy garden and later on 'Bongie' and I went sightseeing with Rodd. The latter, whom I have always liked and admired, ever since I met him seventeen or eighteen years ago for a few minutes at Nauplia in Greece, always improves on acquaintance. He is really an ideal representative for us in Italy. A friend and admirer of the Italians; tremendously popular with all classes—for he seems to have as many friends among the lower as among the upper strata of society; artist, archæologist, student, and a veritable mine of knowledge of all things Italian; possessed of great personal charm. Both we and Italy owe him very much. I felt he was a worthy companion to the Prime Minister, whose vast store of knowledge on all classical and historical matters fills me with amazement and envy. However can he remember it all amid his tremendous burden of State affairs? . . . The Prime Minister stayed at home for a

rest he must need, but he is in tremendously good form and thoroughly enjoying himself.

A lunch by Salandra, the Italian Premier, at the Hotel Excelsior, to which were invited Ministers and ex-Ministers from all parties. Fine robust speech by the Prime Minister, admirably delivered. As one of the Italian Ministers remarked he is a splendid representative of England, typifying all that is best in the race. . . .

We left Rome the same evening after a motor trip to Tivoli.

On the whole the visit has been a gigantic success, and at the station a number of people went out of their way to say what a good impression the Prime Minister has made. I feel glad that no other Minister was with him and that he had it all to himself. Personally I did not feel that the ministerial and upper circles whom we met had any real enthusiasm for the war; they are in it up to the neck and know they have to go through with it, but they have no great . . . confidence in themselves and lean to an extraordinary extent upon us, and will continue to do so more and more. They have an unbounded belief in our strength and greatness (which is justified on the whole), but we shall continually have to support them more and more both in a material and moral sense.

April 3rd. In the morning I awoke to find another glorious sunny day lighting up a gorgeous panorama of snowclad, ethereal-looking mountains, rising like a wall from the flat Venetian plain. As I was breakfasting we heard the roar of an aeroplane overhead. Lo and behold, it was an Austrian! Our time-table was so well advertised that I have no doubt it meant to attack our train. Luckily though there was a new anti-aircraft battery close by, placed for the defence of some airship sheds, and the guns came into action and drove the intruder off, chased by some Italian aeroplanes.

Soon we arrived at Udine, the Italian General Headquarters, where we had a reception of unstinted and clamorous enthusiasm from the populace. Udine is a most delightful old-world Italian town, which I really must explore one day with Adeline. We drove to a villa outside the town, where the King lives, and waited outside an hour or so while the Prime Minister had a long 'heart to heart' with the King.   During this period we watched a most interesting bombardment of an enemy aeroplane by anti-aircraft guns. We lunched with the King. He speaks English perfectly; is a much older man than I had expected; and lives in great simplicity. His bedroom is furnished with two straw-seated chairs and a camp bed—no carpet nor pictures except photographs of his children and wife. He rises at 5.30 a.m. in summer and almost always lunched in the field.

After lunch the King took the Prime Minister, and we others followed, to the mountain front. After driving across the flat plain through some most delightful walled towns—perfect pictures everywhere—we penetrated deep into the mountains, first by the valley of the Tagliamento, and then up the

long Raccolano valley, where the Italian Army have built a marvellous mountain road. Unfortunately we did not reach the trenches on the col and had to turn round about 1,000 feet below the top, but we saw the whole of the rear organization—the corps depots, communications, some 12-inch howitzers, etc., all of which was admirable. I was much struck by the men, who were well set up, healthy, in first-rate spirits, and obviously had an excellent understanding with their officers. O'Beirne and I were in a car with General Elia, Under-Secretary for War, a nice old fellow, who kept stopping the car to talk to the men—often in their own dialect. . . .

Dinner at Cadorna's GHQ. And so to bed; my quarters in the dingy-looking Albergo della Croce di Malta turned out to be far more comfortable than I expected.

April 4th. Up early to start at 8 a.m. (the King arriving as he always does punctual to the moment) to see the Isonzo front. We witnessed a number of aerial combats—three or four at least—and during one of these I penetrated into the command post of the battery, where an officer tried to explain the system of fire control—not entirely successfully, my Italian not being equal to anything quite so technical. We went to a high hill, where there was an observation post, from which we could see Gorizia and the Carso and had a bird's eye view of the whole position. The guns were very quiet that morning but we saw considerable damage to a house close by the observation point, which had been inflicted at the same hour on the previous day, presumably in honour of our arrival, and I spoke to a girl whose sister had been badly wounded. There were also many bloodstains. What impressed me most on this front was the admirable lines of defences in rear of the army—ten lines at least, concreted where they were in low-lying ground. (Memo. Why don't our people concrete their trenches?) Today, as yesterday, I noticed the excellent bearing of the men and the way they saluted—and they were not expecting us as the King had kept back the programme until the last moment. It was pleasant to drive for a whole morning in *enemy* territory. The Italians had built splendid roads everywhere, made partly by their Territorial troops (old stagers) and partly by civilian labour, hired on three months' contracts and employed in military formations. (Memo. Why not hire Italian labour on short engagement and in military formations to work on our docks, railways, and mines? Germany had three to five million Italians working for her when Italy went to war with Austria, and won't let them go. She gets more work out of the Italians than we do. Yet the economic state of Italy depends entirely on us!) The villages were much less knocked about than those behind our lines in France and Flanders. I only saw one badly cut up. The population of both the Italian and occupied territory looked contented and prosperous; very handsome women with beautiful complexions.

Lunch with Cadorna and then good-bye. Elia and Radcliffe came with us as far as Turin. The latter is a great success as head of the British Military

Mission. He gets on well, talks Italian perfectly, is a man of character, and obviously has great influence. I had many very long talks with him and Rennell Rodd, both of whom accompanied us from Rome to GHQ.

Rather an amusing incident occurred on the way back. We received word that there was to be a great popular demonstration at Milan, where we were due to arrive toward midnight. Asquith made up his mind to deliver a speech in Italian, and much of the journey was passed in translating the proposed speech. On arrival at Milan, however, it turned out that the 'demonstration' was by the small English colony only, and instead of being delivered as intended to a vast concourse of Milanese citizens the speech was thrust into the hands of a solitary Italian Press representative!

During this trip I was thrown much into the company of O'Beirne, for whom I formed a great admiration. He had spent part of his diplomatic career at Petrograd and he more than once said how much good a visit of the same kind would do to Russia and how pleasant it would be if the same jolly informal party could do the trip.

On our return journey we were met at Paris by Briand and Ribot, who demanded not only a loan of £60,000,000 but also that Haig should concert an offensive with Joffre in order to relieve the pressure on Verdun. One more extract from my diary to illustrate the vicissitudes of travel in war-time:

At Boulogne we had to wait from 5 p.m. until midnight, as the destroyer sent to fetch us ran ashore in the entrance, so that we missed the safe period of the tide for mines. Arrived in London 4 a.m. and I went to the Charing Cross Hotel. They all laughed at me because I tied a heavy iron bar on to my despatch box so that it would sink in case of emergency. '*Quelques simples preparatifs pour la voyage*' was my remark.

As a matter of fact the weighting of despatch boxes containing secret documents is a matter of great importance in war-time, and there have been instances of valuable secrets being lost and gained from the flotsam and jetsam of the sea. We ourselves obtained at least one great intelligence coup from this source. At the time of which we are speaking I used to borrow heavy bars from the stoke-hold and lash them to my despatch boxes before sailing, but a little later I had made a number of heavy steel boxes, weighted and perforated for use in these cross-Channel trips. They were a great nuisance to carry, but were absolutely certain to sink if we were caught by a mine or submarine. So far as possible I always kept a duplicate set of all papers in the office.

Not very much actual business was accomplished during Asquith's visit to Italy, but it demonstrated to the Italian people that Britain was closely interested in their fortunes, and gave Asquith the opportunity to size up the personal factor in Italian leadership, both civil and military, and *vice versa*. Probably the visit was not without influence in determining Italy to declare war on Germany, which she did on August 28th.

CHAPTER XLVIII

THE WAR AT SEA
U-BOAT WARFARE—JUTLAND

'Never earth nor sea beheld so great a stake before them set.'

(SWINBURNE, *The Armada*, II.)

IT is a curious fact that up to the end of the year 1915 the Navy, which was our main hope and standby for winning the war, was not in any way a preoccupation to the Supreme Command and occupied but little of its energies. In comparison with the enemy our main fleet was so powerful, and its normal role was so sedentary, that it did not come much into the limelight. Far away in northern waters, out of sight and out of mind, the battle fleet kept its silent and sleepless vigil. Mostly it lay in the advanced base at Scapa Flow, but now and again it would emerge to carry out firing practice or some manœuvre, to sweep the North Sea, or to support some movement by the battle cruisers.

In the early days of the war, both the German and British fleets had shown some enterprise in the North Sea, but for more than a year the main fleets never established the smallest contact. They resembled a pair of boxers sparring for an opening, but never striking. Germany lost no capital ship but we lost from submarine warfare the pre-dreadnought battleships *Formidable* (January 1, 1915), and *King Edward VII* (January 6, 1916). In its effect on the balance of naval strength the loss of these old ships was almost negligible, but it was a portent, and the moral effect was appreciable. One result was an ever-increasing demand from the fleets at sea for more destroyers and mine-sweepers. This involved a prior claim on our national resources which were already so severely strained in building up the Army and Air Force.

Meanwhile economic warfare, by which sea-power secures its main results, was slowly but steadily increasing in intensity. The wide interpretation given by the Allies, in reply to German breaches of the laws of war, to the definition of contraband and to the rules on destination in October 1914, had been used by the Germans to justify the declaration of a submarine blockade of Britain on February 18, 1915. The British Government had retaliated by the Order-in-Council of March 11, 1915, the effect of which was to debar neutral merchant

shipping from entering or leaving German ports, except at considerable risk, and to secure that goods with enemy destination or of enemy origin in neutral bottoms should be liable to discharge in a British port. The list of 'absolute' contraband was still further extended. Thereafter the German U-boat warfare had steadily increased in frightfulness. At the beginning of March 1916, with the aid of new and larger submarines, the Germans were able to extend their radius of action far out into the Atlantic and the danger area now included the whole of the North Sea and Channel, the Atlantic from 100 to 150 miles from the Fastnet on the north, and Ushant on the south, and the whole of the Mediterranean. Losses of British merchant ships were heavy and continuous and in April 1916 no less than forty-three British ships of 140,000 tons were sunk—thirty-seven by submarine and six by mine. As yet, however, our tonnage had not diminished, and in April 1916 I was able to submit to Asquith in some notes for his speech in Secret Session the following remarkable coincidence of figures:

Sunk by the enemy up to April 19, 1916, 423 ships of 1,410,000 tons.
Now on the stocks, 424 ships of 1,423,000 tons.

Meanwhile the British and Allied 'blockade' was going better, and the monthly reports compiled in the Foreign Office showed a steady increase in the economic pressure on both Germany and Austria. Moreover, on February 23rd Robert Cecil had been appointed to the new Ministry of Blockade, and it was hoped that this would result in a still greater stiffening up of our economic pressure.

About this time the Germans seem to have come to the conclusion that there was something amiss with their naval policy, and it was not a matter of great surprise when on March 16, 1916, we learned definitely that three days before Tirpitz had been replaced by Capelle. It now became increasingly probable that a more enterprising policy would be attempted. It was inconceivable that the German people would tolerate that their great High Sea Fleet should remain for ever supine without an attempt to break through the steel curtain which shut off Germany from the outer world.

Meanwhile Jellicoe had been making representations about the insufficiency of light cruisers, destroyers and minesweepers in the Grand Fleet. He was asked to come to Town to report to the War Committee. On February 11th, the first date selected, he could not come owing to 'restlessness' in the German Fleet. He did manage to get away, however, for a meeting on February 17th and there was a full-

dress discussion by the War Committee, which was followed up at a series of later meetings. There was no dispute that the Grand Fleet was short of the classes of ship mentioned. The distribution of ships throughout the world was carefully scrutinized. Some battleships were brought home from the Mediterranean with a view to economy in coal and supplies, but no cruisers could anywhere be spared except those attached to the Italian Fleet under the agreement on which Italy entered the war, and owing to Italian susceptibilities it was not considered possible to withdraw these. Jellicoe had to content himself with the light cruisers and old armoured cruisers which he already possessed. Similarly, an examination of the distribution of destroyers revealed that none which were of a type suited for work with the fleet could be spared from their stations. In the case of minesweepers Jellicoe had to be satisfied with promises of new vessels as they left the builders' hands. The Admiralty claimed that these shortages were the direct result of the drain on our man-power. The Army was swallowing up not only skilled artisans, but men who supplied the raw material, the fuel, and the semi-raw material on which our shipyards depended. And what was true of the Royal Navy was even more true of the Mercantile Marine, which was also being depleted by losses and by requisition for war purposes.

Although the Admiralty made good their case, confidence was undoubtedly a little shaken. My predecessor, Ottley, the last man to complain about the service in which he had been brought up, came to me at the end of February to speak about the slackness in naval construction, which he as a managing director of a great armament company was in a position to judge. Another day, Philip Watts, formerly Chief Constructor to the Navy, came on the same errand. There was ample evidence from inside the Admiralty that there was not much drive or punch. Runciman was receiving similar reports from shipbuilding circles and a conference was arranged between the Admiralty, the Board of Trade and the shipbuilders on March 6th. Fisher was tremendously on the rampage and was invited to state his case at the War Committee. He merely confirmed Jellicoe's reports. On March 7th Churchill, who was on leave from the front, delivered an impassioned attack in the House of Commons on the Admiralty and appealed for the recall to office of Fisher, who was sitting in the gallery like a sphinx in his favourite seat behind the clock. The attack was well received by the House, but not the suggestion to reinstate Fisher. Altogether people were not very happy about the Admiralty. It was felt

that they had not made great enough efforts to insist on the retention of skilled craftsmen in the shipyards and affiliated industries; that there was a lack of driving power; and that the Board, which contained no flag officer who had had sea experience during the war, and no member of which was ever heard of as visiting the Fleet, was out of touch with the sea service. Perhaps Balfour, splendid and invaluable as he was as a counsellor on general policy, was temperamentally unsuited to an administrative post requiring incessant drive and initiative. Perhaps Jackson too closely resembled his chief. As yet, however, no change was to take place.

On April 25th the Germans gave the first sign of a change in policy. After an interval of fifteen months the plan of 'tip and run raids' was resumed with a cruiser raid on Lowestoft and Yarmouth. On May 31st the expected happened. The German Fleet put to sea to fight.

May 31st had been a relatively quiet day, occupied, so far as I was concerned, in adjusting some minor differences over the conclusions of the previous day's meeting of the War Committee.

May 31st. At 6.15 p.m., just as I was about to go home, I received a message from the Admiralty, from Masterton Smith, asking where I should be that evening, as he might have some news of interest to communicate. I went across at once, guessing that there must be a fleet action imminent. I was shown into the First Lord's room. Balfour was obviously in a state of very great excitement and showed me a succession of wireless messages, ending with one from Jellicoe to the Admiralty saying that 'a fleet action is imminent'. I then arranged to stay the night with Bonham Carter, and went down to the House to tell the Prime Minister the news. He was in the House listening to a debate and I sent in an urgent message asking him to speak to me. I then delivered my message. I was most impressed with the way he took it. He showed no sign or trace of anxiety or nervousness, but only delight at having brought them to action with some fear that they might manage to flee without a fight—as subsequently seems to have happened, so far as can be judged at present. I was at the Admiralty until past midnight with Balfour, Masterton Smith and later Bonham Carter, but the news was vague, conflicting, and indeterminate, pointing to a breaking-off of the action. Before going back to bed at Bonham Carter's I sent a few lines up in pencil to the Prime Minister, who was playing bridge as though nothing had happened!

June 1st. News trickling in all day at the Admiralty. *The Warrior*, Robert Arbuthnot's flagship sunk, the *Warspite* arrived at Rosyth and docked, and

R

another dreadnought battleship injured, but whether the two latter were injured by the enemy or had collided was not certain. Some destroyers also lost. But there is strong evidence that the 'Bosches' have lost more heavily —three ships said to be sunk and a battleship badly injured. Lunched with Balfour.

June 2nd. Unfortunately as news came in of the fleet action it became worse and worse. All day I was acting as intermediary between the Admiralty and the Prime Minister as the news trickled in. Jellicoe's full report did not arrive until about 4 p.m., when it transpired that we had lost three battle cruisers, three armoured cruisers, and ten or twelve destroyers, against one German battleship, probably a second German battleship, and a few light cruisers and destroyers.[1] The Prime Minister was not in when this news arrived. It is a terrible disappointment as our battle cruisers were nine to five against theirs and ought to have wiped them out. In fact, it shows that they were superior to us in fighting power. The battleship action, so far as it went, was satisfactory, as we seem to have knocked them about without receiving much ourselves. As a whole, however, this, the first trial of strength between the two fleets, has been the most bitter disappointment of this terribly dis-appointing war. Nevertheless even in this moment of disappointment I ask myself the question—is our general sea-power impaired? Is our power to maintain the blockade adversely affected? The answer is in the negative. In every class of vessel we have still the superiority. It is rather one's confidence, perhaps an over-weening confidence in the power of the fleet, that is shaken a bit. God forbid that it should have a bad effect on the morale of the fleet.

June 3rd. The news of the battle much better. It is tolerably clear from secret information that the 'Bosches' got a tremendous hammering and lost far more than they have admitted to. In fact, it is by no means impossible that they lost two dreadnought battleships and three battle cruisers. I do not think that they will venture out again. Then we know that one of their battle cruisers has been beached. We have also discovered the reason why our ships blew up—viz. defective arrangements for preventing the effect of a shell bursting in the turret from reaching the magazine. We are now secure against invasion; the Russian right flank is safe, and the east coast towns will not again be bombarded; and our blockade will be as effective as ever. I asked to be invited to 10 Downing Street to lunch, as I knew great depression would prevail among the ladies. . . . The Prime Minister, Masterton Smith, Bonham Carter and I had them all quite cheerful and almost hilarious before lunch was over. From this focus I hope that a more cheerful spirit will spread all over

---

[1] The actual losses, according to *Naval Operations*, III, App. E, were:

								British	German
Battleships	..	..	..	..	..	..	..	—	1
Battle cruisers	..	..	..	..	..	..	..	3	1
Cruisers	..	..	..	..	..	..	..	3	—
Light cruisers	..	..	..	..	..	..	..	—	4
Destroyers	..	..	..	..	..	..	..	8	5

London society. . . . Personally I am inclined to let the Germans buck on the principle that he laughs longest who laughs last.

Most of these anticipations proved correct. Never again did the High Sea Fleet put to sea to fight. Never again were the east coast towns bombarded. Never again did we have a moment's anxiety about our general command of the sea. We suffered much from the depredations of submarines, just as after Trafalgar we suffered for years from the *guerre de course*. From the point of view of the grand strategy, however, Jutland was as sweeping a success as Trafalgar, and this will be more and more recognized. On the morning that followed the battle Jellicoe found himself in undisputed possession of the North Sea without a sign of an enemy, and to all intents and purposes this state of affairs continued (apart from U-boat warfare) until the German Fleet sailed to Scapa Flow to surrender. Victory is measured not by a comparison of casualties or losses, not by tactical incidents in the battle, but only by results.

CHAPTER XLIX

PREPARATIONS FOR
THE WESTERN OFFENSIVE—TANKS

'The invention all admired, and each, how he
To be th' inventor missed, so easy it seemed
Once found, which yet unfound most would have thought
Impossible; . . .'

(MILTON, *Paradise Lost*, vi, 497.)

ON December 28, 1915, it had been decided that every effort was to be made to prepare for carrying out offensive operations in the spring in the Western theatre, but final sanction had not been given for the offensive to be undertaken. For some time there were some members of the Supreme Command who hoped that the great assault would not be undertaken. Even Kitchener, in January, did not intend, if he could help it, that a great and prolonged offensive should be embarked on. He merely contemplated an intensified policy of attrition in order gradually to use up the German resources. The generals continued very properly to base their preparations on the assumption of a great offensive, and they had behind them the whole of the Commanders-in-Chief and General Staffs of the Allies. More important than their persuasions was the pressure of events, and, above all, the remorseless energy of the German attack on Verdun and the heartrending losses and moral sufferings of our French Allies. 'We are being crucified', Briand said. Even the French military command sometimes suffered from extreme depression—small blame to them—though it did not diminish the obstinacy and gallantry of their resistance. At one time (May 25th) we learned that the French had lost 600 field guns and 100 heavier guns in the last few days and that losses in guns were so great that the whole output of the French factories was required for replacement only, so that the equipment of fresh batteries had to be suspended.

Shortly after the opening of the battle of Verdun on February 21st, the British Government asked in what way they could best help the French Army in this time of trial, and at the French request we had taken over the defence of an additional slice of the line. When on April 5th Briand and Ribot tackled Asquith on his return journey from Rome and asked that instructions might be given to Haig to concert an offensive with Joffre, only one answer was possible. No alternative plan was

forthcoming from any responsible quarter—and the most ingenious plan would have failed if the generals did not believe in it. Haig's proposals had already reached London when Asquith arrived on his return from Rome, and two days later (April 7th) the Commander-in-Chief was given the authority for which he, no less than the French Government, was asking.

The decision, though inevitable, was not given without a good deal of misgiving. The attack was to be preceded by an intensive bombardment of several days' duration, the object of which was to shatter the enemy's trenches, to destroy his barbed wire and machine-gun posts, to silence his guns, and thus to prepare the way for an advance by divisions of infantry massed for the purpose. In this way a gap was to be made in the enemy's lines, through which was to pour an 'army of pursuit' composed of cavalry, closely supported by infantry. Once through the gap the 'army of pursuit' was to strike at the enemy's communications, seizing and if necessary destroying vital strategic points; meanwhile the forces pouring through were to 'mushroom' out, widening the gap, rolling up the enemy's line, thus bringing trench warfare to an end and initiating a war of manœuvre in which we should have the advantage of the initiative.

The critics of this plan were frankly derisive. They said it had really been tried before by both sides without success. Even the German attack at Verdun, terrible as it was for France, was probably proving no less costly to Germany. The initial stages were too difficult. It might be possible, they admitted, at great cost to break through the first line of the enemy's defences. But the range of guns was not sufficient to ensure the destruction of the successive lines of any one section of these defences, which were constructed in depth. While our guns were being moved forward over the broken and pitted lines of our first advance in order to prepare the attack on the next position, the enemy's reinforcements and reserves would be coming up. Fresh trenches would be constructed and the battle would have to begin all over again. Even if, *per impossible* a gap were made in the enemy's line, he had ample reserves wherewith to form an 'army of manœuvre' to deal with the 'army of pursuit'. There were some who continued to believe that for the present the best plan was to limit ourselves to a series of operations of a comparatively limited scope.

One factor which was not without influence and was at the back of some men's minds, was the knowledge that a new instrument of warfare was rapidly approaching fruition. These mysterious machines were

still spoken of with bated breath, if they were spoken of at all. Little was known, which perhaps added subconsciously to the hopes which were built on them. The few decisions which had been taken on the subject by the War Committee had been recorded by me in manuscript and had not even been communicated to the Cabinet. Those, however, who had seen the 'armoured caterpillars', as the tanks were still generally termed, had been profoundly impressed.[1]

I have already told[2] how Swinton explained to Tulloch and myself how our Army in France was held up by the combination of machine-guns and barbed wire and threw out the idea of armouring 'caterpillar' tractors with a view to producing an effective reply. Later Churchill had been fired, partly by my so-called 'Boxing Day' Memorandum, to take up the evolution of technical appliances, including tanks, to over-come the difficulties of trench warfare. In July 1915, when I was sent on a mission to the Dardanelles, I had advised Asquith to bring Swinton back to replace me during my absence. In doing so I had the specific idea that on my return he should devote himself largely to the promo-tion of inventions to combat trench warfare in general and in particular to the tanks, of which from the first he had been the principal pioneer. Thanks to the persistent efforts of Churchill, Swinton, Tennyson d'Eyncourt (the Chief Constructor of the Navy), Colonel Bertie Stern, Lieutenant W. G. Wilson and Mr W. Tritton (the actual designers of the tanks and tracks respectively) and others, models were completed early in 1916 and a test was arranged to take place in Hatfield Park on February 2nd. So great were the precautions for secrecy that Salisbury, who had kindly allowed his park to be used for this purpose, told me long afterwards that he had no idea of what was taking place. My own part in the 'chain of causation' of these weapons had from the first been the comparatively modest one of propagandist. On the occasion of the Hatfield demonstration I felt that the best help I could give would be to secure the personal interest of the Chancellor of the Exchequer, who held the strings of the national purse. I accordingly persuaded McKenna to lunch with me and to proceed immediately after to Hatfield, where Kitchener, Balfour, and Lloyd George were also present. The three latter were all enthusiastic, and Balfour insisted in riding in a tank—just as years before, at an early demonstration of aeroplanes, I remem-

---

[1] The designation 'tank' was part of the ingenious system of camouflage adopted to conceal the real purpose of these engines not only from the enemy's spies, but even from those engaged on their construction. The machines were known as 'tanks for Russia' and had this written on them in English and Russian. This was Swinton's idea.

[2] *vide supra*, p. 227 and p. 246.

bered him insisting on taking a flight. But Kitchener remained profoundly sceptical in spite of the manner in which the larger of the two tanks surmounted trenches, barbed wire, ditches and other obstacles. The military officers, however, sent from the War Office and GHQ to witness the trials were impressed and ten days later the War Office, at the request of GHQ France and with the approval of the War Committee, placed an order for one hundred of the new machines. A few days later I had to surrender the services of my 'chief of staff', Swinton, who was required by the War Office to raise and train the personnel for manning the tanks—a task for which he was well qualified by the zeal and industry with which he had surmounted what is described in my diary (February 2nd) as 'a mountain of apathy and passive resistance'.

I still continued to do what I could to help those concerned with the development of the tank, which was proceeding apace in the spring of 1916 under Swinton's inspired driving force. Thus on April 27th I find an allusion in my diary to a letter I had recently written to Robertson, urging

... postponement of the offensive until August, when the 'caterpillars' are ready; meanwhile, to compel the Germans to keep their reserves in the west, instead of going east to smash the Russians, by making every preparation for a great offensive up to and including the artillery preparations. After we had done this once or twice the Bosches would say 'these fellows are not for it' and would go east. Then we should make our real attack with 'caterpillars'.

Next day Robertson told me he had sent my letter on 'caterpillars' to Haig.

I followed up my letter to Robertson by another addressed to David Henderson, the Director-General of Military Aeronautics:

April 29th. Spent part of morning writing letter to David Henderson suggesting formation out of surplus weak aeroplanes[1] suitable only for instructional purposes, of a corps of 'grasshopper' aeroplanes, to work in conjunction with Swinton's caterpillars and attack heavy guns with bombs, flying at low altitudes and armoured.

What I had in mind, as fully developed in the letter, was to supplement the surprise effect of tanks by the use of aeroplanes for low flying. This would, I thought, be a method of overcoming the resistance of heavy

---

[1] I had been given to understand that at the moment there was a surplus of such machines in the R.N.A.S.

guns, which were at that time expected to prove the worst enemy of the tank.

Neither of my proposals was adopted. The first proposal, to postpone the Somme offensive until August in order that the tanks might be used with full effect, which appeared attractive in April, must have proved impracticable in July. Joffre, who had originally fixed the date of the opening bombardment of several days' duration for July 1st, found himself in mid-June constrained by the seriousness of the situation at Verdun and the resulting political crisis in Paris to advance it to June 25th. In these circumstances it would have been impossible for Haig to insist on postponing his attack, and, if he had done so, the carefully kept secret of the tanks might easily have leaked out. This is the more true because in the event the tanks were not ready to go into action until mid-September. What perhaps Haig might have done was to prepare his plans in such a manner as to use the tanks to open up a new front after the German reserves had been drawn into the Somme area. But here again it has to be remembered that Haig was an optimist, and hoped that by the time the tanks were ready the German front would have been broken and the 'army of pursuit' would have burst through and caused the whole of the enemy's line to fall back.

The second proposal to use a mass of low-flying aeroplanes to support a massed attack by tanks did not commend itself to the Director-General of Military Aeronautics, and, so far as I know, produced no effect at GHQ. Henderson's view was that aircraft could be better employed to support the tank attack by directing the fire of our artillery on to the enemy's guns. The official historian of the War in the Air, in describing the battle of September 15th, while paying a warm tribute to the value of aircraft employed as Henderson advocated also shows how individual aeroplanes on occasions rendered notable services by diving low to attack batteries holding up an advance.[1]

It is perhaps permissible to argue that, if a massed attack could have been carried out by tanks on a new front, where the ground was less broken up than on the Somme, and supported by a mass of low-flying aeroplanes, both methods being employed for the first time and as a

---

[1] *Air Operations*, II, p. 276, describes such an attack at Courcelette. On p. 291 it describes an incident on September 25th at the Grid Trench covering Gueudecourt, where a single aeroplane, working in conjunction with a party of bombers and a tank, after first bringing artillery fire to support the attack—'dropped to three hundred feet and flew along the trench raking the unhappy occupants with machine-gun fire. Their endurance snapped, and they waved arms and white handkerchiefs in surrender to the airmen. This fact was transmitted to the infantry by message bag, and they advanced and accepted the surrender of eight officers and 362 men. The total British casualties in this brilliant little action numbered five.'

surprise without prolonged artillery bombardment, a notable success might have been achieved.

Once the decision had been taken that Haig was to concert an attack with Joffre, the preparations took on a more objective character. These were enormous in scope. They ranged from the local preparations opposite the front of attack to the adaptation thereto of our military and foreign policy all over the world. The former were, of course, the duty of the Commander-in-Chief and his staff. They involved rest after the long winter in the trenches, the preparations and intensive training of the troops selected for the attack, arrangements for their unobtrusive concentration and accommodation at the moment of attack, the accumulation of vast dumps of ammunition for the guns and howitzers, the massing of the batteries, the preparation of elaborate communications by road and rail in order to maintain the stream of munitions and supplies for a prolonged battle; the provision of aerodromes and the concentration therein of the aircraft required to maintain aerial supremacy; water supply, drafts of men to replace casualties, dressing-stations, sanitation and a thousand other details, all of which had to be carried out as far as possible in secrecy and concealment from the lynx eyes of the German spies and aircraft. Away behind the front dumps and depots, sheds and railways, hospitals and rest camps had to be brought into existence right away down to the base ports, where elaborate arrangements were necessary to avoid stagnation and congestion. It was all extraordinarily well done, especially when the comparative rawness of many of the staffs and the inconvenience of sea transport are taken into consideration.

The War Committee's main share in these preparations was to give Robertson and Haig all the help and support they could. Robertson's main conception was to concentrate every man and gun in the main theatre, and to adopt a quiescent attitude in all other theatres of war, from which as many divisions as possible were to be withdrawn. This involved investigations and decisions affecting all these theatres by the War Committee, sometimes in concert with our Allies, with whom, unfortunately, we did not always see eye to eye.

The British offensive could not be considered by itself. It was only a part of a concerted offensive by the Allies as a whole. However well prepared might that offensive be, it must fail unless the other Allies

R*

were in a condition to play their part. Every Austrian division that Italy could draw down to the Southern Front meant one less division to oppose the Russians. Every German division needed to hold up the Russian attacks was one less to oppose the Anglo-French offensive in France. The equipment of Russia, therefore, was one of the main pre-occupations of the British Supreme Command. These tasks fully occupied the War Committee during the spring of 1916.

One of the first necessities was seen to be to bring the last of the out-lying British theatres of war under a central control. Up to the end of 1915 the responsibility for the direction of the Mesopotamian campaign had been delegated to the Commander-in-Chief in India. Early in 1916 the War Committee decided in principle that in future the Commander-in-Chief in India was to receive his orders on military operations whether in Mesopotamia or Persia from the Chief of the Imperial General Staff in exactly the same way as the Commanders-in-Chief in other theatres of war. India was to remain the principal base of these forces, and the Commander-in-Chief in India was only to indent on the War Office when he could not obtain what was needed from Indian resources. These arrangements came into operation on February 16th. Events in this theatre, however, had for the moment got out of hand, and Robertson was unable to avert the fall of Kut-el-Amara (April 29th). Apart from the blow to our prestige this disaster did not give cause for any great anxiety, for by this time the Turks were threatened from other directions.

In the Caucasus the Russians had captured Erzeroum (February 16th), and on April 17th Trebizond. Further advances were anticipated. Moreover a relatively small force under Baratoff had penetrated into Southern Persia, and about a fortnight after the capitulation of Kut, had occupied Khanikin, whence it constituted a threat to Baghdad itself. If no troops could be withdrawn from Mesopotamia the position there was not sufficiently serious to make a drain on the concentration of force on the Western Front.

In Egypt also the position was quite secure. The long expected Turkish attack on the canal had been repulsed in the third week in April and was not likely to be renewed. The Arab revolt had broken out early in June. The Sheriff of Mecca had proclaimed the independence of the Hejaz; the Turkish garrison of Mecca had surrendered on June 10th. So far as the Western offensive was concerned, however, the question that arose about Egypt was not one of sending reinforcements, but solely of how many divisions could be drawn from

there for France. On June 6th it was decided to bring a single British division from Egypt to France. The Australian and New Zealand divisions also were brought to France in time to take a prominent part in the battle of the Somme, and, thanks to the personal intervention of Hughes, who was on a visit to this country, they remained under the command of their redoubtable leader Birdwood.

March 13th. . . . Robertson thanked me for coming but appeared upset about something. I learned from his A.D.C. that he had had a bad morning with Hughes, who had insisted that Birdwood should command the Australian Corps coming to France. . . .

We have already seen that our military authorities had always looked askance at the maintenance of a large Allied force in the Salonica theatre. The abandonment of that theatre would have set free five divisions of British troops for the Western offensive. Unsuccessful in persuading our Allies, the General Staff set their hearts on detaching at least a part of these divisions for use in the West. An opportunity for making the attempt occurred about the middle of March when our assistance was invoked for transporting the Serbian Army from Corfu, where a considerable remnant had been brought by French initiative after the great retreat through Serbia and Albania. In January we had agreed that the responsibility for re-equipping and reorganizing the Serbian Army should rest with the French, and about the middle of March they had asked us to help in transporting the Serbian Army to Salonica. The suggestion was then made that, on arrival at Salonica, the Serbian divisions might replace an equal number of British divisions, which could be brought to France. The subject was brought up at a special meeting during the March Paris Conference, but once more we failed to obtain the acquiescence of our Allies. The French had already agreed that the transport of British divisions from Egypt to France should take precedence over that of Serbian divisions from Corfu to Salonica, but beyond that they would not go. In the middle of May the French Government proposed that an offensive operation should be undertaken at Salonica. This was too much altogether for our military authorities! The proposal was immediately rejected. We were not prepared to dissipate our forces in an operation from which there appeared nothing to gain and everything to lose. Vainly the French argued and implored. Their military advisers urged an offensive; their public opinion expected it. Early in June we heard that Sarrail had been ordered to prepare an offensive—which was felt to be rather sharp

practice more particularly as the matter was about to form the subject of a special conference. This drew from Grey a sharp reminder that we had not agreed to the principle of an offensive in the Balkan theatre.

On June 9th the whole question was ventilated at a special Anglo-French Conference held in London at which Asquith was accompanied by practically the whole of the War Committee, and Briand by Joffre and Roques, his Minister of War. The French urged that the great army of 350,000 men, composed approximately of equal parts of British, French and Serbians, could not remain in the Balkans doing nothing to justify their existence. Russia, who was about to undertake a great offensive, and who had actually sent a detachment, now *en route* to Salonica, expected that something should be attempted in the Balkan theatre to assist her. Italy, who had sent troops to Valona in Albania as a contribution to the Allied cause in the Balkans also expected some action on our part. If nothing was done the Serbian Army would melt away and the Serbian Government would listen to the blandishments of the Central Powers to make a separate peace. The French did not claim that it was possible to gain a sweeping victory and to occupy Sofia itself; but there were, in their opinion, enough men and guns to bring about some considerable local success, which would make a stir in that part of the world. The British reply was that there was no prospect of a big military success. If the Allies had 350,000 troops, the Bulgars, who were stubborn fighters, could put 300,000 men in the field against them. This number, well entrenched as they were, would be quite sufficient to hold up our attack, for which the number of heavy guns at the disposal of the Allies was totally inadequate. Nor had the Serbian Army yet recovered its full efficiency after its terrible experiences and could not as yet be reckoned man for man as equal to the Bulgarians. Some part of the Allied force, also, would have to be kept out of action against the Bulgarians in order to watch the Greeks, whose attitude was becoming ever and ever more equivocal. Added to all this the argument that an offensive would involve too great a strain on our hard-pressed shipping was deployed with great ability by Curzon. As for Russia and Italy, they had sent their blessing to the Salonica campaign, but not much more. The French claim that Italy wished for an offensive there was dramatically disposed of at the end of the conference by the arrival of a telegram showing that Cadorna pretended to no local knowledge and was content to accept Robertson's opinion.

The result of the conference, which was embodied in an exchange of

notes after its close, was that the French agreed to a postponement of the offensive on condition that we for our part should not refuse to examine the possibility of an operation in this theatre when the local conditions were more favourable, and that, in the meantime, so far as was consistent with our main munitions policy, we should hasten the equipment of our army at Salonica. The net result, then, of all these negotiations and conferences was the maintenance of the *status quo* in the Balkans. The British Government did not succeed in withdrawing a man or a gun for use in the Western theatre, and had been hard put to it to avoid an increased commitment.

Few subjects occupied the War Committee during the first half of 1916 more than the supply of war material to Russia. Once her teeming millions could be properly equipped, Russia was a tremendously important element in the coming concerted offensive, but there was a serious apprehension that, if something effective was not done, the Russian Armies might collapse. Russia's own supplies were totally inadequate, and such as these were, they seemed incapable of making the most of them. In April it was learned that the shortage was more serious than ever, partly owing to a strike at the Putiloff works, and the French Government sent Albert Thomas and Viviani to Russia to make inquiries. Their reports indicated that the Russians had formed the habit of relying too much on imported supplies, a fatal error when the inadequate means of entry and communication are considered. There were at that time only two ports of entry—Vladivostok, involving the endless transport over the Siberian railways, and Archangel, which was closed for half the year by ice, and which was served by a railway by no means adequate to the needs of the situation. In March the Admiralty decided to build some ice-breakers for Archangel, to be placed in charge of a Canadian expert. In March also the Shipping Control Committee was instructed to work out a special programme of shipping for the transport of supplies to Archangel. As a result no less than 100 ships were in April allotted for this purpose, apart from the available Russian ships. Russia was short of everything, and it was an impossible task to give her more than a fraction of what she asked. Nevertheless, a good deal of war material was sent, including 300 4·5-inch howitzers before the end of June. One of Russia's greatest needs was for rifles and in April it was decided that as soon as our own needs had been met, the surplus output of British rifles (large numbers of which had been ordered in America) should be put at her disposal. This, however, would not affect the position before 1917. Altogether the situation was

disquieting and was the main reason for the despatch of Kitchener's mission.

Next to Russia, Italy was the ally whose supplies caused the Supreme Command the greatest concern. Italy seems to have organized her industries well; her field gun was in some respects the most ingenious in Europe. She had, however, to import all her raw materials—coal, steel, etc., as well as a very large proportion of the wheat and other foodstuffs required for the Army and the civilian population. Apart from the drain which this made on our shipping, the danger to which merchant vessels were exposed in the narrow waters of the Mediterranean made Italy's demands a special cause of embarrassment. Early in August Runciman attended a special conference at Pallanza at which satisfactory arrangements to govern the situation were drawn up.

These demands from our Allies could only be met by placing increasing burdens on our own population. Runciman drew up a plan for restricting imports by 4,000,000 tons deadweight in the course of the year—some of which involved us in difficulties with neutrals; a movement was started for replacing imported pit-props by home-grown timber, and the Shipping Control Committee devised many expedients for economizing shipping.

Thus the whole of our efforts during the first half of 1916 were dominated by one idea, namely the concentration of all available resources on what was termed the 'decisive theatre of war' in accordance with the principles laid down on December 28, 1915. Whatever may be said in criticism of the First Coalition Government, at least it cannot be said that they failed to do all that at the time seemed humanly possible to carry out their policy, though the question of whether that policy was right or wrong will always remain the subject of controversy.

CHAPTER L

THE DEATH OF LORD KITCHENER

'Such was he: his work is done.
But while the races of mankind endure,
Let his great example stand
Colossal, seen of every land,
And keep the soldier firm, the statesman pure.'
(TENNYSON, *Ode on the Death of the Duke of Wellington*.)

ON the morning of June 6th, I arrived early at the office, and found that Churchill had arrived there still earlier; he was sitting in my room consulting some records of the War Committee or War Council to which he had been permitted access. Shortly after, while he was still in the room, my telephone bell rang. Masterton Smith of the Admiralty was at the other end of the wire. He had rung me up to tell me, in cryptic language of course, of the dreadful tragedy to the *Hampshire*, which had been mined or torpedoed in the North Sea and had sunk with almost all hands, including Kitchener and his whole staff. He added that the news must be kept confidential at the moment as no decision had been taken on the time or method of publicity. Remembering the attempt to keep secret the loss of the *Audacious* I endeavoured to preserve a perfectly calm demeanour at this shocking news in order that my visitor might not guess that anything sensational had happened, and I tried to reply to Masterton Smith as though our conversation were on some routine matter. Churchill must have recognized some unexpected quality in my voice, for he pricked up his ears and asked if there was any news. I refused to be drawn. I am not sure that he ever quite forgave me. But I think I was right. Churchill, it is true, was a Privy Counsellor, an ex-First Lord, the repository of many secrets, an intimate friend. But he was out of office. The information was given to me by the First Lord's authority in the strictest confidence as likely to affect the proceedings of the War Committee that morning. I was not entitled to reveal it to anyone outside the War Committee. Moreover, the fewer people who know a secret, the less risk is there of its being divulged, whether by chance or design. The news was published officially the same morning.

The War Committee met an hour or so later. At first there was a tendency to adjourn as a mark of respect to Kitchener, but on the whole

it was felt that, in war-time, when men's lives or victory itself may turn on the promptitude with which business is despatched, it would be more proper to carry on.

The circumstances in which Kitchener came to start on this ill-starred voyage can be narrated very shortly. For some time past a good deal of disquiet had been felt about the state of affairs in Russia, and more particularly about the condition of her armaments. The reports of our military attaché had been disturbing. On April 28th, Albert Thomas called on Lloyd George early in the morning to tell him that the French Government had learned that there was a very serious shortage of munitions in Russia; that in spite of this shortage Russia was about to take the offensive, and it was feared that they would merely waste what ammunition they had and repeat the disastrous experiences of the previous year; Thomas and Viviani were on their way to Russia to try to ascertain the facts of the situation. That afternoon, while the Prime Minister and Lloyd George were in conversation, the former called me to join them and said he had come to the conclusion that Lloyd George ought to go to Russia. Lloyd George said he wanted some officer well up in all aspects of the military situation to accompany him and looked meaningly at me. I had no particular desire to go with him, at a time when important developments were approaching in the Western theatre, so I merely looked stupid and suggested that he should take Callwell. After Lloyd George had gone Asquith told me he had asked for me. Later on that day Ellershaw, who was doing Russian work at the War Office, came to see me to say that Kitchener wanted to go to Russia. I at once passed this information on to Asquith, who was rather amused.

Early in May the question of Russian credits became acute. Credits granted in the previous September had become exhausted, yet huge demands were being received for further supplies, both from this country and America. No one in Western Europe had the necessary detailed knowledge of the situation in Russia and the only way to deal with this question and that of supplies appeared to be by the despatch of some emissary of the highest status and rank to investigate the situation. It was on May 4th that Kitchener's name was first mentioned officially in this connection. He asked for time to think the matter over, though I had no doubt myself that he intended to go. On May 9th I had a long talk with Lloyd George at Edwin Montagu's house in Queen Anne's Gate, where Montagu, after giving us lunch, had left us alone together. He pressed me very hard to go with him to Russia to 'try and

get to the bottom of the situation there'. I reported our conversation to Asquith. For the next fortnight the composition of the proposed mission to Russia remained *sub judice* but as late as May 17th it was still uncertain whether the mission should consist only of Kitchener, or whether one of his colleagues (probably Lloyd George, for no other name had been suggested) should accompany him. Meanwhile Kitchener had received an invitation from the Czar to visit Russia, but he had not yet decided whether to accept.

On May 12th Asquith went to Ireland to deal with the situation arising out of the Dublin outbreak, remaining away for a week. On May 19th, the day of Asquith's return, Ellershaw called on me to discuss Kitchener's projected visit and to ask me to arrange for the Prime Minister to see Gourko, the President of the Russian Council of Empire. As late as May 23rd Lloyd George was still taking a special interest in Russia, for on that morning I breakfasted with him to meet Bernard Pares, who had just returned after many months spent on the Russian Front, and gave a depressing view of prospects there owing to lack of heavy guns. On May 25th Asquith announced in the House of Commons that, at the unanimous request of his colleagues, Lloyd George had undertaken to devote his time and his energies to obtain an agreement with Ireland. Thereafter there was no further question of his going to Russia, and my name also dropped out. Next day the actual composition of Kitchener's mission was decided on by the War Committee, and on May 27th Kitchener telegraphed his acceptance of the Czar's invitation.

Kitchener's party left London on June 4th. Among the members of his staff was O'Beirne, who during Asquith's visit to Rome[1] had spoken enthusiastically of a hypothetical visit to Russia. Afterwards, however, he shifted his point of view. When it had been decided that he was to accompany Kitchener I asked him if he was pleased. He displayed an obvious unwillingness to go. He saw no particular object in his going and said that he was very happy in the work he was doing in the Foreign Office and for the War Committee, which he had no desire to leave. He said the same thing to others as well as to myself. When the day came his luggage was taken in error to Euston instead of King's Cross; he lost the train and was confronted with complete separation from the party. However, he chartered a special train for Edinburgh (which must have cost him a lot of money) and unfortunately overtook the rest of the party before they embarked in the *Hampshire*. It is

[1] *vide supra*, p. 486.

difficult to believe that he did not have some presage of misfortune. Fitzgerald, Kitchener's wise counsellor and friend, whom I saw the day before their departure, was less enthusiastic than usual, but he was perhaps anxious about Kitchener's position in London during his absence.

To say that Kitchener's death was a tragedy is a mere platitude. To say, as some have said, that the last years of his life were a 'tragedy' is a folly. Granted that by character and training he was an autocrat and that for this reason he did not fit easily into a Cabinet; granted that he was by nature secretive and (not without reason) mistrustful of the capacity of others to keep secrets on which the lives of soldiers and the success of operations might depend; granted that he made mistakes—and who did not in those bewildering days; granted that towards the end he lost the confidence of many of his colleagues in the Cabinet; granted all these things, he nevertheless showed himself the most far-sighted soldier and statesman of his time. It was he who at the beginning of the war foresaw and declared that we were in for a long war. He it was who conceived as in a flash the great armies which bore the brunt of our cause in the later stages of the war. He it was who raised, and before his untimely death had brought to completion this great engine of military power. Whether he would have done better to build on the foundation of the Territorial Army; whether he made mistakes in the organization of the supply of munitions and war material; or whether he was not well served in this respect—these are matters of detail. The great outstanding fact is that within eighteen months of the outbreak of war, when he had found a people reliant on sea-power and essentially non-military in their outlook, he had conceived and brought into being, completely equipped in every way, a national army capable of holding its own against the armies of the greatest military Power the world had ever seen. That is the achievement beside which all else pales. That is the standard by which Kitchener's place in history must be measured.

After the appointment of Robertson as Chief of the Imperial General Staff Kitchener's position necessarily diminished in importance. He was no longer the principal adviser on military operations and he no longer signed the instructions to the Commanders-in-Chief in the various theatres. Neither Kitchener nor Robertson believed theoretically in the system under which the Chief of the Imperial General Staff with these powers had above him a soldier as Secretary of State. But, whatever they believed in theory, they made it work in practice. Each had a high respect for the other's qualities, which grew into a real regard. I never

remember hearing of any serious friction between them, though neither was the easiest man in the world to work with. Kitchener, however, never quite liked the position and was always looking out for some alternative plan. It was probably this feeling of unrest that led him to accept the mission to Russia, where he thought he might really do some good—as would almost certainly have been the case had he survived.

If it be true that Kitchener had to some extent lost the confidence of many of his colleagues he never lost that of the people whose confidence he valued most, and who knew him best—the King, and the Prime Minister, and even more important the soldiers and peoples of the British Empire. To the rank and file of the British and Dominion forces his death was a staggering blow; as an Australian soldier put it to me, 'it was as though a great light had gone out'. Throughout the East also his prestige remained undiminished and unassailable to the last. Mark Sykes, who was attached to my office at the time, described to me how on one of his numerous trips to the East he told an Arab sheikh of Kitchener's death; the sheikh replied: 'Lord Kitchener can never die'.

CHAPTER LI

THE SUMMER OFFENSIVE, 1916

'Battles, in these ages, are transacted by mechanism; with
the slightest possible development of human individuality
or spontaneity; men may even die, and kill one another,
in an artificial manner. Battles ever since Homer's time,
when they were "Fighting Mobs", have mostly ceased to
be worth looking at, worth reading of or remembering.
How many wearisome bloody Battles does History strive
to represent; or even in a husky way to sing:...'
(CARLYLE, *The French Revolution*, Part I, Book VII, c. 4.)

'I LIKE a bit of Russian sauce for my breakfast', remarked Grey on
whom I had called one morning. The date was June 12th; the occasion
the cumulative evidence of Brusilov's successes over the Austrian Army
in Galicia. The Allied offensive had opened brilliantly. Alexeiev, who
was virtually Commander-in-Chief, had originally intended to open
his campaign a little later. But the concentration of many Austrian
divisions in the Trentino, and the beginning of an offensive there, had
led him to anticipate the date. Within a few days of the first attack on
June 4th Brusilov's army had captured tens of thousands of prisoners
and his army had advanced a distance of about thirty miles at the maximum depth. A fortnight later, farther to the south, Czernowitz had
been recaptured.

Following as it did the depression caused by the battle of Jutland,
the death of Kitchener, the losses inflicted by the extended submarine
campaign, and the German hammer strokes at Verdun, these Russian
successes were peculiarly welcome, the more so as they were unexpected. Nor was this satisfaction confined to the general public. Those who
were best informed knew that Brusilov's attack was of a secondary
character, and that the main Russian offensive was to begin some
weeks later, and farther to the north, on the other side of the Pripet
marshes, in the vicinity of Baranovichi. This attack began on the same
date as the battle of the Somme (July 1st). Here, however, the Russians
had to deal with German instead of Austrian troops, and in spite of
heavy fighting, which was renewed later in the month and continued
until the middle of August, they never succeeded in making much
headway. Brusilov unfortunately had not at his immediate disposal
sufficient reserves to exploit his first success to the full, and though he

was able to force his way to the Stockod River and the Russian line farther south was advanced to the crest of the Carpathians, his offensive was gradually brought to a standstill. The Russians, however, not for the first time, had done more than had been hoped, and had made an effective contribution to the Allied offensive, which must always be considered as a whole.

On June 17th the Italians, after some local counter-attacks, opened their main counter-offensive in the Trentino, which was continued until July 7th with some local successes.

On June 25th the bombardment began on the Somme, and on July 1st the long-prepared Anglo-French offensive in that region started. Considerable successes were achieved at first; our troops advanced for a short distance and large numbers of prisoners were captured. It has to be admitted, however, that on the whole the critics were justified by the event. The first lines of the enemy's defensive system were obliterated by the bombardment; the broken, unrecognizable ground was occupied by our troops, but only at the cost of heavy losses. The German 'GHQ was surprised at first'[1] but there was nothing in the nature of a breakthrough. The 'army of pursuit' never came into action. Our forces were held sufficiently firmly to enable enemy reinforcements to arrive on the scene. There was nothing to be done but to move up the guns and repeat the process with new objectives. From that time onwards until November 18th, when the advent of winter brought the operations to a close, the battle of the Somme degenerated into a mere 'slogging match', in which we always had the upper hand, but were never able to obtain a big strategical victory. Division after division took its turn, each adding to its escutcheon the name of some captured town or village, hitherto unheard of and already unrecognizable, or maybe of some scraggy eyesore of a wood, High Wood, Delville Wood, Mametz Wood, etc.—otherwise unknown to history—where imperishable deeds had been performed:

> Not verdant there
> The foliage, but of dusky hue; not light
> The boughs and tapering, but with knares deform'd
> And matted thick; fruits there were none, but thorns
> Instead, with venom filled. (DANTE, *Inferno*, XIII, 3.)

Into this inferno we cannot penetrate; there is 'no admission except on business'. Possibly, however, the following impression

[1] Ludendorff, I, p. 244.

of a visit with Asquith to the threshold, as it were, might be of interest:

September 6th. Accompanied by Major T., one of Haig's aides, who was attached to the Prime Minister for the visit, we motored out to Fricourt. It was a glorious hot day. As we approached the battle of the Somme, the roar of the guns, which had been continuous and loud even at Beauval, became tremendous. We stopped a few minutes at Albert. The cathedral is an extraordinary sight. At the top of the tower was a gigantic gilt figure of a Virgin and Child, which has been hit by a shell and is actually hanging horizontally over the road, face downward, a most pathetic sight. The French say that the day it falls the war will come to an end. The rest of the cathedral, a hideous red brick building, is badly knocked about, as is the whole town of Albert. It was shelled the day before we arrived. After leaving Albert we came out on to bare rolling country with low hills. As far as we could see in every direction was an extraordinary collection of booths, dug-outs, horse lines, 'sausage' balloons, waggons, supply and ammunition dumps, field hospitals, huts, tents and all the paraphernalia and impedimenta of a huge army, intersected with field railways. The roads were all 'chock-a-block' with huge columns of motor lorries, ambulances, water carts, guns and troops. They were changing divisions up at the front, which made it particularly crowded on that day, and we were constantly held up for long periods. The roads were frightfully cut up, and the weather had been heavy, so that the movements of troops were mainly confined to the roads.

Such was the Somme battlefield as it presented itself to me. One could appreciate the advantages of the mastery of the air, for all this medley of men, animals and stores (resembling the Epsom course on race day) was within easy artillery range, but could not be seen by the enemy owing to the intervening ridges, so that without aircraft observation his shell fire could only be unobserved. One shudders to think of the effects if the whole had been visible.

Near Fricourt we met Raymond Asquith, the Prime Minister's eldest son, who was waiting at a cross roads, having ridden over on horseback to meet us. As we jolted up the broken shell-smitten road to Fricourt, which lay close to a shell-blasted wood, I heard the curious whizz of a large howitzer shell—sounding, as they always do, as though it rotated eccentrically and not on its axis. It passed far overhead and burst some hundreds of yards away. By this time we were in the middle of our own guns, and some long 6-inch were firing over our heads, cocked up at extreme ranges. I noticed they were in wire cages, camouflaged to conceal them from aircraft observation. As we came through the 'street' at Fricourt—as a matter of fact there was literally not one stone left on another—another shell came and burst not more than a hundred yards away. We got out of our cars and hurried to a 'dug-out'. Just as we arrived a third shell greeted us and landed not fifty yards away—

but I am not sure that it burst. We had to wait some considerable time in the 'dug-out' until the shell shower had passed over. The member of our party who had the worst time was the Prime Minister's valet,[1] Bull, an elderly man, who had come out on the box of one of the motors. He was too shy to come into the 'dug-out', and without our notice remained out among the shells until he could stand it no longer, when he crept in. The Prime Minister was as usual quite composed, but I thought his hand was trembling rather, and no wonder. The 'dug-out' was the famous three-storeyed one so often described, boarded with matchwood, and lit by electric light. What was mainly of interest to me was that a battle was actually in progress and this was the headquarters of the 7th Division, which was engaged. Bonham Carter's brother was on the staff of the Division, taking in telephone messages from the actual front. The Corps General was also there. In a neighbouring dug-out, they told me, was Lieutenant Weber, a German officer who was killed in the act of getting into his trousers, and whose body had been left unburied in this absurd posture.

September 7th. After spending the night at Haig's advanced HQ and lunch at Montreuil, we motored to Crecy where by some curious chance Montagu,[2] who had been to a conference in Paris, passed us opposite the lonely cross which commemorates the battle; actually the death of the blind King John of Bohemia. The Prime Minister was much amused because Montagu did not seem to have heard of the battle of Crecy! Then we drove on to see the 'caterpillars' of which we found about sixty-two, painted in grotesque colours. While we were there a German aeroplane, flying at a great height, came overhead and the whole of the tanks took cover under trees, etc., or were covered with tarpaulins painted to resemble haystacks.

In the evening at dinner I tackled both the Chief of Staff, Kiggell, and Butler, the sub-Chief about the 'caterpillars'. My thesis is that it is a mistake to put them into the battle of the Somme. They were built for the purpose of breaking an ordinary trench system with a normal artillery fire only, whereas on the Somme they will have to penetrate a terrific artillery barrage, and will have to operate in a broken country full of shell-craters, where they will be able to see very little. They were not very receptive, but Butler gave me a hint that they might be used to open up a new front as well, and next day I met Frank Lyon, the Brigadier-General on the Staff, 7th Corps, and he told me he was to have the next twenty 'caterpillars' and to use them in the region of Gommecourt on September 20th, whereas the big attack on the Somme is to be on the 15th.

Asquith urged the same point of view about the use of tanks on Haig with equal lack of success.

[1] Actually head messenger at 10 Downing Street, and a very good fellow.
[2] He had just succeeded Lloyd George as Minister of Munitions, the latter having succeeded Kitchener as Secretary for War on July 7th.

In the representations I made on the use of the tanks I knew that I was voicing the views of Swinton and of all the others who had been concerned in the production of these new engines. In fact it was mainly on this account that I had left my work at the War Committee to accompany Asquith on his visit to the Somme. It was, however, very difficult for anyone from home to influence those on whom fell the day-to-day responsibility of fighting this great battle. One could not pretend to knowledge of local conditions and one's status was necessarily that of an amateur, or at best of a professor, an academic student without practical experience. Yet in this instance (as the attack at Cambrai proved) the amateurs and 'professors' were right and the 'professionals' were wrong. The tanks came into action a week after the events described above (September 15th). Instead of being used *en masse*, as we had urged, they were employed in groups. Instead of opening up a new front, on ground where they would have had a decent chance, they were put in on the crumbling shell-pocked battlefield of the Somme. Of about fifty, which were to have been employed, only thirty-two surmounted the difficulties in reaching the starting-point. Fourteen more were ditched or broke down from mechanical trouble. Of the eighteen which were engaged, nine did not succeed in keeping up with the infantry. Even so they struck terror to the enemy and enheartened our own men. But the well-kept secret had been given away without giving the new weapon a fair chance. They had been used under conditions which afforded them nothing like a decent prospect of success. A great opportunity had been lost. For the remainder of the fighting season the tanks were used for the most part in small groups. To those who promoted and designed them this misuse of the tanks came as a cruel disappointment. The refusal of the Staff to listen to their views aroused indignation.

And so the weary summer of 1916 dragged on. Each week brought its tale of minor successes, but decisive victory ever eluded us, dancing ahead like some will o' the wisp. Meanwhile week by week the casualties were steadily mounting up. Within three weeks of the opening of the battle the British casualties on the Western Front amounted to 120,000 men, exceeding the total casualties of the eight months of the Gallipoli campaign. By November 18th, when the battle came to an end, they exceeded 400,000.[1] Few families escaped and people dreaded to scan the endless casualty lists published daily in the Press. Within a few days of our return from the visit to the Somme, Raymond Asquith, the

---

[1] *France and Belgium 1916*, I, p. 497.

witty, blithe and gay, had fallen. Just a month later I learned the news of the death of my brother Donald, whose book *A Student in Arms*, proved helpful to many, and whose life and character were an inspiration to all who knew him. He was the second member of the family to lose his life in battle. Both he and Hugh, my eldest brother who fell at Paardeberg in the South African War, were at the time of their deaths officers in the Royal Warwickshire Regiment.

The question has been asked again and again: Was the battle of the Somme justified? In support of the contrary view it has been urged that the result was a foregone conclusion; that, even if the generals believed in it, the members of the War Committee did not; that it did not of itself disengage Verdun, since it was not until after the entry of Roumania on August 27th that the attack on Verdun was called off; that it did not enable the Russians to conquer in the East, notwithstanding attacks renewed again and again until the fighting season was over; that it did not even save Roumania from sharing the fate of Belgium and Serbia; that the Germans were able to hold us up with their left hand, while they punched into Roumania with the right.

If a narrow view is taken of the Somme there is much to be said for this line of argument. It might be said that the capture of large numbers of prisoners, and the occupation of some few square miles of shell-pocked mud, even augmented by the withdrawal by the Germans during the winter to the Hindenburg line some fifteen kilometres to the rear did not justify the tremendous loss of life and material. On a wider view, however, the matter takes a different complexion. If the war is considered as a whole it will be realized that the German desistence from the prolonged assault of Verdun was the result, not solely of the entry of Roumania—though that did compel her to send divisions eastward—but also of the attacks of the Italians (who drove the Austrians back beyond Gorizia in August, and continued their attacks on the Carso until November), *plus* those of the Russians (who caused the enemy many anxious moments and at one time threatened to overrun the plain of Hungary), and *plus* the Somme, which was one of the principal factors in these encircling attacks on the Central European redoubt. It was the pressure of these combined operations on the enemy that enabled our French Allies between October 24th and December 14th to recapture almost all the ground which they had earlier lost at Verdun. Moreover, the moral effect must not be lost sight of. If the collapse of Roumania was a grievous blow, against this must be set the fact that our new, hastily improvised volunteer army (for the Com-

pulsory Service Act can have produced few, if any, soldiers in time to take part in this battle) had shown themselves a match, and perhaps a little more than a match for the most highly trained and organized army that the world had ever seen. Ludendorff bears eloquent testimony to the anxiety which these attacks occasioned him after he and Hindenburg had on August 29th taken control of affairs. 'Not a single man could be spared from the Western Front', he writes.[1]

Mistakes there undoubtedly were in the execution of the battle, and perhaps the worst mistake was the misuse of the tanks; but these were inevitable, especially with a new and hastily improvised army. The battle of the Somme repeated the lesson of the Marne in bringing home to the enemy that his army was not only not invincible but that he had no monopoly of the offensive. More especially must this realization have come home to him now that the failure of his attacks at Verdun had revealed the unwelcome fact that the war had become one of attrition.

---

[1] Ludendorff, I, p. 248. Later he writes: 'Not only did our *morale* suffer but, in addition to fearful wastage in killed and wounded, we lost a large number of prisoners and much material' (p. 267), and farther on 'The army had been fought to a standstill and was utterly worn out' (p. 304).

CHAPTER LII

THE DARDANELLES AND MESOPOTAMIA COMMISSIONS

'I say, then, that the question which we now have to consider is one of the most important that has almost ever
occupied the attention of Parliament—not because it
involves the existence or overthrow of the Government,
but because you are about to set a precedent, dangerous
if you carry it out, and disappointing to the nation if you
let it drop and merely use it as an instrument for over-
throwing the Government of the day.' (Extract from a
speech by Palmerston opposing the appointment of the
Roebuck Committee during the Crimean War.)

BEFORE the Gallipoli campaign had come to an end there had been
pressure in Parliament for the publication of papers relating to the
operations at Suvla Bay. The demand was refused by the Government,
but on May 2nd, after the fall of Kut, it was announced in the House of
Commons that they would lay papers and on May 30th, pending the
compilation of complete papers which it was recognized would take
time, an advance instalment was laid dealing with Townshend's
appreciation after the battle of Kut-el-Amara. This precedent was
immediately seized on in the House of Commons as an excuse for
demanding the laying of papers on the Dardanelles. It was urged that,
if papers could be laid in connection with the Mesopotamian campaign,
which was still continuing, *a fortiori* they could be laid with greater
justification and less risk on the Dardanelles campaign, which was
over.

On June 1st, Bonar Law, who was acting as Leader of the House at
the time, referring to the Mesopotamia Papers, in the Government's
name conceded the principle of publication of papers on the
Dardanelles. It would be difficult to find a better example than this of
the faulty system under which we were still working, whereby the last
word in the Supreme Command in War lay in the hands of a purely
civilian Cabinet, which was not attended by any professional advisers.
Whether the subject was really discussed in Cabinet at all, Heaven alone
knows, for in those days the Cabinet kept no records. That it was not
discussed adequately is highly probable when it is remembered that the
incident occurred at that supreme moment when the news of the battle

of Jutland was trickling in and occupying men's minds to the exclusion of everything else. But what is absolutely certain is that no expert adviser, whether of the Admiralty or War Office or Foreign Office or any other department of State, was consulted. The decision was taken by politicians on political grounds alone. The rich experience of the past in such matters was unknown to those responsible for the decision. And if history was overlooked, the effect of the publication of papers on current operations was ignored. It was a decision that could only have been taken by a body working without an Agenda paper, and without any systematic documentation.

The effect of the announcement in the great departments of State was staggering. I was besieged by telephone calls inquiring how the decision could have been reached, but I knew no more than anyone else.

June 3rd. I also discussed with Balfour the question of issuing Papers to Parliament on the subject of the Dardanelles, which was foolishly promised by Bonar Law last week. We agreed that I should ask the P.M. to withdraw the promise, on the ground that we cannot lay papers without explaining our plans in detail, including our intentions after the Dardanelles were past,[1] so that the Turks would then either know that we would never again attempt the passage of the Straits, or would make plans to defeat our action in case we got through. I can imagine nothing more foolish than to do this during the progress of a great war.

June 5th. In morning wrote a long Memo. to the Prime Minister protesting against the proposal to lay papers on the Dardanelles expedition before Parliament. . . . In the evening Winston Churchill turned up at the office to give me his views on these wretched Dardanelles Papers. I gave him my views on the objections from the point of view of public policy to laying papers. He became quite furious and asked where he came in. 'Whenever I open my mouth in Parliament,' he said, 'someone shouts out that I am the man who let us in for the Dardanelles mistake, and the papers are perpetually repeating it. My usefulness in Parliament is entirely ruined until my responsibility is cleared on the subject. No doubt it is very convenient for members of the present Government to leave the responsibility on my shoulders,' etc. etc.'

Churchill was undoubtedly being very hardly treated in Press and Parliament at this time, but this did not alter my view that the laying of papers would be a first-class mistake from the wider point of view.

---

[1] It was always in my mind that we should keep the Turks guessing whether we might make a fresh attack on the Dardanelles, so as to immobilize a strong garrison in the Gallipoli Peninsula, and keep it away from other fronts. By revealing our earlier plans by publication we should be indicating that we never intended to renew the attack.

June 6th. . . . He [the Prime Minister] also returned my Memo. *re* the publication of the Dardanelles Papers, saying that he agreed with it, but that Parliamentary pressure was so great that he would have to publish something.

I continued, none the less, to press the difficulties, for the more closely the matter was investigated the greater were the objections found to be.

July 7th. Occupied in fixing up conclusions of yesterday's War Committee in morning. Otherwise spent most of the day in dictating a long Memo. on the proposed Mesopotamia and Dardanelles Papers for the information of the War Committee, as the subject is to come before them next week.

The first of the difficulties in publication was that the Foreign Office flatly declined to publish any papers bearing on the diplomatic side of the history of the Dardanelles campaign, which was of paramount importance. They had good reason. Roumania, for example, was in negotiation with the Allies with a view to intervention in the war, and no one could foresee what might be the effect on the negotiations of publishing these earlier papers on Balkan affairs. This was particularly awkward because, in an answer to a supplementary question, Bonar Law had promised that, if there were any relevant diplomatic correspondence, it would certainly be considered as well. Also the omission of the diplomatic history would have removed the background without which the Government's decisions could never have been understood, and frustrated Bonar Law's promise to the House that 'if a story is to be told, the whole story must be told'.

On the military side even more cogent objections were raised to the publication of these papers. The masses of telegrams, despatches and reports contained full details of everything that had militated against the success of the operations; full particulars of our own plans and organization, the relative value of our fighting units, and the extent to which their value had been impaired by losses; details of our intelligence services on all aspects of the campaign, including secret sources, and a full appreciation of our ideas for winning the war. By publication of papers all this information would have been placed at the disposal of our enemies in the most convenient and authentic shape. In these circumstances the Admiralty and War Office were just as strongly opposed as the Foreign Office to publication.

The precedents also were not encouraging. The principal precedent for publishing papers to Parliament while a war was still in progress was the laying of papers on the Walcheren Expedition in January 1810.

Publication on that occasion was followed by debates in Parliament which lasted without intermission from January to March 17th thus, as Alison observes, absorbing

... nearly the whole time both of the Government and of the country at the very moment when the concentration of all the national thought and energies was required for the prosecution of the gigantic campaign in progress on the Continent.[1]

In view of the important military and military-diplomatic considerations raised the question was referred to the War Committee.

July 11th. I am thankful to say we managed to get a decision not to publish Dardanelles and Mesopotamia Papers. I think this was mainly due to my Memo. All the afternoon I was being rung up from different departments by people thanking me for managing this. . . .

The decision of the War Committee was not announced immediately. Probably the Prime Minister thought it necessary to bring it before the Cabinet. Asquith was a good deal troubled about its probable reception. His premonitions seem to have been justified:

July 18th. War Committee in morning. Had hasty lunch, dictated conclusions and then hastened to House of Commons, arriving just in time to hear the Prime Minister's statement refusing to lay Dardanelles and Mesopotamia Papers. The P.M. got sniped a good deal from all sides of the House—more, I think, than would have been the case if he had confined himself to the draft that I gave him. . . .

The refusal of papers was followed immediately by a demand for a Select Committee.

July 19th. Saw P.M. at House of Commons about 4 p.m. He told me he intended to resist the proposals for a Select Committee and asked me to get together precedents. As a matter of fact I had had Storr and Corbett at work looking up precedents all the morning, so I went back to my office and prepared a very fine case full of apt quotations from speeches by Porchester (1810), Gladstone, Palmerston and quotations from Alison, Napier and Kinglake. It took me until 9.30 and I got home by the last train very tired.

The historical precedents told even more strongly against inquiry during the continuance of hostilities than they had against the laying of papers. The precedents of Walcheren, with its inquiry by Parliament itself, and of the Crimean War were equally discouraging. Lord John

[1] Alison, *History of Europe 1789–1915.* Vol. XIII, p. 88 *sq.*

Russell resigned when he found that the Roebuck Committee of Inquiry 'into the condition of the Army in the Crimea' could not be resisted. Aberdeen's Government resigned in consequence of an adverse vote in the debate, and Palmerston, the chief opponent of the inquiry, was called on to form a Government. But, when he subsequently consented to the inquiry being held Gladstone, Graham, and Cardwell resigned their offices.[1]

In obedience to the instructions of the Roebuck Committee, two special Commissioners went to the Crimea, and after the lapse of a year their Report was laid before Parliament. It contained 'animadversions' on the conduct of certain officers, who applied for an opportunity of exposing errors detected in the Report. Their demands were granted and a new tribunal of seven generals was appointed to examine into them. After an inquiry lasting for three months, each of the assailed officers was absolved from the blame expressed or implied in the animadversions of the Commissioners, and the sufferings of the Army in the Crimea were eventually traced to the want of land transport, which in turn was attributed to the insufficient supply of forage by the Treasury!

From these precedents, which I presented to them, the Government could judge what the demand for inquiries into the Mesopotamia and Dardanelles campaigns was likely to involve. On the political side dissensions in the Cabinet, resignations, the paralysis of the Government, with a likelihood—or, as some of us thought, a certainty—of its eventual fall. On the military side it meant that the whole of the administration of the Admiralty, War Office, Foreign and India Offices would be diverted from the paramount task of winning the war to raking over the ashes of a dead past. Nor was this all. It was clear that any exhaustive inquiries must lead (as they actually did) to the diversion of effort from the winning of the war, to injury to the morale of the Army, and to a lowering of the prestige of the Supreme Command both at home and in the field—and all this risk was to be run at a time when the nation and the Empire were fighting for their very existence in conditions of intensity which had never been encountered before in the history of our race.

On this occasion, however, my efforts proved vain. I fought a losing battle.

[1] Kinglake (*History of the Crimean War*, VI, p. 352 *sq.*) says: 'The Committee was directed to enquire . . . and it enquired with a vengeance. . . . It seems to have examined almost everyone from the Prime Minister downwards. . . . It asked 21,421 questions and received, one may say, a much more than corresponding quantity of answers.'

July 20th. War Committee at 11.30. The professional members, i.e. Robertson, Oliver, as well as Jones and self were turned out for quite an hour while the Cabinet members discussed the Dardanelles and Mesopotamia Papers. They decided after all to grant the inquiries, which however were not to be parliamentary. . . . Lunched at 10 Downing Street. . . . Hastened back to dictate the minutes of the War Committee . . . and then hurried down to the House to hear the P.M.'s speech. He made my speech, giving many of my quotations, and then—anti-climax—gave the show away by promising the Committees!

I was profoundly depressed at this decision, all the consequences of which were so clear before my eyes. The only thing left to be considered was how the evil effects were to be mitigated. The Mesopotamia Inquiry was mainly a matter for the India Office, since the responsibility for the campaign had until quite recently rested with the Indian Government. It was far otherwise with the Dardanelles Inquiry. The War Committee, the Service Departments, and the Foreign Office were all in it up to the neck. The different elements in the case were inextricably mixed up. If each department was left to present its own case without co-ordination the Dardanelles Commission would never get a fair picture. The inquiry would simply become a *sauve qui peut.* It was essential that a general case should be presented in which all the elements should appear in proper perspective, round which the Ministers and other representatives of the departments could group their own evidence. But who was to prepare the case? Clearly the Prime Minister could not do so without taking his attention irretrievably away from his direction of the Cabinet and War Committee. A barrister, let loose among the masses of documents, would require months as well as an immense amount of guidance. Coming back from a tank display near Thetford,

July 21st. Lloyd George alarmed me by suggesting that I should go to the Dardanelles Inquiry and speak for the War Council. But I alarmed him by reminding him of his part in it, and asking him how he would like me to say it all at the Committee. Last night I hardly slept a wink, and all day I was much depressed about these Committees, as I fear it may be very difficult to protect the P.M.

I toyed for a day or two with the idea of merely giving the Commission the Minutes of the War Council, but there were strong constitutional objections to this course.

July 24th. In morning dictated Memo. to P.M. offering, though most

reluctantly, to present the Government case for the inception and conduct of the Dardanelles expedition at the secret Committee.

Asquith accepted my offer with alacrity.

Then began one of the most dreary tasks that has ever fallen to my lot. From July 24th until September 27th, when I first appeared before the Dardanelles Commission, every free hour in the evening, every Sunday that I was not on duty, and every moment I could snatch was devoted to the preparation of the case. If I went abroad to a conference, if I undertook a railway journey, even in my daily travelling between my home and the office, I had to take with me a section of the papers I had to summarize and arrange in order. That my own legitimate work as Secretary of the War Committee suffered goes without saying, and, of course, the August holiday of which I stood in such urgent need—I had only had about a week's leave since the summer of 1913—had to be sacrificed. Actually, during these two months I spent 174 hours on this work. I am bound to say that the Commission treated me handsomely. I had put my evidence in the shape of a Memorandum in three parts, which had been submitted to and approved by the Ministers and departments concerned, and of course I was called to answer questions on the subject, which took two days. After I had given my evidence Cromer, the chairman, came to me and, after thanking me, said that he personally had been very much impressed by it. The Government also expressed their gratitude. Asquith said it was the greatest State paper he had ever read, and Curzon wrote an effusive letter of congratulation accompanied by an invitation to my wife and myself to a week-end party to meet the Queen of the Belgians—an invitation which we were unable to accept.

An interesting point arose in connection with my evidence. The Commission demanded that I should produce the minutes of the War Council, Dardanelles Committee, and War Committee. Acting on instructions I refused on the ground that they were equivalent to Cabinet proceedings and were privileged. The Commission pressed their point. The question was adjourned to enable me to consult the Prime Minister. For reasons of secrecy[1] the minutes, which were very full, had been kept in manuscript, and only the conclusions had been printed or circulated to Members, and this only after the establishment of the War Committee, i.e. in the later stages of the campaign. The minutes, therefore, were only an unchecked secretary's note and could

vide supra, pp. 325, 361, 432.

S

not be treated as an exact record of the views expressed. As an *aide-mémoire* to Ministers and others giving evidence they were, of course, invaluable, but they did not pretend to be a record on which a man's reputation should be staked. Moreover, though persons still living were in a position to correct any mistakes they might detect, Kitchener, one of the persons most closely concerned, was dead and no one could check the record of remarks attributed to him. The central case I had presented on behalf of the Government had been built up round these minutes, which constituted the sole record of the Supreme Command, and I contended that this, supplemented by the evidence of witnesses who had refreshed their memories by reading the minutes, should suffice. Eventually it was agreed that the minutes should be placed at the disposal of the chairman, to enable him to check whether there was any discrepancy between them and my evidence, or whether there was anything of substance which I had omitted. I learned with satisfaction that the chairman had no criticism of this kind to make.

There are occasions when a *limited* inquiry into a partial episode may be useful even in time of war. I myself in 1942 advocated an inquiry into the fall of Singapore, stipulating that it should be confined to the responsibility of the Supreme Command and opposing an exhaustive inquiry comparable to the Dardanelles and Mesopotamia Commissions. Personally, though I was almost the only person who received some sort of faint commendation in the report of the earlier Commissions I never discovered any advantage of any sort or description which was obtained from these two inquiries. No controversy was finally settled— for controversy on these matters has continued ever since and will continue to the end of time. On the other hand, an immense amount of suffering and injustice was inflicted on men who had done their best to serve their country in conditions of terrible responsibility and with inadequate means at their disposal, in the confident belief that the country would see them through. At least one brilliant officer was consigned to the 'scrap heap' so that the country lost the benefit of his services and experience for the remainder of the war.

The Australian public, farther away and more detached, though deeply concerned, showed itself wiser than the British.

July 29th. Saw P.M. at 1 p.m. to obtain his initials to War Committee conclusions. Again urged him to retain Counsel and gave him a Memo. on the subject. Showed him two newspaper telegrams from Australia to the effect that Australia did not approve these inquiries and thought we ought to get on with the war. He told me that the Commonwealth Government had

actually sent a telegram to the effect that Fisher, the High Commissioner, had no authority to sit as Commonwealth representative, but only as a private individual.

Perhaps those both inside and outside the Government who supported the holding of these inquiries would seek to justify them by the fact that they did in the end help to bring down Asquith and his Government. Certain it is that the Coalition never recovered from its decision. For the last five months of its existence the function of the Supreme Command was carried out under the shadow of these inquests. Men whose actions are the subject of prolonged inquiry, on the result of which their whole future and their reputation before posterity may depend, are not in good fettle to direct a nation in a great war. Their nerve may be shaken. Their style is cramped. In this case also a good deal of mutual suspicion was engendered. Such homogeneity as the Government had possessed gradually weakened. The cracks visibly widened. Before long, as we shall see, the power of decision in difficult questions was affected. Disintegration set in, and before the first of the Commission's interim reports had been published Asquith's Government had come to an end. Added to this the report of the Mesopotamia Commission led to the resignation of Austen Chamberlain, one of the most useful members of the Coalition, and the country was deprived of his services as Secretary of State for India at a critical juncture, when the vital question of Indian reforms was coming to a head.

Of course the Government ought to have resigned rather than submit to this humiliation. Had they been homogeneous this is what they would have done. Some of the wiser heads took this view:

August 4th. Saw Grey in afternoon in order to explain necessity for stating diplomatic case in Dardanelles Inquiry. Found him very disgusted at the weakness of the Government in granting the Inquiry and threatening that, if people were taken away from their war work on account of it, he would resign in order to show the country it was preventing us from winning the war. He agreed with me that the Government ought to have resigned rather than give in to it. . . .

Balfour took much the same view; unfortunately, however, some members of the Cabinet took a different one.

February 15th (1917). I took home with me an advance proof of the Dardanelles Commission Report, which I thought a very unfair document and much too hard on Asquith, dwelling insufficiently on the difficulties of the times and the tiresome personalities whom Asquith had to handle—also

sketching in much too lightly the diplomatic history, which was intimately bound up with the expedition—our fears as regards Serbia, and our hopes and apprehensions as regards Bulgaria, Italy, Greece and Roumania, and the dangers of the Eastern situation.

I myself, as already mentioned, had nothing to complain about in my treatment by the Dardanelles Commission:

February 10th. The Dardanelles Commission especially thank me for my evidence—but it is quite possible, I foresee, that the papers may try and treat me as mixed up in the defects of the Asquith War Council. If so I have my defence. . . .

Nevertheless I was bitterly opposed in the public interest to the publication of the Report, notwithstanding the promise that had so rashly been given when the inquiry was agreed to. I did not hesitate to express my view both officially and in private. In Ministerial circles, however, apart from Balfour, I met with little support. Massey, the New Zealand Prime Minister, and his colleague Joseph Ward, shared my view and openly expressed 'marked disapproval of the decision to publish the Dardanelles Report'. In fact they were 'very outspoken . . . of the bad behaviour of our Parliament towards the war' and their views in this respect were shared by some other members of the Imperial War Cabinet. Owing to the strong representations of Government Departments and myself the War Cabinet obtained the permission of Parliament to edit some of the more dangerous passages out of the Report.

March 18th. Another tiresome minor matter has been the preparation of paragraphs to replace the portions excised from the Report of the Dardanelles Commission for publication. I was on a committee with Bonar Law, Asquith, Carson, Jellicoe, Churchill and Maurice on this.

Two days later I find this note:

March 20th. One matter which has given me a great deal of trouble lately is a statement made by Robertson in regard to the Calais agreement a week or so ago, which I included, together with the P.M.'s reply, in an Appendix to the Minutes of the meeting. Robertson insisted on my printing a statement handed in by him, which was based on notes he had at the meeting. But Ll.G. declared this was not the statement to which he had replied. After infinite negotiation I have not been able to reach an agreement between the two obstinate creatures, and the question still remains open. *This, I take it, is an aftermath of the Dardanelles Commission. Everyone is so frightened of*

committing himself, that he wants to cover himself by all sorts of statements, protests, or counter-protests.

My earlier anticipations that there might be animadversions on myself did not materialize:

March 20th. There was a debate this afternoon in Parliament on the Dardanelles Commission's interim report, and Longhurst tells me that my name was received with loud applause in the House of Commons when Asquith mentioned me. I was too busy to go down to the House myself.

This, however, did not in the slightest degree remove my repugnance to the whole affair.

Nearly three months elapsed between these events and the production of the Report of the Mesopotamia Commission, but when it did appear it wasted even more of the time of the Supreme Command than had the Report of the Dardanelles Commission.

June 4th (1917). Spent whole day reading the Report of the Mesopotamia Commission.

Between that date and mid-July, the War Cabinet discussed the matter at numerous meetings, several of them being devoted solely to this subject. Most important decisions were held up in order that the deplorable 'head-hunting' proclivities of some Members of Parliament might be satisfied. The question became really acute at the beginning of July, as the Parliamentary debates approached. Thus on June 30th I refer in my diary to the 'disgusting vindictiveness of ... Parliament and Press about the unfortunate victims of the Mesopotamia Commission'. After referring the matter to a Cabinet Committee the first intention of the War Cabinet was to take disciplinary action against one officer only. The others impugned were merely to be shelved. But early in July, yielding to the irresponsible clamour of a section of the Press and of certain Members of Parliament, their mood hardened, and they began to seek a scapegoat.

Head-hunting, however, was found to involve considerable technical difficulties.

July 11th. If once you decide on head-hunting the problem is really perplexing. The soldiers can very easily be dealt with by court martial—but, as the Mesopotamia and Dardanelles Commissions Act provided for complete

indemnity to witnesses, and much of the evidence was given by the persons impugned, the Report and its evidence cannot be used as evidence in a court of law. Consequently the whole of the evidence must be taken afresh if disciplinary action is to be taken, and, as the statute of limitations expires in November and the summary of evidence, which by law must precede a court martial, will itself take several months to prepare, as the witnesses are scattered all over the world, the whole thing will perhaps be null and void before the court could assemble. Nor is this the only difficulty, for the scalp hunters demand that civilians shall also be indicted. But a civilian cannot be tried by court martial, and in fact the lawyers advise that no charge can be laid against any civilian. If the Government had any 'guts' they would flatly decline to take proceedings, and merely put the officers concerned on the retired list where necessary, and take no action against Hardinge, who they all agree deserves no great blame. . . . Nevertheless the Government decided . . . to endeavour to proceed by Court of Inquiry under the 'Barret' Act, whereby a military court, with judges on it, but appointed by the Army Council, would try civilians. Obviously it was a miserable expedient that would not hold water, but having promised a statement in the afternoon they rushed into any decision, however bad, rather than take a courageous course. To my disgust I was asked to prepare a statement for Bonar Law and Curzon. . . . Bonar Law made it in the House of Commons, and I had to get it from him directly it was read to take it to Curzon in the House of Lords. On entering the Lobby of the Upper House I met several of my acquaintances who said: 'Oh, you cannot see Curzon. He has to make an important state-ment in a few minutes,' to which I replied, pointing to an untidy bundle of papers in my hand, 'but here is the statement', which evoked much laughter!

Of course both Houses shouted at the proposed new court, and the Cabinet had to meet again from 6.30 to past 8.30. . . . I walked afterwards with Balfour to Dean's Yard where he was dining. He was in a great state of righteous indignation at the whole proceeding and threatened to resign.

July 12th. In the late afternoon I went to the Talking Shop to hear some of the speeches. . . . Chamberlain made a fine speech announcing his resigna-tion. Balfour, curiously enough, entirely failed to reproduce his form . . . and made a miserably halting speech, which damaged Hardinge, whom he sought to defend.

July 13th. Once more the fatal Mesopotamia Report dogs the work of the War Cabinet. . . . Among the questions which are held up are: the decision about the next offensive; the control of merchant ships . . . ; future policy in the Balkans, Egypt and Mesopotamia; policy in Ireland, where there is dangerous unrest; prices of bread and meat; the appointment of Eric Geddes as First Lord; Indian reforms, which for a month or more the Indian Govern-ment have maintained is critically in need of a decision; the working out of the merchant shipping programme; the gun programme for 1918. These

questions, all of first-rate importance and great and immediate urgency, have been held up. . . . Surely all this reveals an incredible loss of perspective on the part of Parliament and Press.

It is unnecessary to pursue the matter further here, except to mention that Hardinge demanded a judicial inquiry and offered his resignation as Permanent Under-Secretary of State for Foreign Affairs no less than thrice; but the Government, showing wisdom for the first time in this deplorable affair, refused to accept it on the ground that it would be against the public interest. Lest it should be thought that this commentary is biased it is worthy of mention that the author of the Official History[1] (with whom the writer never discussed the question) is hardly less outspoken in his condemnation of the whole proceeding.

[1] *Mesopotamia*, IV, pp. 28 *sq.*

CHAPTER LIII

NEW ALLIES

'Foolish nations; doomed to settle their jarring accounts in that terrible manner! Nay, the fewest of them had any accounts, except imaginary ones, to settle there at all; and they went into the adventure *gratis*, spurred on by spectralities of the sick brain, by phantasms of hope, phantasms of terror; and had, strictly speaking, no actual business in it whatever.' (CARLYLE, *Frederick the Great*, Book XII, c. 11.)

IF the Commissions exercised a somewhat cramping effect on the Supreme Command during the last five months remaining to the Asquith Government, there was not much in the course of events to supply a counter-stimulus.

In German East Africa, it is true, Smuts was gradually wearing down Lettow's sturdy opposition and it was only occasionally that Robertson found it necessary to consult the War Committee on this campaign. The echo of the Dardanelles evacuation was, however, still reverberating in the East. The Germans had sent parties through Southern Persia to make trouble there, and in Afghanistan and India. Indeed the possibility of war with Afghanistan was so serious that two divisions were earmarked in Egypt for despatch to India in case of necessity, and the plans to be adopted in this contingency were considered by the War Committee. Among other steps taken was the despatch of a small Anglo-Indian force to Eastern Persia which was used with the acquiescence, if not at the request, of the Persian Government to screen India and Afghanistan. In Mesopotamia, since the fall of Kut (April 29, 1916), matters had remained at a standstill. After an interchange of telegrams with India and Mesopotamia it was decided that the policy of our forces should be to cover the Karun oilfields, to retain control of the Basra Vilayet, and to deny access as far as possible to the Persian Gulf and Southern Persia. The communications by road and river were to be improved by degrees and the General Officer Commanding was to maintain as forward a position as possible, so that, if and when an advance to Baghdad should be deemed possible and advisable, it could be undertaken. He was warned, however, that he would receive no reinforcements, but on October 27th he was authorized to initiate further operations within the capacity of his forces and on the distinct

understanding that these would not be increased. This was one of the first fruits of the appointment of Maude, who had taken over the command in August.

It was not only in Mesopotamia and Persia that the effects of the evacuation manifested themselves. In mid-July 1916, the Turks actually launched an attack against the Suez Canal and Egypt. The attack was repulsed without very much difficulty, but it emphasized the disadvantages of a purely defensive attitude in these regions. This attack, however, did not occasion any anxiety to the Supreme Command, because of the revolt on June 5, 1916, of Hussein, Sherif of Mecca, an occurrence resulting in the birth or re-birth of one nation and fraught with destiny to several others. As early as October 31, 1914, Kitchener had sent him a conditional guarantee of independence. Negotiations had been opened on July 14, 1915, and on October 24th the British Government had sent a letter defining the territorial limits of the proposed Arab State. The credit for this extraordinary development must ever be associated with the name of Mark Sykes, who was throughout the moving spirit within. For more than a year before this event this witty and talented politician had nominally been attached to my staff at the Committee of Imperial Defence. But in practice he was always a freelance, acting as the agent now of one Government office, now of another. His association with my office had begun with Maurice de Bunsen's Committee on British Desiderata in Turkey in April 1915. After that he had been engaged, with Georges Picot, the French diplomatist, in a series of negotiations which took him sometimes to Egypt, sometimes to Paris, once as far as Petrograd. These negotiations culminated in the conclusion between April 26 and September 1, 1916, of a series of agreements between Britain, France and Russia on the eventual disposal of Turkish territory.

Within less than a week of the commencement of the revolt Medina had been besieged, and the Turkish garrison of Mecca had surrendered. It was clear that our new auxiliary must be supported, so instructions were sent to Egypt to deliver to the Sherif a battery of field guns complete and some machine-guns, and the War Committee concerted an active policy with a view to furthering the movement. The most important element in this policy was a decision to prepare to advance from the Suez Canal to El Arish and Akaba; forces at these two places would threaten the communications of the Turks as well as afford efficient protection to the Canal. At the same time the construction of a railway from Kantara on the Canal to El Arish was to be begun. These

s*

decisions preceded by a fortnight the unsuccessful Turkish attack on the Canal.

Thus, by the early autumn of 1916, the Supreme Command in the Eastern theatre of war had already been compelled by force of circumstances to depart from the decision of December 28, 1915, to adopt a passive role in these outlying campaigns.

There was a similar development in the Balkans. The French Supreme Command had constantly been pressing the British Supreme Command to adopt a more active role in Macedonia and the British Government had stubbornly refused to comply with their wishes. This controversy had continued all spring and well into the summer. Early in July 1916, however, an event occurred which at last overcame British resistance. For on July 6th Roumania made a tentative and somewhat hedging offer to join the Allies. There followed six weeks of palavering, negotiating secret treaties, military agreements and the like, and on or about August 18th the Treaty of Alliance got itself signed. On August 27th Roumania declared war on Austria-Hungary.[1] There were hopes that advantage might be taken of this opportunity to induce Bulgaria to desert the Central Powers, and some obscure negotiations took place, but Russia was difficult and nothing came of it, and after a few days' delay Bulgaria declared war on Roumania on September 1st. Even after this event the idea of detaching Bulgaria was not abandoned and it formed the subject of a kind of Protocol between Lloyd George and Briand, the object being to bring home to Russia that it was only through the Balkans that an effective and continuous line of communications with her Allies could be opened. It was proposed that a bargain should be struck whereby, in return for a large consignment of heavy guns, Russia should make a big effort against Bulgaria through Roumania. But Briand afterwards repented of his bargain as the guns could not be spared for Russia.

To some it was strange that Roumania should have staked her existence at that time after holding off so long. It had been expected that she would have entered the war at the same time as Italy, but that opportunity was lost. Why did she come in fifteen months later? Probably she was influenced but little by events in the west. The real reason, rather, was Brusilov's victory in Galicia which inflicted a

---

[1] It should be noted that Italy, who had hitherto resisted the pressure of her Allies to declare war on Germany (though at war with Austria-Hungary, Bulgaria and Turkey), regularized the position by declaring war on Germany on August 28th, the same day as Germany declared war on Roumania.

terrific blow on Austria; presumably Roumania thought it was a case of 'now or never'.

Whatever her reasons, the accession of this new force was hailed by the Allies with the greatest satisfaction—though it was destined to be short-lived. Materially a reinforcement of a State with a population of over seven millions and an army of a quarter of a million men, neither exhausted nor war-weary, and prepared to take the offensive on a new front, to which the long line of trenches and barbed wire did not extend, was not to be despised. Morally, the fact that a nation, hitherto neutral, had decided after long hesitations that the cause of the Allies was the winning side and that the moment for intervention had come, was of importance. So great was the satisfaction that the British Supreme Command at last decided to abandon its policy of obstruction to the Salonica offensive and even to co-operate in some fashion therein. The decision came about in this wise.

On or about July 18th, the French Government proposed that a conference of the Allied Staffs should be held in Paris in order to consider the terms of the military convention to be concluded with Roumania, and that simultaneously there should be a Governmental Conference to consider the action to be taken. The British Government accepted the invitation to the staff conference, but declined the political conference on the ground that this was purely military business which ought to be settled by soldiers. This, it may be remarked, was in principle a wrong decision, for military operations on the large scale involved in the advent of a new ally must inevitably react on the national resources—money, shipping, munitions, man-power and the like—and it is the duty of governments to satisfy themselves on these points at the earliest possible moment. The military conference accordingly took place; Robertson was our delegate and was accompanied by a shipping representative. It then transpired that the Roumanian representative had no power to sign a treaty, and the conference had to content itself with preparing a draft. This document provided, *inter alia*, for an attack to be made by the Allied armies at Salonica on condition that the Russo-Roumanian armies should similarly take the offensive against Bulgaria. This, however, did not fit in with the Roumanians' plans. They were so sanguine as to hope that they might avoid war with Bulgaria. Nay, a few days before they declared war against Austria-Hungary their Premier was said to be in Sofia, supposedly with the errand of seducing Bulgaria from her alliance with the Central Powers. Thus for the moment the idea of a joint offensive against Bulgaria hung

fire. So important, however, was it felt to be not to lose this opportunity for securing Roumanian co-operation, and so anxious were we to avoid anything which might render Bulgaria less amenable, that the condition of a Roumanian attack on Bulgaria was waived and the British Supreme Command, in full agreement with its military advisers, agreed to co-operate in an offensive at Salonica.

The Supreme Command was at once involved in a number of intricate problems. Roumania proved to be short of every kind of modern equipment. We had to send heavy guns, machine-guns (ultimately 400 in number), rifles, aeroplanes, munitions, and war material of all kinds. Transport presented a most difficult problem, as the only available routes were by Archangel and Vladivostok, both of which were already congested with war material for Russia. One difficulty was to make sure that the material intended for Roumania reached its destination and was not intercepted on its way by the hungry Russians. Another was to equip the Salonica forces for offensive operations in this difficult country, where ordinary military transport had to be supplemented by mules and what-not, and where mountain guns were needed as well as the standardized heavy and field batteries. A third problem was to find at short notice the immense additional tonnage required for Archangel (which might be closed by ice before the autumn was far advanced) and for Salonica along a route which was peculiarly vulnerable to submarine attack; the shipping problems were dealt with by Curzon's Shipping Control Board.

Our efforts were of no avail. Events proceeded with catastrophic rapidity. First there was the advance into Transylvania by several Roumanian columns more or less isolated from one another. On August 29th Hindenburg succeeded Falkenhayn as Chief of the German General Staff. Within about a month of that event, notwithstanding the incessant pounding on the Somme, fresh attacks on the Isonzo (seventh battle of the Isonzo begun September 14th and eighth battle begun October 22nd) and renewed fighting with the Russians in the Carpathians, Hindenburg got together sufficient troops to settle the Roumanian business. And the Allied attacks from Salonica, begun October 5th and continued until December 11th, which resulted principally in the capture of Monastir on November 19th, did not prevent the Bulgarians from taking the Dobrudja, notwithstanding the arrival there of several Russian divisions. The Austro-German counter-attack on Roumania began about September 26th; Bucharest capitulated on December 6th; in the meantime the Bulgarians had taken Silistria on

September 10th, ten days after declaring war, and before the end of October Constanza and Cernavoda, and were masters of a great part of the Dobrudja. Roumania had thus gone the way of Belgium, Serbia and Montenegro, and above all Germany and Austria, both short of food and suffering from the blockade, had obtained actual and potential supplies which would stand them in good stead for many a long day. They had also obtained for the future something almost more valuable to them—oil. And this they would have obtained at once, but for the British Supreme Command, who, on my initiative, at the beginning of November, put strong pressure on the Roumanian Government to make dispositions for destroying their oil wells, before they had to abandon them, and, better still, sent out Norton Griffiths to co-operate with Thomson, our Military Attaché, in doing the job; these officers accomplished their mission with a thoroughness to which Ludendorff bore witness in his memoirs:[1]

> The stocks of oil we found in Roumania were not large. The boring plant had been absolutely destroyed, and the wells were cleverly blocked up. The English Colonel Thomsen [sic] had admirably fulfilled his duty of making it difficult for us to use the oil fields.

The Supreme Commands of the Allies did not watch the disaster to Roumania with indifference or with hands folded. In the way of direct assistance, beyond pushing forward supplies, there was comparatively little they could do to assist so inaccessible a country. Russia managed to send substantial reinforcements into Roumania, and an effort was made to assist from Salonica. The forces in this theatre at the beginning of October 1916 consisted of five British, four French, and three Serbian divisions. In addition, a small Russian force had been brought from Archangel 'to show the flag'; it arrived at Salonica on July 30th. Early in October, when the Roumanian debacle was in sight, and after the Allied attack in the Balkans had begun, the War Committee took the first step towards sending a reinforcement. A series of questions was addressed to Milne, now commanding the British forces at Salonica, and to Joffre, whether the Roumanian position could be bettered by action from Salonica; how an advance could be effected; and what maximum result could be achieved if the forces at Salonica could be considerably increased. Milne replied in effect that with a reinforcement of ten divisions the Allies would have a fair chance of a big success. With fifteen divisions of reinforcements the odds would be in their favour unless the

[1] Ludendorff, I, p. 358.

Bulgarians were reinforced by Germans and Austrians, sufficient heavy artillery being presupposed in both estimates. Joffre, though holding that the Western Front was still the principal theatre, considered that the importance of the Balkan theatre had been considerably enhanced by recent events and that two French and two British divisions should be sent. In his view the role of the Salonica army, in conjunction with the Russian divisions which Alexeiev had sent to the Dobrudja, was now to inflict a decisive defeat on the Bulgarian Army—a statement which led to expostulations by the British Supreme Command. After considering these views and those of their own military advisers the War Committee decided to send a mixed force of about 21,000 rifles (with four or five heavy batteries), most of which were scraped up from the Mediterranean, with two battalions and a number of drafts from home. At the same time they decided to press France and Italy to reinforce the Salonica theatre. This led to a conference at Boulogne on October 20th. We were represented by Asquith, Grey, Lloyd George, Balfour, Robertson, Haig, and Maurice, with myself as secretary; France by Briand, Roques, Lacaze, Ribot, Leon Bourgeois and Albert Thomas, Joffre and Pellé and Margerie of the Quai d'Orsay. The British representatives (except Lloyd George, who rather embarrassed his colleagues by making a strong plea in favour of sending large reinforcements to Salonica) adopted as usual rather an obstructive attitude towards the French proposal to reinforce on a large scale; urged that it was too late in the year to do any good in that quarter, and that we could best assist Roumania by hammering on the Somme, and so forth. Eventually, however, they had to agree to consider sympathetically and promptly the French proposal that, pending an exhaustive examination of the whole question by the Allied General Staffs, the number of British divisions at Salonica should be raised from five to seven, and the French from four to six.[1] Both Governments agreed to put pressure on Italy to send troops. Somewhat reluctantly the French proposal was agreed to by the War Committee; its opponents were only able to salve their consciences by having it laid down that the reinforcements were to be sent with a view to the moral and political effect on Russia and Roumania rather than for military reasons, and a *caveat* was entered that we reserved the right to withdraw a division to France if need be in the spring of 1917. As a result of these decisions the Western Powers were able to inform Russia and Roumania that some ninety thousand men were being sent to the Balkans—a communica-

[1] *vide Macedonia,* I, p. 201.

tion which would have been more reassuring if it had been made some months earlier.

Reinforcements were also being built up in the Balkans from another quarter, for a new ally was gradually coming into being there. Greece was, so to speak, coming into the war in detachments. She wanted to be on the winning side, but she could not make up her mind which side was winning. Broadly speaking, whenever Venizelos was in power Greece's inclination was to join the Allies; when King Constantine was in control her attitude was one of dubious neutrality. And during 1916 the pro-German party had been in the ascendant with the result that her neutrality became more sinister than ever. Ever since the landing of the Anglo-French forces at Salonica on October 5, 1915, the position *vis-à-vis* the Greek Government had been a delicate one. As early as December 6, 1915, owing to the obstructive attitude of the Greek Government towards the military requirements of the Allies at a difficult time, the British Government had been compelled to put economic pressure on Greece by the application of 'export restrictions' and by detaining ships and cargoes bound for Greece at Gibraltar and Malta as well as at home. A week of this treatment had sufficed to produce a more conciliatory attitude and on December 13th these restrictions had been partially removed. In January Greece had refused to consent to the occupation by the Allies of Corfu as a place of refuge for the Serbian Army and in April had refused to allow that army to use the Greek railways during its transportation from Corfu to Salonica with the result that they had to be conveyed by sea through waters infested with submarines. At the end of May, Greek ill-will was manifested in even more striking fashion, for on the 26th the Greeks surrendered to the Bulgarians without fighting Fort Rupel, a key point on the Bulgarian frontier.[1] On June 1st it was learned that Greek troops had withdrawn still farther on the Bulgarian border, enabling the enemy to advance within striking distance of the Xanthi–Demirhissar Railway, thus threatening to frustrate the naval blockade of the short stretch of Bulgarian coast on the Mediterranean. In consequence of this last act the Allies on June 6th began a 'pacific blockade' of Greece[2] and all coal

---

[1] The surrender at Fort Rupel was undoubtedly considered by the Allies at the time as an act of gross treachery, but the Official Naval History shows that it was understandable, since it was in conformity with an understanding reached between the Allies and Greece in December 1916, according to which, if the Anglo-French Army remained on Greek soil, the Hellenic Army would not help it to attack its adversaries, or impede the Central Powers from advancing against it. (*Naval Operations*, IV, p. 133.)

[2] Cf. *Naval Operations*, IV, p. 135.

shipments from Great Britain to Greece were stopped. The French then proposed far stronger measures—first a naval demonstration, to be followed immediately, if this did not suffice, by a joint Anglo-French occupation of the Piræus and Phalerum, the cutting of communication between the Peloponnesus and Greece at the Corinth Canal and other measures of the same kind, with still more drastic steps in reserve for application if required. Just at the moment when these proposals were being considered the pro-German Greek Premier, Skouloudis, resigned (June 21st) and was replaced by Zaïmis, who was of a more anodyne temperament. On the same day the Greek Government accepted the demand of the Allies that their army, which had been mobilized since September 23, 1915, should be demobilized and orders to this effect were issued on June 27, 1916, though the demobilization actually was far from complete. The 'pacific blockade', having done its work, was accordingly suspended on June 22nd and put into cold storage.

All this time Venizelos had not been inactive. Exactly how he was employing himself I do not pretend to know, but shortly after the events just recorded the results became apparent. On August 30th a Venizelist revolt against Constantine's Government began in Salonica and spread rapidly, more especially in the islands. On September 29th Venizelos and Condouriotis proclaimed a Provisional Government in Crete. Shortly after (October 9th) this Government moved to Salonica, and on November 23rd formally declared war on Germany and Bulgaria. Thus a new ally, or, shall we say, part of an ally had joined the ten nations (more or less) who were already at war with the Central Powers. Venizelos lost no time in getting together an army, and by October 26th we learned that within ten days the first of the Venizelist divisions was to take the field alongside the British Army.

The defection of a large part of his kingdom did not incline King Constantine to become more reasonable. Following an attack by the Bulgarians on August 17th to 19th, rumours came from Athens that this attack, which had been made in the region of Florina, in the far west of Macedonia, was a step in a general plan by the enemy to force his way into Greece. The rumour was not considered to be sufficiently probable to justify precautionary action on our part directed against Greece. On August 27th, the day Roumania declared war, the Bulgarians occupied the whole of the district east of the Struma down to the sea without any opposition from the Greek forces. At the end of August also the French made a serious complaint that everything which happened in the Salonica army was at once reported by the Greeks to

the enemy, and, after communication between the two Allies, it was decided to demand from Greece that Schenck, the head of the German secret service in Greece, and his agents should be ejected, and that the postal, wireless, and telegraph stations in Greece should be put under Allied control. The French would have liked to demand in addition the cession of ports and railways, but the British Supreme Command was not prepared to go so far at this stage. Moreover the French wanted to support the demand by a display of force, but the British Government were unwilling to do more than to make a naval demonstration, which in fact proved sufficient. A few days later (about September 4th) the Greek Government made an apparent *volte face*, and, without committing themselves to any particular date, made inquiries whether the Allies would be disposed to help them with cash and war material in the event of their deciding to join them. As this overture came immediately after Roumania's entry into the war and was associated therewith, and as it also came close on the heels of the Venizelist revolt in Salonica, it did not evoke much surprise and most people considered it as an attempt by the King to forestall Venizelos. A week after this approach, however, the anodyne Zaïmis suddenly, mysteriously, and for no apparent reason, resigned, and was replaced by Kalogeropoulos in whom the Allies felt less confidence. On September 17th it was reported from Athens that King Constantine had been playing with us in making these overtures and that the discovery of this had led Zaïmis to resign. Subsequent events immediately confirmed the King's bad faith, for on the very next day (September 18th) the Greek Army Corps at Kavalla surrendered voluntarily to the German forces, and allowed itself to be taken away for internment at Goerlitz in Saxony. Next day the Allies replied by extending the blockade of the Bulgarian coast westward to the mouth of the river Struma. This surrender was immediately followed by yet another overture by the King of a tentative, hedging and conditional character, to mobilize his army with a view to joining the Allies. This evidence of duplicity was too much altogether; it was felt that the King was simply manœuvring for position and the British and French Governments were agreed that nothing less than an unequivocal and immediate declaration of war would meet the case. On October 10th the Allies delivered an ultimatum at Athens demanding the surrender of the Greek Fleet—an ultimatum which was accepted next day by the Greek Government. Kalogeropoulos, having resigned on October 3rd, was replaced on October 10th by Lambros, a more friendly person.

On October 9th, the day preceding the demand for the surrender of the Greek Fleet, news came of a Greek military concentration of troops at Larissa in the north of Thessaly, a most sinister development in view of the King's dubious attitude, since a force at Larissa was on the flank and rear of the Allied Army and dangerously near to Salonica. There followed an interchange of views with Paris on the precise nature of the communication to be made to the King. Curiously enough at this juncture the attitude of the two Governments towards Greece rather changed. The French Government, which had again and again proposed forcible measures against Greece, wished to make what we considered an ineffective representation, while the British Government, which had hitherto always had its hand on the brake, considered that, in view of the unfriendly attitude of the King, a much sterner attitude was required. The whole question was thrashed out at the Boulogne Conference on October 20th. The result was a compromise between the two views, and Greece was told in effect that Greek co-operation would be welcomed only if Greece were on her own initiative to recognize that the Bulgarian action in occupying Kavalla and Florina, both in Greek territory, put her at war with Bulgaria.[1] Note was also taken of undertakings already made by Constantine to reduce the Greek Army to its normal peace strength, to move the troops concentrated at Larissa to the Peloponnesus, and to disperse the supplies concentrated there, under Allied supervision. It was also decided not to recognize Venizelos' Government as yet, but a loan of ten million drachmas made to him by Greek banks was to be guaranteed jointly by the two Governments.

British public opinion was by no means satisfied with the neglect to recognize the Government of Venizelos, who was popular and respected in this country; Asquith's reference in sympathetic terms to the Venizelist movement at the Guildhall banquet evoked the greatest enthusiasm. Early in November therefore the British Government made further representations to Paris. The French Government again refused to grant recognition. The subject was raised again at a big inter-Allied conference, which was held at Paris on November 15th and 16th. It was pointed out that the Venizelist troops coming into the line ran the risk of not being accorded belligerent rights by the enemy, if Venizelos' Government was not recognized. They might even be shot as outlaws, if captured. At best, they could only be regarded as a band of volunteers without recognition. Then it transpired that, in conversation with

[1] *vide Macedonia*, I, p. 219.

a French Senator who had been on a visit to Athens, King Constantine had made further overtures, and had offered to withdraw his troops from Thessaly on condition that the territory evacuated was not handed over to Venizelist troops; to surrender the whole of the Greek war material (including some 200 mountain guns with 1,000 rounds a gun, which would have been very useful at Salonica); and to put his fleet at our disposal (apparently this had not resulted from the demand for surrender on October 10th). The bait thus offered by the faithless Constantine was so tempting that Asquith was unable to induce his French colleagues to accord recognition to Venizelos, and it was not until after the fall of the First Coalition Government that British recognition was given.

This chapter cannot be closed without a brief reference to yet another ally—Portugal—who had come actively into the war on our side in creditable and honourable circumstances. At the end of October 1914, German troops had made an unprovoked attack on the Portuguese colony of Angola in West Africa. The Portuguese Government had responded by announcing their intention to co-operate with Britain in the near future, and had sent an expeditionary force to defend Angola. In February 1916, at the request of the British Government, the Portuguese Government had seized the German merchant ships which had taken refuge in the Tagus with a view to their being used by the Allies. Germany responded by declaring war on Portugal on March 9th, and Austria followed her example a week later. Towards the end of June 1916 the Portuguese Government approached the British Government with a proposal to send an expeditionary force to France to act in co-operation with the British Army. After a short period—not of bargaining like most of our Allies—but of purely business arrangement, the Portuguese Government announced its decision on August 8th. The first contingent landed in France on January 3, 1917, and came into action on June 17th. Thus did Portugal honour her ancient alliance with Britain, an alliance dating back to the time of Edward III (Treaty of 1371, confirmed and extended by the Treaty of Windsor, 1386), one which had more than once been honoured and observed by both parties in the intervening centuries.

The last year of the First Coalition Government thus saw four new Allies added to our cause—Portugal, our oldest ally among the nations; Arabia, an ancient nation reborn; Roumania, a State ruled by a Hohenzollern, but closely connected in the person of its beautiful and

talented Queen with our own Royal Family; and Venizelos' Provisional Government, which exercised sway over a large part of Greece. Twelve nations were now at war with the Central Powers, Britain, France, Italy, Belgium, Russia, Japan, Serbia, Montenegro, Roumania, Portugal, Arabia and part of Greece.

CHAPTER LIV

ORGANIZATION OF THE SUPREME COMMAND AT THE END OF 1916

'Our dealings with the Imperial Government were frequent, and not too pleasant. We did not meet with that spirit of accommodation which was so necessary when we told the Government what the successful prosecution of the war demanded of them, if the German people were to be rendered capable of victory. The representation of military interests in all questions of foreign policy during the war and in connection with the conclusion of peace meant frequent dealings, and much friction also. The machinery of government in Berlin gave the impression of being extremely clumsy. The various departments worked side by side without any real sympathy or cohesion, and there was infinite "overlapping". The left hand did not know what the right was doing. A Bismarck could have made these departments co-operate properly, but the task was beyond our War Chancellors.'
(LUDENDORFF, *War Memories*, I, p. 263.)

THE organization of the British Supreme Command under Asquith's direction may not have reached the same high level of efficiency as it did later under Lloyd George, but it was certainly superior to the German system, as described above. Our generals could not complain of lack of 'spirit of accommodation'. The presence of the Foreign Secretary and the chiefs of the naval and military staffs at the War Committee ensured that our foreign and military policies were co-ordinated. There was no excessive overlapping in our system and the distribution of information was good enough to ensure that the left hand *did* know what the right hand was doing. Nor could the machinery of government in London be described as 'clumsy'.

The organization of the Supreme Command which had come into existence in November 1915 with the formation of the War Committee was a great advance on what had gone before. But, as the range of the war extended and the drain on the nation's resources increased, this particular form of organization gradually in its turn became inadequate. With a loyal and united team it might have been adapted to the requirements of the day. But, with a Government composed of members of opposite political parties who had never been able entirely to forget

their differences and in an atmosphere poisoned by the Dardanelles and Mesopotamia Commissions, this proved impossible even under so patient and experienced a leader as Asquith.

The machinery of the War Committee[1] was at this time working smoothly. An Agenda paper was issued before each meeting. Full records were as before kept in manuscript. The conclusions after being approved and initialled by the Prime Minister—in this matter Asquith was prompt and punctilious—were circulated to the Cabinet whose members were thus kept fully abreast of what was going on. The Government Departments kept the Committee thoroughly well posted with information. At one time things had been less satisfactory but, at the end of May 1916, I prepared a private Memorandum for Asquith on the subject—to my embarrassment Lloyd George, who had received a copy, read it to the Committee—and after a rather thundery meeting the various Ministers agreed to furnish regular information. A new plan, too, was adopted under which the Chief of the Imperial General Staff gave the latest news at the outset of each meeting and answered any questions that might be put, and the First Sea Lord did the same for the Navy. It is a curious coincidence that these new arrangements were made at the end of the last meeting of the Committee attended by Kitchener who had always been suspected by his colleagues of keeping back information, and that this was the last Committee conclusion that was sent to him; before the next meeting he had gone down in the *Hampshire*.

The War Committee was admirably served by Robertson who was a tower of strength to them. His policy, if not very inspired, was always definite and his advice, therefore, always consistent. He was an admirable administrator and, once a decision was taken, the Committee could rely on him to carry it out. He proved far more adaptable than had been expected to political considerations, and in cases where these were paramount, he was willing to recognize that fact and to conform his policy without giving way on what he considered essential. His relations with Asquith and the Committee were, therefore, as good as could be wished. But although the War Committee as a whole liked and trusted their Chief of Staff and invariably backed him up, there were in some quarters misgivings about his policy. Great doubt was felt— especially by Lloyd George—whether the policy of hammering on the

---

[1] The War Committee was now composed of the Prime Minister, McKenna, Lloyd George, Bonar Law, Balfour, Grey, Crewe, Curzon, and Austen Chamberlain. Other frequent attenders were Runciman and Montagu. Henry Jackson and Robertson were always present as experts.

Somme could produce results commensurate with the effort, and the doubters felt that they were justified by the results, more particularly when Roumania collapsed. Their views were further strengthened when the course of events compelled even the extreme 'Westerners' to see the necessity of taking the offensive in the Eastern theatres. They maintained that proved them to have been right all along, that the decision to reinforce Salonica had been taken too late and that, if only they had been listened to earlier, the war in the East might have taken a very different turn.

It was the change of policy in 1916 and the course of events in the Eastern theatres which tended to widen the scope of the Committee at the expense of the Cabinet. To begin with, the intensification of operations in the outlying theatres and the need for furnishing additional supplies to the East involved an additional strain on shipping, and, before they took their decisions, it was essential that the War Committee should inform themselves whether the supplies could be found and shipped. In an island nation the moment you touch shipping you raise all the problems of national life, which depends for its existence on imports and exports. Since the resources of our shipping were already severely strained, the additional demands of the military authorities could only be found by the adoption of new methods.

The most obvious method of improving the shipping situation was to build new ships. At no time up to now, however, had it been found possible to bring the output of shipping up to the losses. In 1915 822,000 gross tons of new shipping were brought on to the register compared with losses of 1,103,000 gross tons; the corresponding figures for 1916 were 544,000 gross tons new shipping against losses of 1,498,000 gross tons—an even more unsatisfactory comparison. In order to increase the output of shipping two things were required— more men and more steel. Something was done to make more men available, but this involved detailed investigations of man-power. Steel for shipbuilding could only be obtained at the expense of naval requirements or of munitions, and this brought the War Committee into the heart of these problems. Eventually the Minister of Munitions agreed to find all the steel the shipyards could use during 1916, and it is partly to this that must be ascribed the fact that the output rose from 118,000 tons in the third quarter of 1916 to 220,000 tons in the fourth quarter and 326,000 tons in the first quarter of 1917.

Another method of improving the situation was to charter merchant ships of neutral nations to carry the requirements of the civil popula-

tion and of our Allies, but, as the German submarines did not discriminate between Allied and neutral merchant vessels, this was a matter of some difficulty. Nevertheless Runciman accomplished a great deal in this direction.

The enemy shipping in British, French and Russian ports had long ago come into employment. Italy had put most of the enemy ships in her ports in service before the end of 1915. Portgual seized the German ships in the Tagus in February 1916. Every effort was made to obtain, by purchase or by diplomatic pressure, the use of enemy shipping lying in ports of neutral countries.

Yet another direction in which improvement was sought and found was in the use made of the available shipping. British shipping trading between ports in distant countries was called in for employment of more immediate service for the war, at the risk of losing for ever this valuable carrying trade. Moreover, the use made by the fighting services of the ships allotted to them came in for very close scrutiny. Admiralty colliers were alleged to be held too long in Scapa Flow and other bases. At Basra, Salonica and elsewhere the Army was said to be holding up ships unnecessarily. A large amount of tonnage was found to be employed in the transport of oats for horses in France, although the prospect of using cavalry was clearly remote. Haig was brought over from France to discuss this matter with the War Committee and some alleviation was found, but not much. Proposals were considered for altering the Plimsoll load line, so that ships could be loaded deeper, for increasing the numbers of men carried by transports, and for carrying men in freight ships. At one time, when the wheat situation was threatening, the emergency reserve of shipping which was always kept ready at Southampton for military purposes was used to bring over a supply of wheat from America.

Steps were taken also for turning the ships round quicker. These included an extension of the system of Transport Workers battalions; towards the end of November 1916, a proposal was approved to raise further battalions up to a total strength of 10,000 men. The possibility of importing foreign labour for service in the ports and on the railways, etc., was often discussed, but the risk of antagonizing British labour was felt to be too great.

Inevitably consideration of shipping problems brought up the question of food supply, which in turn involved the whole question of agricultural policy. In May 1916 Selborne, the Minister of Agriculture, put forward proposals for increasing the output of wheat, but the War

Committee felt that, if the enemy's submarines should succeed in interrupting our supplies, the raising of a small amount of extra food was not likely to save us and rejected the scheme. During the summer of 1916 the British losses from submarines somewhat diminished. In June they fell to 36,000 tons, and in August 43,354 tons, compared with 141,193 tons in April. The figures for neutral losses were relatively high and our own losses increased during the autumn months, but a more serious feature in the situation that autumn was the failure of the North American harvest, which drove us to Australia for a larger proportion of our supply, and the additional length of voyage became a serious matter. On the whole, however, the War Committee were unwilling to consider the adoption of a big food production policy, and contented themselves with measures for releasing soldiers temporarily for bringing in the harvest, and shipping dispositions such as the use of the Southampton reserve.

The work of the War Committee, beginning with shipping, had thus extended into nearly every department of our national life. Once these questions had been brought before the Committee and decisions had been taken, the higher questions of policy connected with them tended to remain with that body rather than with the large unwieldy Cabinet. There was really not very much left for the Cabinet, although to the last it was taking decisions, of which there was no record—which was apt to cause some inconvenience, if not worse.

It must not be supposed that the War Committee allowed itself to be overwhelmed with matters of detail. It was only the larger questions of policy that came before it, though these were very numerous, particularly after the change of military policy. During the last year of the first Coalition Government some very important developments took place. In February 1916, for instance, it was decided to set up a Ministry of Blockade in order to strengthen and co-ordinate the machinery for exerting economic pressure, and Robert Cecil was appointed Minister with a seat in the Cabinet, combining the new post with the Parliamentary Under-Secretaryship of Foreign Affairs, which he had previously held. The general policy of the Ministry was based on the principle of rationing the imports of neutral countries in contact with Germany, combined with purchase schemes for their exports, e.g. we would say to Holland, Denmark, or Norway: 'Unless you stop sending supplies to Germany we will not let you have the coal or sugar which is essential to you. But if you will stop sending supplies, or limit them, we will buy them ourselves at a fair price, and in addition we will let you

have as much coal or sugar as you can prove you require for your own consumption—always on condition that you don't send it on to Germany.' During the year 1916 the new Ministry fully justified its existence by concluding a number of new agreements of this kind. We may also note that our foolish old friend, the Declaration of London, which ever since the beginning of the war had been dying by inches as one Order-in-Council after another was launched to cancel one or other of its provisions, received the *coup de grâce* by an Order-in-Council dated July 7, 1916. It was only the ruthless disregard of international law by the enemy which enabled us to jettison it on the plea of retaliation. It is a standing example of the need for extreme caution in entering into international agreements for the restriction of action in the event of war.

In January 1916 an important step in the co-ordination of shipping was taken in the appointment of a Shipping Control Board, the function of which was to decide on the allocation of British ships to essential requirements of the Allies as well as of the United Kingdom, and to make representations to the Cabinet on the tonnage required for naval and military purposes. Curzon was chairman with Faringdon (chairman of the Great Central Railway), Thomas Royden (deputy chairman of the Cunard Co.), and F. W. Lewis (deputy chairman of Furness Withy & Co.) as members and with Clement Jones (a director of the Booth Line), a most efficient person, as secretary. This powerful committee with so important a Terms of Reference, soon acquired great authority and was constantly turned to by the War Committee for advice on all shipping matters, and itself frequently found it necessary to consult the War Committee or to make suggestions on large questions of policy. In spite of its efforts, to say nothing of those of the Port and Transit Committee, the Shipping Department of the Board of Trade, and other bodies dealing with the more technical details of shipping matters, the shipping situation relative to the ever-increasing demands was constantly deteriorating. In November 1916, therefore, Lloyd George urged the appointment of a Director of Merchant Shipping, or Shipping Controller (the term was not used until later), who, under the President of the Board of Trade, should have a free hand to organize the disposition of all available shipping and its construction, but he was unable to carry his colleagues with him.

The idea of 'Controllers' was always a favourite theme with Lloyd George. Had he not demonstrated the theory with unmistakable success in his own person in the matter of munitions? A day or two

after his failure to persuade the War Committee to approve the appointment of a Shipping Controller he was successful in inducing that body to approve in principle the appointment of a Food Controller to help the Ministry of Agriculture in stimulating agricultural output by the organization of labour and machinery, for avoidance of waste, control of food prices, etc. This approval in principle, however, was not translated into practice until after the fall of the First Coalition and there was a good deal of passive resistance to the idea.

Another very important item related to aerial matters. The co-ordination of aerial action between the Navy and Army from the first proved, and until long after the war remained, a matter of the utmost difficulty. In the early years of the war the competition between the Admiralty and the War Office for the limited output of aeroplanes and engines, etc., was almost a scandal. In March 1916 a Joint War Air Committee was set up under Derby's chairmanship to tackle the question. The Committee failed in its task mainly for the reason that the members could never agree. After eight meetings Derby and Montagu of Beaulieu, the only unofficial members, resigned, and something else had to be devised. The preparation of a scheme was left to Curzon and myself and early in May the War Committee approved a plan we had drawn up for the establishment of an Air Board. The President was to be a Cabinet Minister and there was to be a second Parliamentary member to represent the Board in the other House to that in which the President sat. Besides the naval and military representatives there was to be some person of independent administrative experience. Where the proposed Board differed from previous Air Committees was that it was to be advisory in respect of its president, in whom the power of decision and of report to the War Committee in cases of disagreement was to lie. The general functions of the Air Board were to cover matters of general policy relating to the air, combined operations of the naval and military air services, recommendations on types of machines, co-ordination of supplies of material, prevention of competition between the two services, and the interchange and pooling of information and ideas between the two air services and such bodies as the Naval Board of Inventions, the Inventions Branch of the Ministry of Munitions, the Advisory Committee on Aeronautics, the National Physical Laboratory, etc. In announcing this decision in Parliament both Curzon and Bonar Law made it clear that the new Board was to prepare the way for the formation of an Air Ministry—in doing which they certainly went farther than some of their colleagues intended.

Curzon assumed the presidency of the Air Board in addition to his chairmanship of the Shipping Control Board. His non-official colleagues were Sydenham and John Baird as spokesman in the House of Commons. The new Board at once became tremendously active, meeting several times a week, and did a great deal to relieve the War Committee. Before long, however, they got at loggerheads with the Admiralty, whom they found unhelpful. The general point of view of the Admiralty was that naval aeronautics was a matter just as much under their own control as any other department of naval warfare, whether on the surface of, or beneath, the sea. They must have complete responsibility for operations (which no one disputed), and the logical and inevitable consequence was that they must also have entire responsibility for the design and supply of material. They continued to order their own aeronautical material without consulting, and sometimes without informing, the Air Board. Further, the organization of the Admiralty in aeronautical matters was entirely different from that of the War Office. The latter department had concentrated all aeronautical matters in the hands of the Director-General of Aeronautics, who was a member of the Army Council and was responsible for the supply of material, personnel, training, etc. The Admiralty, on the other hand, had divided the work between the different members of the Board: e.g. the Second Sea Lord, who was responsible for personnel generally, was also responsible for air personnel; the Controller, who was responsible for ship construction, was also responsible for aerial construction, and so forth. The Director of Naval Air Services was a relatively subordinate officer and not a member of the Board. Consequently no naval representative on the Board could speak authoritatively on all aspects of naval aviation, as the military representative could for military aviation, which further hampered the work of the Air Board. Perhaps also the Air Board itself adopted rather a high-handed attitude towards the Admiralty, instead of attempting to proceed gradually in a conciliatory manner to establish itself.

After the Air Board had held some twenty-five meetings these difficulties came to a head. Curzon presented a report to the War Committee in which he poured forth all his grievances against the Admiralty. He did not as yet propose the formation of an Air Ministry, but he did propose that the Admiralty should create an organization similar to that of the War Office, that they should adopt a more helpful attitude, and, finally, that the Admiralty and War Office supply services should, so far as aerial material was concerned, be concentrated and placed under

the Air Board. These proposals gave rise to a terrific controversy, which was complicated by the arrival on the scene of a third party, the Ministry of Munitions, with a claim that, if the supply services were to be concentrated, the work should be undertaken by the Ministry and not by the Air Board. The Admiralty were hotly opposed to both proposals, and there arose one of the acutest inter-departmental controversies of the war. No one who read them will ever forget the series of Memoranda that were exchanged between Balfour and Curzon—an amazing dialectical duel, rapier versus bludgeon. In the last days of November 1916 the Admiralty agreed to promote the Director of Naval Air Services to membership of the Board, but the main controversy could not get itself settled in spite of much discussion and the preparation of many formulæ, and still remained unsolved when the Government fell.

The last of the new administrative organs set up by the War Committee was the Man-Power Distribution Board, which was established in August 1916, on the recommendation of a committee presided over by Derby. The function of this Board was to settle all man-power questions and to co-ordinate the action of the various Government Departments in the economical utilization of men and women. Austen Chamberlain was chairman. Some of the machinery for detailed investigation of the various aspects of man-power was retained in subordination to the Man-Power Distribution Board, for example, the 'Reserved Occupations Committee' and the 'Badge Committee', but a Cabinet conference, which had hitherto dealt with exemptions from military service, was superseded by the new authority. Before the fall of the First Coalition the Man-Power Distribution Board had presented some half-dozen important reports to the War Committee.

During November 1916 the pressure on the War Committee became very great indeed. The number of meetings, which from January to October had averaged about six a month, rose in November to fifteen. Yet the Committee was still failing to keep abreast of its work, and the list of subjects awaiting decision was continually increasing. During the last week of its existence, in a desperate attempt to catch up arrears, the Committee held five long meetings. At the last but one of these a most important decision was arrived at. Germany had just declared a *levée en masse* of the population, whatever that might mean; she was engaged in the deportation to Germany for labour purposes of a large part of the population of the occupied territories, lately increased by the occupation of Roumania; the Central Powers had announced (November 5,

1916) the formation of an 'Independent State of Poland', where they intended to raise an army of some hundreds of thousands of men; our own shipping resources were becoming more and more strained, and our financial resources in America appeared to be nearly at an end; for both reasons it was desirable to increase our home production of essential needs to the utmost, if only to reduce our purchases abroad. In these circumstances the Committee took the tremendous decision in principle that compulsory service, not merely military service, but labour in the field, factory or dockyard, etc., in a word 'industrial conscription', should be introduced for all males up to the age of sixty. A committee was appointed to work out the details; and to consider the extension of the principle to women; the necessary legislation was to be introduced before Christmas. Before this policy had been announced the War Committee, and the Government itself, had ceased to exist. This expiring effort was never translated into action.

Before closing this chapter on the final development of the Supreme Command under the ægis of the War Committee, attention is invited to one feature in this organization, which distinguished it from the methods afterwards adopted by Lloyd George. Whereas Lloyd George preferred to work through Ministries, Asquith worked through committees or boards. In such matters as shipping, aerial navigation, manpower, the pressure, scope and magnitude of the problems had long outgrown the capacity of the older departments. In each case a committee or board, with a Cabinet Minister at its head, had been appointed to deal with them. In time they would probably have grown into Ministries, as had already occurred in the case of the Ministry of Munitions (under the personal direction of Lloyd George) and the Ministry of Blockade, both of which had started on the committee plan. Asquith never showed any objection to the formation of a new Ministry, where the necessity was shown, but some of his colleagues disliked the system, which consequently received no further extension until after the change of Government. There is no doubt, however, that the formation by Asquith's Government of powerful committees under Cabinet Ministers paved the way to the later great developments.

CHAPTER LV

THE FALL OF THE
FIRST COALITION GOVERNMENT

'To decide about ambition whether it is bad or not, you have two things to take into view. Not the coveting of the place alone, but the fitness of the man for the place withal: that is the question. Perhaps the place was his; perhaps he had a natural right, and even obligation to seek the place. (CARLYLE, *Heroes and Hero-worship*, Lecture 6.)

IN November 1916 the atmosphere in the Government, as in London itself in that gloomy season, was becoming daily more sulphureous. There was friction everywhere—in the Cabinet, the War Committee, the Admiralty, the War Office and in Parliament. Nothing particularly sensational was happening at sea except the daily sensation of the loss of some hundreds or even thousands of tons of shipping. No panacea had yet been found for dealing with the German U-boats, which were continually extending their radius of action as the narrow seas became too hot for them, and were especially active in the Mediterranean. Jellicoe was becoming profoundly disturbed at the increase in the losses, and on October 30th he wrote a letter to the Prime Minister on the subject; rather a strong step this, for the Commander-in-Chief to write to the head of the Government instead of to the First Lord of the Admiralty! It gave the impression that in his opinion the latter course was not likely to produce much result! On November 2nd Jellicoe conferred with the War Committee on the whole question. The possibilities of convoys were discussed for the first time, but all the experts, both naval and mercantile, were against them. The Admiralty held that convoys were useless unless there was one escort to each vessel, which was out of the question. The mercantile experts objected that the convoy had to proceed at the rate of the slowest ship, which led to longer average time on voyages, and that the simultaneous arrival of such large numbers of ships would lead to greater congestion than ever in ports. Convoys, therefore, were rejected. The most urgent need at the moment was deemed to be more guns wherewith to arm our merchant ships, and the estimated requirement was for no less than 3,000 guns. The Admiralty were told to confer with the Ministry of Munitions on the subject, and in mid-November the War Committee took the decision in principle

that the provision of guns for merchant ships should be a first charge on our artillery resources.

All these inquiries had produced a feeling, not for the first time, that all was not well with the Admiralty. They were too complacent. There was lack of driving power. The pressure had had to come from outside —from the Grand Fleet and from the War Committee. Moreover in Parliament and elsewhere there was a good deal of dissatisfaction with the Admiralty.

During his visit on November 2nd Jellicoe made an offer to Balfour to come to the Admiralty without a seat on the Board in order to devote himself entirely to anti-submarine work. Next day he repeated his offer to the Prime Minister, but a few days later (November 7th) he withdrew it in a letter to Balfour. Very little came of the conference between the Admiralty and the Ministry of Munitions about guns for merchant ships, beyond the handing over of a certain amount of iron scrap to the former. The Admiralty at that time seemed incapable of asserting themselves. The fact was that Balfour and Jackson, though admirable people in themselves, were unsuited to run in harness. Probably, therefore, Asquith did rightly in requiring, as he did at the end of November, that Balfour should make a change at the Admiralty—though he insisted that Balfour himself should retain his post as First Lord. Anyhow, the immediate result was that Jackson resigned on December 3rd, and Jellicoe was appointed next day First Sea Lord, having already handed over command of the Grand Fleet to Beatty on November 29th. The Admiralty crisis thus got itself solved just as the Cabinet difficulties had reached their crisis.

About the same time a crisis arose at the War Office. If the Admiralty crisis may be described as external, since there was no internal friction, the War Office crisis was internal, though reacting externally. If at the Admiralty Balfour and Jackson were in some respects too much alike to make a good combination, at the War Office Lloyd George and Robertson were too different. From the first I realized that they would not work together very easily, and so it turned out. Lloyd George had never been a partisan of the Western Front policy pursued alone, and had from very early days been a strong advocate of the Salonica expedition. Consequently the losses on the Somme, the collapse of Roumania, and the half-hearted efforts (as he considered them) to retrieve the situation in South-Eastern Europe were more than he could stand, and during the autumn of 1916 he was becoming daily more discontented with the policy of his Chief of Staff.

David Lloyd George in 1917

May 9th. I lunched with Montagu to meet Lloyd George. Montagu left us alone after lunch and we talked for an hour, at first about the offensive. . . . Ultimately he became very confidential and told me he was seriously thinking of leaving the Government, as he thought he might do more good outside than inside. Parliament, he said with great truth, is the only thing the Government are afraid of. They will always reach a decision quickly and put their whole energies into a matter which is about to be settled in Parliament, even if it involves leaving other and more important questions unsettled. I had to agree, as I have seen the truth of this illustrated again and again, but I did my best to persuade him to remain in, pointing out how much he had effected. He pressed me very hard to go to Russia with him in order to try and get to the bottom of the situation there. I saw the Prime Minister in the evening and told him of my talk with Lloyd George.[1] He was in bad spirits.

September 26th. After lunch Robertson asked me to see him. . . . He told me that Lloyd George made the worst possible impression on his recent visit to France. He spent most of his time with the French. He asked Foch's opinion of the English generals, whom he himself criticized severely. Foch promptly telephoned the whole thing to Haig and Joffre. Consequently when he went to see Joffre, the latter refused to see him without Haig. Robertson also said that Lloyd George was making a lot of trouble in the War Office both with him and the Q.M.G. Robertson said he would do anything for the Prime Minister.

October 13th. . . . I had an hour and a half's conversation with Lloyd George, who had asked me to talk with him about the evidence he was to give at the Dardanelles Commission. Very soon, however, we got to the subject of the war. Lloyd George, who has been much attacked in the papers lately, was very depressed about the offensive, which he does not consider to have produced results commensurate with the effort. He is evidently longing to carry out a big offensive at Salonica—his old love, is very apprehensive about Roumania, but cannot get his generals to agree with him. I told him I had very great sympathy with his point of view, and that I had always had precisely the same misgivings about the Somme offensive. Nevertheless I had deliberately muzzled myself because I wanted Robertson to have a perfectly free hand. I said that the Dardanelles expedition had failed because the soldiers did not believe in it, and consequently had insisted on the best of everything being sent to France. Salonica would fail in exactly the same way unless he could induce the soldiers to see that it was the best course and to go for it hard. In military affairs you are dealing with flesh and blood and men's minds, and not with mere machines. It was better to have a second best plan and to conform your whole policy to further it, than to have a plan that your soldiers didn't believe in.

----

[1] I had, as I always did, told Lloyd George I would do so.

T

October 28th. Had a long talk with the Prime Minister before lunch about the war generally. Lloyd George had just been to him very depressed, very disappointed with the lack of imagination of the General Staff, and very disgusted at the heavy losses involved in the offensive on the Somme as contrasted with the relatively small successes achieved. I could not offer much comfort. . . .

November 1st. Lunched alone with Lloyd George at Arthur Lee's house, like cuckoos in another bird's nest. . . . Lloyd George considered that the Somme offensive had been a bloody and disastrous failure; he was not willing to remain in office, if it was to be repeated next year; he said that Thomas, Bissolati, and others thought the same; they would all resign simultaneously and tell their respective fellow-countrymen that the war was being run on wrong lines, and that they had better make peace rather than repeat the experience of 1916. . . . He said that the staff might believe in their plan, but the rank and file of the Army did not and he instanced the vote of the Australian soldiers against conscription as evidence that the rank and file were 'fed up'. He was most gloomy about our prospects. His plan is to send 500 heavy guns to Russia for Roumania and many heavy guns to Salonica in order to crush Bulgaria next spring. . . . I saw the Prime Minister at the House of Commons before dinner, but after I had told him something of my lunch with Lloyd George he was called into the House.

November 3rd. The War Committee met in the morning without any experts or secretaries—just the Cabinet Ministers composing it. . . . After the meeting I saw the Prime Minister and urged on him the importance of having a record of the conclusions. He referred me to Lloyd George, whom I saw by appointment at 5 o'clock. Lloyd George was very delighted at the result of the meeting, as he had found a general agreement that the Somme offensive had been too costly, and he had persuaded them to propose an Anglo-French-Italian conference at Paris next week, without any experts, to be followed by a military conference in Russia, to be attended by Robertson, Joffre, and Cadorna. He gave me his rough notes and described what had happened at the meeting. Then he sent for his shorthand writer and demanded that *I* should dictate a telegram for Grey to send to Paris. Hardly had I finished when Grey's draft arrived, which we 'vetted' together, after which I had to run round to see the Prime Minister and Grey and Lloyd George again, before the draft was finally settled.

November 7th. . . . Saw Robertson in afternoon. Found him intensely indignant because the War Committee want him to go to Russia. He thinks it is a plot of Lloyd George's to get him away, and play 'hanky-panky' behind his back. He says he won't go.

I felt certain that Robertson was wrong in his suspicions of the intentions of the War Committee in desiring him to attend a conference in Russia. Even if Lloyd George desired to get rid of him, which I was

certain was not the case because he had no one in view to replace him, the remainder of the War Committee, in spite of the failure of his policy to accomplish much, believed in and trusted him, no one more so than the Prime Minister. There was no doubt that the War Committee as a whole genuinely thought that a visit by Western generals to Russia during the winter months would produce a wider outlook on the war as a whole, and result in improved co-ordination and mutual understanding.

November 9th. .... Arrived at office early and wrote a long letter to Robertson explaining the reasons why the War Committee want him to go to Russia, in order to try and allay his suspicions. War Committee at 11.30. While they were assembling Bonar Law told me he considered the political situation very precarious. 'Lloyd George', he said, 'is at the same time the right hand man to the Prime Minister, and the leader of the Opposition.' Lloyd George asked himself to lunch with me. I told him that his first task was to remove Robertson's suspicions. He said they had no foundation whatsoever in fact, and to prove it he said he was willing to accompany him to Russia. All that he wanted was that there should be a real collaboration and understanding between East and West. After lunch he read me a long document he had prepared for the conference in Paris next week. It was a most gloomy document, but hard to controvert. I told him that personally I never had the smallest illusions about crushing Germany. The best I had ever hoped for at any time was a draw in our favour, and a favourable peace extorted by economic pressure. He then said: 'We are going to lose this war.' He wanted me to write up his paper from his notes, but I said I hadn't time. I begged him to get right with Haig and Robertson by visiting the former in company with the latter. In the evening I had a letter from Robertson saying bluntly that he would not go to Russia and that he was out for a row without kid gloves on.

November 10th. On arriving at office I wrote another letter to Robertson telling him of my lunch with Lloyd George, assuring him that I did not believe that Ll. G. wished to send him to Russia to get rid of him, and that he had assured me to the contrary, and urging the great dangers of a row, which would probably result in the resignation of one or the other—Robertson's disappearance being a military disaster of the first magnitude and Lloyd George's a political disaster which would smash the Government and perhaps the Alliance. At 11.30 yet another War Committee. These have been really dreadful War Committees. .... The War Committee is hopelessly congested, great questions dealing with Man-Power, the Air Board, Food Supply, and Finance all urgently awaiting settlement. Yet I could not get a meeting for tomorrow, because X was going for a day's shooting, Lord Y for a week-end, and Lord Z to address his former constituents. I managed to

get a meeting for Monday, but the Prime Minister said 'You won't get any-one'. Today's meeting had to end soon after 1 p.m. to enable Ministers to attend official luncheons.

November 11th. Lunched with Lloyd George. He told me that he could not continue to be responsible at the War Office unless the strategy was changed, and that he would tell the people his reasons if he went. He also said that he would not desert the Government 'like rats leaving a sinking ship', but would take some post like 'Food Dictator'. I went from him to the Prime Minister, who takes a much gloomier view of the general situation.

November 12th (Sunday). Lloyd George had lent me his motor car—Kitchener's by the way. Adeline and I picked up Mrs and Miss Lloyd George and motored first down to Lloyd George's country house at Walton Heath, where I went with him through his Memo. for the Paris conference—a most lugubrious and pessimistic document, though difficult to answer in detail. Then Adeline and I motored on alone to the Asquiths at Sutton Courtney, where we lunched. After lunch I went through the paper with the Prime Minister. He flatly declined to include the greater part in his statement for the conference,[1] and the reasons Ll. G. had given me did not appeal to him at all. He thought that the paper would outrage Robertson and do no good. So we motored back to Town, where I rang up Lloyd George on the telephone and told him how the land lay. He then decided to hand the paper to the con-ference himself. At 8 p.m. Mantoux, the interpreter, turned up to take the document for translation, and I was uncommonly glad to be rid of it.

We started for Paris on November 14th. Asquith and Lloyd George were the only Ministers to attend the conference, but Robertson and Maurice accompanied us as they were to attend the conference of generals and staffs, which was to be held simultaneously with the politi-cal conference but at Joffre's headquarters at Chantilly. In spite of the peculiar delicacy of the situation we were an extraordinarily cheery party. Here was a Prime Minister, beset with incredible difficulties, both external and internal, with a disunited Cabinet, and subjected to bitter and acrimonious Press attacks; a Minister of War, an active critic of the policy of the Government of which he was a member, and at logger-heads with his own Chief of Staff; and finally the said Chief of Staff, who was out for war with his chief 'without kid gloves on'. Yet, as Lloyd George was fond of recalling, it was an extraordinarily har-monious and almost hilarious party which travelled that day to Paris. True, a shadow came over the party as we passed the great war cemetery at Etaples, already terribly full, and Asquith's thoughts, we

---

[1] My diary fails to explain that the object of my mission was to induce Asquith to incorporate the 'lugubrious' document in his own principal speech at the Conference.

all felt, had turned to his brilliant son Raymond who had lately fallen on the Somme. Shortly after, however, Robertson restored general merriment by calling out 'There's a fine pair of pants for you, Prime Minister', pointing to some backyard, where there hung on the clothes line a pair of unmentionables of gigantic proportions and indescribable hue!

November 14th (Paris). After dinner at the Crillon, George Clerk and I had to buckle down to a long evening's work, getting the Prime Minister's speech into final shape. It was a desperately complicated business, as first it had been dictated by Lloyd George, then so amended by the Prime Minister that Lloyd George had decided to make it himself, and had it translated by Mantoux (Sunday night) in the original. Then, on Monday morning early, before the War Committee, I had been summoned to Montagu's house to discuss it with Lloyd George and Montagu, with the result that it had been decided that the Prime Minister should deliver it, a long passage written by me being interpolated in the middle, and the Prime Minister in the train had gone through the whole thing and made many alterations. Thus Clerk and I had the heavy task of altering Mantoux's original translation, incorporating the Prime Minister's alterations, cutting out the long excised parts and sub-stituting my part, which first had to be translated into French. Then Mantoux came in about midnight and insisted on altering all our French translation. Finally it had to be typed by my shorthand writer, whom I had luckily brought, but who knew no French, so that he was very slow and his work had to be carefully checked and the accents put in. Thus it was 2 a.m. before I got to bed very tired. Matters were not facilitated by the Prime Minister coming in from the Embassy at about midnight in a very talkative and communicative mood, and telling us a lot of interesting information he had picked up from Briand.

November 15th. A gorgeous, crisp, sunny day. Notwithstanding my late session I was sent for about 8.15 a.m. by Lloyd George, who had had a 'brain-wave' and wanted some resolutions to be drafted to be placed before the conference, the principal point being that the Allies in the west should re-equip the Russian Armies for 1917, even if they had to go short them-selves—a proposal which had my cordial sympathy. As there was not much time I had to dictate this while I shaved. However, it was well done and eventually accepted by the conference, practically without amendment.

This was the first example of a method of collaboration at international conferences, which afterwards became a fixed habit between Lloyd George and myself. Instead of leaving the conclusions to be drafted after a long and unsatisfactory discussion, or maybe never to be drafted at all, which was sometimes the case up to this period, we used to come

to the conference with resolutions ready drafted, sometimes in alternative forms. I would watch the discussion attentively, and, if necessary, amend the original draft in manuscript, and at the appropriate moment Lloyd George would produce 'out of his hat' and hand round a number of copies, retyped by Sylvester, if necessary, in the ante-room.

November 15th (continued). This made me late for breakfast, but before I had been more than five minutes or so at breakfast a messenger came to say that the whole hotel had been scoured for me, as the Prime Minister wanted me immediately. So off I had to go to . . . the Prime Minister, who was breakfasting in a private room. . . . The Prime Minister showed me a letter he had just received from Robertson urging that he should not be sent to Russia owing to the very great importance of his work at home. I knew all about this, as Robertson had consulted me about it, both personally and through Maurice in the train on the previous day, and the letter had been sent on my advice. Then Lloyd George was called in and agreed that Robertson could not go, and with great enthusiasm announced his intention of going himself. He asked the Prime Minister's permission to take me, which the Prime Minister flatly declined to give.

Then we had to go to the conference at the Quai d'Orsay. This was merely a 'heart to heart' talk between the Prime Minister, Lloyd George, Briand, and Lacaze. Bonham Carter, George Clerk and I were not admitted and spent the morning kicking our heels on very uncomfortable gilt chairs and sofas, and going out in pairs to smoke on the embankment by the Seine. The Prime Minister and Lloyd George had to attend an official luncheon and we lunched comfortably with Doumayrou (who is half paralysed and is a pathetic figure with a beard, very different from the former dapper little French officer). The Prime Minister told me that at the morning conference they spent most of their time in abusing the narrow-mindedness of the British and French generals. . . .

It was at this hole-in-the-corner, informal, unrecorded conversation that the famous speech, on which so much lavish care had been spent, got itself made. Instead of stirring to their depths the hearts and souls of the representatives of all the Allies in solemn conclave, with stenographers, procès-verbal writers, protocolists, interpreters—and all the paraphernalia of a great international conclave, this momentous document (and even in the 'bowdlerized' and attenuated form to which it had been reduced, it still was a remarkable document) was communicated only to this small and discreet group. It sounds as though Asquith had made an ingenious move to side-track an embarrassment, but this was not the case. When he went to the Quai d'Orsay that morning Asquith did not know that it was only for a small informal meeting. It

is conceivable that Briand, who probably knew all about the Memorandum from the interpreter, arranged matters in this way, but as it was his usual practice to precede a formal conference by a private discussion with his British colleagues, the incident may have been fortuitous. At any rate the virtual suppression of his carefully prepared speech did not tend to soothe Lloyd George's ruffled feelings.

In any event the Memorandum did produce some result, for when the conference met (including also Isvolski, the Russian Ambassador in Paris, Carcano, Italian Finance Minister and the Italian Ambassador) the first meeting was devoted mainly to a discussion of the relationship of Governments to soldiers, and the gist of it was that Governments must not allow themselves to be run blindly by their General Staffs, but, having the responsibility, must undertake the direction of the operations on the technical basis provided by their Staffs—which was, in fact, pretty much what had been happening since the beginning of the war. The Russian conference was also approved in principle, subject to the agreement of the Czar.

Meanwhile the generals had been in conference at Chantilly and had drawn up a report, the gist of which was very much on the lines of their report of December 1915, namely, that the next offensive should be *prepared for* by the first fortnight in February. The date was advanced as compared with 1916 in order to avoid being again forestalled by the Germans; the actual date of starting was left for later decision. Once an attack had been let loose by one army, the other attacks were to be attuned thereto, i.e. they were to start within three weeks of the first attack. Close liaison between all the armies was to be assured. In the Balkans an effort was to be made to put Bulgaria out of action by combined operations by the Russo-Roumanian Armies on the north and the Salonica 'Army of the Orient' (as it was grandiloquently termed) on the south. The latter was to be raised to twenty-three divisions. In case of serious misadventure to any of the Allies in any of the main theatres the other Allies were to be prepared to come to the rescue, either by direct or indirect action.

These proposals were considered at the second and last meeting of the political conference and were approved. The French were throughout this conference in an optimistic frame of mind, as Nivelle had recently attacked the reduced German forces at Verdun and had recovered almost all the ground lost in the German offensive earlier in the year.

Lloyd George, however, did not catch the infection of optimism and was by no means satisfied with the results of the conference. In his view

the Salonica force had never been properly supported. The total supplies of munitions in that theatre of war had, he used to assert, never exceeded what would be expended in two days' fighting on the Somme. There had never been sufficient heavy guns there. In short, the Salonica expedition, like the Dardanelles expedition, had been starved of what was needful for success. Something of his disgruntlement was observable before we left Paris.

November 17th. At an early hour Lloyd George sent round to me, but I was in bed and eventually breakfasted with him and Thomas. Lloyd George has quite made up his mind that Roumania is going to collapse. Thomas told him that in this event the French Government would fall! This at once caused Lloyd George to say that he would not go to Russia, as he would be required at home. This places the Prime Minister in a great dilemma. Lloyd George has forced this subject forward, has raised all this dust, including the Paris conference, has quarrelled with Robertson in his endeavour to make him go, has released him in order that he may go himself, and now refuses to go! It really makes us look very silly, but the Prime Minister always said this would happen.

In his own memoirs Lloyd George makes clear that this conference was decisive in bringing home to him the need for some action to improve the conduct of the war, and, according to his account, some remarks of mine brought him to this point. He begins by mentioning how he 'left the conference feeling that after all nothing more would be done except to repeat the old fatuous tactics of hammering away with human flesh and sinews at the strongest fortresses of the enemy'. Then he goes on to describe how he and I went for a walk before dinner 'to talk matters over'. After indicating the general coincidence of our views on the need for 'a change in the conduct of the war', and the dangers of a collapse either of Russia or Italy or of a failure on our part to check the losses in the submarine campaign, he continues:

I was in favour of an immediate resignation to rouse Allied opinion to the actualities of the position. To this Sir Maurice was opposed until some other means of effecting a change in the war direction had first been attempted. I can recall that as we passed the Vendôme Column, Sir Maurice paused and said: 'You ought to insist on a small War Committee being set up for the day-to-day conduct of the war, with full powers. It must be independent of the Cabinet. It must keep in close touch with the P.M., but the Committee ought to be in continuous session, and the P.M., as Head of the Government, could not manage that. He has a very heavy job in looking after the Cabinet and attending to Parliament and home affairs. He is a bit tired, too, after all

he has gone through in the last two and a half years. . . .' We both agreed that it was important that Mr Asquith should continue to be Prime Minister. His great prestige and unrivalled authority in the House of Commons would be assets which were regarded as indispensable. It was decided, therefore, that on my return to England I should place the proposition before the Prime Minister; but that before I did so it would be best to sound Bonar Law, whose goodwill and approval it was essential to secure. I wired from Paris to Lord Beaverbrook, asking him to arrange a meeting between Bonar Law and myself the following evening.[1]

Curiously enough I did not record that particular conversation in my diary, but Lloyd George's account is supported both by my recollection and by other evidence in my possession of the views I held at that time on the conduct of the war. Moreover, the proposition which Lloyd George says that I enunciated opposite the Vendôme Column corresponds very closely to a proposal I put to Asquith on December 2nd. In addition my diary for this conference records several other conversations with Lloyd George and that 'all this time Ll. George was intensely friendly to me and continually asking my advice about this, that and the other'.

While on our journey home on November 17th Asquith was recognized on the quayside at Boulogne by a number of British soldiers and given quite an ovation. This looked as if the attacks on him by the halfpenny Press had had less effect than might have been expected, at any rate so far as the Army was concerned.

Soon after our return home the War Committee decided that the British representatives at the proposed Russian Conference should be Grey, Austen Chamberlain, Revelstoke (representing finance), Henry Wilson, Kiggell, an artillery general, and Layton (Ministry of Munitions).

The Russian Conference, however, as planned by the First Coalition, was never destined to take place, though the idea was taken up shortly after under the new régime, for within a fortnight of the conclusion of the Paris Conference the British Supreme Command was plunged into a crisis of the first order, which Asquith failed to survive.

Up to this time the internal troubles in the Supreme Command had taken the form of a more or less vague discontent among some of its members, some objecting to the policy pursued, others dissatisfied with the failure of the policy and out to make trouble, to say nothing of a

[1] *War Memoirs,* II, p. 963.

T*

general undercurrent of dissatisfaction with the inability of the War Committee to reach decisions with reasonable rapidity and to keep abreast of its work. After the Paris Conference, however, the disgruntlement took a more definite form and became directed against the personnel of the War Committee.

November 22nd. I lunched alone with Lloyd George at my club. . . . He wants to . . . secure a new War Committee—himself, Carson, Bonar Law, and Henderson—the latter in order to conciliate Labour. Personally I agree that some new procedure is necessary, as the War Committee wastes a tremendous lot of time. . . . I told Lloyd George that I liked his proposal in principle, but not his personnel. I said frankly that I had not a high opinion of Carson or Bonar Law in council. After thinking it over I added that it would put absolute power into his (Ll. G.'s) hands, and that he might find his colleagues a useful check when he was too exuberant. Lloyd George is, of course, more gifted with ideas than any member of the War Committee—but they are not always good ideas. Under his scheme Asquith will remain Prime Minister, so I saw no disloyalty in discussing it, and a change is urgently necessary. I flatly declined, however, to dine with him, Carson, and Bonar Law this evening as that, I thought, would savour of disloyalty.

November 23rd. . . . At 2.30 I saw Bonar Law by appointment. He outlined to me the Lloyd George scheme for a new War Committee. I told him I agreed in principle, though doubtful about personnel. He was very confidential and told me of all his difficulties with his party.

November 25th (Saturday). . . . Lloyd George asked me to see him before lunch, but when I arrived he was just off to see Bonar Law. I told him I could not come in the afternoon as I wanted a rest and was a 'squeezed lemon'. He replied, 'Well, I am a desiccated lemon!' It has been an extraordinarily heavy week.

November 28th. . . . I lunched with the Prime Minister. After lunch he told me that he had received the Lloyd George–Bonar Law proposal. On the whole he supported it, but asked me to consider it and ponder over it, and let him have my views before the Cabinet meeting next day. (This I did, my views being as before, viz. right in principle, if the personnel could be got right.)

The Cabinet met next day (November 29th) and decided to form a 'Civil Committee' to take in hand such questions as Foreign Labour, Control of Mines, etc., and generally to do for the internal situation what the War Committee was supposed to be doing for the war. Lloyd George was to be chairman, with Runciman, Samuel, Austen Chamberlain, and Robert Cecil as members. This was obviously not a plan which would in any way satisfy Lloyd George, who was just as

dissatisfied with the management of the war as with the civil side of affairs, and he very soon rebelled against it.

December 1st. War Committee at 12.45. I noticed that the Prime Minister was rather piano and I learned afterwards that Lloyd George had delivered his ultimatum,[1] practically threatening to resign unless the War Committee was reconstituted with himself as Chairman, and demanding that Carson should have a place in the Government and Balfour leave the Admiralty. It is all an intolerable nuisance, and is precipitated by the tragedy of Roumania's collapse.

December 2nd. During the day the political crisis became very serious. . . . I suggested a solution to the Prime Minister, but it was not well received. I lunched at 10 Downing Street, but very shortly after lunch the Prime Minister left by motor for Walmer Castle. It was very typical of him that in the middle of this tremendous crisis he should go away for the week-end! Typical both of his qualities and of his defects; of his extraordinary composure and of his easy-going habits. After lunch, at Mrs Asquith's request, I saw Bonar Law, and learned from him that he had called a party meeting of Unionist Cabinet members for the following day, and that he would probably 'send a letter' (viz. of resignation) after it. He explained that he must do this in order not to appear in the eyes of his party to be dragged at the heels of Lloyd George. . . . Bonar Law told me that he might put off his party meeting if he was sure that Lloyd George would not resign first—and so give the unfortunate Prime Minister time to think it out. So I went after Reading, who had been commissioned by the Prime Minister to use his personal influence with Lloyd George in this direction. Reading, however, had only been able to persuade Lloyd George to postpone action until tomorrow. I went back to Bonar Law, but this was not good enough for him and he decided to go on

---

[1] The ultimatum took the form of a Memorandum which has been often published; it is quoted here from Spender, II, pp. 252 *sq.*, 264.

1. That the War Committee consist of three members two of which must be the First Lord of the Admiralty and the Secretary of State for War who should have in their offices deputies capable of attending to and deciding all departmental business, and a third Minister without a portfolio. One of these three to be chairman.

2. That the War Committee shall have full power, subject to the Supreme Control of the Prime Minister, to direct all questions connected with the war.

3. The Prime Minister in his discretion to have power to refer any question to the Cabinet.

4. Unless the Cabinet on reference by the Prime Minister reverses the decision of the War Committee, that decision to be carried out by the Department concerned.

5. The War Committee to have the power to invite any Minister and to summon the expert advisers of any Department to its meetings.

Asquith's counter-proposal, in a letter to Lloyd George on December 4th, was as follows:

The Prime Minister to have supreme and effective control of war policy.

The Agenda of the War Committee will be submitted to him; its Chairman will report to him daily; he can direct it to consider particular topics or proposals; and all its conclusions will be subject to his approval or veto. He can, of course, at his own discretion attend meetings of the Committee.

with his party meeting. So back to Downing Street where we arranged that Bonham Carter should follow the Prime Minister to Walmer and bring him back tomorrow morning. I walked home with Reading. We both agreed that the whole crisis is intolerable. There is really very little between them. Everyone agrees that the methods of the War Committee call for reform. Everyone agrees that the Prime Minister possesses the best judgment. The only thing is that Lloyd George and Bonar Law insist that the former and not the Prime Minister must be the man to run the war. The Prime Minister quite properly says that, if he is not fit to run the War Committee, he is not fit to be Prime Minister. The obvious compromise is for the Prime Minister to retain the Presidency of the War Committee with Lloyd George as Chairman, and to give Lloyd George a fairly free run for his money. This is my solution.

Under the plan I submitted to Asquith he would have retained the leadership of the House of Commons, continued to preside at the Cabinet, and remained as President of the War Committee with the absolute right to attend whenever the questions on the Agenda paper were of sufficient importance to warrant it. But the essence of the scheme was that he should leave the mass of day-to-day business to his colleagues under the chairmanship of his active and ingenious War Minister. Thus the dignity and general control would have remained with the Prime Minister, while full scope would have been given to the extraordinary energy and driving power of Lloyd George.

December 3rd (Sunday). After tea I went down to 10 Downing Street to find out if I could help in any way in the political crisis, having heard that the Prime Minister had come back to Town. Lloyd George was closeted with the Prime Minister. In Bonham Carter's room I found assembled Montagu, Bonham Carter, Masterton Smith, Davis, and Marsh. At the Unionist Ministers' meeting in the morning a resolution had been passed demanding the resignation of the Prime Minister, which Bonar Law had transmitted, but no one seemed to regard it as more than a bluff to force the Prime Minister to give Lloyd George the Chairmanship of the War Committee. Shortly after I arrived Lloyd George came out, and after a short palaver with Montagu, asked to see me, as he was awaiting the arrival of Bonar Law, who had been sent for. Lloyd George then told me that the Unionists had insisted that he should become Prime Minister, but he had flatly declined, and had insisted that he would only serve with Asquith. Apparently the Prime Minister had agreed with him in principle on the question of machinery, and that Lloyd George should have a free hand with the War Committee, but there was a difficulty about personnel. Lloyd George insisted on Balfour's leaving the Admiralty. He himself intended to remain Secretary of State for War and he saw that the First Lord in this event must also be a member, but he would not

agree to Balfour. . . . The Prime Minister, however, is in a difficult position in getting rid of Balfour, because, when he forced him a week or two ago to substitute Jellicoe for Jackson as First Sea Lord, he added his strong wish that Balfour should remain in office. Lloyd George wishes the War Committee to consist of Bonar Law, Carson, and Henderson the Labour man. Apparently the Prime Minister will put up with this but boggles only over Balfour, who cannot be left out if he remains at the Admiralty. . . . Then Bonar Law arrived and he and Lloyd George were closeted with the Prime Minister for half an hour or so. Eventually they agreed that the Cabinet should resign and the Prime Minister should reconstruct on the basis of the Lloyd George plan.

As I walked home that night I believed that the crisis was well on the way to a solution, and so I thought until well on into the next day; and so also thought Lloyd George. About midday next day (December 4th) Lloyd George sent for me, and after forcing my way through a mob of journalists with cameras at the entrance to the War Office and a number of 'dim-looking people' in his anteroom, I was ushered into 'the Presence'.

December 4th. . . . I found 'the Presence' lying back in an armchair by the fireside looking very tired. He and I were then both under the impression that his scheme was accepted. He asked me to draft some 'rules' for the new War Committee, which could be communicated to members of the new Cabinet before they took office, and after hearing his views I undertook to do so on the understanding that I should first talk them over with Montagu, as they were to include a statement on 'industrial compulsion' on which Montagu is working day and night.

On seeing Montagu, however, I learned that the Prime Minister was now backing out of his agreement with Lloyd George. This was due to the appearance that morning of a leading article in *The Times* purporting to give full details of the new plan, and denouncing it. Everyone believed that this leading article had been inspired by Lloyd George, and in these circumstances neither Asquith nor his Liberal colleagues were willing to go on on the new terms. The tragedy of it was that Lloyd George was totally innocent of *The Times* article. He wrote to Asquith at the time to say so, but I fear he was not believed.

Long after I learned the true history of this episode. It was at dinner at Reading's house on Sunday, December 15, 1920, on which I wrote in my diary:

There was much interesting talk. Perhaps the most interesting item was contributed by Lloyd George, who said that on the previous week-end he

had learned the true history of *The Times* article which, four years ago, wrecked Asquith's Government. Geoffrey Dawson had told him that he wrote the article himself at Clieveden (the Astors' place on the Thames) without prompting from anyone, and without communication of any sort or kind with Northcliffe, and because he disliked the arrangement agreed between Asquith and Lloyd George. The particulars of the proposed arrangement had been given him by Carson. This disposes finally of the story that Lloyd George, or someone round him, had prompted the article. If this had been known to Asquith and his friends four years ago, history might have been different.

The later stages of the crisis have no bearing on the methods of the Supreme Command and are not even of much political interest. It is sufficient to recall that on the evening of December 5th Lloyd George resigned, and Asquith, unable to retain the support of the Unionists, also resigned. The same evening the King sent for Bonar Law, who undertook to try to form a Government. That evening I saw Lloyd George, who was still anxious to be reconciled with Asquith, if it could be managed. Meanwhile Bonar Law had invited Asquith to join him in forming a Government, but Asquith had declined. Bonar Law then gave up the attempt. On December 6th the King saw Asquith, Lloyd George, Bonar Law and Balfour together, but did not succeed in effecting a reconcilation, and on December 7th His Majesty sent for Lloyd George, who undertook to form a Government. The First Coalition Government was at an end. The Supreme Command had passed to other hands.

Asquith's resignation was an overwhelming blow to all those who had worked with him. Not only was he gifted with a peculiarly kindly nature, but his character was essentially one to inspire respect. His encyclopædic knowledge (always bursting out unexpectedly), high statesmanship, disregard of purely party considerations when great matters of State were at issue, untiring patience in dealing with difficult colleagues, unswerving loyalty both to colleagues and subordinates, his perfect judgment, serenity and unfailing courage in all circumstances compelled admiration. Even his contempt of personal attacks was an endearing quality. He always treated them with indifference and even with jocularity. Such was his disregard that he would rarely even take the trouble to use such influences as Governments can exert to get on the right side of the Press so far as he personally was concerned. Before the war he was a perfect chairman of the Committee of Imperial Defence, and, while always maintaining peace as his main object, did

not hesitate to prepare our defences to such a pitch as averted all danger of invasion or starvation and maintained the integrity of the British Empire the world over. After the war came he never wavered in his unswerving determination to see it through to final victory. If he did not remain in office long enough to see the victory consummated, he did at any rate build up—from almost nothing at all—a military machine, which was not only able already to hold its own, and a little more, with that of the most militaristic nation of modern times, but on which his successor in office was able to build so successfully as to achieve final victory within less than two years of Asquith's fall. As a Parliamentary leader Asquith had few equals. His powerful and sonorous eloquence enabled him to exercise a leadership which was at the time unsurpassed in any of the nations at war. In this respect the whole of the enemy countries were completely eclipsed by Asquith, as later by Lloyd George, and this quality of leadership was one of the factors in eventual victory.

It has been said that Asquith lacked foresight. This was not the case. He was not a man of any great initiative, but he surrounded himself with persons of initiative, and exercised his incomparable judgment to correct mistakes on their part. We have seen how consistently he encouraged the defensive preparations of the Committee of Imperial Defence, and how wisely he guided them.[1] It was the same during the war; for example, during 1916 he set up a Reconstruction Committee and a sub-committee of the Committee of Imperial Defence to study peace terms, and before he left office a good deal of progress had been made towards the formulation of our attitude towards peace, in case the moment for negotiation should suddenly arrive. He had authorized me to send a circular letter to all Government Departments, Committees, etc., inviting them to make a complete record of their experiences during the war, in order that they might be available for the future. In our pre-war defensive preparations we had suffered considerably from the lack of proper records of what had been done in past wars on administrative questions of all kinds, and we owe it to Asquith's judgment that after the war the Committee of Imperial Defence had a mass of invaluable historical material, compiled by those responsible for what was done, to work on. A copy of the circular letter was sent thereafter to every new department and committee that was brought into being, and at the end of the war a reminder was sent under Lloyd George's authority in order that, before the various war organizations

[1] *vide supra*, p. 144.

were demobilized, their experiences should be collated and edited for the guidance of future generations. Many other instances could be given of Asquith's foresight if space permitted. It is sufficient to mention the care with which the campaign for 1916 was explored before the end of 1915 and the completeness of the preparations: and that as early as November 1916 he had called for Memoranda on the general situation from all departments concerned, with a view to deciding the policy to be pursued in 1917. Yet another instance is the prompt action taken to destroy the Roumanian oilfields before their capture by the Germans. Certainly the idea that Asquith lacked foresight can no more be sustained than the idea that he lacked energy.

It is, of course, true that towards the end of his term of office the Supreme Command had deteriorated. This was not due to any lack of vigour on his part. Even as things were, the output of decisions by the War Committee was prodigious compared with anything that had been known within living memory and the number of meetings, all of which were presided over by Asquith himself, was in the last few weeks of his Government very large. We must seek other causes for the First Coalition's failure; we shall find them in an inherent political weakness rather than in the leadership. The party controversy before the war had been too acute to admit of complete fusion of parties so soon. There were too many rancorous memories, too deep a distrust and only the loftiest minds, such as Asquith and Balfour, could overcome these obstacles. In a word it was a coalition that never coalesced.

Asquith left office on December 7th. With him went many who have hitherto appeared prominently in these pages—Grey, McKenna, Runciman, Samuel and others. Thus was fulfilled Fisher's prophecy in 1911 that Asquith would remain in office until 1916.[1] This great Prime Minister—one of the greatest of modern times—now makes his bow and leaves our stage. He will in the later acts of the drama appear only dimly, lost in the shades of opposition where he pursued his role as leader with the same sturdy patriotism as in office, but his fellow-countrymen will ever remember him as one of the outstanding figures of the Great War.

[1] *vide supra*, p. 146.

THE WAR CABINET AND
THE IMPERIAL WAR CABINET

CHAPTER LVI

DICTATORSHIP IN COMMISSION

'The flexibility of the Cabinet system allows the Prime Minister in an emergency to take upon himself a power not inferior to that of a dictator, provided always that the House of Commons will stand by him.' (JOHN MORLEY, *Walpole*, c. 7.)

December 10th (Sunday).... On the night of the 7th I was summoned by Lloyd George to the War Office at about 10 p.m. He informed me that he was now Prime Minister, though he didn't much like it, and we had a long talk about the personnel of the new Government, the procedure of the new War Committee and the future of the war. He and Bonar Law, who was there part of the time, consulted me on many points and I almost thought they were going to offer me a place.

To say that Lloyd George did not much like being Prime Minister at that moment is to put it mildly. He described himself as 'the most miserable man on earth'. The responsibility was indeed great for, though as yet he did not realize it, he had taken upon himself a power not inferior to that of a dictator, subject, of course, to the condition that Parliament would stand by him. But he had also the vision to share his power with others and virtually to put it in commission.

If the matter is considered aright, in times of national emergency a dictatorship of some kind, provided it is operated in constitutional forms and with reasonable deference to Parliament and public opinion, is not inconsistent with democracy. To quote Hobbes:

And as a Child has need of a Tutor, or Protector, to preserve his Person, and Authority: So also (in great Commonwealths) the Sovereign Assembly, in all great dangers and troubles, have need of *Custodes Libertatis*; that is of Dictators, or Protectors of their Authoritie; which are as much Temporary Monarchs; to whom, for a time, they may commit the entire exercise of their Powers; and they have (at the end of that time) been oftner deprived thereof, than Infant Kings by their Protectors, Regents, or any other Tutors.[1]

The elder Pitt held somewhat similar views:

He undoubtedly believed that it was only by complete responsibility of a War Minister that a constitutional country could hope to make war successfully. Such had been his position, and well had he justified the new theory.

[1] *Leviathan*, c. 19.

But it was one which the Constitutional Whigs could not possibly accept or endorse.[1]

It may be observed that the Constitutional Whigs of Lloyd George's time were no more amenable than were those of Chatham's day. They never ceased to criticize the new system, and they pursued their *quondam* colleague relentlessly and long after the events which we are now considering had passed into history, carrying the vendetta to the point of almost destroying one of the great historic parties of the nation. But, in the light of after events one sees that something approximating to a dictatorship was inevitable. Unless there had been some single mind, working though it was with others, to direct the policy of the nation and above all to take decisions and drive the machine along, the gigantic effort needed to secure victory could never have been made. The same need was found in the other leading nations of the alliance. Clemenceau and Woodrow Wilson were just as much dictators as was Lloyd George, a fact recognized by Ludendorff:[2]

> Our War Chancellors did nothing to repair the damage or enlighten the people. They had no creative ideas and did nothing to hold the people together and lead them, unlike the great dictators, Clemenceau, Lloyd George and Wilson.

Surely it was one of the glories of democracy in a war fought for the existence of democracy, that, in the three greatest democratic countries of the world, the people temporarily ceded their power to a near-dictatorship, recognizing that by these means alone could they accomplish their aim!

In each of the cases mentioned it was a civil and not a military dictatorship. At no time did Lloyd George, Clemenceau or Wilson attempt to dictate naval and military policy. They might criticize the operations proposed by their naval or military advisers; they might force them to justify their proposals by convincing arguments or insist on the examination of alternative suggestions; they might point out that their plans would make too great a drain on the total resources of the Allies or have disastrous political reactions; they might make such dispositions as they thought best for the exercise of the Supreme Command in the field, even to the point of putting the Commander-in-Chief of one army temporarily or permanently under the command of another; they might dismiss an admiral or a general in whom they no

---

[1] Julian Corbett, *England in the Seven Years' War*, II, p. 205.
[2] Ludendorff, I, p. 370.

longer felt confidence; in the interests of the war as a whole, when the naval or military advisers of the various nations took different views, one or other might become parties to a joint decision against the advice of their respective generals—but rarely on any purely naval or military issue of a major character did the civilians attempt, either individually or collectively, to override a consensus of agreed naval or military opinion. Moreover, all of them kept a sharp eye on public opinion, and governed through constitutional machinery; Lloyd George, indeed, as already stated, fortified himself with a band of brothers, who worked with him so harmoniously as to amount to a 'Dictatorship in Commission'.

Before 1914 Lloyd George had displayed no conspicuous interest in the science of war. He had not been a very active member of the Committee of Imperial Defence. When war broke out, he had to find his feet in a world that was new to him, and he did this characteristically by visits to the theatre of war and by frequent conversations with all and sundry, whatever might be their rank or station in life, who were in daily contact with the hard realities of the situation. His independence of judgment is shown in his unceasing condemnation, in opposition to the views of all our leading generals, of the policy of concentrating on the Western Front.

In stature Lloyd George was rather small, but he possessed the stocky solid frame of many of his fellow-countrymen, and his healthy complexion gave evidence of a sound constitution. His head was square and large, with a wealth of black hair gradually turned grey by the cares of office. The dominating feature of his face was his eyes, ever changing, now tender with emotion, now sparkling with fun, now flashing with anger; eyes astute, unfathomable. And from the man there emanated an extraordinary sense of power and strength, such as I have never encountered in any other. Hundreds of times I have watched him listening quietly while some seemingly insoluble problem was debated. One view after another would be expressed; one solution after another proposed and rejected. When all had spoken, Lloyd George would often intervene with some novel and ingenious proposal, which his fertile mind had thrown up, and which he would urge with such logic, conviction and conscious power that opposition would cease and his decision would be accepted in silence or with a few muttered words of assent.

It was believed at the time that Lloyd George read nothing, and he seemed almost to encourage that idea at times. In fact he was an

omnivorous reader. He usually woke early. His official papers were placed by his bedside overnight, and at an early hour he would apply himself to them. If one wanted to ensure that he read a particular paper, this could be put beyond doubt by persuading his private secretary to place it high up among the documents on his bed table. By breakfast time the Prime Minister had mastered the contents of a mass of official and unofficial documents, and had skimmed through the whole of the London Press as well as a good many provincial newspapers, especially the Welsh ones, and was ready to begin—what was really his main fount of knowledge—sucking the brains of the best men he could get on every subject. This was a continuous process. At breakfast, lunch, dinner and between meals, whenever opportunity offered, Lloyd George was engaged in picking up knowledge from every sort and kind of person, in fact, from anyone who had knowledge to impart—and especially knowledge bearing directly or indirectly on the war. Not that he did not enjoy his moments of relaxation, which he often mixed up with his business in the oddest way. A social evening would convert itself unexpectedly into a conference of the most serious kind, and conversely a serious discussion would develop on unconventional lines. Great organizer and administrator though he was, he was not enamoured with official routine. This made him rather a difficult man to serve in an official capacity. He required constant studying and humouring. One had to be ready for anything at the shortest notice. Frequently, almost daily indeed, I used to be invited to breakfast, lunch or dinner, or sometimes all three, for Lloyd George, like Asquith, was extraordinarily hospitable. The conversation would take a serious turn. One person after another would be sent for until the meal had become a conference of the most important kind requiring a formal record. To feed oneself with one hand, and to take notes with the other is neither agreeable nor good for the digestion!

One saving point, however, from the point of view of his staff was that Lloyd George rarely held official meetings late at night, which wears most people out quicker than anything else. During the whole period of the War Cabinet, including the Imperial War Cabinet and Supreme War Council and other directing bodies, I have only been able to trace four formal postprandial meetings, and they rarely if ever lasted until midnight.

On Sundays, even when there was no particularly serious crisis on hand, one had to be prepared to proceed at a moment's notice to Walton Heath, and, like the family doctor, I have sometimes been called

out of church for this purpose. But that was the way the genius of the man worked, and so great was his hold on the imagination, so unsparing was he of himself, so disarming his cordiality and friendship, so inspiring his unfailing courage, that neither his colleagues nor his officials complained at his erratic methods, nor gave anything short of their best. Others have written of the charming simplicity of his life at that time, of his devotion to his family and to the things of the country, especially mountain scenery and walks through woods and heaths. He was also fond of good music of a simple kind, especially his beloved Welsh hymns. He was a keen Nonconformist, but not a bigot. He had one further trait—the gift of humour. His joyous mind, finding vent in remarkable outbursts of fun and wit, often helped the Prime Minister himself as well as his colleagues in the War Cabinet and at international conferences to bear their staggering burden and to tide over a difficulty. 'A merry heart maketh a cheerful countenance', and that counts for something in time of war.

Of Lloyd George's colleagues in the War Cabinet the only one who directed a great office of State was Bonar Law, who was Chancellor of the Exchequer. It was not in virtue of this office, but as Leader of the House of Commons that Bonar Law held the vice-presidency of the War Cabinet. Under the new model Lloyd George held himself free to devote the whole of this time to the daily conduct of the war, and for this he deemed it essential that he should be released from the exacting task of leading the House. This duty fell to Bonar Law, and Lloyd George only appeared in Parliament on the more important occasions when it was necessary for the Prime Minister to address the House in person. This was an inversion of the plan proposed, and even adopted in principle, by Asquith just before his resignation, under which he as Prime Minister was to have presided in the Cabinet and led the House of Commons, while Lloyd George conducted the day-to-day business of the War Committee. The new plan was not popular in the House of Commons, which at first resented the frequent absence of the Prime Minister, but it worked well inside the Government, and for the first time since the outbreak of war the Prime Minister really had time to do his job.

Bonar Law was his loyal and devoted supporter. It is not too much to say that his great contribution to the war was his perspicacity in picking out Lloyd George as the one man who could lead the nation to victory, his courage in forcing the crisis which brought his champion into office, and the consistency with which he backed up the new Prime

Minister—sometimes even when he believed him to be in the wrong. This loyalty became a factor of the greatest importance in the direction of the war, and gave Bonar Law an influence on Lloyd George which was wisely exercised and exceeded that of any other member of the Government. The two became close friends. Nos. 10 and 11 Downing Street, where they lived, are not only under the same roof with a connecting door between them, but in addition they look out at the back on a garden which is common to the two, and there was a short cut from the Cabinet room, where Lloyd George usually worked, across the terrace, which overlooks the garden, to Bonar Law's study, and they were in and out of each other's rooms day and night. The intimacy between the Prime Minister and his first lieutenant was a real asset to the Government and the country.

We come next to the two peers in the War Cabinet, Curzon and Milner. Mark Sykes, in the early days of the War Cabinet, once drew a delightful cartoon in which Lloyd George was depicted as a 'rogue elephant' chained between two staid old elephants. One of these bore the features of Milner, the other of Curzon—the latter with a coronet upon his head! Prance and dance as he might, the 'rogue elephant' was firmly held. This cartoon, however, did more justice to Sykes's imagination than to his accuracy, for, in fact, neither Curzon nor Milner ever exercised as much influence over Lloyd George as Bonar Law. They were loyal supporters and acted rather as lieutenants, taking part of the burden of detail off their chief's shoulders. Curzon's tireless energy, inexhaustible industry and unique gift of setting out in proper perspective and with eloquence the facts of a complicated issue were an asset to the War Cabinet. What he lacked was resource in finding solutions to the problems which he could state so well, but this really mattered little because Lloyd George was himself resourceful. His little peculiarities—his pompous manner, ignorance (partly a pose) of democracy, and so forth—were a source of inexhaustible amusement to Lloyd George, who would listen with delight to any addition to the humorous stories and legends which grew up round Curzon during the war.

To me Milner was rather an unexpected man. I had thought to find in him a man of quick decision, with rather a tendency to rashness—'damn the consequences' Milner, as the Radical newspapers used to call him, after a famous speech in the House of Lords. Actually his temperament was quite different. 'People think I am a quick-witted person', he remarked one day. 'They expect me to take in everything that is said at

the War Cabinet, and to make up my mind on the spot. That is not my way. I am rather a slow man.' That was true, but if he was rather slow, he was very sure. This feature was at first a disappointment to Lloyd George, but in justice to Milner it must be remembered that he alone of the new War Cabinet had not been in office in a British Government, and had no inner knowledge or experience of the vast range of perplexing and thorny problems that pressed themselves forward insistently for early decision. All this he had to learn, and he would sit up to all sorts of hours in his little house in Westminster, poring over the vast mass of literature circulated daily from the Cabinet Office. At the week-end he would disappear to his beautiful house at Sturry Court, near Canterbury, there to continue his lonely and assiduous studies. Lloyd George used him, as he used Curzon, for many purposes, including the chairmanship of many committees that were set up by the War Cabinet to inquire into matters involving intricate detail. Later, however, Milner left the War Cabinet to become Secretary of State for War. Both Curzon and Milner remained to the end of the war Lloyd George's unswerving adherents.

The only other member of the original War Cabinet was Arthur Henderson, representing Labour and thus completing the façade of national unity. Henderson lacked the lustre of his more famous colleagues' achievements, but he was an honest, God-fearing, out-spoken, common-sense man, inspired by a strong determination to win the war. Unfortunately he went off the rails on an important occasion, and had to sever his connection with the War Cabinet, though his atti-tude remained correct and dignified. He was always a good friend to me to the end of his life and our association is a pleasant memory.

With the exception of Bonar Law the members of the War Cabinet were all Ministers without Portfolio. The theory was that they were to devote all their time and energy to the central direction of the British war effort, on which the whole of the energies of the nation were to be concentrated. To enable them to keep their minds on this central problem they were freed entirely from departmental and administrative responsibilities. All the other Ministers, whatever department they con-trolled, were outside the War Cabinet. They retained the rank and status of Cabinet Ministers, though they were not whole-time members of the War Cabinet with which the last word rested. But the Depart-mental Ministers did attend the meetings of the War Cabinet whenever subjects which affected their respective departments were under dis-cussion, and while present they took part in the discussion as Cabinet

Ministers and were expected to take their share of the responsibility for the decision. The War Cabinet never intentionally took a decision in the absence of the responsible Minister, except in rare instances when two or more Departmental Ministers were at loggerheads and it was necessary in order to get on with the war to give an arbitral decision. But as soon as the particular business in which a Departmental Minister was concerned was disposed of, he was expected to leave the War Cabinet and to return to his department. Just as the members of the War Cabinet were expected to give their whole time to the central problems of the war as a whole, so the Departmental Ministers were intended to devote their whole time to the affairs of their departments, and to see that the policy of the War Cabinet, on which they were kept fully informed, was carried out. Another innovation was that Ministers were allowed to bring with them permanent officials and other experts to facilitate the business, and chairmen of committees were also invited when the affairs they dealt with were under discussion.

This plan was not so novel as might at first sight appear. All that had happened was that a system already tested, first on a small scale at the Committee of Imperial Defence, and later on a larger scale at the War Committee, had been extended to enable all the affairs of the nation to be dealt with on the same method. Gone were the scrambles of Ministers to get their pet subjects discussed at chaotic Cabinet meetings. Gone were the endless rambling discussions with no one to give a decision. Gone was the exasperating waste of time while the affairs of a department were discussed by people who knew little of the matter and had received no Memoranda on the subject. Gone were the humiliating and dangerous doubts of what the decision was, or whether there had been a decision at all. Although it was not realized at the time, the old Cabinet system had crashed—never, let us hope, to be resurrected.

From now onward the Cabinet was destined to work to an Agenda paper. The discussions were to be prepared for by documents emanating from the responsible Ministers and circulated beforehand, and a reasonably rapid decision was ensured by the existence of a nucleus of unbiased men, unhampered by departmental prejudices, whose sole standpoint was that of winning the war. Moreover, the decisions were to be recorded and circulated the same day to all concerned by an organized secretariat.

Of the Ministers outside the War Cabinet, Balfour was not officially a member of the War Cabinet; but foreign policy was so vital a factor in the war and so closely bound up with most of its work, that the

Foreign Secretary was deemed to be concerned in almost every question, and Balfour claimed and exercised the right of attending any meeting. Carson and Derby were also frequent attenders. The Chiefs of Staff of the Admiralty and War Office attended at the outset of each meeting to give the latest information on naval and military affairs, and remained until all the naval and military questions on the Agenda paper had been disposed of. Sometimes their statements of fact with which the meetings opened would give rise to important but unforeseen discussions, and a hasty telephone message would have to be sent to their political chiefs to bring them to the scene. Walter Long, the Secretary of State for the Colonies, and Austen Chamberlain, the Secretary of State for India, were other frequent attenders. The former, one of the old school, took unkindly to these newfangled methods, particularly in the early days when the machine was apt to creak, but he was always reasonable and pleasant to deal with. Austen Chamberlain eventually became a member of the War Cabinet himself, and will ever be remembered as a good friend to the Secretariat.

These were the men who, with no interval for rest or preparation, suddenly found themselves face to face with the responsibilities and perplexities of the Supreme Command in December 1916.

CHAPTER LVII

THE SECRETARIAT

'And the first opinion which one forms of a prince, and
of his understanding, is by observing the men he has
around him; and when they are capable and faithful he
may always be considered wise, because he has known
how to recognize the capable and to keep them faithful.'
(MACHIAVELLI, *The Prince*, c. 22.)

THE men who made up the Secretariat of the War Cabinet not only fulfilled the condition of being 'capable', but, as they came to know Lloyd
George, fell under his spell and became the most faithful servants that
any man could wish to have around him. Their first duty was to ensure
the secretarial services of the War Cabinet itself, but their functions
soon extended farther afield.

At first, owing to the large amount of business that had accumulated
during the political crisis, the War Cabinet used to meet two and sometimes three times a day. And except on Saturdays and Sundays, when
meetings were ordinarily not held, it met on an average of at least once
a day throughout its existence. Moreover, one of the first acts of the
new War Cabinet was to summon an Imperial Conference, part of
which met as an 'Imperial War Cabinet', the needs of which were also
provided for by the War Cabinet Secretariat. Both the War Cabinet
and the Imperial War Cabinet set up many committees, some permanent and very many *ad hoc* for the study of particular questions, and
the Secretariat was responsible also for providing their secretarial services. The Prime Minister had a habit of summoning personal conferences at all hours, not excluding meal-times, and I myself was nearly
always summoned to act as secretary on such occasions. Finally, the
system of inter-Allied conferences, which had been started by Asquith,
was greatly intensified. Meetings became more and more frequent,
until they culminated in the establishment of the Supreme War Council. Beginning with a conference with the French Government at
10 Downing Street on December 26th to 28th, I was called upon to
provide the British side of the secretariat of these international meetings and eventually was closely associated with the Supreme War
Council itself, and the British Section of its Secretariat which was under
my control.

The catering for so many Cabinets, councils and committees would, even in normal circumstances, have been a very heavy task. But in the case of the War Cabinet there were features of exceptional difficulty, owing to the fact that, while there were only five members, other Ministers, whose departments were concerned in any way in the business, had to be invited for the discussion of that particular business. In order to avoid these Ministers having to hang about while other subjects were discussed, I devised a special system. In issuing the Agenda paper we appended to each item an estimate of the approximate time at which the subject would be taken. This did not pretend to provide more than a rough guide for the Minister on the time when his presence would be required. During the discussion of each subject I used to keep a careful eye on the rate at which the business was proceeding, and at what I deemed the appropriate moment I sent word to a telephone clerk outside the room to summon those concerned in the next subject on the Agenda paper. The list of those concerned in each item was typed on the back of the Agenda paper and the clerk would summon by telephone all those who were not already in the room. On arrival at 10 Downing Street, they would wait until the War Cabinet reached the subject for which they had been summoned. Thus, as each question on the subject was tackled in turn, there would be some change of personnel, some leaving and others entering the Cabinet room. It was not always easy to decide who was concerned in every subject, as there might be ramifications unknown to the Secretariat, but after two and a half years of war we had a fairly good knowledge of such and we usually played for safety by inviting a Minister if there was any doubt. As, however, new Ministries were constantly being established (Labour on December 11, 1916; Shipping, Food and Pensions on December 22, 1916; Reconstruction, August 21, 1917, National Service, November 1, 1917; Air, January 2, 1918; Information, February 21, 1918), and there were well over 100 interdepartmental committees, whose number was constantly increasing, and whose chairmen might be required as experts—experts as well as Ministers were often invited to the War Cabinet—the assembling of meetings was continually becoming more difficult and complicated.

Save in matters of extreme secrecy we used to send every Agenda paper to all Ministers outside, as well as to members of, the War Cabinet, and they were invited to assist the Secretariat in this part of the task by examining the subjects and letting us know at once if they ought to be included in the list for some particular subject which

affected their respective departments, or if they had been included where they were not concerned. Subjects were as far as possible grouped on the Agenda paper so that the subjects in which any particular Minister outside the Cabinet was concerned would come in sequence; the purely naval and military subjects, for example, were always placed first on the list in order that the Service Ministers and Chiefs of Staff might be released as soon as the Cabinet passed to civil affairs, and so that they, at any rate, never had to hang about awaiting their turn. Moreover, the business always began by statements on the naval and military situation by each of the Chiefs of Staff who were allowed to send subordinates if the news was of secondary importance or if they were absent on duty. By this means the War Cabinet was kept well up to date on the day-to-day progress of events. Occasionally the arrival of some item of news just before the meeting, or during the meeting, would compel the War Cabinet to depart from the Agenda paper and concentrate on some emergency decision that had to be taken and in that event I would instruct the telephone clerk to notify that the whole or part of the Agenda paper was cancelled. I usually had two telephone clerks, and they were given a code word which gave priority over all other messages, so there was not much time lost in telephoning. On the whole, once we had got into our stride the system worked sufficiently well and complaint of delays and misunderstandings were less frequent than might have been expected.

When the list of subjects to be discussed at a meeting had been arranged, and the list of Ministers and experts for each subject had been fixed, the next thing was to ensure that all who were to attend had the necessary documents. In most cases they would have received them before the subject came on to the Agenda paper at all. The moment a Memorandum was received in the Secretariat for consideration by the War Cabinet, a distribution list including every person affected was drawn up, and a separately numbered copy was sent to each person on the list, to whom it was officially charged in our office records. Unless the matter was of exceptional urgency a day or two would be allowed to elapse before it was placed on the Agenda paper to give time for its consideration and for other departments or members of the War Cabinet to circulate further information, suggestion or criticism on the subject. As a further safeguard a list of all subjects on the 'waiting list' was circulated once a week to all Ministers and certain other persons, containing opposite each item a list of the Memoranda already circulated on the subject (including sometimes a précis of all previous decisions

and proceedings on the subject), as well as a list of the persons to whom these Memoranda had been sent. It was from this list that the Agenda papers of the War Cabinet were made up. Ministers, therefore, were largely responsible themselves that their claims to be present at the War Cabinet were not overlooked. They received a weekly list (sometimes it was bi-weekly). If they were not on the list for a subject which in any way concerned them and had not received the Memoranda, it was their business to tell the Secretariat. But if they and their staffs had overlooked the weekly list, they still had a second chance of correcting a mistake when the Agenda paper came round. Mistakes did not often occur, and after a few weeks the lists for distribution and so forth were to a great extent standardized.

Let us suppose that the Agenda paper has been issued with the time-table and the list of those invited appended thereto and the meeting[1] has begun. The members of the War Cabinet are grouped in the centre of the long table, near the Prime Minister but on both sides of the table. Other Ministers and experts sit on either side of them. The secretary sits on the Prime Minister's right hand with assistant secretaries to his right. I had to insist on permission to bring assistant secretaries, except when matters of special secrecy were under consideration, as it would have been impossible for me to undertake the actual drafting of the whole of the War Cabinet's Minutes. As it was, I had to take single-handed all the more secret meetings both of the War Cabinet, of the Prime Minister's own conferences, and of international meetings. In order to expedite the business—for in war-time Minutes may make the difference between success and failure—the assistant secretary would be changed several times during the meeting. As each assistant secretary left the room and was replaced by his successor I would hand him a rough pencil draft of the conclusions reached while he was present. Returning to the office he would at once dictate a draft of the conclusions, and his successor would follow the same procedure. The moment the meeting was over (or, occasionally if there was no special urgency, after lunch) I would return to the office and the rough drafts would be brought for my approval. When approved, they were roneoed on a wax sheet and circulated as a draft to the War Cabinet, the Minutes on each item being sent in addition to those who had been present only for that item. A copy was also sent for printing under conditions of great secrecy. The drafts had to be returned within twenty-four hours

---

[1] The first few meetings were held in the Army Council's room at the War Office but, as soon as Asquith had moved out, they were held in the Cabinet room at 10 Downing Street.

together with any corrections or suggestions. These were then incorporated in the print, after which final copies were struck off and sent to all concerned. Only the King, the War Cabinet and a small selection of Ministers, Chiefs of Staff, and high officials received the full Minutes, extracts being sent as necessary to others.

In theory the Prime Minister was supposed to approve the Agenda papers, and the draft Minutes before they were circulated, and to initial the final copies of Minutes. But in practice, after the first few weeks Lloyd George, who was too incessantly busy to be troubled with details, left me a free hand to conduct all this business in his name without troubling him except on matters of first-rate importance or when I encountered difficulty. This greatly expedited business but placed a good deal of responsibility at times on my shoulders. If, for example, there was a difference of opinion on what had been decided, I would always try to bring about an agreement by negotiation, rather than trouble the Prime Minister or the War Cabinet. This method obviated the necessity of reading over the Minutes of the last meeting, for which there was not time in view of the frequency of the meetings and the mass of business transacted.

Every day one of the assistant secretaries was appointed as 'officer of the day', a roster being issued well in advance once a week. The 'officer of the day' was responsible to me for all the arrangements of the War Cabinet during his day of duty, from the issue of the Agenda papers on the preceding day to the circulation of the final copy of the Minutes a day or two after the meeting. The 'officer of the day' took my instructions based, of course, on the Prime Minister's authority, on the Agenda papers for meetings on his day of duty on the preceding day. It was his duty to collect the draft Minutes from those of his colleagues who had attended part of the meeting, and to bring them to me as soon as possible after the meeting; to send out the approved drafts to members; to incorporate their corrections; to bring the final prints for me to obtain the Prime Minister's approval (unless I thought it safe to assume this), and to arrange the distribution list. In addition, he had to superintend the final distribution of papers to members of the War Cabinet and others, and to stay until the office was closed. This often involved his remaining until midnight or after. The system of an 'officer of the day', however, was an admirable plan, as it ensured that all the assistant secretaries were thoroughly conversant with the whole machine, and that the distribution of what were often very secret papers was carried out by 'distribution clerks' under responsible and personal supervision.

In fact, the actual locking of the boxes was done by the 'officer of the day'—this duty being known in the office as 'boxing'.

The War Cabinet Minutes were kept in rather a full form and contained a record not only of the actual decisions, but of the reasons for those decisions. I should have preferred the system adopted after the war for the purposes of a normal peace Cabinet, under which the record was limited to a conclusion, and so much brief explanatory matter as was essential to render it intelligible. This, however, proved impracticable in the case of the War Cabinet. The drafting of really good short Minutes is a much higher art than the making of a full summary and requires much practice. My staff, admirable and self-sacrificing as they were, had not much experience of this kind of work. It was often found important to have on the record exactly what had influenced a decision (e.g. to assist Ministers in preparing statements in Parliament), and the simplest way was found to be to make a fairly full summary of the discussion. We had, however, one rule, that the opinions expressed by members of the War Cabinet were recorded anonymously. Ministers who attended for the discussion of particular subjects, Chiefs of Staff, chairmen of committees, and civil servants, etc., were treated as though they were 'experts' advising the War Cabinet, and a summary of their facts and advice was given. But it was considered inconsistent with the principle of Cabinet solidarity to record the differences of opinion which necessarily arose before a final decision was reached on a controversial matter. The arguments used were recorded, but not the names of those who used them. An exception was made, however, in a case where a member of the War Cabinet spoke as an expert—e.g. on behalf of some committee over which he had been presiding, or on some matter on which he was notoriously a great specialist.

In the early days of the War Cabinet I got into rather an amusing scrape in this connection. The subject before the War Cabinet was some matter connected with picture galleries or museums—nearly always a highly contentious topic. A number of experts had been summoned, but at the end Curzon made a powerful statement which settled the question once and for all. When the Minutes appeared Curzon's massive contribution was recorded anonymously. Next day I received a letter from Curzon taking me to task for this. In all innocence I replied by explaining the system on which the Minutes were drafted, adding some such words as the following—'as you spoke, *not as an expert in these matters*, but as a member of the War Cabinet, your contribution was recorded anonymously'. This speedily brought down on

U

me such a catalogue of Curzon's contributions to art galleries and museums and so forth, not only in this country but in India and elsewhere, as took my breath away. It was some time before my lapse was forgiven and forgotten!

One of the difficulties which we foresaw and provided against almost from the first in this system was in keeping the whole of the departmental Ministers and officials informed on the general policy of the Government and the progress of the war. Those who received copies of all the Cabinet Minutes and documents, which included all the telegrams of general interest both inward and outward of the Foreign Office, Admiralty, War Office, India Office and Colonial Office, as well as the weekly appreciations sent out by some of these departments, were, of course, thoroughly well-informed. But it was impossible to send these documents, many of which were ultra-secret, to the Ministers and principal officials of all the departments without imperilling secrecy. To meet this difficulty we compiled and issued from the War Cabinet Office two weekly reports, known as the Eastern Report and the Western Report, which contained the principal developments. They were also sent to the Dominions and received a wide circulation.

There were, of course, certain matters, such as forthcoming operations, tentative or alleged overtures for peace, some questions of foreign policy and so forth, which for reasons of secrecy could not be dealt with by methods involving even so limited a circulation as was given to the full War Cabinet Minutes. When such matters were discussed I was the only secretary to attend. The proceedings were kept either in typewritten form or in manuscript, and the conclusions were only communicated to those who had to act upon them. It was inconvenient to give these specially secret proceedings the serial number of the War Cabinet Minutes, because those who received a full set of the latter must have discovered that the series was not complete and would have demanded copies. I hit upon the expedient of giving them the same serial number as the last Minutes with a letter following, thus: War Cabinet Minutes No. 345 A—a plan which was also found useful at the Paris Peace Conference.

One rule which I always insisted on in the drafting of all conclusions was that they should make clear who was responsible for taking the action decided on. This was a matter of great importance in dealing with so many Government Departments, some of them newly organized and staffed by comparatively inexperienced Ministers and officials.

On the night when Lloyd George told me how he meant to run his Government I foresaw at once that my staff would not prove adequate. It was a difficult task to collect an efficient staff and to house them, literally without any notice at all, more especially as the new War Cabinet at once plunged into prodigious activity. But the small staff I already had rose to the occasion in the most wonderful manner. Lloyd George gave me *carte blanche*. I at once got the Office of Works to commandeer the houses on either side of 2 Whitehall Gardens. Then began a terrible turmoil of knocking holes in walls and re-arranging accommodation to take the new office. How my staff managed to carry on in those days is still a mystery. Working three or four in a room, one would be dictating, trying to make his voice heard above the din of hammering and sawing; another conducting a business interview on some high matter of State; a third trying to compile a Memorandum. They were a loyal and enthusiastic team or they never could have done it.

The Secretariat was now divided into two sides—one military, the other civil. Swinton, my *alter ego*, was the head of the former and was assisted by Dally Jones, a staunch veteran, and Lancelot Storr, who had been bequeathed to me by Kitchener when he sailed on his last voyage. One addition was the importation of a naval assistant secretary. I had for long done without a naval assistant secretary, looking after that side of the work myself. Hearing, however, that my old shipmate Philip Rowe was free I gladly seized the opportunity to bring into the new Secretariat one whom I knew to be an indefatigable worker, and who had held the important and responsible post of principal secretary to a number of distinguished admirals. Another importation on the military side was Lawrence Burgis, formerly secretary to Esher, who came to me from GHQ, France, and a year or two after the war became my private secretary and the custodian of all my secrets almost until my retirement.

The civil side had as its first head G. M. Young, then a brilliant young civil servant. He did not stay long as his services were required elsewhere. He was succeeded by Tom Jones, who was for many years after the war my deputy secretary in the Cabinet Office.

December 12th. I breakfasted alone with Lloyd George. He is very anxious to foist on me a Welshman called Tom Jones, whom I interviewed after breakfast. . . . I rather liked the man and I think I could use him on the industrial side. Anyhow he had ideas, and as the result of our interview I caught on to a scheme of organization of the office

into two groups—machinery and ideas—which may fit in with these people.

So began a long, valued and intimate friendship.

The Secretariat of the War Cabinet, though it made its contribution to the stock of ideas, remained principally concerned with machinery. But before long Lloyd George added to his personal staff a number of brilliant young men whose task was to contribute ideas. They included Philip Kerr, Lionel Curtis, and W. G. Adams. They were housed in some corrugated iron buildings run up in the garden of Nos. 10 and 11 Downing Street, and usually known as the 'garden suburb'. We worked with them on cordial terms. The civil side of the War Cabinet Secretariat was completed by Clement Jones, of the Booth Shipping Line, who was the first person I asked to join my staff. I had had my eye on him for a long time for he had been the very efficient secretary of Curzon's Shipping Control Board which came to an end when the Ministry of Shipping was formed. My choice at once justified itself. He was one of the pillars of the new Secretariat and became a lifelong friend, working with me again during the war of 1939.

A number of distinguished M.P.s also joined the staff of the office. In Asquith's time I had had the assistance of Mark Sykes and Harold Baker. The latter who was an adherent of Asquith left when Lloyd George came into office, but Mark Sykes remained. Very soon Amery, at Milner's behest, was brought home from Salonica and attached to the War Cabinet. At first I was not quite happy about it, as I had a suspicion that he might be intended to replace me, a suspicion that was strengthened when, a short time after his arrival and in my absence with Lloyd George abroad, I read in a newspaper that in future Mark Sykes, Amery and I were to be joint secretaries of the War Cabinet. However, Lloyd George assured me there was no foundation for the story and continued to show me unabated confidence; Leo Amery proved to be a most loyal colleague and we became and remained firm friends to the end of his life. Possibly Milner, in bringing him home, was 'insuring' against a failure on my part to fill the bill, but I am sure he never suggested this to Amery. Later Ormsby Gore, and Leslie Wilson, joined the staff and did admirable work. All these M.P.s had distinguished careers afterwards, and it is a pleasure to think that the War Cabinet Secretariat was a nursery for so many famous men.

The organization of the clerical staff from a tiny nucleus, as well as of the housing arrangements, was undertaken by Longhurst. Up to now

he had been my private secretary, but I now required his services as 'establishment officer', a post that he filled under difficulties with the greatest efficiency and tact. He was ably assisted by two head clerks, Sergeant Ives (who had been in the office before the war and whom I got back from the front), and Sergeant Rawlins. Both remained on after the war, became pivotal men on the clerical side of many an international and Imperial conference, and rose to the rank of lieutenant-colonel.

As my private secretary I selected to succeed Longhurst one of my stenographers, Sylvester. He more than justified my choice and travelled with me to international conferences all over Europe. He was a first-rate stenographer and a wonderful typist. I have often dictated to him travelling in the train and never had to stop even in the dark when going through tunnels; in those penurious days there were no lights. Such an efficient man made an immense difference at the inter-Allied conferences to which one could only take a very small staff, and it was partly due to him that Lloyd George was able to obtain so dominating a position at these conferences. We used to have him sitting outside the conference door with his machine. Sylvester was worth three or four ordinary typists. He even taught himself French. A few years after the war (in 1921) Lloyd George carried him off as his own private secretary. My second private stenographer, F. W. Owen, was also a tower of strength. After the war he typed the Cabinet Minutes for me for years and years, a most responsible duty, until, having passed the age limit during the second German War, he retired, with the respect and affection of all who knew him.

We were a true band of brothers. As head of the office I received the bouquets at the end of the war, but no one knows better than I what I owed to the devoted and untiring zeal of my colleagues of all grades.

CHAPTER LVIII

PROBLEMS OF THE WAR CABINET

'I have heard ofttimes that it is more safe to hear and to take counsel than to give it.' (THOMAS À KEMPIS, *The Imitation*, c. 9.)

WRITING on December 10th, when I was summarizing the events of the previous few days during which I had been too busy to write my diary as usual, I noted:

Lloyd George asked me on December 7th to write a Memo. giving my views on the war. I spent the greater part of the 8th dictating it to my two shorthand writers alternately amid many interruptions up to about 8 p.m.

That Memorandum never became an official numbered paper. It was treated as personal between Lloyd George and myself. I gave it to Milner to read—probably at Ll. G.'s request—and I have reason to believe that most of his colleagues in the new War Cabinet also read it. I was concerned really to give in some detail what I thought should be the subjects for discussion and decision in that Cabinet, and began by saying that any general review of the war must commence with a comprehensive examination of the naval situation based on the principle that the maintenance of sea supremacy makes the first claim on the resources of this country. I also asked that in framing policy that principle should not only be considered from the point of view of warships, but equally of merchant ships, and that maintenance in this sphere should be a first charge on our resources. I made various suggestions for combating the U-boat and urged that an inter-Allied Naval Conference was desirable. I also recommended that, at an early date, the War Committee should confer with the Board of Trade, the Admiralty and the Controller of Food Supplies on measures to be taken for the construction of new merchant shipping; the State control of all shipping; relief of congestion in the ports; watching the experiment which the French were trying, of using foreign labour in their ports with a view to the collection of information for its introduction here; greater ruthlessness in the restriction of imports; pressure on neutrals to release interned enemy ships and kindred measures.

On the military situation I pointed out the likelihood that the military policy for 1917 based on the 1916 plan was now rendered obsolete

as a result of the defeat of the Roumanians, and that it was now much less possible to carry through any great offensive from Salonica. I suggested that the General Staff be asked to report on the advisability of adopting a defensive attitude there with the ultimate idea of falling back to a shorter line if we were attacked and on the expediency of arranging a transfer of troops from there to Egypt with a view to intensifying the operations to be taken in that region. Further, the General Staff should be asked to report on the expediency of an operation in the Italian theatre and on a scheme for reinforcing the Italian Armies by heavy guns should they be attacked. I thought we should prepare for a great offensive in the West next year and to transfer some of the home defence forces to France; also that the General Staff with the Admiralty and the High Command in France should work out a scheme for the return of divisions to this country should emergency arise.

In the economic field I did not feel that any immediate action was necessary beyond what had already been decided by the new Government. Time should be given to allow the Food Controller, the Director of Shipping and others concerned to take stock of the situation.

Discussing the political issues, I pointed out that one of the greatest services that could be rendered to the Allied cause would be a settlement of the Irish question. Not only would this release 150,000 men for service with the Irish divisions and the division at present locked up in Ireland, but it would have an immense effect abroad in the Dominions, where recruiting would be much facilitated and in the United States, where the whole financial situation would probably be most favourably influenced. I concluded this political section by emphasizing the importance of maintaining good relations with the United States as the great difficulty of our blockade policy had been to carry it out without antagonizing opinion on the other side of the Atlantic; the problem was especially important in the immediate future owing to the power which our dependence on America for supplies placed in the hands of President Wilson.

The War Committee, I suggested in conclusion, should begin with the discussions of the military questions. Jellicoe had only just commenced work at the Admiralty and discussion of naval questions should be postponed for a few days. Equally those concerned in economic questions were new to their work.

Lloyd George was, of course, familiar with the main issues, and the Memorandum was intended simply to focus his attention on the chief

points. Many of my proposals commended themselves to him, e.g. the proposal for an international Naval Conference, and those for the standardization of merchant ships, the use of foreign labour at the ports and the further restriction of imports. He naturally agreed with me on the importance of solving the Irish question and of maintaining the best relations with the United States. But the proposal for restricting operations in the Balkans did not commend itself to him though the shortage of shipping actually forced it upon him for a time. Nor was the continuation of the offensive in France very congenial, although he was all in favour of the temporary transfer of heavy guns to Italy with a view to an offensive and of intensifying the war against Turkey.

As might have been expected, the War Cabinet took some time to settle down to the new system and my diary, patchy as it was in the pressure then existing, indicates that at times I was rather exasperated at what seemed their lack of businesslike habits.

December 10th (Sunday). By the 9th it was 'off with the old love and on with the new' and I spent the whole day with the new 'War Cabinet', the completion of the Minutes keeping me at the office until 9 p.m. I now find myself Secretary, not of the War Committee, but of the Cabinet, which consists of Lloyd George, Curzon, Henderson, Milner and Bonar Law. An odd turn of the wheel to take place in seven days! Today I stayed in bed until 11.30, being much exhausted, and then motored down to lunch with Lloyd George at Walton Heath. He had a bad cold. After lunch we smoked a cigar together and he rehearsed to me the great speech he intends to make in the House next Thursday and I gave him many suggestions. We also discussed future plans for the war, and he was delighted with my Memo. He is awfully down on Robertson and I more than fear lest he should 'out' Robertson and put me in his place—a job for which I have no desire at all!! Bonar Law turned up before I left. . . . Then on return to Town I had to see Milner by appointment and spent two hours with him. I have always hated his politics but found the man very attractive and possessed of personality and we got on like a house on fire. I had the mission of asking him to go to the conference in Russia and he consented. I left him the Memo. I had written for Lloyd George.

Lloyd George's cold kept him away from the Cabinet for several days, which was a disadvantage at this critical time.

December 11th. Lloyd George . . . could not come to the War Cabinet so Bonar Law took the chair in the afternoon. I lunched alone with Ll. G. who discoursed mainly of his plans for a big military coup in Syria. I did not feel very happy with the new War Cabinet, who do not know much of admini-

stration and seemed to think the only thing to be done is to build up a gigantic office of satellites and clerks. I am getting hold of them one by one. . . . But I got home very late and rather depressed.

December 13th. No time for the diary these days. This was my day— breakfast alone with Ll. G. at 9.15 a.m.; War Cabinet at 11.30; lunch in the office dictating conclusions the while; War Cabinet at 3 p.m.; dictated conclusions during the tea interval; War Cabinet at 6 p.m. Killing! Ll. G. only at the first War Cabinet.

December 14th. Ll. G. has crocked and can't see anyone for twenty-four hours. . . . Only one War Cabinet. . . . I am, I feel, gradually getting the confidence of the new War Cabinet.

December 17th (Sunday). . . . On the 16th I saw Lloyd George, who was still in bed and discussed the war. . . . I went for a walk on Hampstead Heath with Ursula (my daughter) and to the Temple Church in the afternoon. After church I went to Lloyd George's house to tea, having arranged to meet Montagu there. We tried to persuade Montagu to join the Government.[1] After dinner I sat up until midnight working up my new organization for the development of my secretariat into a War Cabinet secretariat. War Cabinet today at 11.30. Arthur Henderson and Montagu lunched with me. We were both at him the whole time to induce him to accept the post of Director of National Service. In the afternoon Milner called to discuss a number of questions affecting the War Cabinet.

December 24th (Sunday). In the intense rush of work this week it has been quite impossible to keep a diary. My ordinary day has been to breakfast with the Prime Minister, remaining with him until about 10.30. Then an hour in the office to read up the day's telegrams, set going a hundred things that Ll. George has given me instructions on, and start the organization of the War Cabinet meetings of the next two days, and attend to any office business. Every day a meeting of the War Cabinet from 11.30 to 2 p.m. In the afternoon another War Cabinet, or sometimes two, or else to attend one or two informal conferences between Lloyd George and some head of a department —the Food Controller, or Director of Shipping, or Director of National Service. I have more than doubled my staff, and have had to train in the new hands to their difficult and exacting duties. I have had to delegate the drafting of Minutes to the assistant secretaries, and have had to keep rather a tight hand on revising the drafts and seeing that the decisions reach all the people affected by them. All this extra work is being done in my old quarters, as I cannot get into my new quarters for two or three weeks, and the organization of the clerical branch, enormously expanded, registry, etc., is carried out under extraordinary difficulties.

December 26th. I found Robertson in a very disgruntled state threatening

---

[1] For some days at Lloyd George's request I had been working with him to try and induce my friend Edwin Montagu to join the Government.

U*

to resign. The new War Cabinet are really up against it, as they don't believe in Robertson's 'Western Front' policy, but they will never find a soldier to carry out their 'Salonica' policy. Moreover, the complete breakdown of shipping renders the latter policy impracticable and they won't recognize it. I am inclined to think they will come a cropper before long. . . . I was on the verge of toothache all day, but can't find time for the dentist.

As years went on, I became accustomed to the teething troubles of new Cabinets which included Ministers unaccustomed to Cabinet business. The symptoms often resembled those already described—a tendency to insist on the preparation of un-needed papers, lack of consideration for their staffs, the holding of more meetings than were really essential. But in December 1916 I was inexperienced in actual Cabinet business and very much overdriven. Moreover, my devotion to Asquith naturally inclined me to be critical of his successors. It detracts in no way from the outstanding merits of Lloyd George and his War Cabinet to show that they were subject to the frailties and weaknesses of human beings, and underwent the usual experiences of Cabinets in shaking down.

CHAPTER LIX

WAR AIMS, POLICY AND PLANS FOR 1917

> 'We cannot be bound beyond what we are able to per-
> form, by reason that effect and performance are not at all
> in our power, and that, indeed, we are masters of nothing
> but the will, in which, by necessity, all the rules and
> whole duty of mankind are founded and established.'
> (MONTAIGNE, *Essays*, Cotton's translation: 'That the
> Intention is Judge'.)

LLOYD GEORGE'S intentions were clearly defined from the moment
of his taking office. His only aim was victory and to that everything was
to be subordinated. He was convinced that this could be achieved only
by real and effective co-operation between the Allies, co-operation that
must exist not only between the heads of Government but throughout
all branches of the war effort. From the first he aimed at something
more like the control which he believed Germany exercised over her
allies, though perhaps he rather exaggerated the strength of this. Even
his agile mind had probably hardly come to believe that complete unity
of command was as yet within the sphere of practical politics. But that
was his goal and for real co-operation he was prepared to make
considerable sacrifices of national *amour propre*.

In the sphere of strategy Lloyd George's ideas were strongly coloured
by this idea of unity of command. He had no use for the strategy
favoured by the military men, wherein each commander-in-chief
devised an attack with all the force he could muster from his own
command to be directed against some point in the line held by the
enemy opposite to his own army, co-ordination of the whole being
limited to some general synchronization in point of time. It was not by
such methods that, in his opinion, victory was to be won. His conception was that of a single front stretching on the west from Flanders to
the borders of Switzerland; continued on the south across the Italian
and Balkan fronts to Egypt and Mesopotamia, where it linked up to an
eastern section spreading from Persia to Transcaucasia and from the
Black Sea to the Baltic. As the front was one, so, in his view, the armies
were one, and must be treated as such in approaching the strategical
problem. If the rearming of the Russian Army, with its huge framework
and inexhaustible reserves of man-power but with its deplorable lack of

war material and the means to produce it, was likely to make some great contribution to the common cause, then he was prepared to put a large proportion of the manufacturing resources, finance and transport of the Western Allies at Russia's disposal. If he felt satisfied that better results to the common cause could be achieved by putting a British general under a foreign general, he would do his utmost to bring it about. If he thought that heavy batteries, or even divisions, could achieve more in Italy or the Balkans than in France or Flanders he was prepared to send them. The Salonica campaign, for the very reason that it was a joint one, where the troops of five Powers were placed under the command of a single commander-in-chief, made a special appeal to him.

Lloyd George held that the British Army, a magnificent improvisation in which the few survivors of our splendid pre-war professional army were very thinly spread, was not yet sufficiently armed or trained to undertake the offensive on the Western Front with prospects of success; nor was the leadership, in his view, as yet equal to the task. He never excluded the possibility of an eventual advance on that front, but he held strongly that the time had not yet come to attempt it. The enemy must be weakened by blockade and distracted by attacks elsewhere, where the line was held by Germany's less tenacious allies. For the moment he did not desire to go beyond a generally defensive role in France and Flanders but an active, not a passive defensive. Pétain's policy of '*petit paquets*', attacks limited in time and in objective, corresponded closely with Lloyd George's ideas of the correct strategy in this part of the single front.

Meanwhile, in his view the big offensive movements should be carried out on fronts where the enemy was weaker. Perhaps in Russia, where the memory of Brusilov's victories died hard in spite of subsequent reverses: in the Balkans with a view to eliminating Bulgaria from the war, atrophying Turkey, and joining with Russia in an attack on Austria: or in Italy, where the enemy's front was in the main held, and was always likely to be held, by Austrian troops of distinctly lower calibre than the Germans. 'We ought to attack the weaker and not the stronger parts of the enemy's line', he used to say. Holding these views so strongly as he did it was a humiliation to Lloyd George that some of the most sanguinary and unsuccessful attacks of the whole war were undertaken in his first year of office. But, although on general principles his views were in the main shared by his Cabinet colleagues and received a sympathetic hearing from the political heads of the Allied

Governments, he could never persuade the generals to adopt them, and the Governments were rightly unwilling to impose on them a strategy in which they did not believe; he was, indeed, 'master of nothing but the will'. In the long run he got his own way—to a sufficient extent, at any rate, to secure the final victory, but only after we had twice been brought to the verge of disaster; twice we shall see that he was able to use disaster to bring about reforms in organization which he had not been able to achieve by other means. Until the autumn of 1917, however, we shall see nothing but the bitterness of failure and defeat, in circumstances which would have daunted the spirits of a lesser man.

The new Prime Minister never lost sight of the advantages he might hope to derive at the eventual peace conference from the acquisition of the territory of our enemies. He wanted assets to bargain with against those of the enemy. The coalition led by Germany was still in firm occupation of most of Belgium, an important part of France, Poland, most of Roumania, almost the whole of Serbia and Montenegro and vast tracts of Russia. Command of the sea they had definitely lost, and most of the German colonies had fallen. Among the other assets which seemed to the Prime Minister to be obtainable from our enemies without too great a drain on our resources were German East Africa which was still holding out, Palestine, perhaps Syria, and Mesopotamia. This is an aspect of the matter often lost sight of by those who inveighed against the 'side-shows'; it was certainly present to the mind of Lloyd George as it had been to his predecessor.

Before they had been a week in office this side of the question was brought somewhat prominently before the War Cabinet, for on December 12th the German and other enemy Governments communicated to the u.s. Government identical notes containing overtures for peace negotiations. These notes created a political situation of the first importance. If genuine, they might have led to an early peace, as all the world desired. It was by no means unlikely, however, that they might be merely a trap set by the Central Powers with the object of cashing-in their successes before sea-power achieved its slow but inevitable triumph.

As soon as the German note was available the War Cabinet met to consider it. The first step was to ascertain the reaction of our Allies and of neutral nations. All our Allies formed much the same impression as we did, that it was a boastful and vainglorious piece of propaganda, designed to encourage the peoples and armies of the Central Powers and correspondingly to discourage the Allies. The absence of any

indication of terms did not encourage anywhere a belief that the note could be intended as a genuine peace offer. Neutral countries, though not much more sanguine than the Allies about the *bona fides* of the enemy's note, held generally that it would be unwise merely to reject the German offer.

When the War Cabinet met on December 18th[1] to consider it they had before them a heavy documentation, which included besides the comments of Allied and neutral opinion, a formidable series of Memoranda on various aspects of Peace Terms, which had been prepared for Asquith's Cabinet a few months before in connection with the Lansdowne letter; these I had been instructed to circulate. The decision of the War Cabinet was that the best plan would be for the Allies to concert an identical reply to the German note and that this should be signed by their representatives in Paris and handed by the French Government to the American Ambassador. The idea underlying this procedure, which was eventually adopted, was that opinion in the United States was always less suspicious of Paris than of London, and it was important to avoid any impression that a 'fire-eating' British War Cabinet was goading France and the other Allies to continue the war against their will. On the day following (December 19th) Lloyd George announced the general lines of the Government's attitude in Parliament, where it was well received.

Events were now moving rapidly, for on December 20th, before it had been possible to concert the joint reply by the Allies to the German note, we received a peace note from President Wilson dated December 18th, in which each of the Allies was asked to state its war aims. 'The President is not proposing peace'; the note stated 'he is not even offering mediation. He is merely proposing that soundings be taken in order that we may learn, the neutral nations with the belligerents, how near the haven of peace may be for which all mankind longs with an intense and increasing longing.'

The War Cabinet took the matter up at once. At the time I was desperately overworked and critical of its methods and I find the following rather peevish note in my diary:

The new War Cabinet are very tiresome and exacting. They are making the mistake of 'bustle for business'.... They are getting very unpopular among Government Departments and are causing too much waste of effort. All this has been very exhausting... and it was a terrible blow when we

received a telegram tonight that three French Ministers had started from Paris to join us in a series of conferences lasting over Xmas.

The Frenchmen did not come for Christmas after all, and the hard-driven War Cabinet and its harder-driven staff (still in the throes of expansion and reorganization) had a short respite over Christmas Day, though a good deal broken into by office business.

The Anglo-French Conference which had been in contemplation for some time had not been easy to arrange. Lloyd George had suffered for some days from a severe cold and perhaps even more from a nervous reaction to the political crisis that had brought him into office, and was not in very good fettle. Apart from that it was almost impossible, so soon after assuming office, for him to leave London, where so many matters required his personal attention. He therefore asked Briand to come to London. But Briand was in no better case. Paris also had been in the throes of a political crisis, and Briand had had to reorganize his Government. On December 12th, only a day or two after Lloyd George, he too had formed a War Cabinet, with Lyautey as Minister of War; Nivelle had succeeded Joffre as Commander-in-Chief of the French Armies; Joffre (who received the well-deserved *baton* of Marshal of France a fortnight later) had become Technical Adviser to the French Government, a more or less honorary post, and disappears from these pages. In these circumstances Briand, who was also indisposed, could no more leave Paris than Lloyd George could leave London, and it was Ribot, the septuagenarian Minister of Finance, who on Boxing Day headed the French delegation, which also included Lloyd George's friend Albert Thomas, Philippe Berthelot of the Quai d'Orsay, and some staff officers.

Although the ostensible object of this conference was to discuss the prosecution of the war, especially in Italy and Greece, advantage was taken of the opportunity it afforded for preparing the replies to the German and American notes. It is interesting to recall that in both cases the drafting of the final text was entrusted to French hands, not so much because Cambon and Berthelot were recognized as particularly competent draftsmen, but so as to ensure that the text should bear an unmistakable French impress.

The reply to the Central Powers rejected the peace overture as empty and insincere, and, without setting out in detail the peace terms of the Allies, tended to over-emphasize the aspects of reparation, guarantees and safeguards for the future.[1] In view of the urgency of leaving public

[1] *War Memoirs*, III, p. 1109.

opinion in no doubt it was decided to communicate it to the American Ambassador in Paris without waiting for the concurrence of the other Allies in the final text.

The reply to the President's note was treated with greater deliberation and left the London Conference in the shape of a draft for consideration by the other Allies and for textual completion through their diplomatic representatives in Paris. In form it was sympathetic to the President's high-minded initiative, but it made clear that, in the opinion of the Allies, the moment was unfavourable to peace negotiations. It contained the usual denunciation of Germany's responsibility for the war and German atrocities in its conduct. Then, after indicating that the final terms 'with all the compensations and indemnities equitable to the damages sustained' could only be formulated at the moment of negotiation, it gave an outline of the aims of the Allies—the restoration of Belgium, Serbia and Montenegro with the compensation due to them; evacuation of the invaded territories of France, Russia and Roumania with fitting reparation; a reorganization of Europe secured by a permanent system based on the principle of nationalities, and the full security and free economic development of nations great and small; safeguards to land and sea frontiers against unprovoked attack; restitution of provinces previously torn from the Allies by force or contrary to the wishes of their inhabitants; liberation of Italians, as well as of Yugoslavs and Roumanians, Czechs and Slovaks from foreign domination; liberation of the populations submitted to the tyranny of the Turks and the casting out of Europe of the Turkish Empire. Poland was provided for by a reference to the Proclamation issued on behalf of the Czar by the Grand Duke Nicholas on August 14, 1914, promising autonomy. The note contained a disclaimer of any intention to exterminate the German people or to bring about the political disappearance of Germany. The intense desire of the Allies to secure peace on principles of liberty and justice and the inviolable sanctity of treaties was strongly emphasized, and the document ended on a note of determination to fight on until victory was achieved.[1]

Were mankind gifted with second sight Germany must perforce have accepted these terms, which bear a fairly close resemblance to the main results of the Treaty of Versailles. What loss of life and treasure, what hideous suffering might thus have been avoided! Under the inscrutable decrees of Providence this was not to be. For two more dreary years the world was to go on working out its penance in misery

[1] *War Memoirs*, III, pp. 1113 *sq.*

and horror. Great empires were to crash; millions were to suffer violent death; civilization itself was to be brought to the verge of dissolution—in Russia it was to fall for a time beyond the verge—before the end so clearly foreseen in the note to President Wilson was to be reached. Those who inveigh against the Peace Treaties are apt to forget that the principles were set down and solemnly agreed to at the close of 1916 with the general assent of public opinion in the Allied countries, and that the unparalleled sacrifices of the next two years were made in order to accomplish those very ends!

Apart from the peace notes, the most urgent (though not the most important) questions that came before the London Conference related to Greece. Although Asquith had failed to convince our Allies of the necessity to give formal recognition to the Salonica Government at the Paris Conference in November, Lloyd George's War Cabinet on December 19th decided to take this step. Meanwhile the attitude of the remainder of Greece, which still acknowledged Constantine's rule, was more equivocal than ever. At the November conference the Allies had agreed to demand the dismissal from Athens of the intriguing Ministers of the Central Powers. The danger of the German submarines using the deep indented bays of the Greek coast for refuelling purposes and of the Greek Army at Larissa on the left rear of the Allied Army, coupled with the King's previous record, had been considered to justify this strong step. On December 1st (the day on which Asquith's War Committee held its last meeting) the Greek Government refused the demand and a small Allied force which had landed at the Piræus on the previous day was compelled to re-embark after sustaining some casualties in an encounter with Greek troops. On December 8th the Allies declared a blockade of Greece—a most serious step in the case of a country so dependent on sea imports and sea communications. On December 11th a Note was presented to Greece demanding demobilization, and three days later a further Note was sent demanding a withdrawal of the Greek Armies from their menacing position in Thessaly. This demand was accepted by the Greek Government on December 15th.

When the Anglo-French Conference met on December 26th the French representatives insisted that the Greek Government was not carrying out its undertaking to withdraw from Thessaly and that the left flank of the Salonica army was exposed to the risk of attack from the Germans and Bulgarians in front and the Greeks in rear. In these circumstances Sarrail was clamouring to make a sudden attack on the

Greeks in Larissa and to occupy Thessaly. The British Government's information did not support the view that Greece was not carrying out her engagements, and, especially in military and diplomatic circles, Sarrail's attitude aroused suspicion. To give him a free hand would, it was felt in London, involve us in a war with Greece, and unite the country against us at the very moment when Venizelos' movement was full of promise, and place us in an invidious position *vis-à-vis* neutrals in general and America in particular. An awkward disagreement was disclosed, which was particularly embarrassing to Lloyd George's plans for closer co-operation between the Allies.

Another question before the conference was the strength of the Allied Army in the Balkans. For some three weeks the French had been urging us to send two more divisions to that theatre and this demand was again pressed. But the issue became complicated by yet another French demand. At an early stage of the conference, it was learned that Ribot had come with instructions to make a strong plea for an extension by twenty-five miles of the 125 miles of front already held by our Army on the Western Front. Haig had so far agreed to take over only four miles and with a proper Scottish caution objected to take more until he knew what the strength of his army was to be. Then the cat came out of the bag, and it was discovered that the object of the desired extension was to enable Nivelle to release from the trenches the French forces required for a breakthrough of the German line and in addition to create an army of manœuvre to exploit the initial success he hoped to achieve.

The situation as a whole arising out of the French demands was not an easy one. The extension of the British line was supported by strong arguments, which (apart from the proposed offensive) appealed to the War Cabinet on merits. Moreover, an extension of the line might curb the British High Command's incessant desire to plunge into new offensive operations of the type that made no appeal to Lloyd George and his colleagues. But to grant the extension there and then would be to quarrel with Lloyd George's own military advisers, and would be virtually an endorsement of the Nivelle plan, of which, as yet, the War Cabinet knew practically nothing, and to postpone indefinitely the adoption of Lloyd George's own ideas. Again, both he and the War Cabinet were not averse in principle to sending two more divisions to the Salonica Front with a view to an offensive there or, at least, to securing the line now held. In this, however, they were violently opposed by their military advisers, who held that no advantage was to

be gained in that theatre and that the proper course was to fall back from Monastir to hold a shorter line covering Salonica and thus to release troops for the Western Front. The Navy was equally averse to any increase in the force at Salonica owing to the difficulty of maintaining the communications against submarine attacks. The shipping authorities were also opposed, and submitted calculations to show that the necessary shipping was not forthcoming. Finally there was much mistrust of Sarrail, and no one could say what he might not do if he was reinforced. It was felt to be by no means unlikely that he might use the reinforcements for a *coup-de-main* against Greece, and expose the Allies to the same opprobrium as Germany had justly been subjected to as the result of the occupation of Belgium.

From these embarrassments Lloyd George extricated himself, after profound thought, by a characteristically ingenious method. On the extension of the line he undertook to instruct Haig to meet the French requirements as far as possible, and promised that, if the generals could not agree, the question should be further discussed between Governments. On the two divisions he reserved his opinion. On Greece, he insisted that the first step was to ascertain the facts, and he secured acceptance of a plan to send French and British officers from Salonica to Greece to find out what was really happening there. But his main proposal was that there should be a further and immediate conference in the south of Italy of all the principal Allies. A moment's reflection will show the importance of this proposal. On the three main questions time had been gained without any breach with France. The new conference[1] would provide an opportunity for furthering his general policy of co-operation between the Allies. The journey to Italy in company with the French Ministers would enable him to learn all that was known of Nivelle and his plans. In the south of Italy he would be able to meet with Sarrail who could easily cross the Adriatic for the purpose without being absent too long from his command, and decide for himself the truth about that much discussed general and his real intentions. He could also bring to Italy, Milne commanding the British forces in Macedonia, Elliot the British Minister in Athens and Fairholme the experienced military attaché, and so learn all about the situation in Greece and in the Balkan army. Above all the conference would give him an opportunity to ventilate his own strategical ideas, before the Allied Governments were irretrievably committed to the plans which had emerged from the November conferences at Chantilly and Paris.

[1] Cf. *Macedonia*, I, p, 246.

Those ideas, which contemplated a big offensive in Italy, and/or in the Balkans, as well as in Russia, should, he hoped, receive powerful reinforcement from the presence of Cadorna and the generals from the Balkan theatre. Such, it would seem, were the motives which inspired the Prime Minister in proposing the conference in Italy, a proposal which was accepted by the Allied Governments; Rome was selected as the rendezvous.

Lloyd George prepared for the Rome Conference with characteristic thoroughness and laid down on broad lines the methods which were destined in the coming years to make him easily the leading figure in Europe. The War Cabinet held a number of preparatory meetings. All the Government departments concerned produced Memoranda. Rennell Rodd was summoned to London at the shortest notice to advise the Government. I was instructed to prepare under the Prime Minister's own directions a Memorandum in which he set forth his policy for the information of the conference. After passing through many editions it was translated into French for the benefit of those who could not speak or read English and circulated just before the Rome Conference began.[1] Lloyd George chose Milner as the colleague to accompany him. There was a special reason for this. As early as December 10th, Lloyd George had wished Milner to head the forthcoming mission to Russia and, after demurring at first, the latter had consented and the War Cabinet had confirmed the arrangement; Lloyd George was especially anxious that the Petrograd Conference should form a continuation of the Rome Conference, just as the Rome Conference was a continuation of the Christmas conference in London. The Prime Minister also took to Rome with him Henry Wilson, a member designate of the Russian mission. Robertson was, of course, taken but not Haig.

We left London on New Year's Day and spent January 2, 1917, in Paris where Lloyd George occupied himself the whole day in collecting every kind of information bearing on the military and political situation. That evening we started for Rome in a special train with the French delegation consisting of Briand, Albert Thomas and Lyautey with a number of staff officers and Philippe Berthelot. Lyautey was the most remarkable character in this party. His claim to fame was as a highly successful administrator of Morocco. At the moment his reputation was high in Paris, where he was spoken of as a possible military

---

[1] The Memorandum is published in full in *War Memoirs*, III, pp. 1414 *sq*. It included *inter alia* the proposal contained in my own Memorandum of December 8, 1916, to prepare a scheme of assistance to Italy in case she was attacked by Germany. This scheme was adopted and saved the situation after Caporetto.

dictator. Whatever his talents for colonial administration, he proved a misfit as a Minister of War in a parliamentary Government. The journey was an incessant series of conferences in conditions of great discomfort owing to the heat and noise. When we were all retiring to bed in a state of complete exhaustion we received a message that Lyautey wished to discuss another important matter. We dressed again and trailed down the swaying and jolting train to his saloon, where we found the general studying a large map of Egypt and Palestine. We listened while he rapped out in sharp, staccato sentences an interminable series of platitudes on the campaign in the Sinai Peninsula. No one made any comment and we retired as soon as we could to our sleeping berths. As we retraced our footsteps Robertson growled out to Lloyd George —'That fellow won't last long!' And he didn't! A few weeks later he got into trouble for refusing information to a parliamentary commission and was packed back to Morocco.

The Rome Conference began in a vast and highly decorated salon at the Consulta, attended by hordes of secretaries, officials, experts, staff officers, in fact by everyone in Rome who had sufficient claim, or 'pull', or bounce to force an entrance. The vast majority were either not required at all or only for some single item on the agenda paper. Lloyd George and Briand who hated great assemblies, and were there for business, soon exploded this method and adjourned the conference into *'petit comité'*.[1] The remainder of the three days of conference were spent in a small room at a round table. Only principals were admitted— Boselli, Sonnino, Scialoja, Lloyd George, Milner, Rennell Rodd, Briand, Albert Thomas, Lyautey and the French and Russian Ambassadors in Rome. Aldrovandi, Berthelot and I undertook the secretarial duties. Cadorna, Robertson, Henry Wilson, Sarrail and Milne and other experts were present at different stages as required. I myself sat behind Briand who occupied himself during the conference in drawing a wonderful caricature of Albert Thomas as Rasputin.

Almost immediately after our arrival at 7 a.m. on January 2nd, I was sent by Lloyd George to sound Cadorna on a proposal to send him a strong reinforcement of heavy guns during the early part of spring, when conditions made an offensive possible on the Italian Front but were unfavourable on the Western one. This was a mission with which, in the ordinary course of events, Robertson should have been entrusted, but he had made no secret of his hostility to any project of the kind. Early as I was, Robertson had been there before me.

[1] There was also a military conference which proved unfruitful.

January 5th (Rome). Lloyd George spent his morning and the first part of the afternoon in official visits, and I did not accompany him. However, he sent me off first thing to see Cadorna, the Italian Commander-in-Chief, in order to sound him how he would take Lloyd George's proposal for artillery concentration on the Carso. It was rather embarrassing for me. On the one hand I knew that Lloyd George was intensely keen on this project, and on the other hand I knew that Robertson was bitterly opposed to it. On inquiry I learned that Robertson was at the moment with Cadorna, and I decided to intrude myself on them, so that there should be no suspicion of concealment. However, when I reached Cadorna's house—a sufficiently simple villa— Robertson had left him and I had my interview alone, except for Delmé Radcliffe to interpret, as my Italian is a little rusty. I was very careful to explain my precise position as Secretary to the War Cabinet, and that I was not there as a technical military expert, nor to poach on Robertson's pre- serves, but merely to sound him whether he would receive Lloyd George's proposal favourably, if made. Cadorna, who is a particularly agreeable, straight fellow, was not nearly as enthusiastic as he ought to have been; he said, of course he could not have too many heavy guns, but he made a number of technical difficulties, and it was clear that he had been 'got at' by Robertson.

Apart from these technical difficulties, Cadorna's main preoccupation was how long he would be allowed to keep the guns. If they were liable to be recalled to France for the summer campaign, he did not seem to want them. He did not readily grasp Lloyd George's conception of a smashing blow with the object of breaking the stalemate of trench warfare and passing to a war of movement.

In spite of Cadorna's lukewarm reception of his proposal and Robertson's unconcealed opposition, Lloyd George included it among his principal suggestions at the conference. Owing to delays in getting his Memorandum translated into French, it had only been possible to circulate it just before the conference met, so he felt bound to set forth his proposals verbally and at great length.[1] He developed his case with great skill. He recalled in clear but moderate terms the failure of the Allied offensive of 1916, emphasizing the relatively small effect it seemed to have produced on the enemy, who had not been prevented by his preoccupations on the Western, Southern and Eastern Fronts from smashing Roumania. He alluded prophetically to the possibility that Russia might prove unable to hold up the Central Powers. The guns trickling through Archangel and Vladivostok would now have to be spread over a front extending from the Baltic to the Black Sea and

---

[1] Cf. *War Memoirs*, III, pp. 1413 *sq.*; *Macedonia*, I, p. 254.

would not prove sufficient. Something more must be done to enable Russia to arm her vast man-power—but that was a matter for the forthcoming conference in Petrograd. If Russia went under, there were several courses open to the Central Powers. They might exploit their successes in Russia itself, advancing to Petrograd and Odessa. Or they might concentrate on the Balkans and drive us into the sea. Greece would then fall under their control, and their submarine campaign in the Mediterranean would be intensified to threaten the essential communications of the Allies in the Mediterranean, including those of Italy, who was so critically dependent on overseas supplies for the means of carrying on the war and for existence itself. Yet a third course on which Lloyd George dwelt, again prophetically, was that the enemy might turn to Italy itself, where, as Cadorna had pointed out, the left flank was threatened from the Trentino. How was all this to be met and countered, Lloyd George asked. The French Government's solution was that Britain should send two more divisions to the Balkans. We could not do it. The shipping was not available. Already we had thousands of men awaiting shipment as drafts for Salonica, Egypt and Mesopotamia. France was clamouring for coal and for British ships to carry it. Italy also needed coal, and steel and wheat as well. To deal with the Balkan situation he urged that Italy, who had so much to lose from a collapse of the Balkan Front, should send reinforcements to the Balkan theatre. Italy was nearest; the voyage was but a short one; and little shipping would be required. He also seized on an idea thrown out by Briand that a new overland route should be developed from France to Brindisi, thence by short sea route to Santi Quaranta on the Adriatic, and from there by road to Monastir. He made an impassioned appeal to the Italians, the descendants of the greatest road-makers in history, who had themselves accomplished some great road-making feats on the Alpine Front, to recreate the old Roman road to the Balkans. Lloyd George also pressed that plans should be worked out for reinforcing the Italian Front by British and French troops. He urged this as a measure of insurance against an attack by Germany in case she succeeded in disposing of Russia. But at the same time he begged the generals to consider it as part of an offensive project. Winter ended earlier in Italy than in the north. The guns could be massed there first to smash in the front, and later, if they were not required to exploit some great strategical success there, they could be returned to France or Flanders. By adopting this plan we should for once gain the initiative in a new theatre. In Italy we should be attacking where Austrians and not Germans would

predominate, where the front was weak—as proved by the Italian successes—instead of where it was strongest. And we should not be taking risks in the Western theatre, since we should only be using, so to speak, that surplus of guns which we intended to concentrate for our own offensive later. Great results might follow. Apart from Cadorna's plan of pressing towards Laibach and Vienna, we might hope to exploit the situation in the Istrian Peninsula, forcing the Austrian Fleet to choose between coming out to give battle and surrendering in harbour at its base at Pola. In this theatre we should be destroying Austrian and not French or Belgian villages as we advanced. The Balkans and Russia would automatically be relieved by a success in this theatre in a manner which it was impossible to achieve by attacks of the orthodox kind on the almost impregnable fortifications erected by the Germans on the Western Front.

Lloyd George's plan must be treated as a whole. With an unerring instinct he put his finger on Russia as the weak point. The only way in which we could help Russia directly was by sending war material, and that he strongly urged, though the details had to be worked out at the Russian Conference. But he also wished to help Russia indirectly. He could see no hope of effecting this by attacks on the Western Front. That plan had been tried out on a full scale in 1916 and had failed. The Balkan theatre attracted him, but he was obliged to reject it for the present for shipping reasons, but he was providing for the future in that theatre by developing the overland route. There remained Italy, and it was there that he fixed his main hopes of breaking the single front.

Our Prime Minister was listened to respectfully and sympathetically, but every kind of objection was soon raised to his major proposals. Offensive operations take long to prepare; they are like a great industrial enterprise. The preparations for carrying out the plans drawn up in November at Chantilly and approved at the Paris Conference were far advanced. It was too late to embark on a new plan this year. The guns would be of no use on the Italian Front unless their retention there for some months could be guaranteed, since months would be required in order to organize and achieve the initial success and to exploit it. Meanwhile Nivelle's plans would be dislocated. Even the road from Santi Quaranta to the Balkan theatre was at first resisted on the ground that the necessary engineers could not be found.

After a good deal of haggling the conference agreed on conclusions which may be summarized as follows: Closer co-operation and more frequent conferences; the rearmament of Russia accepted as essential to

the success of the Allied cause, details being remitted to the Petrograd Conference; development of an overland route for British and French troops to Brindisi, approved and remitted at once to experts to be worked out in detail; development of the Santi Quaranta–Monastir road accepted by the French and Italian Governments; ultimatum to Greece demanding the withdrawal of all her forces within a fortnight to the Peloponnesus;[1] defining of Sarrail's powers in the coercion of Greece on the basis that each General Officer Commanding was to comply with Sarrail's orders on military operations, subject to the right of direct communication with, and reference to, his own Government. The conference also expressed itself as impressed by the opportunities afforded by the Italian Front for a combined offensive by the three Western Allies, and remitted the question to the military advisers of the Governments concerned. This was tantamount to shelving the plan of a combined offensive, but the plans for reinforcing Italy on a defensive basis were, under Lloyd George's driving force, worked out later on, with results in the following autumn which more than justified his prophetic and prescient insistence on them. Finally it was decided to hold a technical Naval and Shipping Conference in London at the earliest possible date.

The actual drafting of the resolutions fell to my share. The conference nominated Aldrovandi, Berthelot and myself as a drafting committee. Aldrovandi was under pressure of other work at the Consulta. The indefatigable Berthelot (perhaps because most of the proposals were of British origin) showed no alacrity for the task, and, as an inveterate collector, he wanted to spend the afternoon in the Roman curio shops. My offer to prepare a first draft was therefore jumped at. Fortunately I had been blocking in the resolutions all through the conference, and many of them had already been submitted by Lloyd George and adopted in principle. This enabled me in the hour or two which was given to me for the purpose to produce plenty of copies both of the English version and of a French translation made by Aldrovandi. The resolutions[2] were passed with hardly any alteration. The French delegation did not like my draft on the subject of Sarrail's attitude towards Greece and I overheard Albert Thomas say—'*Berthelot, c'est une redaction détestable*'. But they had to accept it in this form: Sarrail was to take no action during the forty-eight hours covered by the ultimatum; if it was refused he was to be at liberty to take such action as he considered necessary for the security of his army; if the ultimatum was

---

[1] The ultimatum accomplished its purpose.   [2] Text in *War Memoirs*, III, p. 1443.

accepted and carried out he was to take no military action against Greece without the consent of the Allied Governments: if the conditions were accepted but not carried out by the Greek Government within the stipulated fortnight he was to obtain the consent of the British, French, Italian and Russian Governments before taking the initiative in any military action.

This solution of what had been a most embarrassing problem, on which the British and French Governments had taken widely different views, had in fact been arrived at 'out of court' at a private interview between Lloyd George and Sarrail:

January 7th (Sunday). On waking I received a message from Lloyd George that he wanted me at the Embassy before 9 a.m. Shortly after I got there Sarrail turned up. His interpreter was very bad and I had to do most of the interpreting. It was a most interesting discussion. Sarrail is a man of quite exceptional charm. He was very frank and said that all he asked was for the British and French Governments to shut their eyes or turn their backs for a fortnight!—intending of course to deal with Greece in this interval. We asked him what he would do if the Greek league of reservists took to the mountains and waged guerilla war on him, and he replied that he would catch a few, refuse them belligerent rights and shoot them. After he had run on in this wild manner for some time Lloyd George took him in hand. He reminded him that he had always been the friend of Sarrail himself and of his expedition, and that therefore he was not coloured by prejudice. He then explained how Sarrail's proposed action would outrage opinion in neutral countries generally and in America in particular, and how it would drive moderate opinion in America into the hands of the pro-Germans and pacifists. He urged that it was better to take a risk in Greece than in America. Sarrail was obviously impressed, and frankly offered to take no offensive against Greece until he had the permission of the British Government. Lloyd George undertook to see that he had fair play and asked Sarrail to send regular reports. Then they shook hands on it dramatically.

CHAPTER LX

GENERAL NIVELLE

'For the rest, one bad general is better than two good
generals. With war, as with governance, it is a question
of tact.' (EMIL LUDWIG, *Napoleon*, p. 67.)

THE Rome Conference had accomplished results which were not
inconsiderable, but they were not those on which Lloyd George had set
his heart. The main plans drawn up at Chantilly and approved at Paris
in November still held the field. The Western Front theory had proved
unassailable; the Prime Minister had no doubts now that the generals
would shelve his plans for an attack on the Italian Front, as they
actually did. Cadorna forwarded a plan promptly, but did not press it
strongly and nothing came of it. In these circumstances Lloyd George
had no alternative but to give his serious attention to Nivelle's plan. He
found it more to his liking than he had expected. Many of the more
objectionable features of the Somme offensive were absent. Nivelle
himself inspired him with confidence, so much so that he was willing
to place Haig under his orders.

On his return journey Lloyd George received at the French frontier
a message that Nivelle was anxious to see him. Assuming that the object
of this desire was to discuss the extension of the British line on the
Western Front, Lloyd George refused to meet the French Commander-
in-Chief in Paris, as he was unwilling to discuss this question without
Haig.[1] He proposed instead that Nivelle and Haig should come to
London; they arrived on January 15th.

Nivelle had much to commend him in the eyes of Lloyd George and
the War Cabinet. His mother was British and he was fluent in the
English language. His promotion from the rank of colonel, which he
held at the beginning of the war, had been rapid, and he had closer
experience of the actual fighting than many officers who had held
higher rank when the war began. He had been selected for his present
post by Briand, who spoke of him in the highest terms. Briand, like
Lloyd George, was inclined to be rather cynical about the accomplish-
ments of military men and commendation from him was praise indeed.[2]

[1] Haig had become a Field-Marshal as from January 1st.

[2] Pétain, under whom Nivelle had served at Verdun, on being asked what he thought of his
appointment as Commander-in-Chief, is reported to have replied, 'Well, he is my best pupil'.

Nivelle was equally successful in persuading the War Cabinet. Unlike the leading British generals, who (with the exception of Henry Wilson) were apt to be rather tongue-tied in the presence of politicians, he was fluent and persuasive. Moreover, he claimed that the plan which he propounded was based on a new theory, and was not open to some of the objections which Lloyd George held to offensives of the 'Somme' type. Nivelle's new plan was simply the application on a large scale of the 'break-through' which he had already accomplished on a small scale at Verdun. By applying the same methods, the feature of which was the meticulous use of artillery on the wide front now selected, with an army of manœuvre to exploit success, the General believed that he might accomplish a smashing victory. The attack was to be delivered on the Aisne front by three French armies, one of which was to be kept in reserve for the purpose of exploiting the hoped-for break-through. There was to be an ancillary attack on the Arras front by the British Army, all the reserves of which were to be used to exploit a success. Moreover, the attack was to be a short and sharp affair. Instead of being drawn out into weeks and months the attack was to be called off if success was not achieved within the first few days. The long drawn-out horror of the Somme was not to be repeated. Nevertheless, in spite of its attractions, the War Cabinet did not decide to support it without mature deliberation. All the afternoon of January 15th they remained in conference with Nivelle. In the early evening Lloyd George decided that the question was too complicated and too important to be settled that day, and begged Nivelle to prolong his stay for another day, to which the General reluctantly assented. That evening the War Cabinet deliberated long among themselves. Next morning they met again, and after further discussion sent for Haig and Robertson, with whom they conferred at considerable length. Eventually Nivelle was sent for and received the War Cabinet's endorsement of his plans. The agreement actually took the shape of a Memorandum signed by Nivelle, Haig and Robertson, and by no one else, which disposes of the rumours that were current at one time that this plan was forced by the politicians on reluctant British generals. As a matter of fact Nivelle's plans were supported by the British High Command and Staff, but they were far less sanguine of results than Nivelle, and the event proved them right.

Under these arrangements the British Army was to take over a considerable length of front from the French Army in order to release French divisions for the assault on the Chemin-des-Dames. In addition

a heavy British attack was to be mounted on the Arras front, to be unloosed simultaneously with the French assault on the Aisne.

Immediately after the London Conference an instruction was sent to Haig emphasizing the importance which the War Cabinet attached to the utmost despatch in carrying out both in the letter and the spirit the agreement made with Nivelle. The Field-Marshal was urged to make sure that the French should not have to delay their operations owing to our preparations being incomplete. Before long, however, the War Cabinet learned that Haig's arrangements were being hampered by the lack of railway facilities. The French railway system in the 'Nord' region was reported to have broken down. Eric Geddes, who occupied the post of Director of Railways with the British Expeditionary Force, with the rank of Major-General, did his best with the French authorities, without achieving success. A formal despatch was then sent to the French Government. Next, Haig conferred with Nivelle, who promised improvement; but, so great was the importance which the War Cabinet attached to France having no possible ground for reproaching us with any failure to carry out the operation to which she had persuaded us, that it was decided to ask for a conference.

The representatives of the two Governments met at Calais, on February 26th and 27th. The conference was preceded as usual by special discussions at the War Cabinet at which Lloyd George was authorized, besides settling the railway question, to obtain full particulars about the operations proposed, to ascertain any points on which there might be disagreement between the two Commanders-in-Chief (of which rumours had reached the War Cabinet); to settle them on their merits with Briand; and to aim more particularly at such measures as might be best calculated to ensure unity of command both in the preparatory stages and during the operations.

February 26th. To Calais with Lloyd George and Robertson. Bacon took us across with quite a little fleet of destroyers to escort us, as the German destroyers had come out from Zeebrugge the night before and were suspected of being in the Channel. Dull conference on railway matters to start with. This was followed at 5 p.m. by a conference that was by no means dull: Lloyd George, Briand, Robertson, Lyautey, Haig, Nivelle and myself alone being present. The French had been invited to bring a secretary also, but paid me the delicate compliment of leaving the secretarial arrangements entirely to me. Nivelle and Haig explained their plans for the forthcoming 'push' in detail. Lloyd George then asked Nivelle if he was satisfied, and if not to explain quite frankly what he wanted. Nivelle got red in the face; talked

generalities; and beat about the bush, Briand and Lyautey failing to help him out at all. So Lloyd George broke up the conference and asked the French to put down in writing what they wanted. Lloyd George and I then went for a walk through Calais. Soon after our return I was sent for to Lloyd George's room, where I found Lloyd George, Briand, Lyautey and Nivelle. Lloyd George handed me the document and said 'What do you think of it?' It fairly took my breath away, as it practically demanded the placing of the British Army under Nivelle; the appointment of a British 'Chief of Staff' to Nivelle, who had powers practically eliminating Haig and his Chief of the General Staff, the scheme reducing Haig to a cipher. I showed no emotion and said I wanted time to consider it. After dinner I was sent for by Ll. G., who had dined alone in his room. He . . . really seemed rather to like the French scheme. I warned him that it was quite impossible. . . . Then Robertson and Haig came in. They of course were aghast at the French proposals and urged every possible objection. . . . When Haig objected that the 'Tommies' wouldn't stand being under a Frenchman, Lloyd George said— 'Well, Field-Marshal, I know the private soldier very well. He speaks freely to me and there are people he criticizes a good deal more strongly than Nivelle.' He more than hinted that Haig would have to resign if he didn't come to heel. . . . It was uncomfortable for me as both Haig and Robertson had the air of regarding me as with Lloyd George against them. They wouldn't see me afterwards, so I went to bed, but before retiring drafted a formula which I thought might suit all parties.[1]

February 27th. I had my formula typed by Sylvester, first thing, and saw Robertson at 8 a.m. He was in a terrible state and ramped up and down the room, talking about the horrible idea of putting the 'wonderful army' under a Frenchman, swearing he would never serve under one, nor his son either, and that no one could order him to. He had not slept, for the first time in the war, he said. I could do nothing with him, so left him. I then went to Lloyd George, who had also slept badly. I tried to frighten him by the probable results of Robertson's and Haig's impending resignations, and he was affected, though he swore he was not going to be beaten over this. Then I warned him he could not fight on the basis of the outrageous French document and he agreed and asked me to draft something on which he could fight. This was the psychological moment to pull my formula out of my pocket. He read it, accepted it, sent for Robertson, who accepted it with intense relief and took it to Haig, who accepted it after palaver. Lloyd George then showed it to Briand, Lyautey and Nivelle, who accepted it. All therefore was well. Robertson and Haig, who had taken no notice of Lloyd George's invitation to them to breakfast with him and me were satisfied; Lloyd George, Briand, Nivelle and Lyautey were equally satisfied—and that had all been effected by my little scrap of paper. Moreover all recognized my effort and thanked me

---

[1] Spears, pp. 147 *sq.* where there is a fuller account.

for it. The rest of the conference was uneventful, but I had to stay late at the office to complete my record of the proceedings. Lloyd George is a restless fellow, and it must have been most trying to Haig to have this happening at a moment when the German withdrawal on the Ancre seems to presage great events.

The 'formula' provided that as the object of the forthcoming operations was to drive the enemy from French soil, and as the French Army was larger than the British, the general direction of the campaign should be in the hands of the French Commander-in-Chief. The British War Cabinet would, therefore, undertake to direct their Commander-in-Chief to conform his plans to the general strategical plans of the French Commander-in-Chief; this was to apply both during the period of preparation and of execution of the operations. If Haig felt that Nivelle's instructions were imperilling the safety of his army or prejudicing the prospects of success he could refuse to conform, but in that event he was at once to report to the British Government. He was to be free to choose the means he would employ and the method of using his troops in the sector allotted to him by Nivelle. An addition agreed to at the final meeting provided that each Government was to be the judge of when the operations of its own army should be deemed to have terminated and when the operations were so terminated, the agreement was to come to an end, i.e. it was on trial for this particular battle only which was expected to last about a fortnight. It was signed by Haig and Robertson as well as by Lloyd George, Briand and the French generals.[1]

On the day following our return from Calais (February 28th) the War Cabinet formally confirmed the agreement. At the same time they sent through Derby a message to Haig explaining that the object of the Calais agreement was merely to secure a clearly defined unity of control, and one which the French Government understood and definitely accepted. It was not intended as an aspersion on the Field-Marshal, in whom the War Cabinet had unabated confidence. This decision probably reflected very fairly the views of the War Cabinet. The situation was indeed not a very pleasant one. The War Cabinet as a whole undoubtedly had complete confidence in Haig; they also had complete confidence in their Prime Minister. But the Prime Minister himself was irritated with the Field-Marshal owing to his reluctance to come under Nivelle's command. The following extract probably explains the attitude of the members:

[1] Text in Spears, pp. 154 *sq.*

March 2nd. Then I had to see Bonar Law, to whom I spoke of Robertson's misgivings *re* the Calais arrangements. Bonar Law replied that he didn't like them much himself, but he regarded Lloyd George as dictator and meant to give him his chance, so acquiesced.

A note made a few days later indicates Lloyd George's attitude:

March 10th. It has been such a busy week that I have never had time to write a line in my diary. In the early part of the week the difficulties have been mainly parliamentary, in connection more especially with the Irish debate, when Ll. George made a dead failure of his speech. I lunched alone with him just before this speech, and my own belief is that his mind was filled with other things—his daughter Megan's attack of measles, and the question whether or no he should get rid of Haig. That evening he asked me to give him my views next morning. Adeline had gone that morning with Robin to Brighton, and I sat up until past midnight writing out my views. Ll. G. refused to read them, so I made him a long speech on the subject, weighing all the pros and cons and winding up strongly in favour of Haig. He didn't like it, as he wanted me to report the other way, and argued and contested my points hotly, as he paced up and down the long Cabinet room. But I met him on every point and stuck to my guns. That is one special merit of Lloyd George that one can speak one's mind to him fearlessly, and, even if he is annoyed at the time, he bears no malice. . . .

How far my views carried weight with Lloyd George it is not for me to say. It is more likely perhaps that the storm at Calais had cleared the air. However this may be, the Prime Minister's relations with Haig improved from now onwards for some time to come, and within a few days he was hotly defending Haig's conduct at a new conference, held once more in London. My diary of March 10th continues:

After this we were snowed under with documents about the results of the Calais Conference. Correspondence between Haig and Nivelle; beginning with a letter sent by Nivelle dated the very day of the Calais Conference, couched in peremptory terms; this is followed by Haig's reply, in which he points out that the actual and anticipated German retirement to the Hindenburg line threatens to 'dish' the Allied plans of attack; next comes a complaint from the French Government that Haig's letter is a mere attempt to upset the Calais agreement. There is no attempt on behalf of the French to recognize that we have made a very remarkable and unprecedented concession, and have asked a great sacrifice on the part of Haig in allowing our army to come temporarily under Nivelle's command.

Balfour sent an admirable despatch to the French Ambassador on this new cause of friction, with the result that on March 12th, Briand,

accompanied by Lyautey, Lacaze, Albert Thomas and Nivelle, came to London.

The situation confronting Lloyd George at this new conference was not an easy one. Nivelle and Haig were badly at loggerheads. This was due in the main to Nivelle's tactlessness, or that of his Staff acting under his authority. Instead of recognizing the *beau geste* made by the British Government and by Haig himself in the orders to the latter to conform to the French Commander-in-Chief's orders during this battle; instead of handling the situation with tact and delicacy, Nivelle had couched his instructions to Haig in terms suited to a general addressing a subordinate rather than the Commander-in-Chief of the largest army that had ever left our shores. Quick to seize on the temperamental differences between Lloyd George and Haig, the French were undoubtedly trying to exploit the situation with a view to getting rid of Haig, whose Scottish caution and halting speech blinded them to his intrinsic merit and capacity. But apart from this there was a real difference of strategical opinion between the two Commanders-in-Chief. The German withdrawal to the Hindenburg line, the first news of which had arrived during the Calais Conference, had to some extent dislocated both their plans (since all the Allied preparations for attack between the river Ailette and Neuville Vitasse, where the Hindenburg line joined the old front, were rendered abortive), and their readjustment had involved difficulties, which had not yet been solved. Haig, even though he did not much like the Calais agreement, was always loyal to any decision of the Government and was undoubtedly doing his best to honour his signature and to carry out the agreement as he understood it. But the French Commander-in-Chief was stretching the Calais agreement far beyond what the Field-Marshal had understood to be the intention. Basing himself on a clause providing for a better liaison system between the two armies, he was demanding the establishment of a British General Staff at French GHQ through which Haig was to receive Nivelle's orders, and which was to report to the Chief of the Imperial General Staff direct and over Haig's head. Taken in conjunction with the rumours of a desire in certain quarters in France to get complete control over the British Armies, this was too much for the Field-Marshal, patient and loyal man though he was. Nor was this the only difficulty. Robertson was almost in a state of rebellion. Scarcely was the ink dry on his signature to the Calais agreement than he was explaining that he had all along disagreed with the principle of placing the British Armies under Nivelle's command, and therefore that his signature

x

merely meant that, given the principle, the procedure involved by the agreement was in his view the one best suited to give effect to it.

The Prime Minister handled the situation with his usual dexterity and resource. First he saw Haig alone—and in private conversation these two generally got on well together. Then he saw Nivelle alone. Having thus prepared the way he saw the two together. Before the conversation was over they were well on the road to agreement. The difficult question of the liaison mission had been practically settled; Henry Wilson was to be its head. He was to report direct to Haig instead of to Robertson in London. Nivelle denied having ever had any intention of claiming the right to inspect the British troops or to issue orders direct to subordinate commanders. The relations of the two Commanders-in-Chief during the battle had been almost, if not completely, cleared up, and on the question of the command of the reserves Lloyd George had himself suggested and obtained acceptance of words in the agreement to prevent British troops from being mixed up with French. A phrase had been inserted to enable Nivelle to get the use of British reserves if he succeeded in breaking through the German line. Having thus virtually secured agreement 'off his own bat', Lloyd George packed the two soldiers off to Robertson at the War Office to draft the formal document, and spent the rest of the afternoon with the French politicians. From them he secured an admission that Nivelle's communications had been too brusque in tone.[1] By the next morning (March 13th) the Commanders-in-Chief had reached complete agreement on every point in respect of their mutual relations except one. The outstanding point was whether, in the event of Haig finding it necessary to exercise the right given him by the Calais agreement to appeal to the British Government in any case where he thought that Nivelle's orders endangered his army, he should be entitled to stop his preparations to carry out the order during the appeal. After some discussion it was arranged that Haig should suspend his preparations during reference to the British Government only in very exceptional circumstances. The two Commanders-in-Chief succeeded also in reconciling their strategical plans and adjusting them to the new situation, and the conference ended in complete harmony, which must have been a disappointment to those disgruntled persons on the British side who had hoped to upset the Calais agreement, and equally so to those on the French side who had sought to secure the disappearance of Haig, and the complete supersession of the British command in the field.

[1] *War Memoirs*, III, pp. 1510 *sq.*

The German retirement to the Hindenburg line had resulted in a considerable delay in the development of the Allied attack as originally contemplated at the Chantilly Conference, when it had been arranged that the armies of the Allies were to be ready to take the offensive at any time after the first fortnight in February, though the precise dates were to be fixed later by agreement between the Commanders-in-Chief. At the London Conference on January 15th a good deal of discussion had taken place on the date. Nivelle and Cambon, speaking with the authority of the French Government, had pressed very strongly for an early date and mentioned February 15th, though under pressure the French Commander-in-Chief admitted that it was scarcely possible to be ready so soon. The British generals had favoured a later date in April or May, in order to secure a better prospect of fine weather, to give time for fuller preparations and the transport to France of additional divisions from England, and to enable the Russians and Italians to strike in co-operation. Lloyd George had preferred an earlier date, one of his reasons being that there would still be time to make other plans for the summer campaigning season if Nivelle's plans did not accomplish all that was hoped from them; this shows that the Italian plan was still at the back of Lloyd George's mind, as a second string to his bow. In the end the question of the date was left to the Generals to determine, and they decided that the offensive should take place not later than April 1st; earlier if possible, or if the general situation necessitated it. In the event the British attack in the Arras region did not begin until April 9th, nor the main French offensive until April 16th. Whether an attack on a really large scale could have been opened as early as February 15th is open to question. Whether it could have achieved any substantial success in the weather conditions of a normal February is even more doubtful; and whether any great strategical consequences could have resulted unless the Russian and Italian armies had been in a position to co-operate (which they were not) is the most doubtful proposition of all. However this may be, the fact remains that, during the period intervening between February 15th and April 5th, a series of military and political events took place, which were almost without exception unfavourable to Nivelle's plan.

First there was the extraordinary leakage of information on the operations. Nivelle's plan was based upon the element of surprise, yet he took singularly few precautions to ensure secrecy. On the occasion of his first visit to London, the only unfavourable comment on him was the extraordinary freedom with which he spoke about his plans, not in

the conference—for Lloyd George saw to it that strategical plans were not described, much less written down, in open conference—but in private conversation. To determine the exact border-line between the needs of secrecy and administration is always a difficult matter. If too much is allowed to leak out, if too many people are privy to the secret, it ceases to be a secret any longer. On the other hand, if the plan is kept within too narrow a circle, the intention of the High Command may not be sufficiently understood by subordinates and it is liable to miscarry. The art of generalship, indeed the art of the Supreme Control in war, depends a good deal on the proper adjustment of this matter. In the present case there is little doubt that Nivelle erred on the side of excessive disclosure to subordinates, with the result that important documents were captured by the Germans on March 3rd and on April 6th, which gave them vitally important information on the French intentions. Moreover the General's plans were known so widely that it used to be said that every shopkeeper in Paris was talking across the counter about the plans, dates and prospects of the offensive. When Painlevé came into office as Minister for War on March 20th he learned, as he himself put it, 'by public voice' that the attack was at that time fixed for April 8th.

Then came the German withdrawal to the Hindenburg line, the first news of which had reached us at the Calais Conference (February 26th or 27th). During the next fortnight news of fresh retirements kept coming in; but the main retirement took place between March 14th and April 5th between Arras and Crouy near Soissons on a front of about seventy-two miles with a depth varying from fifteen to twenty-two miles. The straggling German line was thus considerably shortened, a big salient disappeared and an approximately straight line on selected and strongly fortified positions was substituted for it. The evacuated territory was systematically devastated on a scale far exceeding military requirements and caused the greatest resentment in France, especially the destruction of fruit-trees. As Polybius says:[1]

For my part I never concur with those who indulge their anger against men of their own blood to the length of not only depriving them of the year's harvest when at war with them but even of cutting down their trees and destroying their buildings. . . . Such proceedings seem to me to be rank folly. For while they imagine they are dismaying the enemy . . . they are converting an isolated ebullition of anger into a lasting hatred. . . .

It was one of those psychological miscalculations which the Germans

[1] The Histories, XXIII, 15 (Shuckburgh's translation).

frequently made and which strengthened the set of world opinion against them.

From a military point of view, however, the withdrawal was advantageous to the enemy. Months of preparation would be required before his strong lines could be attacked across the newly devastated area, behind which on the Allied side of the line lay the shell-pitted wilderness of the Somme battlefields. Consequently the enemy was enabled to hold the Hindenburg line with greatly reduced forces, to transfer divisions to those areas which he now knew Nivelle was intending to attack, and to build up a reserve for rapid transfer to any part of the line which Haig might select for assault, a subject on which the German intelligence was as yet uncertain.

From a political point of view, perhaps the most important event bearing on Nivelle's operations was the outbreak of the Russian revolution on March 12th, followed two days later by the abdication of the Czar. This tremendous episode was not at first recognized as necessarily involving the defection of Russia. Some even thought that the escape from the corruption and inefficiency of the Czarist régime and the substitution of a more enlightened administration might lead to a more efficient prosecution of the war, a view which for some time the British and French Governments did their utmost to foster. But a nation which has undergone such a tremendous upheaval is in no position to exert its maximum strength, and soon we received reports of war-weariness, disillusionment, pacifism and even mutiny in the Russian forces. Towards the end of March Alexeiev warned the British and French High Commands that, owing to political commotions, his army was in such a state that he could not undertake an offensive on a large scale, at any rate before June–July, and hinted at the advisability of a readjustment of their plans. Information was also coming in on the transfer of German divisions from east to west.[1] It must be remembered that Nivelle's plan was intended as the French, or Anglo-French, contribution to the general policy of concerted attacks. The inability of the Russian Commander-in-Chief to play his part was a factor of the first importance, since it removed one of the strongest elements of the intended combination.[2] The temporary disappearance of the Russian Army as an element in the coming battles would alone have justified Nivelle in reconsidering his plans. Cadorna too was as yet unready. In a word, the whole basis of the Chantilly policy of concerted attack had disappeared.

[1] Cf. Ludendorff, II, p. 414. [2] Ibid., p. 426.

Just before the battle yet a new complication was introduced, for on April 5th the United States declared war on Germany. We afterwards learned that on April 6th, when the situation was being discussed at Nivelle's headquarters at a conference which included the President of the Republic, French ministers and generals, a postponement of the offensive was urged on the ground, among others, that, with the addition of the United States, the Allies would be able to hold out indefinitely, and that a defensive policy would be appropriate while America was mobilizing her strength. One difficulty, however, was that the bombardment of the enemy which preceded Haig's attack had already been in progress since April 4th. In a sense the battle had begun.

From the point of view of Nivelle's personal position perhaps the greatest misfortune of all was the resignation of Briand on March 17th, and the selection by Ribot, the new President of the Council, of Painlevé as Minister of War and thus Nivelle's immediate chief. Not only did the General lose in Briand the Premier who had backed him through thick and thin and promoted him from comparative obscurity to the proud position of Commander-in-Chief of the French Army, but his new chief was the man who had refused to take office owing to his (Nivelle's) appointment and was known to be opposed to the whole policy of great offensives such as that about to begin.

Nivelle clung tenaciously to his determination to go ahead. Painlevé was not prepared to go to the length either of stopping the offensive or of superseding the Commander-in-Chief. At any rate no such proposal reached the ears of the British Government. Neither was the British Government prepared to intervene in a matter in which the initiative lay primarily with the French. But it was a time of anxiety and apprehension:

March 22nd. I lunched with Lloyd George and dined with him also to meet Derby who had just come back from France and was full of interesting stories of the great German retreat. The soldiers, he said, were in great spirits, but the leading generals were more anxious than he had ever known them.

After some postponement due to bad weather the battle was opened on April 9th by the British attack north of Arras, which took the enemy by surprise, threw him into considerable disorder[1] and resulted in the capture of the important Vimy Ridge with 13,000 prisoners and 200 guns, at the cost of nearly 45,000 casualties up to the night of April

[1] Cf. Ludendorff, II, p. 412.

16th. While Haig was seeking to follow up his success the French Army on April 16th attacked on a front extending roughly from a few miles north of the Soissons–Laon road to north of Rheims. The results were of the usual discouraging type; an advance of two or three kilometres; 21,000 prisoners and 183 guns captured; over 100,000 casualties and so forth; but no breakthrough; no perceptible strategical result.

April 18th (Paris).... I interpreted for an interview between Lloyd George and Painlevé. Painlevé was very downhearted about the failure of Nivelle's offensive, and his whole conversation was a repetition of the fact that he had warned Nivelle that his attack must fail. The fact is that Nivelle had talked so big about breaking through that he had encouraged absurdly high hopes. Moreover, all Paris knew where and when the attack was to take place and the enemy had got wind of it. Painlevé was also much disappointed about the failure of the tanks, or 'tonks' as he called them.[1] He is by trade a great mathematician and seems a decent honest fellow himself.

Notwithstanding Nivelle's repeated assertions that, if success was not achieved within forty-eight hours the attack should be broken off, this did not happen. Haig was so well satisfied with his initial success at the Vimy Ridge that he wished to follow it up. Lloyd George did not object and supported the request. On April 21st, on his return journey from St. Jean de Maurienne, he saw Ribot, Painlevé, and Nivelle, and obtained an undertaking that the French offensive should be continued in order to draw the German reserves off Haig's front. Haig was doing well at the time and naturally wished to exploit his success to the utmost, more particularly in view of the comparative failure of Nivelle's gigantic effort, and Lloyd George wished to give him all the support he could.

Soon after this, however, Lloyd George began to feel doubts on the wisdom of pursuing the offensive on the present lines. In its early stages the British offensive had made a strong appeal to him. The capture of the Vimy Ridge had been a clean cut affair in which a definite and unmistakable tactical success had been won. The second stage of the operation was in its way equally attractive, for, if successful, the operations would put France once more in possession of the important coal mines in the vicinity of Lens or at least extend the front sufficiently to enable work to be started in the Grenay mines, and the Lens–Arras railway to be reopened. To Lloyd George's mind there was all the

---

[1] The British tanks, on the other hand, had been reported on very favourably in the attack on the Vimy Ridge.

difference in the world between a battle fought with definite strategic, tactical or economic objectives and the *guerre d'usure* as typified by the Somme. But as the casualties began to mount up without corresponding advantages his doubts increased. Early in May the British casualties since the beginning of the offensive on April 9th had exceeded 100,000. Moreover the rate of advance had slowed down. The Germans were now making formidable and determined counter-attacks, to which our troops would reply with a rejoinder. The operations seemed to be rapidly degenerating into a mere war of exhaustion of the Somme type. Moreover the Prime Minister was keeping in close touch with Ribot and Painlevé, whose minds were moving in the same direction as his own. Painlevé was known to favour Pétain, who had been opposed to the offensive and had gone so far as to lay his views before the French Government before the battle. The Pétain policy of attacks on a secondary scale, carefully prepared and limited in objective, made as strong an appeal to Lloyd George as to Painlevé. To capture 5,000 prisoners with relatively small loss; to bite off here a ridge, there a crossroads or other vantage-point; to keep the enemy continually harassed by surprise attacks—that was a form of the *guerre d'usure* to which he was prepared to subscribe while the enemy's strength was sapped elsewhere—in Turkey, in Bulgaria, in Austria, until the day came when Germany itself could be attacked from all sides. Soon there were signs that Nivelle was to be superseded; Pétain became Chief of the French General Staff in Paris on April 29th, a promotion which was generally recognized as a preliminary to his appointment as Commander-in-Chief.

The big question on which Lloyd George had to make up his mind before proceeding to another conference as was now necessary, was whether he should press the French Government to continue the Nivelle offensive. There was much to be said both for and against. Against it could be argued that two Allied generals, Pétain and Alexeiev, were now opposed to the policy of a great offensive. Russia was unlikely to be capable of any very great effort that year and consequently the Allies on the Western Front would find themselves opposed to the bulk of the German reserves, and by attacking on the grand scale would exhaust their man-power in an operation offering but poor prospects of success, thereby weakening their offensive capacity for 1918. Neither in artillery nor in man-power were the Allies likely during 1917 to dispose of the superiority necessary for a successful offensive. By 1918 the enemy would be further weakened by block-

ade, the Russian situation would have cleared up one way or the other, and the United States would have powerful forces in the field. It was believed that for some such reasons as these Pétain was advocating a policy of repeated surprise attacks conceived on a less ambitious scale than the previous great offensives. All this line of argument made the strongest appeal to Lloyd George, who also had ever in mind the thought that, after Nivelle's failure, the French nation, whatever the promises of their leaders, could not be induced to sacrifice their depleted man-power in attacks of the old type. Had he known even more than he did of the extent of the demoralization of the French Army, parts of which were on the verge of mutiny (a marvellously-kept secret, considering how many people had knowledge of it), this line of argument would have appealed even more strongly. But Lloyd George's instinct in these matters was almost uncanny, and he did not fail to emphasize that we ourselves had no reserve of man-power sufficient to sustain a combat with the bulk of the German reserves until America could bring her strength to bear, without withdrawing men from shipbuilding. Shipping was our weakest link, and Lloyd George had almost convinced himself that it would be necessary to withdraw men from the Army in order to realize the building programme that was necessary to maintain our shipping at the barest minimum required to sustain the war. In these circumstances he felt difficulty in supporting any military policy that was likely to prove wasteful of man-power.

On the other hand, it was argued that if the Western Allies adopted a defensive policy—and the Pétain policy was regarded by British military opinion as such—the Germans would be in a position to release reserves for a decisive operation against the tottering Russian Army, or against the Italians, who were at the time more and more apprehensive of a German attack and had already made serious representations to their Allies on the subject. Even if there was no great prospect of breaking the German line in 1917 it was arguable that by a process of constant hammering the enemy might be brought into a frame of mind in which he would be only too glad to make peace. At present the Allies were stronger economically than the enemy, but the losses from submarine attack had already reached appalling dimensions and were still increasing. Who could say what the position would be in 1918? What would be the effect of a defensive policy on the morale of the Allied nations and armies? This was the view which prevailed, and Lloyd George went to the conference in Paris on May 4th pledged to press the

x*

French to continue the offensive, though nothing was said about the particular form it was to take.

Accounts have been published of the Paris Conference, which give the impression that Lloyd George fought strenuously for a continuation of the offensive on the lines on which it had already been begun.[1] No such necessity arose. During the morning of May 4th, Nivelle, Pétain, Haig and Robertson conferred, and the results were announced by Robertson to the full conference in the afternoon. It is true that they were unanimously of opinion that it was essential to continue offensive operations on the Western Front. But they were equally unanimous that the situation had changed since the original plan was drawn up, and that it was no longer operative. It was no longer a question of breaking through; it was now a matter of wearing down the enemy's strength and the generals were unanimous that this object could be achieved by relentlessly attacking *with limited objectives*, while making the fullest possible use of our artillery. By this means they hoped to gain their ends with the minimum possible loss. In a word it was the Pétain policy which had prevailed. This feature was very emphatically elaborated by Lloyd George after the principles had been clearly stated by Pétain himself, and the policy was accepted by the French Ministers.[2]

When, therefore, Lloyd George returned from Paris it was with the clear understanding that the Pétain policy, with which he was in full accord, had been adopted. Ten days later (on May 15th) Pétain was appointed Commander-in-Chief of the French Army in Nivelle's place. The latter's grandiose schemes had failed, but, before his retirement into obscurity, he had the satisfaction of capturing Craonne and the Chemin des Dames. This was soon followed by alarming symptoms of demoralization in the French Army, rumours of which reached us from time to time. Considered in conjunction with the information we had received in Paris that the French depots only contained 35,000 men ready for replacing casualties, the situation did not offer much hope that the French Army would be able to pull its weight as before. It was obvious that the new French Commander-in-Chief had a terribly heavy burden to bear.[3]

---

[1] e.g. Mermeix's account on which Churchill bases his version in *World Crisis 1916–1918*.

[2] *War Memoirs*, III, pp. 1558 *sq*.

[3] Here are some hasty impressions from my diary of May 4th: 'At *dejeuner* at the Quai d'Orsay. I sat next to Pétain. I asked him how he liked the change to Paris from commanding a field army. He replied: "During the war I have only applied for forty-eight hours' leave. At the end of twenty-four hours I was tired of Paris and went back. That is the measure by which you can

From the point of view of the development of the Supreme Command these events are of considerable importance. We see a single mind tending to dominate more and more in the central direction of our own war effort. Even when his colleagues in the War Cabinet did not entirely agree in Lloyd George's views, as in the matter of placing Haig under Nivelle's command, we find them subordinating their views to his. On all occasions, however, we see Lloyd George consulting his colleagues and securing their general assent before taking action. Every conference is preceded by long and anxious deliberation in the War Cabinet. In all matters of military strategy, as distinct from questions of command and organization, we find Lloyd George and his War Cabinet acceding in the last resort to the views of their military advisers. But they did not do so until they had convinced themselves by exhaustive discussion that the advice was correct. In cases where they differed from their military advisers at first sight they called them into council and thrashed the matter out. Originally Lloyd George and the majority of the War Cabinet undoubtedly entertained the gravest doubts about the prospects of a great offensive on the Western Front. At the Rome Conference, in conjunction with French and Italian statesmen, the Prime Minister and Milner confronted them with the difficulties and insisted on their considering an alternative plan. It was not until it was clear that the hearts of the military men were not in the alternative that they consented to the Nivelle plan. And when they did consent, it was to a plan which they were assured was not open to the objections which they all, or nearly all, felt towards attacks of the Somme type. Nivelle promised a smashing blow or nothing. Haig, less presumptuous than his French confrère, promised a handsome tactical success with the possibility of important economic advantages to follow. The moment the operations begin to degenerate into the 'Somme' type we find the French, as well as the British, Government bringing the question to the council table, where they found an able ally in Pétain, who seems to have convinced his military colleagues, if they were not already convinced.

The point on which Lloyd George definitely overrode his military advisers (i.e. in the matter of the Command) was one not of strategy or of tactics but of organization. In this the Prime Minister had as much

judge my liking for my new position." He struck me as a very reserved and soldierly man. He wore no decorations. In speaking of military matters he talked in low tones close to my ear, as though he didn't want the civilians on either side of us to know what he was saying. The general atmosphere of Paris struck me as very bad—a weak Government, a tiresome Chamber, intrigue everywhere, and a troubled and rather dejected people.'

right as the generals to claim to be an expert. Whether he treated Haig as tactfully as he might is another question. It may be that his methods were rather drastic and that his manner was too hectoring even for a Prime Minister to adopt. That was my own view at the time, and I was present at nearly all the interviews between them. On the other hand Lloyd George was above all things a judge of men. He knew exactly when to insist and when to persuade. Unity of command was with him a matter of supreme importance in the winning of the war. He could not afford to be thwarted in this test case. Moreover, once he had won on the point of principle, he did all he could to make Haig's position tolerable and to back his views in the Allied counsels.

An interesting point arises whether the Supreme Command ought to have stopped the Nivelle offensive. It has been shown how heavily the tide had set against its prospects. It is easy to see that the Commanders-in-Chief, immersed in their gigantic preparations and worked up thereby to a state of enthusiasm and confidence, would be extremely reluctant to call off the attack. But it can be argued that the Governments ought to have taken a wider view. They were probably better informed than the Commanders-in-Chief about the state of affairs in Russia. They were almost sure that at last America intended to intervene against Germany. Why then did they make no move? The position of the British Government in the matter was peculiarly delicate. They had been persuaded to agree to the offensive not without difficulty. They had, so to speak, put their money on Nivelle. It was difficult for them to stop him so long as he wished to go ahead. Moreover, their military advisers were in favour of going ahead—even Robertson, whose point of view at this stage did not differ widely from their own. They had no ground for intervening. It was far otherwise with Painlevé. He was a definite sceptic about both Nivelle and his plan. He was supported by the advice of the general (Pétain) in whom he did believe. It might have been a strong step to stop the operation on his own authority or on that of the French War Committee or Cabinet. He might, however, well have submitted the matter to a joint Council of the Allies, though it is doubtful whether, if he had done so, the result would have been different.

One more point should be mentioned, the steady growth of the practice of settling difficult questions by the method of conference. The questions between the British and French Governments were of such complexity that they could not have been settled by the ordinary methods of diplomacy. It was essential to bring both statesmen and

generals to the conference table, if rapid and durable decisions were to be taken. By these means effect was given in the most practical way to the principle agreed to at the Rome Conference. The Petrograd Conference had gone one step farther in this matter and had recommended the creation of a central organ by the four Powers represented at the conference, to ensure a rapid understanding on questions affecting the Higher Direction of the war. The conference advocated that this organ should be constituted by regular and frequent meetings of the Prime Ministers of the Powers, though (owing to the difficulty which the Russian Prime Minister would have in carrying out this proposal) provision was made for representation by some other political delegate from Russia, specially selected for this purpose, when necessary. The conference urged that, as far as possible, the meetings of the Central Council should be attended by the same persons. In addition there was a private understanding that the meetings should as a rule be held elsewhere than in a capital city. In these suggestions we can perceive the wise influence of Milner, the head of the British Mission, who later in the year was to see his proposals take shape at the Supreme War Council at Versailles.

CHAPTER LXI

THE SUBMARINE PROBLEM

'If blood be the price of Admiralty,
Lord God, we ha' bought it fair.'
(KIPLING, *Song of the English*.)

IMPORTANT and critical as were these events, they were not the main preoccupation of the War Cabinet during the first half of 1917. Even more urgent were the measures to combat the enemy's submarine campaign. Exposed to the extreme rigours of the Allied blockade our enemies found themselves faced with the danger of economic exhaustion. As each successive harvest approached their anxieties became greater. Only by the success of their operations in Russia and Roumania had they been able to lay hands on the essentials of existence. The strain on the civil population of Germany, and still more of Austria, was already severe. In this emergency it is only natural that they should have sought to subject the Allies to a corresponding economic pressure by striking at the sea communications on which not only their war effort but their means of existence depended. For this purpose the enemy now possessed one weapon and one weapon only. In only one branch of naval activity had they achieved comparative success—in the attacks on merchant ships by submarines and mines. The price paid for this moderate success had been heavy. Public opinion among Germany's enemies had hardened to an extent which made a negotiated peace almost unthinkable, and neutral public opinion all over the world had set strongly against the Central Powers. Every merchant ship sunk by submarines—and especially every neutral ship—was propaganda for the Allies. Nevertheless, in spite of the strong representations of Bernstorff, their Ambassador at Washington, the German Supreme Command in January 1917 decided to adopt a policy of unrestricted submarine warfare. The new policy was announced on January 31st and came into operation on February 1st. On February 3rd the United States severed diplomatic relations with Germany, and on April 6th declared war. The German Supreme Command had pronounced its own death sentence.

The more closely the history of the war is studied, the larger does the factor of sea supremacy loom. At this stage of it nearly every decision which the Supreme Command had to take was found to depend in some

way on shipping. The Western Front was up to now less affected than any other; the enemy had never succeeded in seriously interrupting the cross-Channel traffic which served the British Army. All the other fronts were, however, suffering in a greater or less degree from the shipping shortage. The difficulty of finding shipping to support the Salonica expedition became so great[1] that the Prime Minister and the War Cabinet, rather against their will, found themselves compelled to fall in with the strong views expressed by their advisers in favour of reducing our forces in that theatre. At St. Jean de Maurienne (April 17th) Lloyd George gave the French and Italian Ministers a solemn warning that, if the offensive movement which Sarrail was preparing did not achieve important results, the shipping position would compel us to consider a drastic reduction of the British forces. At the Paris Conference (May 5th) he took an even more drastic step. At that time no less than 150 ships (600,000 tons) were locked up in serving the requirements of the Salonica force, and the advent of hot weather was expected to lead to an additional heavy demand for hospital ships to carry men stricken with malaria. Twenty-two British ships, two of them transports, had been lost in the Mediterranean in the first twelve days of April; the naval forces there had proved inadequate to protect the sea routes to Salonica and Egypt. After Jellicoe and Robertson had made impressive statements on the subject, Lloyd George tabled a series of resolutions outlining the policy which the British Government thought ought to be followed. That Government after continuous study of the shipping situation, and after cutting down imports to an irreducible minimum, had come to the conclusion that the essential needs of the civilian populations of the Allies could only be met by a reduction of the force to that required to hold an entrenched camp surrounding Salonica harbour. The reduction was to be gradual, but notice was given of the Government's intention to withdraw one division and two cavalry brigades beginning on June 1st. This withdrawal would only be reconsidered in the event of Sarrail achieving such success in his forthcoming offensive as to render it reasonably certain before the end of May that Bulgaria could be brought to terms. The French representatives bitterly opposed these proposals. They pointed out that, if the British troops were withdrawn, the French would have to follow; Serbia would then be irretrievably lost; Constantine and his German friends would become masters of Greece; Venizelos would be abandoned, and his cause, which was part of the Allied cause, would be

[1] *Macedonia*, I, p. 302.

ruined; the Bulgarians and Turks would be encouraged beyond their wildest dreams; the Greek harbours would become bases for the enemy's submarines, and maritime communications with Egypt would be gravely imperilled. No French Government could exist which consented to such a state of affairs. What the French Government seemed unable to realize, was that the military situation in the Balkans was dominated by the shipping shortage. Neither at the conference nor in the correspondence which followed it did they indicate that they had grasped this essential and all-important factor.

Moreover, the question was complicated by the Greek affair. Sarrail, although abiding by the decision of the Rome Conference, had never ceased to press the demand he had made before that conference that he should be permitted to occupy Larissa and clear up the Greek situation. At St. Jean de Maurienne the French had made their usual assertions that the Greek military authorities were not playing the game; that we were being hoodwinked about the supposed concentration of the Greek Army in the Morea; and that the rear of Sarrail's army was in danger. On this occasion the Italian representatives, after obtaining substantial, if somewhat hypothetical, political concessions on the ultimate future of Smyrna after the war, had abandoned their previous obstruction to the French policy towards Greece, and left the matter to the British and French Governments. These two then decided that the proposed occupation of Larissa should stand over until after Sarrail's offensive.

At the Paris Conference (May 4th–5th), Lloyd George withdrew his objections to the occupation of Thessaly, if it could be shown to be a real military necessity, but he rejected as contrary to the declaration made by the Allies at the Rome Conference (January 7th) an offer received just before the conference from Venizelos to do the job for us. Eventually, after much discussion, he included with his resolutions on the Balkan campaign proposals for dealing with Greece on the following lines. The Allies were to announce to the Greek Government their intention to raise the blockade, provided they were permitted to purchase the harvest of Thessaly (the granary of Greece) without obstruction. The harvest was to be divided in fair proportions between monarchist and Venizelist Greece. In order to control the harvest the Allies were to have the right to establish military control posts in Thessaly. Not more than 500 British troops were to be employed. The French Government was to issue the necessary orders to Sarrail and they were authorized at the same time to transmit to him the British Government's acknowledgment of his loyal adherence to the under-

taking he had given at Rome. In order to avoid the constant misunderstandings which had occurred at Athens the principle was to be accepted that one Power should undertake the diplomatic lead at Athens. This role was to be assigned to France, who was to send some man of exceptional status, one acceptable to the British Government, who should be recognized as the principal medium of communication on all questions of common policy between the British and French Governments on the one hand and the Greek Government on the other.

This plan (which it fell to my lot to put into words) was devised in order to meet French susceptibilities as far as possible, while retaining all the essentials of British policy. The British Government secured the withdrawal from Salonica of the first instalment of troops on which they had set their hearts. They ensured that the Allied occupation of Thessaly should be carried out in the most pacific manner possible, and that both the *de facto* Governments in Greece should receive fair play. Above all they avoided the additional strain on shipping which their naval and military advisers considered that a forcible occupation of Thessaly would entail. The French Government obtained the guarantees they considered essential for the good behaviour of Greece. The ultimate decision on the withdrawal to a position covering Salonica was virtually postponed, and the French Government, who already held the High Military Command at Salonica, obtained as well the diplomatic lead at Athens.

These proposals were accepted by the French representatives *ad referendum* to the French Cabinet—which, as we ought to have known from previous experience, meant that they would not be accepted at all. The French Government did, indeed, acquiesce in the withdrawal of the instalment of British troops, since they saw that Lloyd George had made up his mind on that. They also lost no time in obtaining our acceptance of Jonnart (an admirable selection) as ambassador in Athens. The proposed policy towards Greece, however, did not satisfy them. They felt that the withdrawal of British troops would encourage Constantine; that the larger the number of troops withdrawn, the greater would be the danger to the left flank and rear of the Allies; and that if troops were to be withdrawn, it was essential that the situation in Greece should be cleared up first. They therefore transmitted personally through Derby a proposal that the Allies should occupy Thessaly, march on Athens, and depose the King. At first the British Government were taken aback by this proposal. Their naval and military advisers were strongly opposed to yet another commitment in the

Near East, which they foresaw would make yet a further demand on shipping. A certain amount of evidence had come to hand, however, that Constantine might not be averse to abdication, especially if one of his sons was selected to reign in his stead, and gradually opinion veered round in favour, not of the French proposals in full, but of steps to secure the King's abdication. A conference was arranged in London for May 28th and just before the first session, at an informal meeting between members of the War Cabinet and Robert Cecil, who was acting as Foreign Minister during Balfour's absence on a mission to Washington, it was decided to support a demand for the abdication of Constantine in favour of one of his sons. Under this plan the abdication was not to be demanded until the Thessalian harvest had been put under Allied control, so that, if the King refused, Greece could be blockaded, by which means the necessary pressure could be exerted.[1]

The London Conference of May 28th–29th was notable for the first appearance of Foch, who had replaced Pétain as Chief of the Staff, and who made a remarkable and clear-headed contribution to the discussions. The French were delighted with the British change of view, but considered it essential, if coercion were required, to supplement the blockade by the occupation of the Isthmus of Corinth. They now admitted that, as we had long contended, practically the whole of the Greek Army was in the Morea, and that the occupation of the Isthmus, combined with the blockade, and with the seizure of the Thessalian harvest, if necessary would enable us to bottle it up effectively, and starve it into surrender. The British naval and military authorities, however, objected to these military measures again on account of the demand they would make on shipping. The general losses from submarines had, it was true, been slightly less during the last week or two, but the shipping position in the Mediterranean was worse than ever: 9,000 troops destined for Egypt and Salonica had been held up at Marseilles for a month for lack of transport, and another 9,000 in England. The British Government had had to give notice to the French Government that 100 ships which had been lent to them must be withdrawn. Eventually it was arranged that, in case of necessity, the French should undertake the occupation of the Isthmus, including provision of the necessary shipping, as well as of the forces required, except for a nominal contingent of British troops to show the flag. Fortunately these drastic measures were not required. Constantine's abdication was called for on June 11th[2] and on the following day he signed it in favour

[1] *Macedania*, I, pp. 351 *sq.*   [2] *Ibid.*, p. 356.

of his second son Alexander. On June 26th Venizelos again became Premier. The prolonged disagreement between the British and French Governments on Greek policy came to an end. The former adhered to their determination to withdraw a division and two cavalry brigades (to Egypt, where they could be more effectively employed), but all further withdrawals were suspended for six weeks, before which a further conference was to be held to consider the question.

In other theatres, too, shipping was an important factor. In Mesopotamia Maude had passed from success to success. Capturing Kut-el-Amara early in February, he had begun his advance to Baghdad and occupied it on March 11th—the one bright spot in the military situation. The strain of maintaining this campaign had, however, been increased by the necessity, owing to the submarine danger, of sending British drafts *via* the Cape. Owing to the longer time involved in the voyage, their strength had to be increased by 5 per cent thus reacting on our man-power.

As a result of Maude's successes, Robertson who, though in principle opposed to 'sideshows', never displayed quite the same aversion for the Palestine expedition as he did for the Balkan operations, proposed in March to instruct Archibald Murray to adopt a more offensive role. This fitted in very well with the views of the Prime Minister and the War Cabinet who from a political point of view were particularly keen to win some success, and it was decided to instruct Murray that they were anxious to capture Jerusalem and to obtain from him an estimate of the forces and transport required. On April 17th Murray, who had completed the desert railway to within four miles of Gaza, attacked the gateway of Palestine but failed to capture it, incurring nearly 3,000 casualties. The War Cabinet then decided to relieve him. The choice of his successor led to an investigation of the whole future of this campaign. Robertson was now less optimistic. The Russians could no longer be counted on to contain many Turkish troops in the Caucasus. The Turks, who had probably written off Mesopotamia, would therefore be able to concentrate on the Palestine Front as large a force as their communications enabled them to maintain there. Smuts was offered the command in Palestine, but refused it because, owing to the Russian revolution, Robertson could not promise to send all that was required for a great offensive campaign there. Eventually, on June 28th, Allenby succeeded Archibald Murray as Commander-in-Chief of the Egyptian Expeditionary Force. By that time the future policy in this theatre had become merged into the question of the major strategy of

the war, which was being examined by a special committee of the Cabinet under the chairmanship of the Prime Minister.

The campaign in East Africa was also making a relatively small but inconvenient drain on shipping. Smuts, after making great progress, had resigned the command in order to accompany Botha to the Imperial War Cabinet meetings.[1] He had handed over his command to Hoskins on January 20th. In mid-April Hoskins, who had some 50,000 troops (including South African as well as Indian troops) under his command, wanted five ships put at his disposal in order to enable him to undertake operations which, it was hoped, would clear up this campaign and release a large quantity of shipping. So serious was the shipping situation, however, that the Shipping Controller found the utmost difficulty in satisfying this relatively modest demand.

Perhaps the most important work of the Petrograd Conference was the compilation of a complete list of Russia's requirements in artillery, ammunition, railway material, aircraft, etc., and the working out of a comprehensive scheme for supplying as much of her needs as possible from Western sources of supply. The figures were colossal, and at best it was only deemed possible to furnish part of the requirements. There were two limiting factors. One was the inadequate port facilities at Murmansk and Archangel (frozen up for several months every year) and the railways connecting them with the Russian armies, while the other was—shipping. As time went on, it became clear that Russia was no longer in a position to play an important role in the war, and the programme of the Petrograd Conference was only carried out in part. Nevertheless, in the first half of 1917 the demands of Russia on our shipping resources were a serious preoccupation.

In Italy the situation was even more serious. We have already noted that Cadorna was not ready to make his attack in concert with Nivelle's operations. The General's precise reasons were not known to us, but there is little doubt that the delay was due to shortage of ammunition, and that this resulted from insufficiency of coal, the cause of which was lack of shipping. The supply of coal to Italy had always been a matter of great difficulty. As the winter went on the deficiency became most serious, and Italy only received on an average 60 per cent of her requirements. In January dall'Olio, the Italian Minister of Munitions, warned an Allied Naval and Shipping Conference that, if Italy did not get the tonnage she required, the production of munitions would be

---

[1] In the event, Botha found it impossible to leave South Africa and Smuts represented him in the Imperial War Cabinet.

stopped in March; the offensive would be impossible, and even the defensive paralysed. He was not exaggerating. In one week in March there was a deficit of 98 per cent of the weekly requirements. Yet the greatest efforts were being made continuously to find the necessary tonnage by the British Government. The War Cabinet had the matter constantly before them. All sorts of expedients were resorted to: 3,000 tons a day were sent overland through France. The Admiralty, who withdrew some battleships from the Mediterranean about this time, made over substantial quantities of naval coal and lent their own colliers to carry it. When Cadorna did start an offensive (on May 12th, contemporaneously with the later stages of Haig's attack on Bullecourt, south of Arras) he achieved a considerable success on the Carso, taking 18,000 prisoners, but he was obliged to desist owing to a shortage of heavy gun ammunition—which, no doubt, must again be attributed largely to the perennial shortage of coal; in this offensive Cadorna had had the assistance of ten batteries of British 6-inch howitzers.

France also during the winter 1916–17 only received 68 per cent of her British requirements in coal owing to the shipping shortage. This was not quite so serious for her as for Italy, as she was not entirely dependent on imported coal, and the War Cabinet felt justified in transferring part of the French ration to Italy for a month or two.

The main reason for this shortage of shipping was the losses due to enemy action and more especially to submarine attack, as shown by the following figures for losses during the first half of 1917:

1917	British Gross Tons	World Total Gross Tons
January	153,666	368,521
February	313,486	540,006
March	353,478	593,841
April	545,282	881,027
May	352,289	596,629
June	417,925	687,507
TOTAL	2,136,126	3,667,531

It will be noticed how the losses leap up after the adoption of the policy of unrestricted submarine warfare by Germany in February. The difficulty was not confined to the effect of the actual losses, but was augmented by the fact that neutral shipping could no longer be tempted

to accept charters on the more dangerous routes. This was more especially the case in the matter of coal for Italy.

The total British losses from the beginning of the war due to enemy action and marine losses amounted to 5,372,000 gross tons up to the middle of 1917. The net loss, after allowing for new ships built and enemy and other merchant vessels brought on to the British register, was 2,891,000 gross tons. For the world the net loss of shipping was 2,005,000 gross tons. The British losses from enemy action in the first half of 1917 (2,136,126 gross tons) were far greater than for the whole of 1916 (1,237,636 gross tons) and vastly exceeded the shipbuilding output (631,000 gross tons for the first six months of 1917).

Every morning I used to find on my office table the list of sinkings for the last twenty-four hours. In April 1917 they sometimes rose above 50,000 tons. This preyed upon my mind, the more so because I was convinced that the Admiralty's arrangements were not what they should be. For the first and only time in the war I suffered from sleepless nights.

CHAPTER LXII

THE CONVOY SYSTEM

'To every action there is an equal and opposite reaction.'
(EUCLID).

UNRESTRICTED warfare on merchant ships was a hard nut to crack in
1917. It was countered by a series of measures of different kinds in
reduction of our dependence on imports, development of home
resources, cutting down consumption and rationing, combined with
technical devices for locating, obstructing and destroying the enemy,
and finally defeated by a device of the old wars—the convoy system.
At their very first meeting the War Cabinet were informed by Lloyd
George that he had appointed as Shipping Controller (a step already
overdue) Joseph Maclay, a canny Glasgow shipowner, who filled the
bill admirably. He was a man of strong character, an ardent advocate of
'prohibition', and knew his job inside and out. Maclay was allowed to
draft his own powers, and, after a sharp tussle with the Admiralty, the
War Cabinet accorded him the responsibility for allocating the available shipping for all national requirements, including Government
Departments. The departments remained responsible for the employment of the shipping allotted to them, but the Shipping Controller had
the right to inquire how the ships were being used, and to make
representations if their employment was not economical. In the last
resort he could bring the matter to the War Cabinet. This measure
proved most fruitful in ensuring the most economical use of shipping.
A fortnight after they came into office, the War Cabinet decided that
all shipping and shipbuilding questions were to be examined on the
basis that the war would last throughout 1918—a useful piece of
prevision, which was more than once repeated.

At first the policy of the War Cabinet may be summed up as follows:

To combat the submarines by every known method. This was, of course,
a matter for the Navy, but the Admiralty had to justify to the War Cabinet
the demands they were making on our national resources, and this led eventually to an investigation of the administration of the Admiralty by the Prime
Minister himself.

An increase in shipping tonnage, by construction, purchase, chartering,
and other measures, such as pressure on neutrals to make use of enemy ships
laid up in their ports.

Restriction of imports, in order to release shipping for our war effort.

Increased production at home, more especially of food and raw materials, in order to facilitate the restriction of imports.

The utmost economy in the use of shipping, not only by private users, but also by the Services and Government Departments, and by our Allies. This was the special task of the Shipping Controller.

Each head of the policy required patient and often prolonged investigation by committees. These were usually presided over by either Curzon or Milner, who were assisted by secretaries deputed from the War Cabinet Office. These questions were, of course, inextricably mixed up with the question of man-power. The stimulation of home production, for example, and of food, iron ore, timber felling, etc., called for large supplies of labour and clashed with the requirements of the fighting services. Each case had to be examined patiently on its merits and in the end the labour would be found, perhaps by releasing men employed in home defence or men in the higher age categories or in the lower categories of physical fitness, by the substitution of women, which was soon going on apace, and, e.g., in the case of timber felling, by the importation of foreign labour.

The policy of a further curtailment of imports was adopted just before Christmas 1916, and a committee under Curzon was appointed to work it out. Early in February Parliament was warned that further restrictions would have to be adopted, and in the middle of the month the War Cabinet decided on detailed restrictions involving a further curtailment of 500,000 tons a month. The most important articles affected were paper (which was still being used in a profligate manner in Government Departments, newspaper offices, for packing purposes, and everywhere), timber, and brewing materials. Even these drastic recommendations did not satisfy Lloyd George, and Curzon's committee was asked to find another 100,000 tons a month. This was accomplished mainly by adopting in principle the exclusion of all imports of timber. A Director of Timber Supplies was appointed under the War Office with an interdepartmental committee to assist him. A great national scheme of timber felling was adopted. Inquiries were set on foot with a view to finding and felling the timber required for the Expeditionary Force from behind the lines in France. Schemes were drawn up for collecting and using waste paper. The Minister of Munitions was set to work to organize increased production at home of ores, nitrates and pyrites. Brewing materials which had already been seriously curtailed were now limited to one-third of their pre-war bulk.

Corresponding limitations were made in the issues from bond of wines and spirits. These restrictions naturally led to many difficulties with the interested parties, and with foreign governments, who protested against the loss of the British market for their wares, and these matters were constantly coming before the War Cabinet. On the whole, however, the long-suffering people of this country bore these privations with the same uncomplaining stoicism as they had withstood still greater physical and moral hardships.

As early as December 1916, measures for stimulating the home production of food were approved in principle, including the fixing of prices for the harvest of 1917, and much time was devoted to consequential measures, including the creation of a new Food Production Department under the Minister of Agriculture, of which Arthur Lee had charge, and above all the Food Production Act. There had been a failure of the potato crop and difficulties arose in February in Lancashire, and more especially in Scotland, where there was a potato famine. The Army was called on to give up requisitioning of potatoes; the soldier serving at home had to share the privations of the civil population in this respect. In December, when the War Cabinet came into office, there were fourteen weeks' supply of grain in the country. Owing to the virulence of the submarine campaign the policy was adopted of importing as much wheat as possible. The Ministry of Munitions was asked to give up certain shipments for a few weeks in order to enable larger supplies of foodstuffs to be imported. Nevertheless the stocks were steadily falling and by mid-April the amount of wheat was reported as down to nine weeks' supply. If stocks were to fall below six weeks' supply their proper distribution throughout the country would become a matter of great difficulty, so that, in view of the increasing losses from submarines, the food position did not offer a large margin of safety (though stocks had sometimes been reduced as low as seven weeks' supply in time of peace). Moreover the whole position of our imports had become very serious. Precise returns were not yet available, but it was estimated that the imports for March 1917 amounted to little over two and a half million tons, compared with over three and a half million tons in the corresponding month in 1916, a deficiency of nearly one-third. Meanwhile the British shipping losses had leaped up from 353,478 gross tons in March to 545,282 tons in April. They were in fact at their maximum. Milner was accordingly asked to investigate the position on shipping priority in consultation with the Ministers at the head of the departments concerned with a view to the accumulation

of the largest possible stocks of food. For the month of June Milner accorded the whole of the claims of the Food Ministry so far as essential foodstuffs were concerned. No allotment was made for tonnage to import timber, and the Ministry of Munitions was asked to cede 303,300 tons. Milner's proposals were adopted by the War Cabinet, and on the same day, May 30th, a proposal, which emanated from the fertile brain of Chiozza Money, the Parliamentary Under-Secretary of Shipping, was adopted in principle for concentrating all purchases as far as possible in the United States, with the object of shortening the sea voyage and facilitating the task of protection.

The question of rationing food had been discussed by the War Cabinet almost from the first moment of assuming office. In January 1917, the statistical position was not considered sufficiently serious to warrant this step. By the end of May the Food Controller (Devonport) had worked out a scheme for general rationing, but even then it was not considered necessary to put it in operation. In March, however, drastic measures for limiting the consumption of food in hotels, restaurants, clubs, etc., were approved. In such places Wednesday was to be a meat-less day; Thursday and Saturday were potatoless days; the amount of meat issuable to each customer was limited to five ounces for lunch or dinner, or ten ounces for a day, including breakfast; and only one ounce of flour was allowed at lunch or dinner. The amounts of food to be served at railway buffets were also severely restricted. In May also investigations were entrusted to Milner on the labour, horses, importa-tions of phosphate rock, etc., required for the agricultural programme of 1918.

Perhaps the greatest difficulties of all in carrying out the anti-sub-marine policy arose in connection with shipbuilding, and the Prime Minister himself was indefatigable on this aspect. One of the root difficulties was the clash between the requirements of the Admiralty and those of the Mercantile Marine. In February 1917 the Admiralty put forward a programme which, if approved, would have reduced the out-put of merchant shipping by 500,000 tons. The matter was thrashed out at the War Cabinet, with the result that the Admiralty were asked drastically to curtail their programme. All their requirements for anti-submarine craft and apparatus were approved, and the battle-cruiser *Hood* was to be completed, but work was to be stopped on her three sister ships unless it could be continued without interfering with mercantile construction. Five light cruisers were cut out of the list. That is a reply to those who say that the War Cabinet allowed the

Admiralty too large a share of the national resources in the later stages of the war.

Meanwhile the War Cabinet had sanctioned the ordering in the United States of forty big merchant ships at an estimated cost of £12,500,000, and had instigated inquiries in Japan and other countries as well as an investigation about the usefulness of the 'British Columbia model', a wooden ship. One ingenious proposal, which emanated from the Admiralty, was for the construction of a 'mammoth' ship—a vessel of vast size, which would ply between deep water ports in Britain and America, bringing huge cargoes of wheat. The Shipping Controller and his Shipbuilding Committee looked coldly on the proposal, but the Chief Constructor of the Navy was ready with a design. In the end the proposal was dropped. A more practical measure was the adoption by the Shipping Controller of 'standard' ships.

During the whole of the early part of 1917 Lloyd George was disquieted about the administration at the Admiralty, which he felt lacked resource and drive. Both the First Lord and First Sea Lord gave the appearance of suffering from pessimism, which was very irritating to an incorrigible optimist like the Prime Minister. Moreover, some very able young officers in the War Staff did not conceal their conviction that the method of routing merchant ships was involving unnecessary losses which could be avoided by the adoption of the convoy system. The Shipping Controller, who inspired great confidence, was continually at loggerheads with the Admiralty, and in private conversation was very outspoken in his opinions of that department. The following contemporary notes give some idea of the situation:

February 8th. The submarine warfare has become frantic. We seem to be sinking a good many submarines, but they are sinking a terrible lot of ships. . . . We discussed today the naval programme of construction. Rather a gloomy business owing to lack of labour and raw materials, which have all gone to munitions.

February 11th (Sunday). Had a brainwave on the subject of anti-submarine warfare, so ran down to Walton Heath in the afternoon to formulate my ideas to Lloyd George, who was very interested. I sat up late completing a long Memo. on the subject. My Memorandum was an argument for convoys, but contained a great number of suggestions.

The Memorandum which was dashed off in such haste that Sunday night, proved to be of considerable importance. Years after the war, when the Official History was being written, doubts were raised in the Admiralty about the correctness of the original draft of the story of the

initiation of the convoy system. As the Historical Section was attached to the Office of the Committee of Imperial Defence the matter was referred to me, but I had already put all the official records of the War Cabinet at the disposal of the Historical Section and could not at first throw any light on the subject. At that point Duff, who had been Director of the Anti-Submarine Section at the Admiralty, recalled vaguely that I had written something on the subject, which had exercised a good deal of influence at the time. Strange to say I had forgotten the episode, but I found in my diary the extract quoted above. A search was made in the archives of my private office and the Memorandum was found. The greater part of it is quoted by the Official Historian who writes[1] that it is

... the clearest and most authentic account of the reasoning which enabled the War Cabinet to sustain their constitutional parts in the conduct of the war; not as technical experts but as responsible leaders bringing in their powers at the decisive moment to carry forward and support their high executive officers.

The gist of it is contained in the following extracts:

The situation created by the enemy's adoption of unrestricted submarine warfare threatens to become so serious that the Admiralty will surely not resent the suggestions of an outsider, who, though well placed as an onlooker, can lay no claim to be a practical expert....

The general scheme ... entails ultimately an entire reorganization of the Admiralty's present scheme of anti-submarine warfare, although it might, in the first instance, be adopted experimentally on a smaller scale. It involves the substitution of a system of scientifically organized convoys, and the concentration on this service of the whole of the anti-submarine craft allotted to the protection of our trade routes, excepting only those vessels devoted to the anti-submarine service of our main fleets. It further involves the concentration on to the convoy system of every means of anti-submarine warfare—the gun, the submarine, the net, the depth charge, the mortar, the hydrophone, and wireless telegraphy. It aims at the effective utilization of the slower as well as of the faster anti-submarine craft for the convoy system, and it contemplates ultimately the provision of special salvage and life-saving craft and plant to accompany the convoys.... The object of the proposals may be summed up as follows: To prevent the enemy from knowing when and where our merchant ships are to be found ... ; to debar the enemy from engaging without undertaking a serious attack and himself running great risks; to obtain the advantages of mutual support; to combine every technical device to increase the chances of injuring the enemy; to concentrate our

[1] *Naval Operations*, V, pp. 10 *sq*.

widely scattered anti-submarine craft on the immediate defence of the merchant shipping they are intended to protect; to bait the trap, thereby compelling the enemy to risk an action if he is to inflict injury—in fact, this is a form of the offensive on our part; to reduce losses to a minimum; to ensure means of saving life and to provide a fair chance of salving torpedoed or mined ships and cargoes.

Admittedly the system cannot come into full operation at once, but it would seem to deserve a trial. For its proper development it is essential that the personnel of the mercantile marine should be nationalized; that the Admiralty should have complete control over convoys; that the personnel of the merchant ship should be trained and for the present should be generously diluted with officers, seamen and marines of the Royal Navy; that large numbers of signalmen should be trained immediately; and, finally, that the sharp dividing line between the Royal Navy and the mercantile marine should disappear.

The sequel to the receipt by Lloyd George of the Memorandum was a summons to me to breakfast at 10 Downing Street.

February 13th. Breakfast with Lloyd George, Carson, Jellicoe and Duff, to discuss my theories as regards the adoption of convoys. They resisted a good deal, but I think that the discussion did good. They admitted they were convoying transports and agreed to inquire about the results of a big convoy of eight transports coming from Australia. They told us many things about anti-submarine warfare. It was interesting to learn that last week, the first week of the so-called submarine blockade, the importation of wheat was the greatest we had ever had.

That laconic extract does scant justice to the embarrassment in which I was placed at this breakfast. Although carefully drawn to set forth the Admiralty's case as fairly as I could, seeing that I did not believe in it, the Memorandum was in effect a strong indictment of the Admiralty's policy. Although I occupied a high office as Secretary to the War Cabinet, from the Admiralty's point of view I was a young Lieutenant-Colonel of Marines, devoid of any constitutional right and unqualified by experience to criticize their policy. My feelings can be imagined when I was asked without warning to read the peccant document to an audience of the First Lord, the First Sea Lord and the Director of Anti-Submarine warfare, and afterwards to attempt to stand up to a barrage of technical objections! It is pleasant to recall that none of the three, either at the time or thereafter, ever mentioned the constitutional point either in public or in private. Neither did it impair in any way our friendly relations.

The objections that were raised were very formidable: if a submarine did locate a convoy it would get a big bag; the value of speed would be lost owing to the need of the convoy going the speed of the slowest ship; zigzagging would be impossible to ships in convoy; cargo ships would never be able to keep station; great confusion would arise in the event of a fog; and, most formidable of all, there were not enough cruisers and destroyers to supply the necessary escorts. I did my best, with such tact as I could muster, to meet every point. But it was a case of *Athanasius contra mundum*. Beyond a point I could not pit my amateur views against theirs on technical issues. Nevertheless I remained unshaken in my own conviction that convoy was the only answer to the submarine attack on merchant ships, and, what was infinitely more important, Lloyd George was of the same opinion, and I have no doubt that from that moment his mind was made up.

As yet, however, even Lloyd George could not drive the matter through. He had other difficulties on his hands. He was at loggerheads with the Chief of the Imperial General Staff about the strategy of the war, and within a fortnight of the breakfast discussion on submarines he was engaged in the desperate struggle at Calais over unity of command. Until that was out of the way he could not afford a dispute with the heads of the Admiralty as well, especially as the Empire Prime Ministers were already assembling for the first meetings of the Imperial War Cabinet. To confront them with such a spectacle of internal dis-union would have been unfortunate. Moreover, the objection that the Admiralty could not provide the necessary escorts was a hard one to surmount. It was not until after the United States had joined in the war, bringing the expectation of appreciable co-operation in the provision of destroyers, that he returned to the subject. In the meantime, however, in his own way he had been adding to his knowledge of the subject, e.g. by a visit to the Grand Fleet, where he found that Beatty favoured the convoy system, and in conversation with the American Admiral Sims, who was of the same view.

March 30th. Personally I am much worried about the shipping outlook owing to submarines and the inability of the Admiralty to deal with it, and their general ineptitude as indicated by their stickiness towards any new pro-posal. I have many ideas on the matter, but cannot get at Lloyd George in regard to it as he is so full of politics. I am oppressed by the fear I have always had that, while moderately successful on land, we may yet be beaten at sea. Something like a million tons of the world's shipping have been lost in the last two months—and that takes a lot of replacement.

April 13th. Was at office until about 8 p.m. and went home to Limpsfield by the 9.5 p.m. train, Lloyd George having gone off to Scotland to visit the Grand Fleet. I could not go with him as there was no spare cabin.

April 14th (Sunday). Spent whole day at home writing an appreciation of the whole war.

This appreciation was an ambitious document bringing up to date the big review I had prepared for Lloyd George when he first came into office as Prime Minister.[1] In it I laid the utmost stress on the importance to the future of the war of dealing with the shipping situation and the submarine losses. It seems to have had some effect on Lloyd George's mind.

April 22nd. (I was travelling back with Lloyd George from a conference at St. Jean de Maurienne. On this day we were motoring from Abbeville to Calais.) We arrived Calais about noon. Lloyd George and I conversed mainly about the war. He had evidently carefully studied the paper I wrote last Saturday and Sunday and at last seemed to have grasped the danger of the submarine question—though earlier in the trip he had said 'Oh, well, I have never regarded that matter so seriously as you have'.

At Calais we found there had been a slight bombardment the night before, a hole having been made in a crane just by the landing-place. It was quite evident they had tried to bag us. Bonar Law had announced our departure in the House of Commons, as he had to do to excuse Lloyd George for not moving the vote of recognition to Congress on America's entry into the war, but had added quite unnecessarily that we should return in three days. Had we not stayed a day in Paris, or had we been in a hurry, we should have crossed that night at high tide to ensure our riding over the mines—precisely the hour at which Calais was bombarded, and we should have arrived off Dover about the time the destroyer action took place. However the Germans lost two or three destroyers. . . .

This was in a very gallant action in which the *Broke* and the *Swift* engaged a number of German destroyers and sank two.[2] The incident emphasizes the importance of thinking out the possible consequences of statements in Parliament in war.

April 29th. In one way this has been one of the most dreadful weeks of the war, owing to appalling mercantile losses from submarines. These have depressed me very much, but at last, when it is almost too late, the Government are taking action. I spent the whole morning dictating a long Memo. to help Lloyd George, who has undertaken to investigate the whole question at the Admiralty on Monday. I also had a long talk on the telephone with

---

[1] *vide supra*, p. 592. [2] *Naval Operations*, IV, p. 373. Dover also was bombarded.

Stamfordham about the Press attacks on the Admiralty, though in my opinion these attacks are largely justified. For example, a few weeks ago they scouted the idea of convoy. Now they are undertaking it on their own initiative, but apparently want weeks to organize it, though this at any rate might have been done earlier. They don't look ahead. As Fisher has recently written to me, the problem is 'Can the Army win the war before the Navy loses it?' My horrible prophesy when Lord K.'s army was first conceived, that we should lose at sea without winning on land, threatens to come true.'

The decision that the Prime Minister should investigate the whole submarine question at the Admiralty had been taken by the War Cabinet on April 25th. Whether as the result of this decision, or spontaneously and on its merits, on the very next day (April 26th) Duff submitted a Minute to the First Sea Lord in favour of the establishment of the convoy system, and Jellicoe approved it on April 27th. That explains the passage in the above extract. Consequently when Lloyd George visited the Admiralty on April 30th he found that his task was greatly simplified.

April 30th. At last Lloyd George has set himself to tackle the submarine question seriously, when it is almost too late. Yesterday afternoon he sent for me to come to Walton Heath to discuss the method of conducting an inquiry into the Admiralty. . . . Lloyd George then carried me off to Town. I supped with him at 10 Downing Street, and worked up into the form of questions a number of Memoranda by Milner, Curzon, Robertson and a long one by myself. . . . This morning Lloyd George and I went to the Admiralty and spent the whole day there very pleasantly, lunching with Jellicoe and his wife and four little girls—Lloyd George having a great flirtation with a little girl of three. I spent the whole evening up to 8.30 p.m. dictating a long report, embodying a large reconstruction of the Admiralty and more especially of the Admiralty War Staff. Then I caught the 9.5 p.m. train to Oxted.

Lloyd George's visit to the Admiralty set the seal on the decision to adopt the convoy system, and, however cautious the Admiralty may have been in adopting that system, they carried it out with the utmost energy and competence.

Up to that moment the submarine campaign had been a matter of the utmost misgiving, but from now onwards, though it did not cease to trouble, it was a less overwhelming preoccupation. For my part I ceased to fear any more that it was likely to prove our undoing.

The story of the convoy system as a whole has been told in the Official History and in various memoirs. Here we are only concerned with the matter from the point of view of the Supreme Command. It

was a characteristic example of Lloyd George's methods. Before undertaking a task of this kind he would obtain the views of the most diverse
people, each of whom would as likely as not be under the impression
that he was the only confidant of the Prime Minister on the subject and
put his whole soul into the task as I did. Having stimulated his mind
in this way Lloyd George would form his own opinions, which would
often have little relation to the suggestions made to him. He then would
proceed to conduct the inquiry in the pleasantest possible way without
any display of officialdom or red tape. Finally he would entrust the
drafting of the report to one of those about him who knew his mind and
could be relied on to give suitable expression to his ideas. In this way he
would grapple with the most abstruse questions with a minimum of
wear and tear to himself. It was only by some such methods that anyone could have borne the fearful strain and responsibility of his daily
task.

Y

CHAPTER LXIII

CHANGES AT THE ADMIRALTY

'It seems to me evident that the time has arrived when
we must be ready to introduce a comprehensive scheme
of convoy at any moment.' (Note from Admiral Duff
to Admiral Sir John Jellicoe dated April 26, 1917: *vide
Naval Operations*, V, p. 198.)

ON his visit to the Admiralty on April 30th, Lloyd George first set
himself to relieve the First Sea Lord of as much detail as possible, in
which he had Jellicoe's cordial agreement. The main difficulty was that
Sir John had found by experience that the material he required for
carrying out his plans was not forthcoming sufficiently quickly unless
he was constantly exercising his personal initiative and drive. Lloyd
George at once saw this was wrong, and that it was of the first importance that the Admiralty should be so organized as to free the First Sea
Lord from having to devote his energy to the supply of material. He
decided that the best way to accomplish this was to appoint a
thoroughly capable business man, of the type which had been so
successful at the Ministry of Munitions, to supervise the whole supply
of naval material. That was his first recommendation. In the event he
extended this plan by appointing Eric Geddes to take charge of all
shipbuilding, not only for the Royal Navy, but also for the Mercantile
Marine.

Having thus released the First Sea Lord from duties and responsibilities which he ought never to have found it necessary to assume, Lloyd
George went on to investigate the duties of the staff. He soon reached
the opinion that the weakest point in the system was the lack of a
division whose special duty was to think out and work out large questions of policy for the First Sea Lord. He asked the question who was
responsible for this function, and received the reply: 'the First Sea Lord
and the Chief of the War Staff' (at that time separate officials). Then he
asked who was responsible for the day-to-day dispositions, drafting of
telegrams, etc., for the numerous forces under the direct control of the
Admiralty, which, in the larger sense, included not only the co-ordination of the main fleets and squadrons, but also the control of various
forces (e.g. at Harwich and the Dover patrol) in home waters. He
received the same answer—the First Sea Lord and the Chief of the
War Staff. The Prime Minister quickly reached the conclusion that this

involved too much centralization and was too great a burden to place on one man, even when he was gifted with such enormous capacity for work as Oliver, through whom all this work passed. He found also that none of the Directors of sections working under him had the specific duty of looking ahead and working out the policy, plans and prepara-tions for meeting the various contingencies that might threaten; only one of these Directors had actual sea experience in the war. To meet these defects he recommended that the Admiralty War Staff should be reorganized *mutatis mutandis* on the lines of the War Office General Staff. The First Sea Lord was to become Chief of the War Staff. He was to have a Deputy Chief to direct the day-to-day movements of ships, squadrons, etc., and to supervise the relations between the War Staff and the administrative side of the Admiralty. A Director of Operations was to be charged with working out, under the First Sea Lord, the measures of policy to meet every development that could be foreseen. A Director of Intelligence was to supply data for the Director of Operations and other Directors. The Head of the Trade Division was to continue to be responsible, as he always had been, to the First Sea Lord for the control of the movements of merchant ships. The Director of Anti-Submarine craft was also to continue the duties he already discharged under the First Sea Lord. Another recom-mendation was that these Directors should include several officers of war experience.

For a long time past the War Office General Staff had been furnish-ing a weekly appreciation on the military operations of the war, which was of great value, not only to the War Office, but also to the War Cabinet. The Admiralty had always demurred to the suggestion that they should furnish a similar report, but Lloyd George recommended that this should be done. He also recommended the creation of a Statistical Department, the establishment of a system of close liaison with the Ministry of Shipping, the training of wireless operators for the Mercantile Marine, joint inquiry between the Admiralty and Ministry of Shipping about the possibility of diverting more shipping from the east coast to the west, an appeal to Japan to send more destroyers to the Mediterranean, and *mirabile dictu* a withdrawal, or at least a diminution, of our Army in the Balkans; additional minesweepers, increased use of seaplanes against submarines, and the construction of mammoth torpedo-proof ships, which was favoured by the Admiralty, but was afterwards dropped owing to the opposition of the Ministry of Shipping.

Needless to say Lloyd George was glad to learn that Duff had completely altered his views on convoy, that the First Sea Lord agreed, at any rate to the extent of an experiment, and that, substantially, the views of the Admiralty on this matter were now in accord with those of the War Cabinet.

Although Lloyd George's report had been accepted by both the War Cabinet and the Admiralty, that department was not yet at the end of its troubles. A good many people had their knife into them and Lloyd George himself was not satisfied with the direction at the top. It was hard to elicit the facts:

June 30th. For the last ten days I have been too desperately busy to keep a diary at all. . . . Meanwhile another great question had arisen. During Haig's visit,[1] Jellicoe at one of the meetings had declared that after this year we should not be able to continue the war for lack of shipping. This example of Jellicoe's pessimism, which had already caused annoyance owing to its effect on Pershing and the Americans generally, caused great irritation. Haig was very seriously alarmed and urged on the Prime Minister that the question could not remain where it was. He and Eric Geddes, who is now Controller of the Admiralty, and Milner breakfasted together next morning with the Prime Minister. Geddes . . . seems to have revealed a very unsatisfactory state of affairs in the conduct of business. This at any rate was the effect on the mind of the Prime Minister. Next day (the 27th), the Cabinet Committee considered the question. . . .

On the morning of the 28th, the Prime Minister having gone to Walton Heath to prepare the speech he intended to deliver at Glasgow the following day, I went to the Shipping Controller's Office in his place to meet the Shipping Controller's Committee. They spent an hour or so abusing the Admiralty and making many rather startling allegations about Admiralty maladministration, particularly in regard to the control of shipping. I made a full written report and telephoned the gist to the Prime Minister at Walton Heath. The result was that the P.M. summoned me to Walton Heath that afternoon and I motored back to London with him. He discussed every alternative for the post of First Lord and had evidently decided to get rid of Carson by the simple expedient of 'booting' him up to the War Cabinet. He rather inclined to Geddes, but was undecided. . . . Perhaps unwisely I asked him if he had ever thought of me in this connection. He simply fastened on to it, and would, I believe, there and then have forced me to accept the post of First Lord, but for my many protests of unfitness in many respects. I pointed out that, while I believed that I could improve matters as regards anti-submarine warfare and produce better results, I should be quite hopeless as

[1] The Field-Marshal had been summoned to Downing Street in connection with the meeting of the War Policy Committee (*vide infra*, p. 673).

regards parliamentary matters, deputations, etc., in regard to which I had no experience. I also pointed out that it would be a fearful gamble for me. I was in a post which suited me and where I was happy, with good future prospects. To enter a rather rocky Ministry in the most criticized post with a rather doubtful staff; to incur the odium of sacking half of them, including some of the most distinguished admirals; to take on the most responsible office, in the most difficult part of the war, in a department that has to a considerable extent failed; these are risks which I would only exchange for my present post, difficult though it is, under pressure of a very high sense of national duty, and under persuasion from the whole Cabinet. Perhaps the strongest deterrent is the base and bitter scapegoat-hunting of the Press, so clearly brought out in connection with the Reports of the Dardanelles and Mesopotamia Commissions. All this and much more I put to Lloyd George on that motor ride from Walton Heath to London. But he was absolutely bitten with the idea, and would talk of nothing else. When we reached London he sent for Milner to dine with him before he went off at 8.30 p.m. to Glasgow, in order that he might discuss the proposal with him. I suspect Milner was unresponsive as he is a very cautious man. Still I am in a somewhat unsettled frame of mind about it all. . . .

July 3rd. As I anticipated Ll. G. sent for me immediately on his return to tell me of his conversations with Beatty. He also told me of his talk with Milner about the question of First Lord. Milner had said exactly what I told Ll. George he would say, namely that I was practically irreplaceable at the War Cabinet; that I should no doubt be quite an effective First Lord; but that the public would not understand the appointment. Ll. G. had evidently cooled on the idea and was for Geddes. But he was hot for getting rid of Jellicoe.

The sequel was not very long in coming.

'*July 6th.* It has been decided that Eric Geddes is to be First Lord. Ll. George has offered it to him and he told me on the telephone he had accepted.

Carson resigned on July 19th and Geddes was sworn in and kissed hands as First Lord on July 20th. Geddes took a long time to settle down. It was not a post that he took to readily and at first he was inclined to be impatient, restless and suspicious of outside interference, but from then on things at the Admiralty tended to improve. Losses from submarine attack were being reduced and by the end of the year had been approximately halved as compared with the preceding period. The First Lord ought to have been satisfied but he remained rather restless; the real trouble was that both he and Lloyd George were still dissatisfied with the First Sea Lord. The situation remained

unsatisfactory for a time, but, on December 27th, Jellicoe resigned and was succeeded by Wemyss as First Sea Lord and Chief of the Naval Staff.

Undoubtedly Jellicoe was one of the great figures of the war. In the eyes of the Ministers who exercised the Supreme Control his worst defect was his apparent pessimism. There was, of course, ample reason for pessimism in the appalling losses from submarines, which were sufficient to daunt even the most sanguine. Moreover, Jellicoe for most of his occupancy of the post of First Sea Lord was grossly overworked. One evening, coming home late from a dinner to some Allied mission which he and I had both been forced to attend, he told me that he still had at least two hours' heavy work before him and that that was his nightly lot. This told on his health in time, following as it did on his long and anxious time as Commander-in-Chief of the Grand Fleet. Like many Service officers also he found the long hours spent with the War Committee and later on the War Cabinet trying. To this must be added a certain exasperation at the difficulty he encountered in getting all the material he required in time owing to the huge competing demands of the sister Service, to which he probably felt that undue priority was being given when the vital importance of the Navy was taken into consideration. I sometimes wondered whether his pessimism was not assumed in order to induce the politicians to make a still greater naval effort. However this may be, he was a great seaman, a great administrator and a great gentleman.

As for Eric Geddes, once the change of the First Sea Lord had been made, he settled down more comfortably:

March 2 (1918). . . . I forgot to mention that I had a talk last night with Eric Geddes. He is very cheerful about submarines and says that the Admiralty have absolutely certain, but very secret, information that they are destroying ten a month and he believes they will master this terrible menace in six months. They are having tremendous success with their mining policy (which I have advocated since the first days of the war), and have sunk or damaged fourteen German ships in the last day or two, upsetting the Huns dreadfully, so that they got up steam in their main fleet.

CHAPTER LXIV

THE IMPERIAL WAR CABINET, 1917

'The outstanding event of the year in the sphere of
Imperial affairs was the inauguration of the Imperial War
Cabinet.' (War Cabinet Report for 1917, p. 5.)

WITHIN nine days of assuming office on December 19, 1916, Lloyd
George, largely on Milner's initiative, informed the House of Commons
that the Government proposed to summon an Imperial Conference at
which the whole position would be put before the representatives of the
Dominions, and to take counsel with them on future action. Lloyd
George had in his mind something differing somewhat from the pre-
war Imperial Conferences. He believed that the representatives of the
Dominions had been far more impressed by the secret meetings of the
Committee of Imperial Defence held *in camera* in 1911, at which the
whole situation on foreign policy and defence had been disclosed without reserve, than by the ordinary sessions of the Imperial Conference,
at which a certain formality and reticence had to be observed owing to
the publicity given to the proceedings. He wished the new conference
to resemble the former rather than the latter. Moreover, the Prime
Minister and his War Cabinet shared Austen Chamberlain's view that
the efforts made by India rendered it essential that India should be
represented. There were difficulties about both these proposals. The
Imperial Conference had a regular constitution, which made no provision for these meetings *in camera* and did not include India in its
membership. The difficulty was surmounted by inviting the representatives to attend a series of special and continuous meetings of the War
Cabinet. For the purposes of these meetings the Prime Ministers of the
Dominions were to be members of the War Cabinet. The object was to
consider urgent questions affecting the prosecution of the war, the
possible conditions on which, with the agreement of our Allies, we
could assent to its termination, and the problems which would then
immediately arise. India was to be represented by the Secretary of
State, with the assistance of three assessors—Meston, Sinha and the
Maharaja of Bikaner. Massey, New Zealand's Prime Minister, and
Joseph Ward, the leader of the other party in the New Zealand fusion
Government, were already in England when this decision was taken
and agreed at once to postpone their departure. Borden and Perley

represented Canada, Smuts South Africa and Morris Newfoundland. To everyone's regret Australia was unrepresented. Hughes found it impossible to attend in the political conditions then prevailing in the Commonwealth; one of his difficulties was the Irish attitude towards the war as a result of the absence of a settlement of the Irish question which had important reactions in the Commonwealth; this was undoubtedly among the reasons which led the War Cabinet to make great efforts to solve it.

It was with some dismay that it gradually dawned upon me that I was expected to do most of the preliminary organization of this Imperial gathering. On top of the heavy work of creating the machinery of the new War Cabinet Secretariat, training on my new assistants, attending several meetings a day, conducting single-handed the secretarial work at all the more secret discussions, attending with Lloyd George and acting as secretary to many inter-ally conferences at home and abroad, preparing Memoranda, notes for speeches and generally dancing attendance on the Prime Minister—on top of all this the preparatory work of the Imperial meetings was a heavy burden. Fortunately I had in Leo Amery an invaluable assistant on this side of my activities. Milner had brought him to me. At first I felt some doubt about adding another M.P. to the staff as their outside contacts and independent methods did not always fit in to the official machine. So it was at first with Amery, but he soon adapted himself to the new conditions. He proved a very loyal colleague and friend, and in this particular work with the Dominions his zeal, energy and knowledge were invaluable.

March 1st. Much trouble in the afternoon about the Dominion Premiers who are to attend tomorrow's Cabinet meeting. Massey and Ward are the heads of a Government formed by the fusion rather than the coalition of the two main parties. Massey has insisted that Ward must be invited to all meetings attended by himself; otherwise Ward will go home and if he does Massey will have to go too; otherwise Ward will upset him. In fact they are a sort of political Siamese twins. . . . So both had to be invited. But then steps in Borden and says that, if New Zealand is to have two representatives, he must also have two—and no doubt the others will follow suit which raises the number to an unwieldy extent. . . . Lloyd George decided the whole caboodle must be asked but was very bored.

This refers only to preliminary meetings of the ordinary War Cabinet to which those representatives of the Dominions and India, who had already arrived, were invited from time to time to justify their presence in England. These meetings, however, were not very numerous, as the

representatives seized the opportunity to visit their contingents in France or training in the United Kingdom. The actual organization of the conference was decided in February on the basis of a Memorandum I submitted to the War Cabinet,[1] one result of which was that the fullest possible information was prepared for the Empire representatives by Government Departments.

I had originally supposed that the secretarial work of the conference would devolve upon the Colonial Office, who maintained a special branch to serve as the permanent Secretariat of the Imperial Conference and to deal generally with Dominions business. When it was decided, however, that the conference was to be an Imperial War Cabinet it became clear that this work must be added to our other duties at 2 Whitehall Gardens. All the strings of the War Cabinet were there already. Although the original basis of the meetings had been to co-ordinate and, if possible, increase the Empire's effort, it soon became clear that they would also have to deal to a large extent with the complex war situation which was being handled from day to day by the War Cabinet. This created a situation between the Colonial Office and myself which contained elements of possible friction but, owing to the tact and goodwill of Fiddes and Lambert, the Permanent Under-Secretary and the head of the Dominions branch, all trouble was avoided. It was arranged that Walter Long should be present at every meeting of the Imperial War Cabinet, accompanied by Lambert, and all post-war business other than terms of peace was remitted to a special War Conference, meeting at the Colonial Office, presided over by Long, with Lambert as secretary. I had the right to attend this conference in person or by deputy. All was, therefore, satisfactorily arranged. We had not yet risen to the level of the Imperial Secretariat, which we inaugurated at the Peace Conference and which became so useful a feature of the post-war Imperial Conferences. For me, however, this was a beginning of a long era of work as secretary of Imperial Conferences, a branch of work which, though originally undertaken with reluctance and some irritability owing to my overwhelming responsibilities, I came in time more and more to appreciate and which for twenty-two years brought me on to terms of intimate friendship with most of the great figures of the day in all the Dominions.

March 18th (Sunday). . . . On Wednesday evening (March 14th) I dined with Milner to meet Smuts, Massey, Joseph Ward, Hythe and Amery. I sat

---

[1] Published in *War Memoirs*, IV, App. B to c. 5, p. 1786.

Y*

next to Smuts, whom I got on with first-rate. After dinner they discussed closer Imperial co-operation; Massey and Ward all for it . . . ; Smuts most reluctant to discuss it at all, and, I thought, very suspicious of Milner. Rather an interesting evening.

March 19th. Lloyd George sent for me in the morning with intent to upset the whole of the Agenda and arrangements for the Imperial War Cabinets, which had been so carefully worked out by Milner, Curzon, Austen Chamberlain, Walter Long, Amery and myself. I resisted strenuously after consulting Milner on the telephone, and was eventually fairly successful in securing adherence. . . . In the evening I dined with Hythe to meet Massey, an old Liberal M.P. named MacDonald, Stewart the Public Trustee, and one or two others. Great talk about Imperial Federation and much argument whether it should take the form of an Imperial Parliament or not.

I was, of course, at that time a novice in these great questions of the constitutional relations of the Empire, and it was interesting to hear them discussed by authorities like Milner and Massey. As the result of pre-war experience at the meetings of the Committee of Imperial Defence in 1911 and 1912 my instincts favoured something savouring of an Imperial Cabinet and the Committee of Imperial Defence rather than an Imperial Parliament.

The way the title 'Imperial War Cabinet' came to be used for these meetings was rather fortuitous. The original invitation was addressed to the Prime Ministers of the Dominions, who were bidden to attend a series of special meetings of the War Cabinet. Nothing was said about the title of the meetings. Almost immediately after it was decided that India should also be invited, and the Secretary of State for India was to be the principal representative. Although Austen Chamberlain was not then a member of the War Cabinet, no breach was involved of the idea of confining the meetings to Prime Ministers and Members of the War Cabinet, since he was to represent India and not the British Government. A technical breach, however, was made when Botha sent Smuts to represent him; also to meet the difficulty of New Zealand's dual representation, the various Prime Ministers and senior delegates had to be allowed to bring one or more colleagues with them if they so desired. When a few days before the opening of the meetings I was instructed to prepare the draft Agenda for the consideration of the War Cabinet, the question of the title was still unsettled and I gave the draft the heading, 'Provisional Agenda for the Imperial War Cabinet'. Lloyd George approved; no objection was raised in any quarter and the title remained for the rest of the war.

It was not until March 20th that the formal meetings were opened. One of the first acts of the Empire statesmen was to send a telegram to Hughes expressing regret at the absence of himself or any representative of Australia. The start of the first meeting was not particularly favourable.

March 20th. The first of the Imperial War Cabinets was held today. It nearly began with a fiasco as X, my assistant secretary,[1] whom I had especially warned to be there early, arrived late with the cards showing people where to sit, with the result that for a minute or two the room was crowded with a welter of Dominions Prime Ministers, British Ministers and Indian Maharajahs, who could not find their seats, and it took some little time to restore order. Next, Lloyd George, when all were arranged, turned round to me and said 'Where are the Staff and the First Sea Lord?' I then reminded him that by a decision of the previous day they were not to be invited. None the less he insisted on their being brought over and crammed into my already closely packed table.

Lloyd George was, of course, right, in view of the title 'Imperial War Conference', to bring in Jellicoe and Robertson at the start of these meetings, even though it involved reversing a previous decision.

From this time onwards until the adjournment on May 2nd the general plan was that the Imperial War Cabinet should meet normally three times a week, namely on Tuesday and Thursday mornings and on Friday afternoons. This left Mondays, Tuesday and Thursday afternoons, Friday mornings and the whole of Saturday and Sunday for meetings of the Imperial War Conference, Committees of the Imperial War Cabinet, and for the ordinary work of the War Cabinet, which was very heavy. This scheme, however, had frequently to be interrupted by other pressing business such as Lloyd George's visit to St. Jean de Maurienne and Paris (April 18th–21st), his inquiry into the Admiralty and the preoccupations of the War Cabinet with urgent matters arising out of submarine losses. I found it extraordinarily difficult to work out and stick to any kind of programme.

The Imperial War Cabinet began,[2] as many later Imperial Conferences have begun, by listening to statements by the British Ministers concerned on the different aspects of the war situation, foreign policy, etc. Each overseas representative contributed an account of the war effort of his own nation, what more it was hoped to accomplish, and what special difficulties had to be surmounted. From the general the

---

[1] Not Leo Amery.
[2] A more detailed account will be found in *War Memoirs*, IV, p. 1727. *sq.*

Imperial War Cabinet soon passed to the particular, and questions such as the size of contingents, man-power, munitions and war material of all kinds, shipbuilding, measures for economizing shipping and releasing it for war purposes and so forth were discussed in detail with our own experts. In addition a good deal of attention was devoted to our war aims and possible and acceptable terms of peace. On the latter subject two very important committees were set up, one under Curzon's chairmanship to consider territorial desiderata, the other under Milner's to examine economic and other branches of peace terms, including such subjects as indemnities and reparations, limitation of armaments, League of Nations, etc. The reports of these committees were discussed at length in the full Imperial War Cabinet. As a result, the conclusion reached was that the policy of the Empire should have the following ends in view:

1. The re-establishment of liberty and public right in Europe and on the high seas, the settlement of the political boundaries of Europe in accordance with the wishes of its peoples, and the liberation of the oppressed nationalities of the Turkish Empire from the Turkish yoke.

2. The security and integrity of the Empire and of the nations of which it is composed.

3. The framing of measures for the preservation of lasting peace in concert with our Allies.

Meanwhile the Imperial War Conference at the Colonial Office had done much good work, particularly in the field of post-war problems.

When the Imperial War Cabinet terminated its meetings there was a strong and unanimous view that the experiment had been a great success. The representatives of the Dominions and India got a first-hand view of the magnitude and complexity of the task of the British Government such as they could have obtained by no other means. The representatives of the British Government learned more of the magnificent spirit and the magnitude of the effort of the Dominions than they could have derived from any number of telegrams and despatches. The summoning of the Dominions and India to share in the Supreme Command met the growing national consciousness of all the self-governing parts of the Empire, and provided a stimulus and tonic to their peoples. The great drain on the time and energy of the British Ministers, and the inconvenience to the overseas representatives in their prolonged absence from home and the dangers which they ran in passing through seas infested with submarines were felt to have been well

worth while. In spite of the difficult situation in which these meetings took place, there was a note of sober confidence and fixed determination to see the thing through which was highly reassuring. No one could foretell what effect the Imperial War Cabinet was to have on the future of Imperial relations, but there was a general recognition that it marked a great change, that the change was wholly for the better and that the Imperial War Cabinet should reassemble within a year.

CHAPTER LXV

STRAIN

'A man's strength has its limits.' (TOLSTOI, *Anna Karenina*, Part V, c. 22.)

In order to deal adequately with such great issues as I have described it is unavoidable to treat them separately; but, for a proper comprehension of the work of the Supreme Command, it is necessary to bear in mind that many of them were being considered concurrently, and that they were interacting upon one another. To complete the picture it is also necessary to appreciate that, in addition to these major problems, there were a host of other problems individually of secondary importance but collectively imposing a considerable burden upon the members of the War Cabinet and sometimes involving political issues affecting the very existence of the Government.

From the very first there was a great deal of criticism of the new Cabinet system. In these early days, while the War Cabinet and its Secretariat were getting into their stride, there was considerable justification for it. My own diary is full of complaints of the unbusinesslike methods of the Prime Minister and War Cabinet. Maybe I was living in a glass house myself and had no right to throw stones! The critics were by no means confined to outside opponents of the Government, but were to be found among Ministers, more especially those who were not members of the War Cabinet.

February 15th. In the morning I had a talk with Walter Long at the Colonial Office. I found him in a very disgruntled state, complaining much of the new War Cabinet system, which he says is unworkable. . . .

Some of the senior civil servants also, and especially those who had worked for years with the former régime, were inclined, and not unnaturally, to sneer at the rough and ready methods of the new War Cabinet Secretariat in this early stage, when we were short of trained staff of all ranks and working in conditions of great discomfort in buildings that were being altered to meet a heavy expansion of personnel. This influenced their subordinates and became the gossip of the clubs, whence it soon passed into Parliament itself.

The House of Commons was not Lloyd George's House but one that he had inherited from his predecessor. The Liberal Party to which

Lloyd George belonged still had a majority, but was hopelessly divided between the two leaders, and Lloyd George was dependent upon the support of the Conservative Party. In these circumstances it is not surprising that the House was difficult to manage. The situation was not eased by the working arrangement under which Bonar Law acted as the Leader of the House of Commons and Lloyd George appeared only on the more important occasions. For the conduct of business in those hectic times this arrangement was essential, but it was not popular with Members.

Some of the questions asked in Parliament were so indiscreet that in February 1917 the War Cabinet decided to approach the Leader of the Opposition and the Speaker with a view to asking the House of Commons to give discretionary power to the Speaker to control them. They also considered making it an offence to publish questions before they appeared on the order paper. Nothing seems to have come of these proposals and eventually the War Cabinet decided that the best way to come to terms with Parliament was to hold a secret session, which took place on May 19th. This cleared the air for a time. Recourse was had to the same expedient after the big daylight air raid on London on July 7th, which made a great stir. The plan of a secret session is one which has its uses in time of war but should not be resorted to too often; once the novelty has worn off its efficacy is largely lost.

The Press, and more particularly the less responsible organs, were also a source of serious preoccupation both to the Government as a whole and to the naval and military authorities in particular. The discretion which had been observed in the early days of the war had long since disappeared from the offices of the more sensational newspapers. The Press Bureau could not exercise an effective censorship. Prosecution had been resorted to once or twice without very beneficial results. In March 1917 one of the weeklies, whose depressing articles had been quoted for propaganda purposes by the German wireless news service, was prohibited from export, a restriction which had been applied by the previous Government to certain extreme and obscure papers. In May, Northcliffe, some of whose newspapers were rather over-critical, was appointed Head of the British War Mission in the United States of America. No one doubted Northcliffe's patriotism. No one questioned his ability. By this masterstroke Lloyd George harnessed this restless and turbulent spirit, and diverted his inexhaustible energies from a direction where they were doing harm to one where they would strengthen our war effort. It was a good minor

example of the Prime Minister's amazing versatility in drawing good out of evil.

During this period I myself was subjected to Press criticism for the first time in the war:

March 12th. At the office they brought to my notice a scurrilous attack on me in . . . the *National News.*[1] The attack itself is contemptible and has no basis of fact, being all built up on a short reference to Roche's Minority Report of the Dardanelles Commission, and I propose to ignore it. But it is annoying as an indication that I have somewhere an enemy who seeks to do me mischief.

The Irish question was another subject of grave concern to the War Cabinet and involved them in prolonged discussions and negotiations which belong to the political history of the Irish question with which happily we are not concerned; it is sufficient to note how great a drain this subject made on the time and energy of the War Cabinet.

By the middle of May, when for several weeks the work of the Imperial War Cabinet had been superimposed on that of the War Cabinet, all concerned were considerably exhausted.

May 14th. Was kept awake all night with excruciating toothache. Had tooth out with gas in the morning. Was too rotten to take part in the War Cabinet, so came home to bed. First War Cabinet or War Committee I have missed owing to ill-health since beginning of war. Feverish attack in evening. Lloyd George strongly urged me to stay away for a few days.

May 17th. . . . In the evening I called to see Lloyd George about next day's meeting, and to my surprise he announced his intention of taking a complete rest until Monday, and in spite of my remonstrances *ordered* me to do ditto. In fact he said that he wanted the whole War Cabinet to go into 'rest camp' in order to freshen up. . . .

But the overworked Prime Minister did not get his holiday, as he had to come up to Town from the country, where he had gone to rest, in order to settle a labour dispute, and until the end of the month the pressure continued as great as ever.

One result of this general exhaustion of the nation's principal organ of decision was that the business of the War Cabinet was falling into arrears. This threatened to produce a situation similar to that which had brought about the downfall of the previous Government. I was so disturbed at the position that I wrote a Memorandum on the subject which

---

[1] A short-lived Sunday newspaper.

Lloyd George instructed me to circulate to his colleagues, and of which
I give the substance:

As Secretary of the War Cabinet I feel bound to call attention to the fact
that the business of the War Cabinet has for some time been seriously in
arrears. At one time the War Cabinet practically caught up all arrears of
work, but latterly they have been accumulating rather alarmingly. . . .

The secretary prepares at the end of each week a list of subjects awaiting
consideration, and this, kept daily and indeed hourly up to date, serves as a
basis for drawing up the Agenda Papers for the following week. The
Immediate List issued on May 6th only contained fourteen subjects. The list
for the present week contains twenty-five subjects; that for the previous week
contained twenty-two subjects.

Questions of some considerable importance have been delayed rather
seriously, and there are a number of minor questions which require to be
dealt with. . . .

. . . For the last few weeks the Weekly List has been scrutinized by the
secretary very carefully, and efforts have been made to get many of the questions dealt with outside the War Cabinet. There is undoubtedly a tendency
on the part of departments to throw decisions on to the War Cabinet which
are well within the competence of departments themselves and could be
arrived at in consultation with other departments without troubling the War
Cabinet. By these (latter) means the War Cabinet has been relieved of a considerable mass of minor business which ought not to engage their attention at
all, and the process is being continued. Many cases occur, however, in which
the departments do not feel justified in acting without a Cabinet decision,
and questions have sometimes been brought before the Cabinet which, in my
personal opinion, could be settled·outside.

'I have been very carefully considering the best method of alleviating this
congestion, and have had the matter constantly in mind during the meetings
of the War Cabinet. The conclusion I have come to is that the accumulation
arises largely owing to the order in which the business of the Cabinet is conducted. I have observed that the daily statements and the discussions which
arise therefrom quite commonly occupy the first hour of the Cabinet meeting. Very often the daily statements give rise to a discussion on some great
question of policy, and important matters on the Agenda Paper are squeezed
out.

After a long list of examples and comments on expedients already tried
the note ended:

The solution which I would submit for the consideration of War Cabinet
is that in future the statements by the naval, military, and foreign political
advisers of the Government should not take place at the beginning of the

meeting but an hour or so later. The first half-hour, and, indeed, the first hour when there are accumulations of work, should be devoted to questions on the Agenda Paper which are not quite of the first importance. Then would come the statements on naval, military and political matters, which would immediately be followed by a discussion of some one great question of policy, such as is at all times before the War Cabinet. Discussions of these larger questions would, when necessary, be continued in the afternoon. It is suggested that it would not be necessary for the whole of the War Cabinet invariably to attend at the beginning of the meeting for the less important questions, but arrangements would have to be made to ensure that at least two Ministers were present. When the accumulation of work is heavy, as at present, the meeting might normally begin at 11 o'clock, but once arrears had been caught up it is unlikely that this would be necessary more than once or twice a week.

I am confident that by means of this slight alteration in the procedure of the War Cabinet a very great improvement would be effected almost immediately in the transaction of business. I am the more assured of this that on days when the usual statements are not given at the beginning of a meeting the War Cabinet invariably gets through its Agenda Paper and usually well before the ordinary time of adjournment.

The circulation of this downright document put the War Cabinet on its mettle and in two days the arrears were cleared off with a view to a much needed Friday to Monday rest. This time we really did get a holiday—in my case a 'busman's' one.

June 1st. Spent a very busy morning dealing with office business of all kinds. In the afternoon I went down by special train with Robertson, Macdonogh, and some railway men—Guy Granet, Sam Fay and Collard—to Richboro', a small port close to Sandwich, which is being developed with marvellous energy and efficiency for cross-Channel ferries and barge traffic. The remarkable thing is that, whereas the Admiralty always said that the barges would sink, they have proved perfectly seaworthy in all weathers.

Thereafter in spite of the heavy work connected with the Flanders offensive, various tentative peace soundings, the distracting episode of the Mesopotamia Commission report, and other matters, the situation improved and I noted:

August 2nd. At the meeting this morning the War Cabinet were actually abreast of their work. I felt like 'Pilgrim relieved of his burden' and as elated as if we had won the war. It is true that it has been done largely by delegating particular subjects to particular Members, in fact by asking some-one else to settle things; but the fact remains that the system I invented for

picking up arrears has succeeded. I actually got away at about 6 p.m. and went home to Limpsfield.

By this date (August 2nd) the War Cabinet had held more than 200 meetings since it came into existence—200 meetings in 235 days, without counting the Imperial War Cabinet, the War Policy Committee, or the many meetings at home and abroad with our Allies. Has any group of men engaged in a great enterprise ever beaten that record?

CHAPTER LXVI

THE WAR POLICY COMMITTEE, 1917

'To fix and limit the objects to be obtained by the war,
and to advise the monarch in respect of these, is and
remains during the war just as before it a political
function, and the manner in which these questions are
solved cannot be without great influence on the method
of conducting the war.' (BISMARCK, *Intentions and
Reminiscences*, edited by A. J. Butler, II, p. 105.)

THE prolonged controversy between the 'eastern' and the 'western'
schools of thought which began with the Gallipoli campaign and has
continued more or less ever since, reached its point of greatest intensity
in the deliberations before the battle of Flanders. The supporters of the
western theory, notwithstanding the carnage on the Somme and
Nivelle's failure, still clung tenaciously to the belief that the war could
be won in France and Flanders and only there. By this time they had
come to realize that the war had become one of attrition, but they
claimed that here alone was it possible to kill Germans, and, if we could
kill enough, the main enemy would collapse and the war would end.
When the war was over they maintained that it was the ceaseless
hammering on the Somme and in Flanders, combined with the earlier
attacks of the French Army, which had brought the victory. Those of
the opposite school held equally firmly to their own theory of the way
to win the war. They regarded the battles that had taken place up to
midsummer of 1917 as mere slogging matches, devoid of all science and
resource. They were able to point to the effect of this policy on France,
whose man-power was so depleted and army so shattered by the efforts
of previous years, culminating in Nivelle's failure, that by August her
Government and generals felt that for the time being their army was
no longer fit to embark on an aggressive operation on the grand scale.
If the British Empire was to pursue this discredited policy for another
season, the critics maintained, it was certain that before 1918 we should
find ourselves, like France, bleeding to death and unable to sustain the
struggle in its decisive stages. In May, we had asked the question—
'France, hast thou yet more blood to cast away?',[1] and though her
statesmen and generals had promised to go on fighting, it had become

[1] Shakespeare, *King John*, Act ii, sc. 2.

clear in the next few weeks that no big effort could be expected of them. Reinforced by these considerations the opponents of the extreme 'western' school made in June and July their greatest effort to secure the adoption of a different strategy. Lloyd George still held to his theory of 'knocking away props'—Austria, Bulgaria and Turkey. Once they were eliminated, which he claimed to be the easier task, the full strength of the Allies could be deployed against Germany in conditions where they would have more elbow room and the citadel of the Central Powers could be stormed.

It has been suggested in some quarters that the civilian War Cabinet had no business to interest themselves in these military matters; that these were questions for soldiers, in which politicians ought not to interfere. This theory will not stand a moment's examination. The War Cabinet were responsible to Parliament, and through Parliament to the nation as a whole for the direction of the national war effort—naval, military, political and economic. They were bound to satisfy themselves that the strategical plans of their military advisers were the best possible for the defeat of the enemy, and would not make so great a drain on the resources of the nation as to reduce us to impotence before our national aim had been accomplished. This was particularly important in 1917, when the strain was already severe. They were entitled also to invite the views of their military advisers on alternative suggestions. Moreover, a number of new factors had just entered into the situation, some political, some military, but all affecting the military problem, which rendered desirable a comprehensive review of the situation as a whole. Among these new factors perhaps the most important was the increasing chaos in Russia, which was rapidly approaching a stage when that country could no longer be counted on to play an effective part in the war. Equally ominous was the accumulating evidence that France was and for some time would be unable to pull her full weight.

June 8th. The new feature in the situation today is that Henry Wilson came to the War Cabinet this morning to warn us that the French would not stick it much longer, and Pétain had to fail in his promise to carry out an offensive on the 10th in support of Haig's attack on the Messines Ridge. This report is confirmed more or less by Esher, and has made us all very anxious.

Another new factor was that Austria was getting tired of the war and inclining towards a separate peace.[1] This raised in Lloyd George's mind the question whether the time had not come to put in operation the plan

[1] *vide infra*, p. 735.

he had urged in January at the Rome Conference for concentrating the main efforts of the Allies on the Italian Front against Austria. Although the plan had then been remitted for study to the military advisers, and had fallen into the background during Nivelle's battle, Lloyd George had not allowed it to be forgotten. Bissolati, who shared the Prime Minister's views on this question, had visited London, and even attended a meeting of the War Cabinet on March 1st, when the question had been discussed and remitted to Robertson and Cadorna for further consideration. Robertson had visited the Italian General Headquarters from March 22nd to March 24th, but was not encouraged as the result of his visit to fall in with Lloyd George's ideas. On the contrary, he had formed so low an opinion of the Italian High Command, mainly owing to the age of some of the generals, that tactful representations had been made by the Foreign Office to the Italian Government on the subject. This had been taken in good part, and some of the older generals had been relieved of their commands. These exchanges with the Italian civil and military authorities had elicited that they were in constant anxiety about the possibility of an attack on their flank from the Trentino (as actually did occur in October), which would gravely imperil their main army on the Carso. In April forty British 6-inch howitzers (ten batteries) had been sent to Italy and had arrived in time to take part in the successful attack on the Carso. A little later thirty-five French heavy guns were sent. In addition arrangements had been made for carrying out Lloyd George's suggestion at the Rome Conference for reinforcing the Italian Front with British and French divisions in case of emergency. The ground, therefore, had been well prepared for executing the Prime Minister's more ambitious projects, if he could persuade the British and Allied High Command to adopt them.

All these things were felt by the War Cabinet to require some special and more comprehensive investigation than was possible in their daily meetings at which so many immediate day-to-day problems had to be settled. On June 8th, therefore, just after their brief 'holiday', they decided to set up a small committee for the purpose of reviewing our war policy as a whole.

The War Policy Committee consisted of Lloyd George, Curzon, Milner, and Smuts (who had just become a member of the War Cabinet), but Bonar Law was kept in the closest touch with their work and was virtually a member. I was the secretary, and I had to carry out this task without any assistance. The Committee had to conduct its investigations without interfering with the daily meetings of the War

Cabinet, where day-to-day decisions had to be taken over a vast field. The new Committee, therefore, used to meet at an early hour and twice the members dined together and continued their deliberations late into the night.[1] The Committee managed to hold sixteen meetings between June 8th and June 20th when the results of the inquiry were laid before a full meeting of the War Cabinet, and the final conclusions were reached. Robertson, Haig, Jellicoe, Webb Gilman, Delmé Radcliffe, and Guy Granet were heard as witnesses and Robertson was present at many of the discussions. I was charged with collecting a large number of reports and preparing summaries; Smuts was good enough to associate himself with me in this heavy task, involving interviews with a very large number of officials.

The common gibe against governments is that they have no policy. Even before this inquiry, however, the policy of the War Cabinet was quite clearly defined. Its object was to secure victory. The Supreme Command never wavered in its belief that the foundation of victory was sea-power. Two primary policies of the Government, therefore, which never varied throughout the war, were to bring economic pressure to bear upon the enemy peoples so as to compel their Governments to come to terms, and to resist the economic pressure applied by the enemy at sea so that we might carry on the struggle in the other elements. Hence, although the immediate object of the inquiry was to decide on the military policy to be adopted for the remainder of 1917, the War Policy Committee approached the problem from the widest aspect, and took the opportunity to review the whole of the machinery for bringing pressure to bear on the enemy.

Broadly speaking, however, the Committee confirmed our naval and blockade policy in all its aspects. The only point on which they at first felt a certain amount of doubt was whether the Navy was not adopting rather too passive a role. In particular they pressed the Admiralty hard whether an intensive bombardment of the German nests of submarines and destroyers at Zeebrugge and Ostend could not be undertaken, as, if these objectives could be attacked by naval means, the military problem would be simplified. It was difficult to use battleships for the purpose as, owing to the numerous shoals and the danger from minefields, they could only fire at very long range. The monitors, which had been used occasionally for this purpose, were fragile, unarmoured ships, which had to keep out of effective range from the coast defence guns,

[1] Meetings of the War Cabinet and its Committees were very rarely held after dinner. Lloyd George believed in keeping his team fit.

and the coincidence of conditions of visibility, tide, etc., favourable to their employment and for their ancillary aircraft only occurred at comparatively long intervals. Moreover, the available objectives, such as dock gates, pumping stations, etc., formed a very small target. The enemy's destroyers and submarines, during a bombardment, could retire by canal to Bruges where they were out of range. The Committee had to accept the Admiralty's technical objections but pressed the naval staff to study the possibility of offensive operations—a recommendation which was eventually given effect to by the famous Zeebrugge attack. The Admiralty were also urged to press on with the development of the convoy system.

The man-power position was, of course, an essential factor in assessing the military situation. Reports showed that, notwithstanding the adoption of compulsory service more than twelve months before, the monthly intake of recruits during 1917 had been far below the estimates, and was insufficient to make good the wastage involved in offensive operations. As a result the strength of the British Army in France in the middle of June was from 20,000 to 30,000 men below establishment. Before the middle of August, however, 150,000 men would become available, and Haig considered the situation sufficiently satisfactory to enable him to carry out his plans. The reason why the man-power estimates had failed to materialize was not due to an actual shortage of men of military age, but partly to the fact that many of them were engaged on work vital to the continuance of the war, such as munitions, coal, shipbuilding, transport, agriculture, etc., and partly also to the intense opposition which was offered to their withdrawal from those industries, which had resulted in strikes and had exercised an appreciable effect on the output of essential war material. Nevertheless lack of munitions was no longer a serious factor in the situation. Our Army was by this time firing a good deal more ammunition than the enemy, and in this respect the tables were turned as compared with 1915.

Although at the January Rome Conference Cadorna had at first shown but little enthusiasm for Lloyd George's plan of a great artillery concentration on his front, his ideas on the subject had gradually matured and he had now worked out the project in some detail. After the comparatively successful actions of the Italian Army at the tenth battle of the Isonzo (May 15th to June 8th), Cadorna had let Lloyd George know that he would welcome a reinforcement of 100 heavy guns (over and above the British and French artillery already referred to) with ample ammunition to enable him to exploit a favourable

situation. At the end of June the Russian Army, from which nothing had been expected, had achieved some gratifying successes, and this gave further encouragement to the idea of some co-ordinated effort against Austria, by Russia from the north and east and from the south by an Italian army reinforced with heavy artillery. The revised plan which Lloyd George brought before the War Policy Committee was based on a proposed concentration of three or four hundred British and/or French guns on the Isonzo front in support of the Italian Army with a view to dealing Austria a smashing blow. Cadorna believed that with his aid he could ensure the capture of Trieste, and he was supported in this view by the head of the British Military Mission with the Italian Army.

This plan had certain attractions. Austria was known to be war-weary and anxious for peace, but it was unlikely that she could surrender Trieste as one of the conditions of peace, and Italy certainly could not have taken less. It was felt that a severe defeat, involving the loss of Trieste and accompanied by heavy casualties, might provide the stimulus necessary for Austria to break with Germany and to agree to terms of peace acceptable to the Allies. If she did so, the consequences might well prove decisive. Bulgaria and Turkey, cut off from help from Germany, were not likely to delay long in making peace themselves. Germany would then be isolated. Large Allied forces would be released for concentration against and encirclement of Germany. The Dardanelles would be opened, enabling Russia to obtain war material and to supply wheat. The German submarines would be unable to maintain themselves in the Mediterranean, and, apart from the cessation of losses in this most dangerous area, the whole shipping situation would be immeasurably relieved. Moreover, one of the attractions of the scheme was that it would make no demand on shipping. Italian infantry in sufficient numbers and all the paraphernalia of the attacking army were on the spot, and the two lines of railway from France to Italy were believed to be sufficient for the transport of the British and French guns and their ammunition. The Italian Army at this stage of the war still had ample men and reserves; its combatant strength was estimated at about 1,770,000 men against Austria's 571,000 on that front. Italy was supposed to have reserves of 531,000 men, exclusive of 580,000 sick and wounded and 280,000 men in the 1900 class, compared with Austria's estimated total reserve of 865,000, which had to supply drafts also for an army of nearly half a million combatants on the Russian Front. The morale of the Italian soldiers was reported to be good. All accounts

agreed that their failure to achieve greater successes was due to lack of sufficient heavy artillery and ammunition. In the matter of field guns they were believed to be superior to their adversary (1,924 to 1,108), but of guns of 4·5-inch calibre and above they possessed only about 2,000 to Austria's 2,360. Above all, however, the Italians had not nearly enough ammunition to blast their way through the enemy's well-entrenched positions. Their attacks had to be carried out with a far smaller expenditure of ammunition than those of their British and French Allies. The British guns also were believed to be superior and to last better than the Italian or Austrian weapons. In these circumstances an advance sufficient to secure the capture of Trieste (already only about twelve miles from the Italian advanced positions) did not seem unreasonable, provided sufficient artillery was made available. Lloyd George and those of his colleagues who supported the plan felt that nowhere on the whole Allied front was there a section where so small an advance could realize such great results. They urged in addition that by adopting this plan we should be striking the enemy at his weakest instead of his strongest point.

Robertson and Haig and those who shared their views raised very powerful objections. If it was to our interest to make a separate peace with Austria, it was Germany's interest to prevent it. The withdrawal from France and Flanders of 300 heavy guns—nearly a quarter of our guns of above 6-inch calibre—would prevent us from continuing our offensive, and Germany would be able either to make an attack in force on the French, who for the moment were in a bad situation, or alternatively to release large forces to support Austria. How, it was asked, would the Italian troops fare if pitted against the redoubtable Germans? The Austrian lines in the Trentino were within twenty miles of the main communications of the Italian Army on the Isonzo—a point which had always aroused anxiety. The enemy's proper *riposte* to a really menacing assault on the Isonzo front was an advance through the Trentino, which would not only at once compel a suspension of the advance on the Isonzo front, but would place the whole Italian Army, including the Allied guns, in jeopardy. The result might well be to transfer the main campaign from France and Flanders to the Italian Front, where the strategical position, owing to the exposed northern flank, was unsound, and where the enemy (possessing five lines of railway against the two lines of the Allies from France into Italy) could concentrate a larger force than the Allies. All this proved prophetic in the light of after events. Robertson considered that there was no chance

of achieving a big success on the Isonzo unless a number of divisions, as well as artillery, were despatched. To mount an attack on the grand scale would be a matter of months, and it was uncertain whether the French railways were adequate for maintaining an army at so great a distance. He doubted if even an artillery concentration, much less a massing of divisions, could be effected without the enemy's knowledge. The Austrian position was one of great strength. Even if Trieste were captured he doubted whether Austria would make peace. The Allied armies would not constitute a serious threat until they were far advanced towards Vienna. Robertson stuck to the view he had always held, that the best military course was to defeat the strongest enemy, since that would bring with it the defeat of the weaker. Only if there was no reasonable chance of defeating the main enemy would it be justifiable to attempt to defeat the weaker, and only then if this were possible. To keep the Germans on our front it was necessary not only to fight but to fight hard, and that we could not do if we sent a large force to Italy. Haig was equally opposed to the Italian project. To divert part of our forces from the Western Front might lead to the collapse of France, and would discourage our own Army.

The plan officially put forward by Haig and supported by Robertson for an attack in Flanders—to which the Italian plan had been proposed by Lloyd George as a possible alternative—had been long maturing. Haig had had it in view practically from the moment he assumed the command, at any rate since January 1916. He had spoken of it to Joffre when discussing the offensive for 1916. The French Commander-in-Chief had expressed approval and intimated his willingness to co-operate. In the spring Rawlinson had been ordered to report on the project. Flanders had come to be regarded as a possible alternative to the offensive on the Somme, if for any reason the latter plan should prove impracticable. In a word, it had long been in the programme. In November 1916 the War Committee under Asquith's presidency had adopted a resolution to the effect that there was no operation of war to which they would attach greater importance than the successful occupation, or at least the deprivation to the enemy, of Ostend and especially Zeebrugge. From that time on Haig had been quietly completing and preparing his plans for the execution of this project. For various reasons he had been unable to put it into execution. First he had been compelled to conform his plans to Nivelle's grandiose scheme. The success which the British Army had achieved in their part of the Nivelle plan had led to a prolongation of the operations in the vicinity of Arras and

Bullecourt. On May 4 and 5, 1917, at a conference in Paris, the British and French Governments had agreed to continue the offensive on the Western Front, and to devote the whole of their forces to this purpose. On this occasion the following principles had been laid down in concert by Pétain, Nivelle, Haig and Robertson:

> It is no longer a question of aiming at breaking through the enemy's front and aiming at distant objectives. It is now a question of wearing down and exhausting the enemy's resistance and if and when this is achieved, to exploit it to the fullest possible extent.

In other words, the British and French Governments, on the recommendation of their responsible military advisers, had officially adopted the policy of a war of attrition.

Owing to the temporary weakness of the French Army Haig had now taken the lead in the main offensive operations against the enemy, and on June 7th, within three weeks of the termination of the battle of Bullecourt (May 17th), had put in hand the first part of his plan for clearing the Flanders coast. This first step, the capture of the Messines ridge, was designed to secure the right flank of his army in its advance. The battle had been opened by the explosion of a number of mines, which for many months had been driven far into the enemy's position, and the whole plan had been carried out successfully within a brief period—one of the neatest and cleanest pieces of work accomplished during the first four years of the war. Both Lloyd George and I, he at Walton Heath and I at Limpsfield, had awakened at the hour the battle was to start in the belief that we heard the explosion of the great mines. Perhaps it was imagination due to foreknowledge of what was to happen, and in my case to the belief that I had been the first person to suggest the adaptation to modern conditions of this ancient method of siege warfare. However this may be, the roar of guns at dawn on that still summer morning was louder in my Surrey garden than on any occasion in the war. At Messines Haig had achieved a big success and was able to confront the War Policy Committee with a happy earnest of his proposed plans.

Robertson, who realized the War Cabinet's objections to undertaking another exhausting operation of the Somme type, made it clear that he did not advocate spending our last man and our last round of ammunition in an attempt to clear the Flanders coast if the opposition encountered showed that the attempt would involve disproportionate loss. The process of wearing down the enemy was to be pursued in a

direction which, if the enemy weakened, would be exploited to great advantage, but which would enable us to modify our operations if the situation demanded it.

The Flanders plan was claimed by its authors to possess great strategical advantages from a naval, military and air point of view. The Admiralty had always insisted very strongly on the importance of ejecting the enemy from Ostend and Zeebrugge. As early as January 1915 they had warmly supported French's plans for this purpose and now, after two and a half years' experience of the difficulties of holding the Channel, they were of the same opinion. Barrages of mines and nets had been laid in profusion in these narrow seas, but mainly owing to the great rise and fall of the tide it had not been found possible to bring to an end the harassing operations of the enemy's submarines. These were small in size and probably did not exceed ten in number. Several were of the minelaying type, and they made the Channel a constant danger to patrols and transports, particularly in winter, when continuous bad weather made minesweeping more than usually dangerous; even the Prime Minister's frequent cross-Channel passages had as a rule to take place at night. But the enemy's destroyers were considered to be a greater danger even than his submarines. They provided a constant menace to the cross-Channel communications and had necessitated the provision of a regular convoy for the ships bringing food from Holland, which were important both from the point of view of our own food supply and from that of preventing the sale of the Dutch produce to Germany. Up to now the enemy's destroyers had not been very enterprising. If, instead of carrying out desultory raids in small numbers, they were to reserve themselves for unexpected massed attacks, they would become very formidable. The Admiralty stated that, if the Belgian coast were not occupied by the Allies by the following winter, it would be necessary greatly to increase the strength of the Dover flotillas at the expense of other hard-pressed services, whereas the occupation of Zeebrugge and Ostend would release considerable forces for other sections of the anti-submarine campaign, where they were urgently needed. In fact, on one occasion Jellicoe stated that, unless we carried out Haig's plan successfully, we should not be able to continue the war in 1918 for lack of shipping.[1]

The military advantages claimed for the occupation of the Flanders coast were no less striking. Anything like a break in the enemy's front in this region would bring us to Ghent and Brussels, whence our Army

[1] *War Memoirs*, IV, p. 2162.

would threaten the main communications of the German Army which ran through bottlenecks north and south of the Ardennes. Even a partial success would render the important base port at Dunkirk immune from the long-range bombardment to which it had long been exposed, and might bring Ostend under our fire and render it useless to the enemy for naval purposes. An advance bringing the Roulers–Thourout railway within effective range of our guns would restrict the enemy's railway communications with the coast to the lines passing through Ghent and Bruges. A short further advance, bringing us within effective heavy gun range of Bruges, might secure the evacuation of the whole coast. Finally, the occupation of the Belgian coast would compel the enemy's aircraft to cross our lines in order to carry out raids on London and the south-eastern corner of England, which would greatly facilitate our defensive plans against this inconvenient though indecisive form of warfare.

Most of the earlier plans of the British High Command on the Western Front, and more particularly the battle of the Somme, had been criticized as lacking any proper strategical objective. This accusation at least could not be directed against Haig's latest conception. The only question was whether it offered a reasonable prospect of success, and it was mainly to this point that the War Policy Committee addressed themselves; they felt it was their duty to probe the plan to the bottom before taking their decision. There was, of course, no question of a 'breakthrough' such as had been hoped for in previous great offensives. The first step, already accomplished, was the capture of the Messines–Wytschaete ridge with the object of securing the right flank of the Army and ejecting the enemy from a position from which he could observe and harass the preparations for a further advance, as well as to improve our defensive position round Ypres. The next stages were designed in an ordered sequence so as to secure one after another the various low ridges—Passchendaele Ridge, Clerken Ridge, etc.— until Ostend was brought under fire. At the appropriate stage, i.e. after the occupation of Roulers, a division was to be landed on the coast in order to cut off the enemy in the coastal region, and for this operation elaborate naval and military preparations were made, though, for reasons of secrecy, no reference was made to the matter in the record of the proceedings of the War Policy Committee. In this manner the whole campaign was plotted in a series of consecutive operations, each of which could be prepared for methodically so that it could be put into operation the moment the previous stage was successfully completed.

The first doubt which assailed the War Policy Committee was whether the Allies possessed a sufficient margin of strength to bring the campaign to a successful conclusion. The combatant strength (rifles and sabres) of the Allies on the Western Front was estimated at 2,611,300 (1,127,300 British, 1,310,000 French, 131,000 Belgians, 25,000 Portuguese, 18,000 Russians) compared with 2,149,000 Germans. The Allied reserves were estimated at 830,000 (330,000 British and 500,000 French) against the German reserve of 1,000,000 for all fronts. The Allied superiority in combatant strength was felt to be set off to some extent by the lack of homogeneity in the composition of their armies. In field guns the Allies were believed to possess 9,126 to the German 4,556. But in heavy guns (4·5-inch howitzer and above) the Germans were believed to possess 7,520 to the Allies 6,614. For the heaviest guns of 5·9 inch and above the numbers were believed to be equal. Having regard to the weakness of the French Army in offensive power after its gruelling earlier in the year, and the despondency of the French people after the dashing of their hopes, and the uncertainty how far the co-operation of the French Army could be counted on, very grave doubts were entertained whether the margin of strength was sufficient.

The next criticism was the extent of the advance required in order to achieve any of the strategical objects of the attack. A total advance of no less than thirteen miles was required before even Ostend could be brought under long-range gun-fire, and a further considerable advance before Bruges could be bombarded. Judged by previous experience this was unattainable. In four months' fighting on the Somme the maximum depth of the advance did not exceed seven miles. But at that time a large French army had been co-operating on our right flank, and the enemy had been hard-pressed by the Russian armies which were trying to follow up Brussilov's victory on the Eastern Front. At Arras the maximum depth of the advance did not exceed six miles, although the main force of the enemy had been occupied in countering Nivelle's attack. Why, it was asked, could we hope to succeed in Flanders, when we should be confronted with the enemy's main forces, when but little French co-operation could be counted on, and when the pressure on the Eastern Front would, at best, be only moderate?

It was pointed out that, as soon as the attack began, the whole world would know what was our objective. Failure would produce loss of confidence everywhere and depression at home, particularly if accompanied by heavy losses as was certain to be the case. A good deal of emphasis was laid by the critics on the importance of not exhausting our

dwindling reserves of man-power before the United States could bring their strength to bear.

To all these criticisms Haig and Robertson were able to give a plausible reply. On the lack of a sufficient margin of strength it was urged that the German Army had greatly deteriorated. The establishment of German battalions had been reduced, and many companies were now reported to be only fifty to seventy strong, compared with an original establishment of 250. Divisions had been broken up for draft-finding and men of the 1919 class were already at the front. Their physique was visibly lower. The economic situation of the German Army was none too good, and the enemy only had thirteen fresh and thirty-five used divisions in reserve. Haig was more optimistic than the members of the War Cabinet about French co-operation. Pétain had promised active co-operation both on the left flank of our Army and by attacks elsewhere. On this point, however, the War Policy Committee felt that it would be necessary to put pressure on the French Government, if they decided to sanction the attack. Haig claimed that if the extent of the advance at the battles of Vimy and Messines had been limited, this had been because the scope of the operations had deliberately been restricted. Our intentions had been accomplished, and this was the best earnest of our capacity in the intended series of battles. As at Vimy and Messines the advance at each stage of the projected campaign was to be limited in scope. Moreover the plan was devised so as to limit casualties as much as possible. No attack would be opened until all the preparations were completed. If we did not attack the enemy, he would attack us, and in the end our losses would be greater. Neither Haig nor Robertson could, naturally, guarantee complete success, but, when asked to consider all the criticisms urged against the Flanders plan and to weigh it against the alternative of an attack on the Italian Front, they both stuck to their guns and advised the adoption of the former plan.

June 30th. For the last ten days I have been too desperately busy to write my diary at all. The heavy work of the Cabinet Committee on War Policy, which for reasons of secrecy I have had to work single-handed, often without even my shorthand clerk, has been an overwhelming burden on top of the War Cabinet work. Haig came over on the 19th and stayed for a week holding frequent conferences with the Committee on War Policy. There was a regular battle royal (conducted in the best possible spirit) between Lloyd George on the one hand and Robertson and Haig on the other. . . . On the evening of the 20th there was a dinner at Curzon's attended by the Prime

Alfred Milner in 1918

Minister, Milner, Smuts and myself, Bonar Law joining after dinner, when we adjourned to the terrace and thrashed the matter out until past midnight. It was a very interesting evening. All the week the controversy went on, but on Monday (June 25th), after the Committee had adjourned to give Robertson and Haig time to think it over, they adhered to their opinion and Lloyd George felt he could not press his amateur opinions and over-rule them, so he gave in, and Haig was authorized to continue his preparations. The final decision, however, was postponed until after a conference with the French, as Lloyd George declines to agree finally until assured that the French will do their bit by attacking simultaneously. A fortnight was left for this, during which Albert Thomas was to do his best to persuade the French Cabinet. All Saturday and Sunday I worked at the report, sitting up until nearly midnight each day.

A fortnight passed and still the intended Paris Conference did not take place. The War Cabinet was immersed meanwhile in the pre-posterous controversy over the Mesopotamia Commission's Report. Day after day the dismal argument went on, wasting the time of the Supreme Command and awakening such violent feelings as almost to occasion the dissolution of the War Cabinet. As the date for beginning the offensive was rapidly approaching a final decision became essential, and this was reached in the following circumstances:

July 16th. In the evening Lloyd George gave a dinner at 10 Downing Street to the War Policy Committee (Curzon, Milner, Smuts and self), Balfour and Carson being also guests. We went over much the same ground as at the last dinner at Curzon's, and the final decision was to allow Haig to begin his offensive, but not to allow it to degenerate into a drawn out, indecisive battle of the 'Somme' type. If this happened, it was to be stopped and the plan for an attack on the Italian Front would be tried.

July 18th. War Policy Committee in the morning, at which the conclusions agreed to at Monday's dinner were confirmed, and I was asked to write a report for circulation by Thursday evening (i.e. the very next evening). I said I could only do it by knocking off all other work. So from 4 p.m. until 9.15 p.m. I worked away at it, locking my door, refusing all visitors and telephone calls, the faithful Longhurst and Sylvester standing guard. Just arrived at the club in time for a whisky and soda before the forbidden hour, but was too late for dinner and had to get a scrappy supper.

July 19th. Worked at report from 10 a.m. until 2.30 p.m. and then on until 5 p.m. when I finished. It was sixty pages long and a very complete production, though I say it who shouldn't.

July 20th. War Cabinet in morning and again in afternoon to consider my Report on War Policy (which, by the way, the Committee have not discussed among themselves) and to arrange the line to be taken at the inter-ally

z

conference next week. Balfour, Curzon and Robertson congratulated me very warmly on the Report, the production of which within twenty-four hours appeared to them an incredible feat. They did not realize that I had been working at it in odds and ends of time for weeks and had begun it after the first of the sixteen meetings.

The decision to allow Haig to undertake the Flanders offensive was taken by Lloyd George and by most of his colleagues with reluctance and misgiving. No one believed that a strategical result could be achieved, and all shrank from the terrible losses which they knew it must involve. But the consensus of naval and military opinion was so overwhelming that the War Cabinet could not take the responsibility of rejecting the advice thrust upon them with so much cogency. It is true that they adopted the Italian plan as a reserve plan in case the Flanders attack failed or degenerated into a mere slogging match. They went so far as to order that staff officers should be sent to Italy, railway time-tables worked out, and that ammunition dumps should be built up for an eventual force of heavy guns. With this in view the progress of the Flanders attack was to be kept under constant review by the War Cabinet.

The Balkan theatre was once more examined in great detail; Webb Gilman, Milne's Chief of Staff, had been brought home to give evidence. The Committee found itself in complete unanimity that the changed situation in Greece, now converted from a suspected neutral into an active ally, rendered it no longer necessary to cling to the policy of withdrawal to an entrenched camp surrounding Salonica—the policy so frequently pressed by our own military advisers and so obnoxious to our Allies. There was equal unanimity that, for the present at any rate, offensive operations offered no prospects of compensation for the inevitable losses involved. Something might be done in combination with an attack by the Russian and Roumanian armies across the Danube but of this there was no prospect. It was decided, therefore, that the best course was to withdraw from the fighting line in the Balkans as many divisions of the British Army as possible, replacing them with Greek or other Allied troops; to send one division at once to Egypt; and to form the remaining divisions withdrawn from the fighting line into a reserve army for service in any theatre where they might be required according as the military situation should develop. This series of decisions, unlike the decision to attack in Flanders which

Pétain had already agreed to, required, of course, Allied concurrence, and it was recognized that in this difficulties were likely to be encountered.

In Egypt Allenby had assumed command on June 28th. Within a fortnight, however, he had adumbrated proposals for an advance into Palestine. He had found the Turks strongly entrenched on a line of thirty miles in length extending from Gaza on the shore of the Mediterranean to Beersheba in order to cover Jerusalem. This line was said to be held by a force of about five divisions with one cavalry division (say 46,000 rifles, 2,800 sabres, 200 guns and 250 machine-guns) with good lateral communications, so that any threatened point could be rapidly reinforced. Opposed to this force Allenby disposed of four divisions and three cavalry divisions, exclusive of a division newly arrived from Salonica and a division in process of formation which would not be ready to take the field for some months. This force was sufficient to frustrate an attack on the Egyptian frontier, but not for a big advance. For this latter purpose it was estimated that a total of seven divisions and three cavalry divisions would be needed. But this was not all, for in addition very extensive administrative preparations were required. For any decisive advance it would be necessary to double the railway line and the water pipe-line east of the Suez Canal. Allenby, therefore, asked for the maintenance of his present divisions fully equipped and at full strength; for two additional fully trained divisions; for a large addition to his aircraft and artillery; as well as for a quantity of railway material, water-pipes, etc. Before a decision could be taken it was necessary to convert these requirements into terms of shipping. Consequently, though his proposals were felt to be very attractive, more particularly as the operations would be carried out after the fighting had died down in the main theatre, the decision had to be postponed. This did not matter much, as in any event there was no question of an advance before November. For the moment the War Cabinet decided that, in addition to the division to be sent from Salonica, the doubling of the railway should be put in hand as well as the doubling of the pipe-line, provided the pipes could be got; that Allenby's force should be made up to full strength; and that he should take advantage of any opportunity to press and harass the Turks.

In Mesopotamia Maude was to continue the policy of establishing British influence in the Baghdad Vilayet, and in German East Africa the war was to be pursued to victory as rapidly as circumstances permitted.

The whole inquiry had taken two months to complete, but provisional decisions had been taken at intervals in order that executive instructions might be issued to those in command. This stocktaking was of great value to the statesmen and our leading sailors and soldiers. The strength and weakness of our position were seen in perspective both from the point of view of the immediate and the more distant future. The decisions may have been right or wrong, or, as is more probable, partly right and partly wrong, but there can hardly be question that Lloyd George had mastered the proper method for the conduct of the Supreme Command, i.e. to separate the investigation of policy (which he delegated to a small committee of the War Cabinet), from the great mass of detailed day-to-day business, partly naval, partly military, partly administrative, partly political, and partly Parliamentary with which the War Cabinet had to deal. It is true that those concerned in both the policy inquiry and the War Cabinet business were badly overworked, but the two classes of work were so interdependent that this was inevitable. Work under such pressure is only possible to Ministers of great mental capacity, trained by long experience in the art of government, and accustomed to make good use of their staffs for working out details. Fortunately, in Lloyd George, with his inexhaustible reserve of energy and buoyancy and power of decision and in less degree in his colleagues—and here we must include Robertson—the nation had thrown up men possessing these qualities and working as a team. But they could never have carried out the task without breaking down unless they had all been freed from the additional strain of administrative and Parliamentary work as heads of departments. In other words unless they had been—to use a continental phrase which some people object to—Ministers without Portfolio. This is a consideration which should be borne in mind for the future.

CHAPTER LXVII

THE BATTLE OF FLANDERS

'The blood of English shall manure the ground.'
(SHAKESPEARE, *Richard II*, Act iv., sc. i.)

THE Conference of the Allies took place on July 25th and 26th. Its avowed object was to re-examine the situation and policy in the Balkans, and this necessitated the presence of representatives of Greece, Serbia, Russia, and Roumania, as well as of the Western Allies at most of the meetings. As all insisted in making interminable speeches this made progress very slow. Nor was this all. The French Government felt that, if part of the Allies conferred together without the remainder, friction and suspicion might result. In consequence a 'Duma' was held at the end of the conference, which was attended by no less than eleven Allies and no real business done.

I asked the secretary of the conference, in jest, if Siam was to be present. He looked horrified and replied '*Non, Mon Dieu! Nous les avons oubliés*' —and rushed off to the telephone!

The United States was not represented at any of the main discussions, but Sims and Pershing attended some of the military meetings. This was the first occasion in the war on which the great associate of the Far West came into the councils of the Allies, but their participation was frowned upon by President Wilson.

The main object of the British representatives, so far as the Balkans were concerned, was to secure agreement to the decision of the War Policy Committee to withdraw a division from Salonica to Egypt. This modest request aroused the most violent hostility and opposition from the French, and to a less extent from the Italians, the Russians, Greeks, Serbians and Roumanians. An interminable discussion started. If the whole of the five British divisions had been in question the pother could hardly have been greater. The withdrawal, it was represented, would be a sure sign to the enemy that the Allies did not mean to attack. The Bulgarians would also be able to withdraw troops and would direct them against Russia and Roumania, already in a parlous condition. It would have dire effect on the morale of the Balkan peoples, who would believe that Britain was abandoning them; the Roumanians would lose hope; the Serbian soldiers would desert the colours and go home;

Venizelos' task in pulling his people together would become more difficult than ever; the enemy would be encouraged. To these arguments Lloyd George, supported by Balfour, had no difficulty in making an effective reply. He stated explicitly (1) that the British Government fully recognized the paramount necessity of preventing a German-Bulgarian advance towards the south; and (2) the desirability of taking the offensive towards the north whenever this should become practicable. As there were some 600,000 Allied troops in the Balkan theatre to 300,000 of the enemy's, it was absurd to contend that the withdrawal of a division would make any difference to the security of the Allied forces. The latter were too numerous for a passive defensive; and too few and not properly equipped for an offensive. In these circumstances it was only right and proper that a small part of the force should be withdrawn and employed where it would be useful. A division would decrease the Allied forces in the Balkans by only 3 per cent, but would increase the Army in Palestine by 14 per cent. At this stage the French offered to send one or even two of their divisions from Salonica to Palestine, if we would leave our division, and Sonnino offered to send 12,000 native troops. These offers were politely refused on the ground that Allenby's army was maintained by a single line of communication across the desert of Sinai, and he would be unable to carry on if he had the forces of three nations, each with its own type of ammunition and its separate supply dumps. Lloyd George laughed the morale argument out of court. No one knew more about war than the Balkan nations, and the withdrawal of one division, which could be brought back at a pinch, was not going to upset them. Moreover, with consummate skill he won the Balkan representatives over on a side issue. The Greek representative had complained that the Italian forces had occupied a triangle of territory in the north of Epirus. Lloyd George and Balfour then made powerful and moving appeals to Sonnino, in the course of which they laid stress on the importance of the proper treatment of small nations as a factor in the moral position of the Allies. Sonnino took the appeal in good part and undertook to withdraw the Italian troops from Epirus simultaneously with the cessation of the Allied military occupation of Thessaly, and to come to an agreement for the re-establishment of Greek administration, though reserving provisionally the right of military occupation of the triangle between Koritza, Santi Quaranta, and the Epirus frontier. Even though the Balkan States were mollified by this episode and intimated privately that they would withdraw their opposition, the French, who are a most tenacious people, refused their

assent to the withdrawal of the division, and the result of two days' wrangling was to postpone the decision to a fresh conference to be held in London on August 5th.[1]

Among a number of detailed and technical reports prepared by experts for the use of the conference the most notable was one by Robertson, Foch, Pétain, Cadorna and Pershing on the policy to be adopted if Russia went out of the war, the possibility of which had now to be considered seriously. The generals took a very grave view of the situation which would present itself in this contingency. If, however, proper dispositions were made, they held that the Coalition should be able to assemble sufficient force to hold up the onslaught of the forces which the enemy could assemble from the armies now on the Eastern Front until such time as the American Army could pull its weight. Those measures would involve a passive attitude in the secondary theatres accompanied by a reduction of the forces there and a concentration on the Western Front; acceleration of the American arrangements for creating and transporting their army (which seemed to be proceeding dreadfully slowly); tonnage arrangements for transporting troops from the secondary theatres; and, most interesting of all, the realization of unity of action on the Western Front by the help of a permanent inter-Allied military organization, which would study and prepare the rapid movements of troops from one theatre to another. This latter recommendation shows how the minds of some of the leading military men were moving towards some central organ for military co-ordination, though as yet it was only contemplated in the event of Russia's defection.

The discussion was resumed at a conference held in London on August 7th and 8th at which the British, French, Italian and Russian Governments were represented, the latter by Nabukoff, their ambassador under the new régime. The Salonica question at last got itself settled. The withdrawal of the British division was agreed to, but in order to secure this concession the British Government had to declare that it recognized the necessity for maintaining the Allied force in Salonica, and to undertake not to withdraw any further British troops unless unexpected events occurred and then only after discussion with their Allies. The French Government also reserved the right to withdraw a division, if necessary, 'because French interests in Palestine and Syria may put upon France a military and moral obligation to make French military representation in that country effective', and the

[1] *Macedonia*, II, pp. 12 *sq.*

Italian Government claimed the same right to send troops to Palestine, if France did. Lloyd George did not object to these reservations, provided the British Government was notified and consulted about the military arrangements before the troops were sent to Palestine. This episode illustrates the sort of difficulties that are constantly arising between Allies, even the most friendly Allies, in the course of a war, and which greatly hamper the effectiveness of the Supreme Command.

We must now turn to an episode which caused considerable distraction to the British Supreme Command and which culminated in the resignation of Arthur Henderson, the representative of Labour in the War Cabinet, who had been sent to Russia in the previous June with a view to bringing good influences to bear on the new régime in that country. The War Cabinet had been at first inclined to think that the adoption of a constitutional system of Government more or less on Western lines might tend to greater efficiency in the conduct of the war than under the Czarist régime, but, as time went on, evidence accumulated that things were going none too well with the provisional Government which we had recognized on March 22nd. Early in June the Foreign Office advised the War Cabinet that a change in our representation in Petrograd might be desirable. Our Ambassador, Buchanan, as the War Cabinet recognized, had rendered exceptional services in circumstances of the greatest difficulty; his appreciations of a most complicated situation had proved almost uniformly correct. The very fact, however, that he had been able to establish an exceptional position with the Czarist Government and with the first provisional Government, which had since been superseded, made it probable that the new Russian administration might have less confidence in him. In these circumstances the War Cabinet, believing that the success or failure of the Allies in the war might very likely turn on what happened in Russia, felt that it would be advisable to send someone there whose experience and personality would be calculated to influence the new Government of that country to pursue the war with energy. Their choice fell upon Arthur Henderson who, on June 5th, was invited by the whole of his colleagues to make the personal sacrifice involved and to go to Russia. The question whether Henderson's visit was to be permanent or temporary was left open but it was arranged that Buchanan should remain for a time at his post. On July 23rd, while Lloyd George was in Paris, we learned that Henderson had returned.

July 3rd. The great subject of the moment is Henderson's visit to Paris with Ramsay MacDonald.

On August 1st, Henderson gave his colleagues an account of his experiences. This was the occasion when, to use his own picturesque phrase, he was left 'on the door-mat' while the rest of the War Cabinet conferred without him. Henderson made a good deal of the incident at the time, but later it became a stock joke and many years after when, on the occasion of a labour dispute, Henderson and other labour leaders were asked to leave the Cabinet room for a few minutes in order that the members of the Government concerned in the negotiation might confer alone, Lloyd George apologized for leaving them 'on the door-mat'. Henderson was the first to join in the laugh. On August 1st, of course, no offence was intended and Henderson's colleagues only wished to confer alone for a short time in order to try to find a way out for their comrade from a difficult situation.

The difficulty arose from the peculiar situation in which Henderson found himself. When he became a member of the War Cabinet he had retained his position as Secretary of the British Labour Party. This arrangement had been considered desirable at the time. It had enabled him to keep in touch with Labour opinion and to influence it, thus contributing towards the maintenance of a united front at home. More than once also he had attended conferences of Allied socialists, where his influence had always been exercised wisely, more particularly the previous Christmas when in the teeth of considerable opposition he had induced a conference in Paris to adopt a view favourable to the continued prosecution of the war. Moreover, members of the French and other Allied Cabinets occupied a dual position somewhat similar to Henderson's. Why then was it that Henderson's attendance at another conference of Allied socialists in Paris caused so much feeling? The reasons were twofold. First the object of the conference was to discuss an invitation from Russian socialists to attend a conference at Stockholm *at which representatives of the socialist parties of enemy countries were to be present,* and arrangements had actually been made to hold the conference on September 15th. And, second, Henderson had travelled to Paris with Ramsay MacDonald, who was regarded as the leading pacifist in this country. The majority of Parliament and of the nation were in no mood to countenance pacifism in any form, and the proposed parleys between Allied and enemy socialists gave rise to proprofound misgiving. On August 10th the Labour Party Conference

z*

passed a resolution by 1,846,000 votes against 550,000 in favour of representation at the Stockholm Conference, and Henderson, contrary to what the Prime Minister and his colleagues had expected, failed to use his influence against the resolution in accordance with the views of the War Cabinet. The result was that Henderson resigned on August 10th.

For my part I was very sorry to see Henderson go. He was a good fellow, a loyal man and a useful and hardworking member of the War Cabinet. Even on resigning he expressed his unabated desire to assist in the prosecution of the war. George Barnes, who had entered the War Cabinet during Henderson's absence in Russia, remained a valued member until the end of the war.

It was in the atmosphere of this exhausting crisis that the War Cabinet took its decisions on the difficult question of Indian Reforms. In a history of the Supreme Command it would be out of place to enter into details of this important episode in the history of the British Empire. Nevertheless in a sense it was a war-time measure and cannot be passed over in silence. The question had been raised by the Government of India in November 1916, and had been discussed in correspondence between the Viceroy and the Secretary of State. It had been brought before the War Cabinet at the end of June 1917, in Lloyd George's absence. India's great services in the war had predisposed men's minds to some advance and in principle there had been no opposition, though the precise formula of any announcement on the subject obviously required most careful drafting. The Secretary of State had undertaken to prepare such a formula, which could be discussed when the Prime Minister could be present. Then there had been a long interval of several weeks occupied by more pressingly urgent war business. On August 15th the subject was at last tackled. Austen Chamberlain had resigned over the Mesopotamia Commission and Edwin Montagu, who had taken his place, was authorized to make the famous announcement, which began:

The policy of His Majesty's Government is that of the increasing association of Indians in every branch of the administration, and the gradual development of self-governing institutions, with a view to progressive realization of responsible government in India under the aegis of the British Crown.

Montagu was also authorized to announce his acceptance of the Viceroy's invitation to proceed to India to discuss the matter with the Viceroy and the Government of India.

All this time, from July 31st onwards, the battle of Flanders had been in full swing. By mid-August it was already clear that the attack was not going to achieve results commensurate with the effort involved and the losses incurred, and that the moment had come to consider the War Cabinet's decision that in that eventuality the whole matter should be re-examined:

August 15th. . . . I had a short talk with the Prime Minister and Robert Cecil. I impressed strongly on the former that he ought to investigate the question of the Flanders offensive, which seems to be rather hung up, with a view to the possible adoption of the alternative Italian plan before Cadorna had started. I found him unresponsive, though he sent for Robertson in order to instruct him to report on Haig's next objective. In this connection it must be noted that Robertson is going to France tomorrow. The P.M. is obviously puzzled, as his predecessor was, how far the Government is justified in interfering with a military operation.

Two days later, on August 17th, Cadorna started the eleventh battle of the Isonzo. It may have been for this reason that Lloyd George did not for the moment pursue the idea. A few days later, however, news of a considerable success by Cadorna gave him the opportunity he sought. Parliament had risen. The business of the War Cabinet had once more been brought up to date. The Prime Minister had left for mid-Sussex for a short rest and I had taken the opportunity to join my family at Eastbourne. The sequel follows:

August 26th (Sunday). Alas, my leave came to an end, although I did not realize it at the moment. Lloyd George had asked Adeline and me up to Lindfield, where he is staying with Riddell, to lunch. With some difficulty we got a car and arrived without misadventure. I found Lloyd George in a ferment of excitement about Cadorna's victory on the Carso. I myself was also excited about it. We strolled round talking about it all the morning before lunch. Incidentally Lloyd George climbed high up a plum tree, and out on to a very rotten branch after plums. Gladstone used to cut them down! Lloyd George climbs them! Most of the afternoon, while Adeline, Riddell and others were at Forest Row Golf Course (where they were caught in heavy rain), Lloyd George, Philip Kerr and I discussed it (Cadorna's victory). Lloyd George then insisted we should stay the night, and we were fixed up somehow. After dinner Lloyd George chanted Welsh hymns, which gradually started a regular 'sing-song' of old-fashioned songs. About 11 p.m. he suddenly decided to write a letter to Robertson about Cadorna's victory, urging that Robertson should go to Italy to investigate, with a view to a big transfer of guns and the exploitation of a great victory. He also wrote to

Bonar Law on the same tack, pointing out the great opportunity opened up, particularly in view of the failure of the Flanders offensive, consequent on the continuous rain. The result was that we were very late getting to bed.

To the Prime Minister the Flanders offensive was a time of unrelieved gloom. On this muddy and bloody battlefield he saw realized all that he had predicted only a few weeks before. The moment seemed at hand to fall back upon the alternative plan for an operation in Italy which the War Cabinet had decided to adopt if the Flanders plan should prove unsuccessful. First, however, he had to persuade military opinion, and that, as he knew to his cost, was no easy matter. Never for one moment was this great issue out of the Prime Minister's mind. In order to get a true picture of how he stood the strain of this difficult time it is necessary to touch occasionally on the human side. Historically the picture would be untrue without it. To continue:

August 27th. Philip Kerr went off by an early train with the letters, and Lloyd George asked me to stay until he returned. Adeline went off at tea-time, but I was kept all day hanging about, and Lloyd George insisted on my staying on, as he wanted me to go with him to the Cabinet next day. Albert Thomas came down to dinner with Reading. The latter was off shortly to America on a special mission to the President. He wanted some knowledge-able official to go with him and Lloyd George suggested I should go, but eventually thought he could not spare me and left me to nominate someone. I selected Swinton. . . . Kerr reported that Robertson had been away, but that Maurice had strongly opposed the Italian plan.

August 28th. Once more I hung about all day at Lindfield in attendance on Lloyd George, who was in a peevish, changeable mood, worried by the shocking weather and afflicted with neuralgia. As no reply had been received from Italy to our telegram regarding stocks of heavy ammunition Lloyd George decided not to attend the Cabinet, and eventually it was arranged that Robertson should come to Lindfield next day, so I was kept on—still, I may remark, without any kit. To add to our troubles the wind broke the telephone lines, and I had to walk with Riddell two or three times to the tele-graph office at Lindfield. Milner came down to dinner and was in substantial agreement with Lloyd George on the Italian question. All day Lloyd George was in a most capricious mood and Kerr and I drafted about ten letters from Ll. G. for Reading to take to President Wilson, but before we had finished one draft he would invariably get a 'brainwave' and want a new one.

August 29th. Robertson and Maurice arrived about 11 a.m. and an agree-ment was reached that a telegram should be sent to the British Ambassador at Rome (who had warned the Government that a great opportunity might arise for exploiting the Italian success), warning him that we could only assist at

the expense of an abandonment of the Flanders offensive; that this would be trumpeted by the Germans as a defeat to our arms; that we could even consider facing this, if we were assured that a really great victory could be won with our aid on the Italian Front; but that we knew by experience the optimism of generals, and we should therefore require a convincing appreciation. Robertson . . . on the previous day had dissented strongly from the whole idea, and I am certain that he only agreed to this telegram because he was sure that the Italians could not convince us. Maurice, with whom I had a talk, was also strongly opposed. He told me that Haig, and still more Kiggell, his Chief of Staff, still believed we could clear the Flanders coast—his reason being that there only remained five German divisions that had not passed through the mill, and that the reserves with which they were filled up were the poorest material. I am bound to say that I could not share this optimism. A private letter I received about this time from a valued former member of my staff, now a brigadier-general and a corps Chief of Staff, described the German shelling as heavier than he had ever encountered, and the difficulties of dealing with the myriads of machine-guns in wooded country as very great. And he, though a sober judge, has always been an optimist. An amusing incident occurred at luncheon. In order to put Robertson in a good temper Riddell had ordered an apple suet pudding, of which Maurice had said he was very fond. When Robertson saw it he expressed the greatest delight; he had two large helpings, and frequently commented on its excellence. Of course we all pretended it was a chance, and there was much suppressed merriment. In the afternoon Lloyd George decided to return to Town and we all motored up in the rain. I had tea with Lloyd George and dined at the Club with Swinton to discuss his forthcoming trip to America with Reading.

August 30th. I spent the evening re-drafting Lloyd George's letter to President Wilson, as Kerr's draft . . . appalled me. Lloyd George had insisted on his putting in all his complaints against the military management of the war; his protests against Western Front policy; his desire to knock out Austria and Turkey; and a new, and not very well-thought-out scheme for an Allied Council and General Staff in Paris to direct the war.

This shows that as early as August 30th Lloyd George was attracted by the idea of a Supreme War Council. But to launch it first in a letter to President Wilson would, I felt, have been a tactical mistake and it was dropped for the moment. A certain amount of preparatory work with his own colleagues, with the military advisers and with the French Government was essential before the scheme could be launched with any prospect of success.

A few days later a most unexpected development took place. On September 3rd, while the War Cabinet were meeting with Bonar Law in the chair (Lloyd George being away at his house at Walton Heath), a

telegram was sent in by the Director of Military Operations from our liaison officer in Paris to the effect that the French Government wanted to send 100 guns to Italy, that Foch and Pétain proposed they should be taken from French First Army, which was attached to Haig's command in Flanders; that Foch was on his way to London to see Robertson about it; and that, if the latter would not agree, the French Government hoped he would be overruled by the British Government!

September 3rd. . . . Robertson was at once recalled from leave; Haig was brought to England; and Lloyd George telephoned up that he would hold a Cabinet after dinner. I lunched with Montagu and dined with Lloyd George and Philip Kerr at the Athenæum Club.

When the War Cabinet met at 9.15 p.m. (one of the very rare instances of an after-dinner meeting), Foch had not arrived and there was no fresh news. That night, however, the famous letter to President Wilson, so often re-drafted, was read and approved. As my diary continues—

. . . in the main, it was a carefully worded plea to President Wilson to take part in the Allied Councils.

September 4th. No War Cabinet in the morning, but in the afternoon there was a War Cabinet first, followed by a meeting with Foch. The net result was that a conference was arranged between Haig, Robertson, Foch and Pétain with a view to scraping up 100 heavy guns for Italy on the basis that Haig should release fifty from the French First Army . . . on condition that fifty more were got together from other parts of the French front, thus making a really important contribution to Cadorna's artillery. . . . I have no doubt that Thomas, who had at Lindfield the previous week shown great enthusiasm for the Italian idea, had inspired the French message. . . . Haig again showed himself very confident, though I could discover no good reason for his confidence. One thing that impressed me was his great desire to capture a ridge from which he could interrupt the Roulers–Thourout railway, which runs parallel to and a few miles behind the enemy's front in Flanders. I asked him why he could not interrupt it with aircraft. He replied that they were no use for this. His opinion strongly supports my own views that the offensive value of aircraft is greatly exaggerated.

Thus, at last, Lloyd George seemed to have succeeded in converting French governmental and military opinion to his idea for a big artillery concentration on the Italian Front. He had worked at it incessantly from the January Rome Conference onwards, never losing any opportunity to press his idea. If adopted earlier the plan might have led to big results. At least it would have had a fair trial. Now, however, as so often

in this war, it was too late. The eleventh and last attack of the Italian Army on the Isonzo ended a few days later (on September 12th). For the remainder of the year and for some time to come Italy was to be fighting for her life on the defensive and thereafter there was no question of sending any more British guns to Italy for an offensive. Two days later (September 6th), suffering from neuralgia and overstrain, Lloyd George went off to Criccieth for a few days' rest. On September 12th he sent for me to join him there.

September 14th. Spent the whole day travelling to Criccieth. Found the Prime Minister had been quite seriously ill with a very high temperature. He was still looking out of sorts and only convalescent. I spent an hour after dinner . . . discussing the general situation, after which he went straight to bed. I found him rather despondent at the failure of the year's campaigning, and disgusted at the narrowness of the General Staff, and the inability of his colleagues to see eye to eye with him and their fear of overruling the General Staff. He was also very annoyed at the way the General Staff twist their facts and estimates to suit their arguments. For example, they had insisted that three months would be required to transfer and mount a large number of heavy guns on the Italian frontier, whereas Robertson yesterday stated that the hundred heavy guns to be sent by the French . . . will arrive within a week.

September 16th. . . . Lloyd George . . . rediscussed military policy. He wants to abandon all activity on the Western Front and to concentrate our efforts against Turkey.

September 17th. Milner arrived this morning. . . . In the afternoon went a walk on the golf links with Milner and had a good talk. In the evening after tea and dinner we all had a good talk, as the result of which it was agreed that our proper course in the war was to concentrate on Turkey, as there is little hope of achieving definite success on the Western Front. I felt it my duty to warn them that the Turkish operation involved considerable risks, viz. the maintenance of a much larger force if we are to advance beyond or even to hold Jerusalem, which would involve a permanent addition to our shipping. At the end I was asked to write a paper recording the results of our conversation.

September 18th. Spent whole morning from 7 a.m. to 2 p.m. writing the Memorandum and most of afternoon reading telegrams and papers arrived from the office and writing letters. Went for a very jolly walk late in the afternoon with Milner on the banks of the river Dwyfur. Useful conversation. Milner seems to have come completely round to Lloyd George's view that the Western Front affords no opportunity for achieving complete success and that it is necessary to devote our main efforts against Turkey. He agrees fully with me, however—having reached his decision quite independently—that

success in the Turkish theatre can only be achieved if the soldiers are in it whole-heartedly.

September 20th. . . . I forgot to mention that yesterday I had at Lloyd George's request written no less than five letters to Robertson asking for information on the Palestine campaign, Mesopotamia casualties, alleged losses of Irish division, and also for a complete estimate of relative forces in western and all other theatres of enemy and Allies. . . .

September 21st. . . . Milner has gone up to Town to sound Robertson and Carson *re* the proposed Turkish campaign. . . . Lloyd George's neuralgia, I regret to say, is not much better.

September 22nd. We have news from our Ambassador at Madrid that the Germans want to open peace negotiations with us, and we have accordingly invited Painlevé to come to London, or alternatively we may have to meet him at Boulogne next week. . . . We also received Robertson's answer to the request for information *re* prospects in Mesopotamia and Palestine. In this connection the Prime Minister was rather perturbed about Mesopotamia, and I had to write to Robertson asking whether it would not be advisable to assist Maude by sending the British heavy artillery now in Italy to Egypt, either to enable Allenby to make a diversion, or to be transferred in case of necessity rapidly to Mesopotamia. Cadorna has announced his intention of making no further offensive, but of awaiting the Austrian attack and then counter-attacking. This is very difficult to account for unless there is truth in rumours of insurrection in Italy, as the French guns were sent for the specific purpose of enabling Cadorna to attack.

Next day (September 23rd, Sunday) we returned to London. The position at that moment was that the Flanders offensive was still in full blast, but without concerted strategical action by the French Army, except for an offensive action at Verdun, which had been in progress since August 30th, and the tactical co-operation of French First Army. The latter, however, had been deprived of many of its heavy guns. The Italian offensive was over. As the season was getting late for fresh operations in the Western theatre attention was being given to the possibility of exploiting the situation against Turkey during the autumn. The Germans had made some kind of a peace approach to the French through Lancken, First Secretary at the Paris Embassy before the war. The War Cabinet decided that Lloyd George should discuss the matter with Painlevé as soon as possible.[1] That evening we started for Boulogne and had rather an exciting journey.

September 24th. . . . At 8 p.m. we started for Dover. On arrival at the station I found that an air raid was imminent and that the warning had been

[1] *vide infra*, p. 734.

received some time before. However, we slipped out of Charing Cross and started dinner. I shared a table with Lloyd George. We remained for some time outside London Bridge Station in momentary expectation of bombs—an exposed and unpleasant situation—but eventually went on. As we left London we observed the start of the artillery barrage fire. We travelled at a snail's pace and arrived at Dover at about 11.30 to find that they had been heavily bombed, part of the railway destroyed (the cause of our delay) and a church and some buildings badly damaged. Slept at the 'Lord Warden'. Wrote Minutes of the morning's meeting in the train.

September 25th. Up at 4.45 a.m., crossed in a destroyer at 5.45. Conference in the train at Boulogne after breakfast between Lloyd George and Painlevé only. I spent the time giving a lecture on how to run a War Committee to Commandant Helbronner, Secretary of the French War Committee, which they are just starting. He was very interested to learn how we can run it, and how we had solved the difficulties that he was meeting with. *'C'est merveilleuse. Une organisation parfaite!'* he said at the end. Lunched with Painlevé in the train, after which a formal conference—Lloyd George, Painlevé, Robertson, Macdonogh, Foch, Helbronner and self. No very important business done.[1] Foch did not show himself very ready to play to Lloyd George's desire for a French expedition to Alexandretta, but promised to send a Memorandum on the subject. Lloyd George in his conversations found Painlevé entirely preoccupied about his political difficulties. Painlevé is not a strong man, and his Government obviously 'rocky'. One fact that emerged was that the French are not fighting at all. They put off their attack on Chemin des Dames from September 1st until today or tomorrow and are postponing it again until October 10th, with the result that all the German strength is being concentrated against us in Flanders. Very fishy. After the conference Lloyd George, Robertson, Philip Kerr, Butler (Robertson's A.D.C.) and I motored up to GHQ in a village outside St Omer. I sat next to Haig at dinner. He was rather preoccupied about tomorrow's attack, which has been somewhat dislocated by a big unsuccessful German counter-attack this afternoon. He only warmed up about the proposed Ministry of the Air, which he objects to as much as I do.

September 26th. Conference in morning with Haig, Prime Minister and Robertson. The Prime Minister told Haig of the German peace offer, and of Germany's apparent intention to take it out of Russia, and asked for his considered opinion of our military prospects if Russia went out of the war. Haig promised a reply in writing. There was a big attack that morning. All the time at the conference messages were coming in from the front. Haig had a great map showing the line we wanted to reach, and it was very interesting

---

[1] The most important decision taken at the Boulogne Conference was that, as Cadorna could not be induced to continue his attack, the British and French guns should be withdrawn. Orders had actually been issued for the withdrawal of the sixty British howitzers before the Conference. But *vide infra*, pp. 747 *sq.* on the extension of the British line.

the way first one bit was filled in on the map, then another, until by the time we finished (11.30 a.m.) the picture was complete except for a small section, where two brigades had been held up. In the evening, when we came back to GHQ for tea *en route* to Boulogne, news came that this bit was also captured, and the whole picture was complete like a jigsaw puzzle. Lloyd George's son turned up at 11.30 from the Nieuport sector, and we went off through Cassel to Fifth Army, lunching *en route* with some very confident Australians —a brigadier and his staff. At Army Headquarters I met Neill Malcolm, the Chief of Staff, who was very busy, but spared me ten minutes. Then we drove on to the rear of the Army through the usual paraphernalia of dumps of ammunition, aerodromes, herds of 'tanks', like great mastodons, roads made of planks, etc. At a cross roads just outside Poperinghe a big 11-inch shell whistled over our heads and burst 100 yards away—too close to be pleasant. Our destination was a cage for prisoners brought down from the day's battle —containing a number of nerve-shattered, tired, unshaved, and dirty men, who nevertheless sprang to attention as though under review by the Kaiser. Thence back to Boulogne and home to Limpsfield at about midnight. I have been nearly a fortnight away.

With this fleeting glimpse of the back areas and of the scene at General Headquarters we can appropriately bring the account of the Flanders offensive to an end. It is true that the battle continued incessantly until November 10th, but, so far as the Supreme Command was concerned, no more decisions were taken and attention was already being given to the next moves.

The question whether the results of the battle of Flanders justified the effort and the tremendous casualties has been and will remain a matter of controversy. Haig to the end of his days believed that the battle had been an essential factor in winning the war. Not long after the war the Field-Marshal was invited to London to advise a subcommittee of the Committee of Imperial Defence on certain technical issues. Before leaving for the night train to the north he gave a small dinner party at which were present Hubert Gough, James Edmonds, author of so many volumes of the Official Military History, another military officer and myself. I took the opportunity of a very frank discussion to ask the Field-Marshal whether, after hearing all the criticisms of the battle, he still felt that the decision had been a right one. He replied without any note of hesitation that he had not the slightest doubt on the matter. Already by 1916, when the Germans had failed to

break through the French lines at Verdun and we had similarly failed on the Somme, the war had become a *guerre d'usure*. Flanders he described as simply a continuation of the battle of the Somme and an essential factor in wearing down the German resistance. On the whole it was less costly in casualties to attack than to defend as was shown by the battles in March 1918, when the Germans, with the aid of reinforcements released from their Eastern Front, had made their last bid for victory. Nevertheless they were so exhausted by the remorseless hammering they had received in the previous two years that their efforts in their spring offensive of 1918 had finished them. This had enabled the Allies, reinforced by American troops, to reap the harvest sown on the Somme and in Flanders. Whether he was right or wrong in this appreciation (which has had to be given from memory) I felt a sense of satisfaction as I bade him good-bye, for the last time as it turned out, that Haig's mind was so completely free from anything in the nature of self-reproach.[1] On the other hand, no one can read Lloyd George's own account without realizing that there is a tremendous case on the other side.[2]

Should Lloyd George then have overruled the generals and insisted on the adoption of the Italian plan? There is no doubt that he was absolutely convinced that the attack in Flanders had not the remotest prospect of success. He foresaw the results with uncanny prescience, and no one who heard him at the time had the slightest doubt about his inner conviction. All his colleagues, too, had grave doubts about the offensive's prospects, though they were probably less sure than the Prime Minister about the prospects of the plan for sending heavy guns to Italy. The criticisms of it by Haig and Robertson had been very telling. Jellicoe's strong support on naval grounds, and his extreme pessimism on what would happen in the narrow seas if the coast of Flanders was not cleared of the enemy, also produced an almost decisive effect. On balance I myself felt at the time that Lloyd George had had slightly the better of the argument, and that, if the question could be decided exclusively on its merits, the Italian plan ought to be tried.

As so often happens in military affairs, however, the statesmen could not decide the issue solely on what they considered to be its merits. It is useless to order a general to carry out a policy in which he wholly disbelieves. Lloyd George and the War Cabinet had entirely failed to con-

---

[1] Many passages could be quoted from German writers in support of Haig's view. Note especially Ludendorff, II, p. 541.
[2] *War Memoirs*, IV, p. 2163.

vince Haig and Robertson either that the Flanders plan was wrong or that the Italian plan was right. At that time both of them undoubtedly possessed the confidence of the Army and of the country. Even if some other generals could have been found who believed in the Italian plan, and were prepared to carry it out, they would not have had the confidence of the Army to anything like the same extent as their predecessors. The fact that Haig and Robertson had been overruled must soon have leaked out, particularly if they had been superseded. There would have been a great outcry in Parliament and the Government would have been upset long before any decisive victory could have been achieved on the Italian Front. It was a case where a possibly second-best plan in which the Army's trusted leaders believed more than did the statesmen, was preferable to what may, intrinsically, have been a better plan, but which must have upset national unity. The decision was unavoidable.

A more interesting point is whether Lloyd George and the War Cabinet ought not to have interfered as soon as it became clear that the Flanders offensive was not getting on. This would have been in accordance with the decision of the War Cabinet that, if it appeared probable that the results of the fighting were not commensurate with the effort and the losses involved, the whole situation should be re-examined. The difficulty was to decide when the exact moment had come for intervening. The official reports were always optimistic and there was usually a considerable lag between events and the arrival of the unofficial information which sometimes helps to elucidate the official reports. My own view was that the moment for re-examining the situation had arrived as early as August 15th and Lloyd George did take some steps to procure some preliminary information about Haig's future intentions. As soon as he heard of Cadorna's success Lloyd George became very active in the matter and did, in his own way, undertake a very thorough re-examination of the position, bringing Robertson and Maurice down to Lindfield, recalling Robertson from leave, summoning Haig from France and doing his utmost to press the soldiers to adopt a change of plan. But he found the generals as reluctant as ever to fall in with his ideas, while their optimism persisted and was maintained until the battle petered out in November. Cadorna's offensive had ended on September 12th.

There remains the question whether, even though they no longer had a second string to their bow in the form of an Italian offensive plan,[1] the Prime Minister and his War Cabinet ought not to have intervened to

[1] vide supra, pp. 675 sq.

stop the offensive before the end of October with a view to the conservation of our resources. Lloyd George did his best to inform himself of the real situation in Flanders by his visit to Haig on September 25th–26th, but he only encountered the usual optimism, emphasized by the picture of steady, remorseless execution of the plan for the day, as witnessed at GHQ, and by the spectacle of numbers of German prisoners in a barbed wire cage to which they had been brought from the front that morning. There was nothing here which could justify him in stopping the offensive. Had he done so either then or any time before the battle petered out, he would have exposed himself to the charge of 'amateur' interference with the responsible Commander-in-Chief and of preventing the latter from reaping the fruits of months of successful fighting. Also it is difficult to stop a Commander-in-Chief who believes himself to be on the floodtide of success.

Lloyd George was already bending his mind towards next year's campaign. I had a long talk with him alone on the subject (October 15th). Neither of us yet had the data to express considered views, and the conversation was preliminary and tentative in character; at Lloyd George's request, I dictated a note immediately after. It shows how far ahead Lloyd George was already looking and the trend of his mind at that time:

The conversation opened by Hankey remarking that he felt in a state of considerable optimism about our war prospects. Pressed by the Prime Minister for his reason for this optimism, Hankey stated it was due to a great many significant events in Germany, such as the present political crisis; the mutiny in the German Navy; and the information we receive of the bad economic conditions in the country. He brought to the notice of the Prime Minister a Memorandum recently circulated by Macdonogh, dealing with the internal situation in Germany, in which he had expressed the view that the German public was beginning to become disillusioned and to lose their confidence in the High Military Command. This, Hankey said, exactly interpreted his own feeling and was the cause of his confidence.

The Prime Minister admitted that disillusionment was beginning in Germany. Between disillusionment and collapse there was a long road to travel. The Germans were a most obstinate and tenacious people, certainly only second to ourselves in this respect. We had won no great military victory, and he suggested that no nation in the world had ever surrendered for economic reasons, unless actually within sight of starvation. Germany, however, would probably never starve, a view in which Hankey concurred; hence, while he believed we could win in time, the Prime Minister could not share Hankey's optimism about the present.

Hankey then proceeded to give his reasons for optimism concerning the effects of the military operations in Flanders. He pointed out that we were not fighting Germany with one weapon only. We were attacking with the military weapon, the blockade weapon, the weapon of morale, and by attacking the allies of Germany. The military operations in Flanders reacted upon every one of these weapons. Haig's operations must be measured not only by the military objects which they achieved, but by their general effect on Germany. They strengthened the effect of the blockade by draining the manpower of Germany, increasing the strain on her manufacturing resources, and thereby reducing the amount available for the civil population, and by the strain on railway communications. The Flanders operations reacted on the morale of the German people by reducing their faith in their military commanders, by the loss of relatives, and by engendering a feeling of hopelessness. Finally, these operations reacted on Germany's allies by showing that the story of Germany's invincibility was a mere fiction. Hence it appeared to him that there was every reason for continuing these operations, viewing it not solely from a military aspect, which was not properly his concern, but from a wider point of view.

Hankey then turned to the question of the military operations of next year. The first point which struck him was that it would be absolutely essential to take some offensive on the Western Front next year; it would probably be necessary to strike hard in order to prevent the enemy from turning sufficient force on to Russia or Italy to achieve great victories elsewhere. If this were admitted as a basis for discussion the question arose of the nature of the offensive. Three alternative suggestions have been made:

(1) To continue Haig's plan of remorselessly hammering the enemy.
(2) To adopt Pétain's tactics of striking here and striking there, always carrying out the first and successful stage of an attack, but never carrying it through to a prolonged offensive.
(3) To carry out (2) in conjunction with a great offensive elsewhere, for example in Turkey.

Hankey suggested that neither (2) nor (3) would suffice to keep the Germans on our front. He also urged that if an offensive was to be carried out at all it might as well have some strategical aim. Pétain's tactics had no strategical aim. On the previous day he had asked Franklin Bouillon and Foch what was the underlying strategical idea, and Franklin Bouillon had frankly admitted that there was not one, and that the plan was based on the theory that big operations with strategical objectives were a mistake in existing conditions. Haig's operations, however, had objectives which were more than strategical. They would react upon the naval and aerial situations by ultimately achieving the command of the coast, and when advanced to a certain point they would threaten the German lines of communication, and per-

haps bring about a great retirement. If the matter was regarded from the point of view of an attack in 1919, it would be an inestimable advantage to have driven the Germans off the coast and to start fair on the second great strategical objective. The advance in 1919 might be no faster than in 1918, and this was a strong reason for obtaining as much as you could next year. Another advantage was that the enemy was compelled to dispute every inch of ground, and to assemble great reserves to meet the attack. If Pétain's tactics were adopted the enemy would probably get to know it. He might retire and so spoil the effect of a carefully prepared attack, or he might meet it with local reserves, setting free the strategical reserves for operations elsewhere.

In supporting the continuance of Haig's plan Hankey reminded the Prime Minister of what had happened at Verdun. The Germans had hammered continuously from February to July, and the French Army had been very hard put to it to hold the attack up. More than one appeal had been made by the French Government that they could not sustain these grievous blows, and ultimately it was only the offensive on the Somme which had called off the Germans from Verdun. It appeared to him that Haig's offensive might be compared to this. He was continually hammering at the Germans, but they were not in a position to mount an attack comparable to the Somme in order to relieve the situation. Hence Haig was hammering, as it were, on a serious bruise, and every blow told with redoubled force on Germany's strength.[1]

The Prime Minister answered in regard to Verdun that the whole point had been that the French were only able to yield five miles of ground. Had the French given more than this, the enemy would have captured Verdun with all that that entailed. The Germans, in yielding the Belgian coast, had from fifteen to twenty miles of ground to dispute. They were, therefore, not in the tight place that the French had been in at Verdun. The Prime Minister drew quite a different lesson from the Verdun attack. At their first onslaught the Germans had gained about half the total amount of ground that they captured in six months. It was a striking demonstration of the fact that an attack at once drew in the reserves and multiplied the strength of the defending force, so that any advance must be very slow and costly. What he wished to avoid in 1918 was the terrific losses that were inevitably bound up with an attack of this nature. He admitted that a continuance of Haig's attacks might conceivably result in bringing Germany to terms in 1919. But in that case it would be the u.s. who would deal the blow and not we ourselves. If our Army was spent in a succession of shattering attacks during 1918, it would, indeed, be in exactly the condition that the French Army was in at this moment, with its numbers reduced and its morale weakened. He was particularly anxious to avoid a situation at the end of the war in which our Army would no longer

---

[1] It should perhaps be said that these points were not put absolutely consecutively but were elicited in the course of conversation. The same applies to the Prime Minister's remarks which follow.

be a first-class one. He wished it to be in every respect as good as the American army, and possibly a revived Russian Army, so that this country would be a great military power in the world. It was not that he could not face losses, but he insisted that the losses must not be incurred without commensurate results. A man took 21 years to make, and human life was very precious. To win a complete and decisive victory it was necessary that we and the u.s. at our full strength, and Russia and Italy with such as remained to them, should attack simultaneously with France in 1919 and overwhelm the enemy. He differed from the view that Hankey had expressed, that victory could never come from purely military victory, and that what we had to hope for was that the combined effect of the various weapons we were using would compel the enemy to accede to our terms. The Prime Minister contemplated an overwhelming military defeat, which would absolutely compel the enemy to submit. This could not possibly be achieved in 1918 by any method. The u.s. Army would not by that time have reached sufficient strength, and there was no prospect that the Russian Army could have revived. Hence the policy that he had outlined to the War Cabinet was based on the fundamental idea that the Allies should reserve their main strength and make a great and terrific effort in 1919. He believed that by means of Pétain's tactics the Germans could be sufficiently occupied on the Western Front to prevent them from dealing decisive blows against Russia, and that this result could be achieved without the great sacrifice in life involved in a continuance of Haig's operations. At the same time he would make every effort to detach Germany's allies from her by combined military and diplomatic efforts in Turkey and diplomatic efforts in Bulgaria. He also was not unhopeful of the possibility of detaching Austria. All this would help towards the concentration of overwhelming forces for the blow in 1919.

Hankey pointed out that in all the expositions of policy that he had heard him make to the War Cabinet, he had never gathered this view, that 1919 was to be the year of the decisive attack. He suggested that the Prime Minister should take an early opportunity to make his colleagues aware of this, as it was fundamental to the whole scheme and must affect anyone's attitude towards it.

The Prime Minister agreed that this ought to be done, but said it was not convenient for him to make a fresh statement of policy that day. He asked Hankey to talk to one or two of his colleagues on the subject and tell them of his conversation.

Hankey undertook to do this and said that the points in the Prime Minister's remarks which had struck him most were the following:

(1) That his plan was to make the main attack in 1919, and for the Allies to conserve their strength for this tremendous blow.
(2) That it was vital to our national policy that, at the end of the war, our Army should not be exhausted and demoralized.

These were the points which he would, in his conversations, explain to such of the Prime Minister's colleagues as he met.

The Prime Minister said he attached so much importance to the carrying out of his plan that, sooner than abandon it, he would be willing to forgo the great position he occupied and see someone else Prime Minister to carry it through.

I saw Balfour, Curzon and Milner the same day and told them the whole story, but without mentioning the Prime Minister's final observation.

THE SUPREME WAR COUNCIL

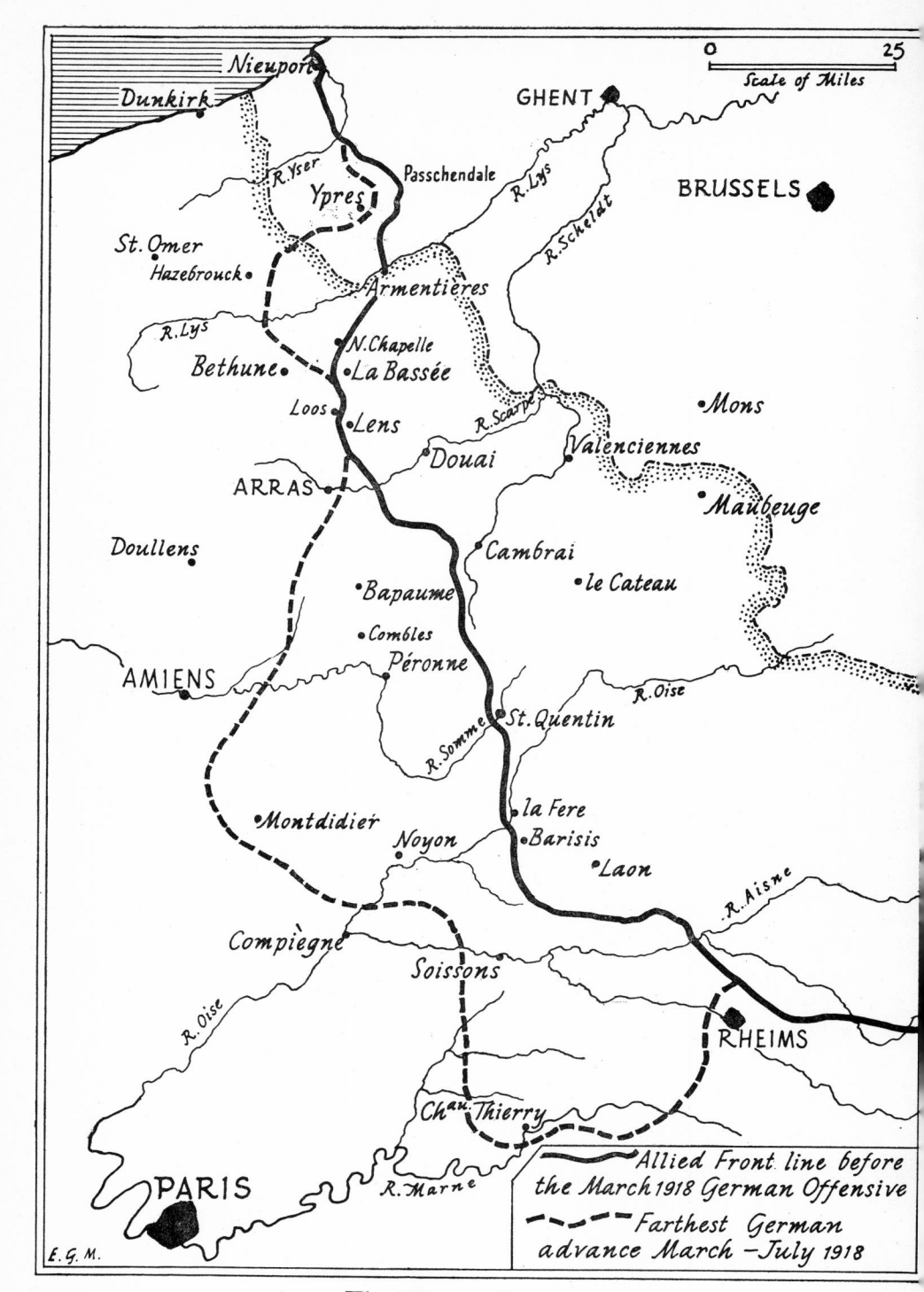

The Western Front, 1918

CHAPTER LXVIII

THE CREATION OF THE SUPREME WAR COUNCIL

'In a single battle the Peloponnesians and their allies may
be able to defy all Hellas, but they are incapacitated from
carrying on a war against a power different in character
from their own, by the want of the single council-
chamber requisite to prompt and vigorous action. . . .'
(Extract from a speech by Pericles. THUCYDIDES,
Peloponnesian War, I, 5.)

THE failure of the Flanders offensive to achieve any immediate strategical result, the terrible losses and the fact that the plan had worked out
exactly as he had anticipated had affected the Prime Minister's usual
buoyancy of spirit. He had begun to feel that that victory could not be
won before 1919. His conviction that the war could not be won on the
lines hitherto adopted was only too strongly confirmed. Yet his professional advisers could suggest nothing better. Every alternative he
had proposed had been rejected. The obvious remedy was to find new
advisers. But where? The General Staff trained at Camberley nearly all
shared the view of their superiors and they held together, a veritable
band of brothers. Their opinion might be right or wrong, but their
unanimity was remarkable. Lloyd George had as yet met no British
general of distinction who shared his convictions; in France, however,
there were signs of disillusionment and of a tendency to take a broader
view.

Realizing the impossibility of persuading the responsible military
authorities to think of anything except the Western Front; disappointed at the failure of the French to give wholehearted support to
the Flanders offensive, in which in their hearts, as he thought, they did
not believe; chagrined at the neglect to give the Italian Army an
adequate artillery support until it was too late; anxious at the steady
deterioration of the Russian situation, Lloyd George's mind was turning more and more towards the idea of some central body to control the
operations of all the Allies. The Allied generals had themselves
suggested something of the kind,[1] though they had only envisaged a
purely military organization confined to the Western theatre of war. In

[1] *vide supra*, p. 689.

an extension of that idea Lloyd George saw the possibility of victory. The heads of Governments, acting in a corporate capacity, ought in his view to take their decisions on the basis of the war situation as a whole. The British, French, Italian and Russian views would all be pooled. Naval, military, political considerations, and the economic factors, such as man-power, shipping, supplies, transport, etc., would all be taken into account. An inter-Allied War Council of this kind would do for the Allies as a whole what the War Cabinet had accomplished for the United Kingdom and the Imperial War Cabinet for the British Empire. The constitutional difficulties, however, in evolving a workable plan were considerable, and Lloyd George realized that time would be required for the proposed Council to achieve efficiency and prestige. It is doubtful whether the Supreme War Council would have come into existence unless he had inclined towards the view that the war might be prolonged until 1919.

During the dreary, soaking wet days of his so-called holiday at Lindfield the Prime Minister obtained a strong confirmation of his views. In accordance with his practice of gleaning information and inspiration from every quarter he had invited French and Henry Wilson to pay him a visit. Both these distinguished soldiers proved to be critics of the Flanders offensive, and both indicated privately their belief in the necessity of some kind of central Allied control. Neither of them, however, was the constitutional adviser of the Government, and without giving mortal offence to Robertson it was difficult to bring their views formally to the notice of the War Cabinet. After mature consideration Lloyd George decided to bring this about by following the precedent set by Asquith at the outset of the war. On October 10th he induced the War Cabinet to summon a Council of War at which Robertson, French and Henry Wilson should be invited to express their opinions. This decision immediately aroused Robertson's suspicions.

October 10th. . . . Lucas, Robertson's *factotum*, arrived in the afternoon at my office and I told him what had occurred. He said Robertson would be very angry at this incident, which he would regard as a vote of no confidence in him. I did my best to make him see it in a right light with a view to influencing Robertson. The Prime Minister saw Robertson in the afternoon, but the interview was unsatisfactory. At 7.20 p.m. Curzon called on me and told me that Derby had told him that Robertson had just offered his resignation. Derby had, in order to gain time, refused to accept it that night, and had asked Robertson to dinner. Curzon had then explained to Derby, as I had already explained to Lucas, that there was no lack of confidence in

Robertson; that the War Cabinet was merely following Asquith's precedent in August 1914 in calling a War Council before taking a great decision; and that it was like calling an independent medical opinion. Curzon then went on to tell me that, if the Prime Minister drove out Robertson, Robert Cecil, Balfour, Derby, Carson, and he himself, probably, would leave the Government, which would then break up. He stayed an hour discussing the whole situation, and I did not get home until 10.15 p.m.

October 11th. Before the War Cabinet I walked round St James's Park with Lloyd George and Philip Kerr. I repeated Curzon's warning in very straight terms and he (Ll. G.) took the hint very quickly. I told Curzon what I had done and he said I had rendered a very considerable public service. Balfour, with whom I walked to the Foreign Office after the meeting, remarked on how admirable the P.M. had been. I told him of my warning to Ll. G. which he warmly endorsed. . . . I lunched today with Montagu who told me that Asquith had got hold of Ll. G.'s difficulties with the soldiers and thinks he may get back.

One result of the meeting was that French and Wilson were asked, each separately, to commit his views to writing.

October 12th. Another walk round the park with Ll. G. before the War Cabinet—rather upsetting to office routine. He asked me to join tomorrow the first weekend at Chequers. . . . I lunched alone with Eric Geddes who told me that Robertson had consulted him about resigning but that he had told him that it would be bad ground for resignation merely because the War Cabinet wanted to have someone else's views. He promised me to use all his influence with Robertson to prevent him resigning.

October 11th. In the afternoon motored down to Chequers. . . . I was pleased at being included in the party which consisted besides myself of the P.M., Balfour, Smuts, Arthur Lee, Painlevé, Franklin Bouillon, Foch and Helbronner. Shortly after our arrival Painlevé decorated me with the order of Commander of the Legion of Honour, making a speech in which he gracefully alluded to my services as Secretary of the Inter-Allied Conferences. The P.M. added his mead of praise and all shook hands with me. Nothing interesting happened after this and Painlevé and Helbronner left for Paris at 10 p.m. We all remarked, as everyone all the week has remarked, on the extraordinary air of distraction of Painlevé. I gathered from Franklin Bouillon and Helbronner that they are much worried about it and that they really got him over to England to escape the worry of the French Chamber and its Commissions, which make life intolerable. I slept in the prison of Lady Mary Grey, sister of Lady Jane Grey, and was quite alone in this part of the house. A dark and eerie stairway communicated with a secret opening in the panels to a room at the bottom of the house. I slept admirably!

October 14th (Sunday). The P.M., Balfour, Smuts, Franklin Bouillon,

Foch and I had an informal conference in the library in the morning. The P.M. horrified me by raising the question of an inter-allied War Council *and permanent General Staff* in Paris. Of course Franklin Bouillon and Foch leaped at it. I had no time to warn the P.M. that in Robertson's present hurt, bruised and suspicious frame of mind he will see in it merely a proposal further to upset his authority and may resign. When I warned him of this afterwards he was astonished, and hardly credited it! . . .

I made a short record of the conversation at Chequers,[1] which, though only semi-official in character, possesses a certain importance owing to the fact that by this conversation Lloyd George committed himself morally to the principle of the establishment of a Supreme War Council and prepared the way with the French Government; and the conversation in the library, however unofficial in character, did in fact form an important stage in the creation of the Supreme War Council. My own criticism of the opening of this issue on this occasion was not so much an objection of principle, though I had my doubts on that point, as one of expediency in discussing the matter with the French representatives before the War Cabinet had taken a decision, and in further embittering Robertson at that particular moment. Looking back, however, I feel that Lloyd George was right to raise it, as it prepared the way for him to bring off his policy two or three weeks later after the Italian disaster at Caporetto.

To return to the Memoranda written by French and Henry Wilson:

October 20th. I have somehow omitted to record that at one of the War Cabinet meetings in the week before last it had been decided at Robertson's request that French's and Henry Wilson's (Council of War) Papers should be sent in to him. I had communicated this to French and Wilson and on the following day (October 13th I think) they had asked me to see them at the Horse Guards, and French had strongly demurred to the idea of rendering his report to the C.I.G.S. on the ground that he had been asked to report to the War Cabinet. The P.M., whom I at once consulted, had declined to give a decision, so I had no alternative but to let the matter rest. This morning Henry Wilson called at my office and handed me two copies of each Report. The Prime Minister had gone out of Town and I was in a quandary whether to send the Reports to Robertson or what. I decided that the proper constitutional course was to pass them through the Secretary of State, so I arranged to see Derby immediately after lunch. The P.M. confirmed this decision on the telephone. The whole subject is so thorny and Robertson is in so prickly

---

[1] Chequers had been bequeathed to the nation by Sir Arthur and Lady Lee as the official country residence of future Prime Ministers.

a state that I did not wish to make any mistake in procedure, a point on which the generals are very fussy. I then settled down to read the Reports, sending the duplicate to be cyclostyled but not circulated until Robertson had pronounced on them. The Reports confirmed my worst anticipations. They both recommended a central council, including a staff of generals in Paris, to be independent of the national General Staffs. This alone is enough to drive Robertson into resignation. They both condemned the continuance of the Flanders offensive next year, which is the course that Robertson and Haig recommend. In addition French's report hit out hard at Robertson and Haig, whose views were challenged in principle and in detail.

The affair dragged on for some days. Derby hesitated to hand the Reports on to Robertson in their original form as he thought it would precipitate his resignation and bring about the fall of the Government. I had several interviews with him and we each tried to devise expedients to get round this awkward corner. Although the Prime Minister had read the reports, they had not yet been communicated either to Robertson or to the War Cabinet.

October 22nd. Derby asked to see me before the War Cabinet and we once more discussed the French–Wilson Memoranda. He was much less hopeful, after reading the papers, of the possibility of achieving a settlement. We discussed the matter for three-quarters of an hour without getting much 'forrarder'. War Cabinet at 12.30. Lunched with the Prime Minister and Milner. The former read me part of his speech for the Albert Hall that afternoon. After lunch I discussed the French–Wilson Memoranda with Milner, who had just been reading them—the P.M. having directed me to show him a copy. His view was that Robertson must see them at once—but he agreed with me that the Government would very likely come down over it. . . .

October 24th. . . . In the afternoon French asked me to call about teatime. He said that the P.M. had sent for him and had suggested that he should soften some of the phrases to make them less offensive to Robertson and he had agreed to do so. At the Prime Minister's suggestion he asked for my co-operation in this. I spent an hour or so with him and Henry Wilson doing this. From what Wilson said when French was out of the room, it was clear that French's reason for agreeing to alter his report was that he wanted to remove the impression that he was bitter against Robertson. He told me, however, that he had declined to accede to the P.M.'s proposal that he should praise Haig's tactical handling of the situation. To sum up, he was critical both of Robertson and Haig and of their combination.

October 25th. . . . Sykes came in to say that Picot had told him in the strictest confidence that Painlevé had told him that there are serious differences between British politicians and their generals. . . . I went to Derby **to**

hand him French's revised report and to notify to him the War Cabinet's decision that he should communicate the French–Wilson Memoranda to Robertson. In the evening I dined alone with Derby at Derby House. He wanted to discuss the French–Wilson affair with me. He was very gloomy and thought it would be very difficult to avoid the resignation of Haig and Robertson in which I agreed. He proposed the following solution: that Asquith should be appointed Ambassador in Paris and permanent British representative on an Allied Council in Paris with Henry Wilson and Maurice as his military advisers. This he considered would reconcile Haig and Robertson to the central council idea and to a change in strategy, as both have great confidence in Asquith. Politically it would be to Ll. G.'s interest to get Asquith out of the way. After some hours' talk I agreed to put this to Ll. G., but without holding out any hope of his agreement.

October 26th. . . . Saw Ll. G. and propounded the 'Derby Scheme' for sending Asquith to Paris. As I anticipated Ll. G. wouldn't look at it. He regarded it as merely a dodge to 'pack' the Central Council of Allies, and outwit the whole plan. He was full of buck, and considered himself strong enough to beat the generals on the central council plan. I tried to put the great danger of a split with the generals. While I was there a message came that Robertson wanted to see him. I tried to persuade him to behave decently to R. Apparently with some success for, in the evening, Derby asked me to call and told me Robertson had come back from the interview very pleased and had said that he had asked the P.M. not to decide either for or against a big offensive next year owing to the uncertainty of the position in Italy and Russia, but to be prepared for either. The P.M. had agreed and, according to Robertson as reported by Derby, had promised to try and get London as the *habitat* of the inter-ally Council of War which reconciled Robertson to it. Robertson also seemed to think that he and Haig could meet French's criticism. Derby was much relieved and so was I. . . . On reaching home I telephoned to Ll. G. at Walton Heath what Derby had told me about Robertson.

The difficult situation between the Prime Minister and the Chief of the Imperial General Staff was thus cleared up for the moment—and only just in time, for the Italian defeat at Caporetto proved to be a disaster of the first magnitude. But the genius of Lloyd George enabled him to snatch advantage out of it by making it the occasion to bring to fruition the scheme that he had for some time been maturing for the creation of a Supreme War Council for the Allies.

October 27th. About noon Fagalde[1] came in to give a message from Painlevé for Ll. G. that the French think an immediate conference is required

[1] French liaison officer.

to consider the Italian situation and the relief of the French line, and that they were prepared to hold it in Paris, Boulogne or London. I replied, after consulting Ll. G. at Walton Heath by telephone, that we were agreeable, but that the conference must be in London. Fagalde also showed me a telegram from the French Ministry of War to Cadorna that if French assistance was required they were ready to march. Ll. G. told me to see Robertson about this and to suggest that we also should send a similar message. I saw Robertson, who told me he had already warned Haig to have two divisions ready, and that he had sent an officer with all papers to Walton Heath. I communicated this by telephone and Ll. George said I must come down at once. So I got a War Office car and went down to Walton Heath, where I found Ll. George at the Golf House closeted in Riddell's room with Steel of the General Staff. After some discussion Ll. G. wrote a letter to Robertson telling him to send a promise of assistance to Cadorna, and warning him that, if we are to get control of our Allies (as Robertson is always pressing we should do), we must give them substantial assistance when in difficulties, as the Germans do, and not by lecturing them at conferences. I copied this letter (taking the precaution to burn the blotting paper)[1] and Steel took it back to London. Ll. George went off to play golf, and I went into the Club dining-room to lunch at 3.15 p.m. Just as I sat down Winston Churchill and his brother Jack turned up, and I sent them off to the golf links. After lunch I joined the party (Ll. George, Philip Kerr, Riddell, Donald of the *Chronicle* and the two Churchills) and walked round the course. They were playing appallingly badly, everyone's mind being preoccupied with the Italian affair. Then back to tea at Lloyd George's. At 7 o'clock another staff officer came down from Robertson with the latest news, and with his telegram to Cadorna, which was good, saying that two divisions were told off and that the Italians, with British and French assistance, would give the Germans a lesson. The French, we learned, were sending four divisions. Lloyd George is anxious to utilize this occasion to strengthen our hold on the Allies, so at my suggestion we rang up the Foreign Office and asked them to send a telegram to Rome to the effect that we were sending substantial assistance. Meanwhile the news from Italy continues thoroughly bad. They are preparing to evacuate all the territory they have captured and to fall back successively to the Tagliamento, and to a position covering Venice. They have lost 650 guns, 500 of which are heavy or medium, and tens of thousands of prisoners. Only three German divisions have been located and not more than seven are suspected as being on that front. The Higher Command, like the Army, is in a panic and is evacuating Udine. Ll. G. and I recalled with satisfaction the Memorandum ... prepared for the Rome Conference last January, insisting on a *defensive*, if not an offensive, plan for Allied co-operation on the Italian Front, which had eventually resulted in arrangements for Allied reinforcements being

---

[1] An odd thing to do in the smoking-room of a strange club.

made. Ll. G. of course is furious. The Germans have struck at the weak link, just as he himself wanted to do on (almost) the very same spot—a plan which the General Staff rejected with contempt. Meanwhile Haig's plan has completely failed, as Ll. G. always said it would. As though to add fuel to the flames Robertson tonight sent down a Memorandum of his policy, which practically amounted to a reaffirmation of his 'slogging on the Western Front' plan. It annoyed Ll. G. intensely. I got away about 7.45 and had a very cold drive home to Limpsfield, where I found Adeline was anxious, as the night was cold and frosty and suitable for an air raid.

On October 30th the plan of an Allied War Council and General Staff was discussed by the War Cabinet and 'practically accepted in principle'. That afternoon Painlevé, Franklin Bouillon and Pétain arrived in London. Next day:

October 31st. . . . The Prime Minister in the afternoon invited Maurice to draft a constitution although Robertson was away. In the evening I dined at 10 Downing Street, to meet Painlevé, Franklin Bouillon and Maurice. Much talk about the Italian situation and the French food situation. The P.M. then gave them the draft constitution for the inter-Allied advisory General Staff. I noticed that Painlevé paid great attention to everything I said, and insisted on its being translated. I stayed at the Club. There was a heavy air raid. My room was in an attic but I was too lazy to go to the basement. The guns made a devil of a row intermittently for three hours, and I missed my 'psychological moment' and scarcely slept all night.

Meanwhile I had been getting busy about the Secretariat of the projected Allied Council, the British section of which I determined must be linked up with the War Cabinet Secretariat. I confided my views to Helbronner, who was now secretary to Painlevé's War Cabinet and had modelled his organization *mutatis mutandis* on our own, suggesting that he should be linked up in the same manner.

November 1st. In the afternoon Helbronner called, and at his request I drafted rules for the secretariat of the new supreme Inter-Allied Council and General Staff.

The French Army had just brought off a successful coup at Malmaison, taking many prisoners and guns. That night at dinner with Painlevé at the Ritz:

I congratulated Pétain on his recent victory, describing it as the cleanest bit of work done this year. No, he said, Verdun was just as clean. He seemed very pleased with himself.

At the moment of the Italian disaster it was particularly encouraging to find that the French were getting their tails up.

On the following day (November 2nd), the French Ministers and Pétain met Lloyd George at breakfast at 10 Downing Street, and they decided to proceed to Italy in order to try to retrieve the situation, which was rapidly deteriorating. That evening Lloyd George summoned the War Cabinet which—

November 2nd . . . approved the scheme for an Inter-Allied Supreme Council and General Staff (advisory) and Henry Wilson's appointment as British representative on the latter.

Before our departure next morning Kiggell arrived from GHQ with a despatch from Haig to the effect that the proper way to save Italy was to renew the attack on the Western Front. The Prime Minister was most indignant and even Maurice disagreed with Haig and thought that the only way was by direct assistance.

November 4th (Sunday). (Hotel Crillon, Paris.) Breakfasted with the Prime Minister, Pershing, Smuts, Wilson and Maurice. The P.M. made a very fine statement on the lack of co-ordination among the Allies and the evils attendant thereon, and urged Pershing to come to the conference in Italy, if only as a spectator with a watching brief. Pershing agreed in the principle of more unity of control, but evidently felt great hesitation in attending the conference in view of the difficulties made by his Government about attending previous conferences. . . . After breakfast the P.M. had a long conference with Haig, which I did not attend, as Ll. G. intended, among other things, to raise the Press question, and it was better it should be a 'heart to heart'. Meanwhile Bertie called and gave me the latest Paris political gossip, namely, that Clemenceau was likely to come into office for a time. . . . The P.M. saw Briand and Haig, but I was not present at either interview. Haig seems as cocksure as ever that he is going to bring off a big *coup* this year. At about 8.45 p.m. we left for Italy. The Italians at first chose Nervi for the *rendezvous* (What a chance for the comic papers in the present state of Italian 'nerves'!), but afterwards changed it for Rapallo.

During the journey to Rapallo 'I was occupied a good deal in helping Henry Wilson to organize his section of the proposed inter-Allied Staff. . . .'

November 6th (Rapallo). It was strange to wake up and look out on this exquisite bay, which I visited last some eighteen or nineteen years ago in my sea-going days, when I was with Charlie Beresford in the *Ramillies*. The

place has grown enormously. I slept badly, being kept awake by mosquitoes, which bit me unmercifully, and I had a bad attack of diarrhoea, which was very trying. In fact I was very seedy indeed most of the day. Before breakfast I had a stroll with Lloyd George, returning before him for a talk at 8.30 with Robertson, who was to breakfast alone with Ll. G. I had promised Ll. G. that I would make it quite clear to Robertson that the War Cabinet was absolutely committed to this scheme of a Central Council of Allies, and that it was useless for him to kick against it. This I did in my interview with R. and I could do it the more sympathetically because at Criccieth I had explained my own objections to the scheme, and I told Robertson this. I think therefore that I did good. Robertson made no secret of his objections to the scheme, and I deduced from his manner that he was half inclined to chuck the appointment of c.i.g.s. Shortly after breakfast the conferences commenced and continued on and off all day. When I was not in a conference I was dictating a *procès-verbal* or concocting a draft resolution or a telegram to England describing the proceedings.

The Rapallo Conference lasted for the whole of November 6th and 7th.

November 7th. I had another rather bad night owing to the mosquitoes. Started work very early, after working late the night before. Once more we had a constant succession of conferences, the intervals being mainly spent in dictating *procès-verbaux*, etc., as yesterday. In the two days I did no less than seven *procès-verbaux*, two of Anglo-French conferences and three of Anglo-French-Italian. The first day was devoted mainly to a gathering up of information on the Italian position, and the second to the creation and constitution of the new Allied War Council. The Italian position proves to be critical in the extreme. The Army has lost at least 200,000 prisoners and 2,000 guns and immense quantities of stores and ammunition. Of the four armies the Second, the largest, is scattered all over the country after throwing away its rifles and losing all its guns. The Third Army has retired behind the Piave, after losing half its heavy and a quarter of its other guns, and is tired out. Two divisions are probably cut off in the mountains. The Vatican and to a less extent the socialists are responsible for an active peace propaganda. It is doubtful whether the Army will stand on the Piave, and if it does not, the rest of the guns will have to be abandoned for lack of transport, and Venice, with the command of the Upper Adriatic, will be lost. The Higher Command has lost all grip of the situation. Ll. George talked with great candour and insisted on the immediate riddance of Cadorna. The Italians agreed, but could not think of a way of saving Cadorna's prestige. At lunch I whispered to Aldrovandi a suggestion that Cadorna be appointed the Italian permanent military adviser to the Supreme (Allied) War Council. This suggestion took effect for at the next meeting Orlando announced that a solution had been

found.[1] I fancy that this suggestion had the double effect of tiding the Italians round a difficult corner and rendering Ll. G.'s scheme of a Supreme War Council more acceptable to them.

The essential condition of getting rid of Cadorna and Porro (his Chief of Staff) having been acceded to, Lloyd George and Painlevé promised ample help to Italy. Eight divisions are under orders (four French and two new British divisions, besides the two previously under orders) and the French have nearly all arrived. The Italians demand fifteen. As the troops under orders will take up all the accommodation for some weeks, it was decided to remit the question to examination on the spot by the Permanent Military Advisers of the Supreme War Council, the Italian Government promising every assistance. The Supreme War Council was formally set up with its permanent military staff.

The doubts which I had previously entertained about the usefulness of the Supreme War Council had gradually been vanishing, and by this time I had become a believer in the scheme:

I can see great possibilities in this institution. During the war the military staff might be expanded to include the study of blockade, munitions, shipping, finance, terms of peace, and all other matters affecting the external relations of the Allies. After the war it might gradually embrace all the nations and become a veritable piece of machinery where all international information would be pooled and where all international differences would be discussed by the parties concerned in the first instance, and settled by arbitration if they could not agree. It is the germ of the real League of Nations.

Robertson persisted in his opposition to the Supreme War Council to the last. During the meeting at which the scheme was being examined in detail he got up rather ostentatiously and walked out of the room, stopping on the way out in order to ask me as secretary to record the fact that he had withdrawn, a request with which I complied.

It has been stated in some of the memoirs that the first meeting of the Supreme War Council was held at Versailles on December 1st. Technically that is incorrect, for in the official *procès-verbal* the last meeting of the Rapallo Conference held at the New Casino Hotel on November 7th at 4 p.m. is described as 'The First Session of the Supreme War Council'. There is also a footnote which states that the Supreme War Council was formally constituted at this meeting

[1] Aldrovandi-Marescotti *Guerra diplomatica. Ricordi e frammenti di diario 1914–1919*, p. 147, 'il soggerimento di Hankey'.

and took its first decisions. Moreover, the 'first decision' begins as follows:

The Supreme War Council assembled at Rapallo on November 7th, directs its Permanent Military Representatives to report immediately on the present situation on the Italian Front. . . .

Immediately after the meeting Henry Wilson left to join Foch and Cadorna in carrying out this mission.

In its original form the Supreme War Council[1] was constituted 'with a view to the better co-ordination of action on the Western Front'. The limitation to the Western Front was adopted in order to keep the situation open *vis-à-vis* Russia. It was impossible to include Russia at that stage, partly because the Russian Government was not represented at Rapallo, and partly because it was becoming more and more doubtful whether that country would play any further part in the war. But it was felt to be of great importance to do nothing which would offend Russian susceptibilities. The question of the formal extension of the constitution to cover other fronts was, therefore, left to the future, but, at Lloyd George's request, it was agreed that the Council should concern itself with all the fronts where the three Western Allies were fighting in common. The organization comprised a Supreme War Council 'composed of the Prime Minister and a Member of the Government of each of the Great Powers whose armies are fighting on that front'.[2] The Supreme War Council had for its mission 'to watch over the general conduct of the war'. It was to prepare recommendations for the decision of the Governments, and to keep itself informed of their execution and report thereon to the respective Governments. The General Staffs and Military Commands of the armies of each Power charged with the conduct of military operations were to remain responsible to their respective Governments, but—and this is important—the general war plans of the competent military authorities were to be 'submitted to the Supreme War Council, which, under the high authority of the Governments, ensures their concordance, and submits, if need be, any necessary changes'. Each Power was to appoint a Permanent Military Representative whose exclusive function was to act as a technical adviser to the Council. The Military Representatives were to receive from the Government and from the competent military authorities of their respective countries 'all the proposals, information, and documents

---

[1] The constitution as approved at Rapallo is given in *War Memoirs*, V, p. 2392.
[2] i.e. the Western Front.

relating to the conduct of the war'. The Military Representatives were to watch day by day the situation of the forces, and of the means of all kinds of which the Allied armies and the enemy armies disposed. They and their staffs were to be established at Versailles, which would be the normal meeting-place of the Supreme War Council, though the latter could meet elsewhere as might be agreed according to circumstances. The meetings of the Council were to be held at least once a month.

AA*

CHAPTER LXIX

THE LAUNCH OF THE SUPREME WAR COUNCIL

'Many fateful events were crowded into 1917.... On December 1st the Allied Supreme War Council (Versailles) was initiated.' (EDMONDS, *A Short History of World War I*, p. 19.)[1]

ALTHOUGH the Supreme War Council had begun work on the very day of its foundation, it still remained to secure its acceptance by the peoples more particularly concerned. The first step was to get the approval of the King of Italy who was entitled to learn at first hand the important decisions that had been taken in his kingdom. To Peschiera on Lake Garda where the King had established his headquarters, the members of the Rapallo Conference set out by special train on the evening of November 7th. I myself saw the King only for a few minutes as everyone except Ministers and interpreters were asked to leave the room shortly after he entered.

November 8th. . . . The little man seemed plucky and in good heart but a pathetic figure with his country tumbling about his ears. He was, however, obviously facing it bravely. He agreed to all we wanted, including the change in the command. Foch and Robertson wanted the Duc d'Aosta, but for dynastic reasons he was rejected and Diaz, a corps commander with only some three months' experience, was appointed. . . .'

The King attributed the disaster at Caporetto partly to thick fog which prevented the Italian Army using its artillery, and partly to the absence of trained professional officers who could properly manœuvre the troops when the retreat began. He was hopeful of being able to hold the enemy on the line of the Piave, an anticipation which proved correct.

The next step was to proceed to Paris, where the new plan was to be explained at a specially organized luncheon. The French Ministers, however, wanted a little time to prepare for this, and Lloyd George, somewhat exhausted with incessant travelling and his exertions at Rapallo, was glad of a few hours in which to prepare the great speech which he intended to deliver in Paris. Consequently we arranged for our sleeping-car to be detached from the train at Aix-les-Bains.

[1] But *vide supra*, p. 721.

While at Aix-les-Bains we had a little mild relaxation, motoring the first afternoon to Annecy, while on the next morning Smuts and I went for a twelve-mile walk.

November 10th. Left at 10.30 p.m. for Paris, having spent the whole afternoon discussing Lloyd George's speech for Monday, which alarms me not a little. I wrote a peroration to it, which he rather liked, but which (hastily dashed off) contained an absurd mixed metaphor.

For this Lloyd George chaffed me for years, whenever I had occasion to prepare a brief for his use.

November 11th (Sunday). Arrived Paris 10.30 a.m.—one and a half hours late. Spent morning at the Hotel Crillon, Ll. G. polishing his speech while I enjoyed the luxury of a real hot bath, the first since we left Paris. Albert Thomas lunched with us. He is no longer a Minister, and, as one of the leaders of the Socialist Party, is making himself rather troublesome to the Government. Ll. G. made a strong appeal to him to sink party feelings and prejudices in the present tremendous crisis and to join the Government, but he did not respond very favourably and is evidently rather *tête montée*.

In the afternoon, Ll. G. went to see Clemenceau at his private house alone. At the end of half an hour I came back to fetch him, and shook hands with this curious old character, this bitter-tongued, political journalist-patriot. The object of Ll. G.'s visit was to get him to support the new Supreme Council in *L'Homme enchaîné*,[1] and he seemed pleased with his visit.

Venizelos was the next caller.

I have long been interested in the remarkable career of Venizelos, and the man himself impressed me a good deal. Vivacious, clear-headed, speaking fluent but not good French, and understanding, but not speaking, English. It was easy to recognize a big man.

What happened with Venizelos is not recorded. In the evening we came back to French politics.

Painlevé and Franklin Bouillon dined with Ll. G. and self at the Crillon and the conversation was wholly on French politics, Ll. G. trying to persuade Painlevé to form a stable party based on the following plan:

(*a*) Painlevé to be President of the Council only, adopting Ll. G.'s plan of a 'Bonar Law' to run the Chamber.

(*b*) Thomas to have the post of Minister of War vacated by Painlevé.

(*c*) Briand to be the French 'Bonar Law'.

[1] Clemenceau's newspaper *L'Homme libre* having been suppressed, he had brought it out under the title *L'Homme enchaîné*.

They seemed to be taken with (c) but said that the Chamber would not stand Albert Thomas as Minister of War.

Next day the famous speech, which Lloyd George had spent the whole morning in polishing, got itself delivered:

November 12th. . . . Lunch at 12.30 at the Ministry of War. I sat between Helbronner and a French deputy, and talked much to Hanotaux, ex-Minister of Foreign Affairs, who was opposed to the new Council on the ground that we wanted a generalissimo and not a new machine. Ll. G.'s speech was very sensational. He delivered it admirably in English, and, though only a few understood, you could have heard a pin drop most of the time. It was a wonderful oratorical performance. Franklin Bouillon read a translation none too well—and the speech lost a great deal in the reproduction in French. But, none the less, its dire, sombre tones made a great sensation, most of the comments I heard being favourable, though there was a very general tendency towards Hanotaux's criticism. . . . At 7 p.m. I spoke to Milner on the telephone to ascertain the reaction in London, without gleaning much. Long walk and talk with Esher, who had seen Robertson and found him in a resentful mood about the new Council. Esher got the impression that the General Staff would starve Henry Wilson as regards information, and that it was absolutely necessary to have Milner or some other 'frock' in Paris, both to ensure information and also to take hold of the French Government. . . .

The speech was a terrible indictment of the lack of unity in counsel and in action by the Allies, as may be judged by the following extract quoted from *The Times* (November 13th).

As my colleagues here know very well, there have been many attempts made to achieve strategic unity. Conferences have been annually held to concert united action for the campaign of the coming year. Great generals came from many lands to Paris with carefully and skilfully prepared plans for their own fronts. In the absence of a genuine Inter-Allied Council of men responsible as much for one part of the battlefield as for another there was a sensitiveness, a delicacy about even tendering advice, letting alone support for any sector other than that for which the generals were themselves directly responsible. But there had to be an appearance of a strategic whole, so they all sat at the same table, and, metaphorically, took thread and needle, sewed these plans together, and produced them to a subsequent civilian conference as one great strategic piece; and it was solemnly proclaimed to the world the following morning that the unity of the Allies was complete.

That unity, in so far as strategy went, was pure make-believe; and make-believe may live through a generation of peace—it cannot survive a week of war. It was a collection of completely independent schemes pieced together.

Stitching is not strategy. So it came to pass that when these plans were worked out in the terrible realities of war the stitches came out and disintegration was complete. . . .

The Italian disaster may yet save the alliance, for without it I do not believe that even now we should have set up a real Council. National and professional traditions, prestige, and susceptibilities all conspired to render nugatory our best resolutions. There was no one in particular to blame. It was an inherent difficulty in getting so many independent nations, so many independent organizations, to merge all their individual idiosyncrasies and to act together as if they were one people. Now that we have set up this Council our business is to see that the unity which it represents is a fact and not a fraud.

It is for this reason that I have spoken today with perhaps brutal frankness, at the risk of much misconception here and elsewhere, and perhaps at some risk of giving temporary encouragement to the foe.

There still remained two important tasks, first, to obtain American support, and, second, to convince the British Parliament. It was important, if possible, to obtain the former in order that the Prime Minister might be in a position to inform the House of Commons that President Wilson was favourable. This the Prime Minister set about doing as soon as he arrived in London on November 13th. At luncheon with Milner and myself, he arranged that the former should attend the next session of the Supreme War Council, which was to be held as soon as the necessary arrangements could be made at Versailles, and that he should remain there for a few days. In the afternoon the War Cabinet met to hear the Prime Minister's report. In the evening House, who had arrived about a week before at the head of an American Mission, dined alone with him. The utmost that Lloyd George was able to wring from the Colonel was that he would advise the President to appoint Bliss as u.s. Military Representative on the Supreme War Council.[1] Although House asked for an immediate decision about Bliss, it did not arrive in time for an announcement of American participation in the Prime Minister's statement in Parliament on the following day.

The Parliamentary situation was an anxious one owing to Robertson's hostility which remained unabated, notwithstanding the fact that Maurice, his right hand man, had prepared the first draft of the Supreme War Council's constitution. On November 14th, the day following our return and the very day on which the Prime Minister had arranged to make his statement, a Memorandum was received from the

[1] House, III, pp. 223 sq.

War Office claiming that they alone had the right to issue instructions to the British Permanent Military Adviser of the Council. The matter was remitted to Carson and Smuts to deal with and—

November 14th. . . . they prepared a reply based on a draft that I had put up, to the effect that the Army Council undoubtedly possessed the right they claim, but that the instructions they would issue must be based on the instructions of the Government and that we relied on their co-operation in this important innovation.

November 15th. War Cabinet at 11.30. I lunched with the Asquiths, having Ll. G.'s consent. . . . Asquith, while talking of the Italian situation, let the cat slip out of the bag, mentioning that he had seen Robertson that morning. I have no doubt that Robertson is intriguing like the deuce. Last night House let slip that Robertson was coming to see him this morning. His private secretary, thinking I was on Robertson's staff, came in to say that Bliss particularly wanted Robertson to repeat to House what he had said to him. Why does Robertson cut the War Cabinet and see House and the Leader of the Opposition? Was it in order to intrigue against the Council? Carson told me this afternoon that he was very sick with Lloyd George's speech and opposed to the Supreme War Council but meant to stick to him because he thought he was the only man to win the war. Had a long talk at tea-time with Strachey of the *Spectator* who had written a violent article against Ll. G. I put Ll. G.'s point of view and he said he was glad he had not seen me before because he would not have written his article.

This tittle-tattle is included just to show the kind of atmosphere which had grown up round Lloyd George's statement in Parliament on November 14th which was followed by a full-dress debate in the House of Commons on the 19th. There was not much enthusiasm for his plan and there was a good deal of genuine opposition. It was just the sort of situation in which his genius and courage came strongly to the fore. In the debate to which I listened in the official gallery, the Prime Minister's speech carried the House and was a decisive triumph for his idea. On that very day he had the satisfaction of learning that President Wilson had issued a public statement in support of it and had instructed House to be present with Bliss at the first meeting of the Supreme War Council in Versailles.

CHAPTER LXX

THE FIRST VERSAILLES MEETING

'Russia will never be really civilized, because it was
civilized too soon.' (ROUSSEAU, *Social Contract*, II, c. 8.)

LLOYD GEORGE had shown peculiar prescience in seeking the
support of Clemenceau for the projected Supreme War Council, for,
on November 16th, two days after we left Paris, he had become
President of the Council. On Clemenceau, therefore, fell the responsibility for establishing the new machinery at Versailles and setting it in
motion.

His arrangements for the first meeting had to be adjusted to other
changes. In Italy Orlando had replaced Boselli as Premier, with
Sonnino as Foreign Minister and Nitti, a broadminded statesman, as
Minister of Finance. House had arrived in Paris from London on
November 2nd with instructions from President Wilson to attend the
Council's first meeting, although his personal attitude towards it was
known to be critical. In addition the United States had asked for an
assembly of the Allies in which their mission would take part. A major
change was the deterioration of the situation in Russia, where Kerenski
had fallen the day before Clemenceau took office, and armistice negotiations with Germany had begun. These events had opened up for the
Allied Governments a number of delicate political questions, unsuitable
for discussion either in a large general assembly or at the first meeting of
a military organization like the Supreme War Council.

Under Clemenceau's admirable management the proceedings began
at 10 a.m. on November 30th—to quote my diary 'an absurd affair with
about 120 persons present of every imaginable race and colour'. Without wasting a moment on eloquent speeches, Clemenceau announced
'*L'ordre du jour est le travail. Travaillons!*' and proceeded to divide up
the work between committees. The most important of these was the
Committee of Heads of Delegations of the principal belligerents
(France, Britain, Italy and, for the first time, the United States with
House as chief delegate). Others, which included members of the
American mission, were to consider improvements in organization and
co-ordination over a wide field: and December 2nd was kept free for
the Supreme War Council.

On the organizational side, following up previous consultations in

London and Paris with the American mission, useful results were achieved, including the setting up of (1) an Allied Naval Council as a companion to the Military Advisers at Versailles, for which I had been pressing; (2) an Allied Maritime Transport Council for the co-ordination of sea transport; (3) a permanent Allied Committee in Paris to co-ordinate the supply and transport of munitions; (4) an extension to the United States and Italy of the system for exchange of information already operating between Britain and France; and (5) an organization for rationing neutrals and preventing them from supplying our enemies. These and other arrangements for strengthening the organization of the Allied and Associated Powers were useful.

At the very important conferences of the heads of the principal Allied Powers, in Pichon's tapestry-hung sanctum at the Quai d'Orsay, the discussions were dominated by events in Russia. Consideration was first given to a suggestion by the British Ambassador at Petrograd that the Allies should release Russia from her original engagement not to make a separate peace, in order to strengthen the moderate party, but this was at once rejected as a most dangerous precedent. Lloyd George, though not enamoured with the proposal, thought it ought to be explored, so the Russian Ambassador in Paris was called into Council. He, too, had no use for the idea, but suggested that war aims might be discussed with a decent Russian Government. He was then asked to try his hand at a draft of war aims. He produced no less than three, Sonnino a fourth and House a fifth, and attempts were made to marry them up, but without success. The root difficulty was that the United States was not a party to any of the treaties which bound the Allies, having, as House put it, 'entered the war for idealistic motives', and could not associate herself in any discussion of them. Everyone agreed, however, that a declaration by the conference without the United States would be useless. So that idea was dropped, and each Power was left to tell the Russian Government in its own way that, while intending to fight on to victory, they were prepared to discuss war aims with any properly constituted Russian Goverment.

The next problem was the possibility of Japanese assistance to Russia. The Japanese Ambassadors in London and Paris were called in to the conversations, but could offer little encouragement owing to lack of national enthusiasm, the smallness of their Army, and material difficulties. Still, they were asked to consult their Government.

The question of the plight of Roumania after the defection of Russia was taken up, and was left for the moment to the French Government

who had always taken the Roumanians under their wing. They were asked to seek support by the British Missions in Russia and Roumania on the question of *ravitaillement*.

Finally, it was felt necessary to do something to avert the danger that the Poles, in their despair, might succumb to the blandishments of the Central Powers, and eventually, on the suggestion of Balfour, the following addition to the war aims of the Allies was agreed to by the conference:

The creation of a Poland, independent and indivisible, under such conditions as will ensure her free political and economic development, constitutes one of the conditions of a solid and just peace, and of the régime of right in Europe.

The last and the most important feature of the conference was the first meeting on December 1st of the Supreme War Council, in the new headquarters allotted to them by the French Government at the Hotel Trianon, Versailles.

Ever since our arrival in Paris on November 27th I had been anxious about this meeting. House was notoriously dubious[1] about the desirability of the Council, and particularly of American participation therein, but had been overridden by President Wilson. On the evening of our arrival, friendly American colleagues had told me that Clemenceau was out to wreck the scheme and was aiming at replacing it by a single Commander-in-Chief; and later in the evening, after reporting this to Lloyd George, I learned from Reading, who had arrived from Washington, and another Englishman in close touch with House, that Lloyd George was now willing to adopt a proposal made by Clemenceau to House 'that the civilian element should be dropped out of the Supreme War Council'. That idea, of course, would have wrecked the whole scheme. Next morning, however, November 28th, I accompanied the Prime Minister to the Ministry of War, where he saw Clemenceau alone and cleared the matter up. He told me also that he had undertaken to Clemenceau that 'I should draft his opening speech for the Supreme War Council on December 1st'. That troubled me not a little, with so many disagreeable rumours current about the attitude of House, Clemenceau, Robertson and others. However, with some aid from Milner, I soon had a draft ready, and on December 1st, sure enough, Clemenceau read it as his opening speech.[2]

[1] House, III, p. 271.
[2] Full text in *War Memoirs*, V, pp. 2755-9; *vide*, too, House, III, p. 276.

Much of it was based on a Memorandum that I had prepared for the use of Lloyd George at a meeting of the War Cabinet just before our departure for Paris, where great stress was laid on the need for framing our policy for 1918 based not only on a review of the military projects, but also on our staying power, which included the naval, shipping, shipbuilding, and man-power outlook on which depended our ability to stay the course.

The speech made clear that the first thing to be done was to set the Military Advisers to work on the nature of the campaigns to be under-taken in 1918, and to prepare recommendations. The first step was for Governments to instruct their respective military advisers at Versailles on their own views and those of their General Staffs. Clemenceau then drew attention to the new factors. The first was that it must be assumed that Russia could not be counted on for future assistance. The second was the grave reverse in Italy, where large British and French forces were now engaged for the first time; this concentration suggested the possibility of an offensive on that front. The third was the potentiality of the gradual accumulation of American forces on the Western Front in 1918. That again depended on a fourth, i.e. the effect of American co-operation in improving the shipping situation. In this connection Clemenceau enjoined the Military Advisers not to forget that the war had become one of exhaustion, as witnessed by the collapse of Russia.

The final objective, he added, now as formerly, was the overthrow of Prussian militarism, but he asked the Permanent Military Advisers 'to consider carefully whether possibly that object might not be brought nearer final achievement by the overthrow, first of all of Germany's allies, and the isolation of Germany. . . .' He also commended the military situation in the Balkans for early consideration by the Military Advisers.[1]

As the result of the discussion, eight resolutions were passed. Four related to the furnishing of information to the military advisers and the establishment by each country of military advisers and a secretariat, the other four to the investigation of the military situation on the French, Belgian, Italian and Balkan fronts.

December 1st. The meeting was a great success; the P.M. and I were in the best possible form. That is to say, while he was speaking I drafted conclu-sions, which he got the Council to accept. Altogether it was a good send-off. . . . At one point the discussion got on to the Balkans and Greece, and began

[1] House's editor comments shrewdly that Clemenceau's opening speech 'was much more in accord with the particular ideas of Mr. Lloyd George than those of M. Clemenceau.'

to deteriorate. Robertson wrote on a bit of paper to Henry Wilson 'We always get on to this subject and waste all our time over it' (or words to that effect). Wilson then wrote 'it gets bloodier and bloodier' to which Robertson replied 'and bloodier'. I felt that the two generals were beginning to get on terms.

No secretaries had appeared from any other country and my little replica of the War Cabinet Secretariat took charge of the secretarial arrangements.

Weygand, the French Military Representative, was a little worried at the way I and my Secretariat (Storr and Amery) took charge, but I said we had only done it to suit our own convenience, and that, as they were not so highly organized yet, we would put all our arrangements at his disposal. Of course my real objects in developing this branch of my office at Versailles so promptly were, first, to get the thing run on our lines, and, second, to get a high standard of execution . . . and make it a success.

As a matter of fact an English-language *procès-verbal* was in the hands of every member of the Council the same evening—a great triumph for the distribution department, considering the distance of Versailles from Paris.

I was busy up to past midnight with the *procès-verbal* and winding up affairs in Paris. Up to the last moment it was in question whether I should leave next day with the P.M., or remain with Balfour (who was to stay for the final winding-up). To bed about 12.30 a.m.

Passing over enthusiastic and highly complimentary farewells from my American colleagues I come to the journey home.

December 2nd (Sunday). Called at 5 a.m. and started to London at 7 a.m. The Prime Minister is talking of sending me to Berne to meet Mensdorff or some other Austrian to hear what proposals they have to make for a separate peace. Fearful crossing. I was appallingly seasick.

CHAPTER LXXI

PEACE PROBES

'War! war! no peace! peace is to me a war.'
(SHAKESPEARE, *King John*, Act III, sc. i).

THE reason why, after the first meeting at Versailles, Lloyd George had gone home so abruptly, leaving Balfour to replace him for the final stage, was that during the secret discussions of the heads of delegations on November 29th he had secured agreement that he should be authorized to probe an Austrian approach for a separate peace. Up to now very little has been said in these pages about such overtures, although the War Policy Committee of 1917 had included in their Report a recommendation that efforts should be made to detach some of Germany's Allies. Since then a whole story of such efforts had been growing up, but necessarily shrouded in great secrecy, as nothing could be more shattering to a Government and to its fighting forces than any suggestion that it is wilting. Tentative feelers had from time to time been received from all our enemies. Those of Bulgaria and Turkey hardly deserve mention, as their authenticity was dubious. The former were dropped after Caporetto, and the latter after Allenby's capture of Jerusalem (December 7, 1917).

Much more important than these was the definite German approach through Lancken, First Secretary of the German Legation in Madrid, news of which had reached Lloyd George at Criccieth late on September 22nd, and in conjunction with military developments brought us hurtling back to London on September 23rd (Sunday). Next evening, with War Cabinet approval, Lloyd George had followed it up by an all-night journey, accompanied only by myself, to meet Painlevé and Foch at breakfast in Boulogne on September 25th.[1]

At Boulogne Painlevé confirmed that the German approach was genuine, but no decision was taken whether it should be followed up; Lloyd George, who believed that the defection of Russia could not be delayed much longer, felt that the decision depended in the main on what was likely to be the effect of that defection on the military situation. At Boulogne Robertson expressed the view that in that event our prospects of victory would vanish, but Foch did not agree. There and

[1] *vide supra*, pp. 698 *sq.*

then Lloyd George decided to visit GHQ, where Haig, who was very preoccupied in conducting the Flanders offensive, sided with Foch and promised a Memorandum.

On September 27th we were back in London, but owing to serious German air raids on London and other delays, some time was lost in getting the consent first of the War Cabinet and then of all the Allies, including Russia, and it was not until October 6th that a despatch was sent to Madrid to the effect that we should be prepared to receive any communication that the Germans might desire to make and to discuss it with our Allies. But on the day after the despatch was delivered in Madrid, Kuhlmann, the German Foreign Minister, made an important public speech in which he made clear that Germany could make no concessions in Alsace-Lorraine and omitted any declaration about the evacuation of Belgium, on which Britain and France had always insisted. That was the end of the German overtures.

Much more authoritative and more sustained were the Austrian approaches in the spring of 1917. The first I heard of them was on April 10, 1917. I had accompanied Lloyd George to Paris on the pretext of a visit to his old friend, Painlevé, who had recently become Minister of War. The story is continued in the following diary extract:

April 18th. .... Lloyd George also had a mysterious interview with a mysterious person, and laid great stress on Painlevé's not knowing who it was, so I had to keep guard and arrange that they should not meet. Later on he told me that it was the brother-in-law of the Austrian Emperor, who had an autograph letter from the Austrian Emperor making peace overtures. Only Ribot (and the French President) knew of it in France, and both they and Ll. George were sworn not to reveal it to the Italians or to their colleagues. Ll. G. told this to me, as he felt that in case of an accident an Englishman ought to share the secret.

Lloyd George then told me that Ribot had arranged with the Italian Government for a meeting of Ministers on the Franco-Italian frontier to discuss the matter. I suggested at once that he should add a representative of the Foreign Office to our party, as I knew little of Austro-Italian relations, and I had never even seen the London Treaty of April 26, 1915, which had been dealt with at the Cabinet and not at the War Council of which I was then secretary; and, having had no warning, I had brought no papers. Lloyd George rejected this proposal as it would involve a wide breach of his pledge of secrecy. He had, however,

brought Macdonogh, who, he understood, knew about the Treaty and its military aspects. We left Paris that evening (April 15th) with Ribot by special train to St. Jean de Maurienne, where we found Boselli, the Italian Prime Minister (who took little part in the proceedings), Sonnino, and Barrère, the French Ambassador in Rome, a first-rate diplomat and linguist but not a good interpreter—the role for which he was cast.

During the whole of the forenoon the Ministers met alone in a steaming hot railway carriage, while Macdonogh and I tramped up and down the railway-siding in the melting snow and sunshine, awaiting a summons that never came. Afterwards:

Lloyd George told me that Sonnino at the morning meeting had been strongly opposed to the idea of a separate peace between Austria and the Allies—which I much regretted. It was a pity they could not tell him of the Emperor's offer. Aldrovandi and I were there as secretaries, but found it difficult to pick up the threads. I have a note, though, that 'during the conference Lloyd George spoke very straight to Sonnino about Italy's inadequate efforts in the war, compared with her inordinate demands'. I sat up until 1 a.m. drafting a report on the conference, for the King and Cabinet.

The main reason, of course, for the comparative failure of the Conference of St. Jean de Maurienne was the pledge of secrecy, and the consequent difficulty in convincing Sonnino, who was completely sceptical, that the Austrians wanted peace talks. Even if the British and French Ministers could have revealed the source of their information I think it unlikely that Sonnino could have consented to concede any of Italy's rights under the Treaty of London—as we were to discover a year or two later at the Paris Peace Conference.

After the failure at St. Jean de Maurienne we received no more definite overtures from Austria for some time. There were rumours in Paris, and a certain amount of leakage during the summer, and a peace proposal by the Pope in August led to some talk of secret negotiations, but nothing came of it, and the first news that reached me of anything more definite was the Prime Minister's intimation that I might be sent to Berne; the circumstances he explained in detail on our journey home on December 2nd. On December 8th, however, I have a diary note that 'my bag has been ready packed with plain clothes all the week'. But that same day, while at breakfast with Lloyd George and Smuts, after discussing the subject at great length, the former decided that he could not spare me as I was needed 'for the new and vitally important War

Cabinet Committee on Man-Power'—a decision that was confirmed a week later (December 16th). So instead of a thrilling mission to Switzerland in search of peace, I was condemned to weeks of concentration on the dreariest and most controversial aspect of our war effort.

Nevertheless I did not lose much, for a fortnight later (December 23rd) Smuts and Philip Kerr, who had accompanied him in my place, turned up while I was talking to Lloyd George, and reported as my diary records:

. . . that Mensdorff had made it clear that Austria could not make a separate peace but had tried hard to discuss a general peace. Kerr, in addition, had had some pourparlers with a Turkish representative, and reported that both Mensdorff and the Turkish spokesman had independently suggested that it would be very useful if the Allies would restate their war aims. Lloyd George at once caught on to this belated idea and on Christmas Day, 1917, when the Central Powers published an account of their preliminary peace negotiations with the Russians, he decided to take action.

On December 28th the War Cabinet got to work on the subject of war aims. After sketching out to me his own ideas on the subject on December 29th, the Prime Minister asked me to produce a Memorandum as a basis for discussion, which I did, and it was circulated to the War Cabinet the same day. On December 31st and thereafter they worked on it hammer and tongs and three alternative drafts were produced by Smuts, Robert Cecil and the Prime Minister respectively. Cecil was then called on to marry them into a final draft, which he did with great skill. At the last moment as I noted:

I persuaded him to drop out adherence to the principle of self-determination by pointing out what a lot of trouble it would give the British Empire.

Before publishing the statement, Lloyd George obtained the assent of the Dominions, Asquith and the leaders of the Labour Party, which had published its own ideas. He then announced publicly the Government's war aims on January 5, 1918, at a meeting of trade unionists—a characteristic touch. It did something towards allaying the spirit of war-weariness, disappointment and unrest that was spreading over the country and to strengthen the basic opinion that we must fight on until the enemy was crushed. Pichon, the French Foreign Minister, made a corresponding statement on December 28th, and on January 8th President Wilson proclaimed his famous fourteen points.

The year 1918, therefore, like the year 1917, was ushered in by

declarations of the war aims of the principal Allies, supplemented this time by the American President's screed. The effect on the enemy, however, was not what we had hoped, for on January 24th the German Chancellor Hertling and Czernin, the Austrian Foreign Minister, made public replies, which banged the door on any hope of peace negotiations.[1]

Nevertheless 'hope springs eternal in the human breast' and on March 5th the War Cabinet decided to send Philip Kerr to Switzerland 'to try and get to the bottom of a message we have had from Czernin, indicating that he wants to meet someone'. Next day the Foreign Office tried to stop him, but the War Cabinet adhered to their decision. On March 12th Kerr sent a favourable report, and Smuts was induced to return to Switzerland. After an interview with Skrzynski, Austrian representative at Berne, he reported that Czernin had cooled off and was now apprehensive that our object was to detach Austria from Germany.

My last entry on the subject was:

March 20th. . . . Philip Kerr came to see me this evening after his trip to Switzerland. He thinks the Austrians will 'bust soon'.

Next day (March 21st) the Germans launched their great attack on the Western Front, and all hopes of an early peace were shattered.

---

[1] As a pendant to this story of peace probes we may quote this passage from the communiqué issued after the meeting of the Supreme War Council on January 30th:

'The Supreme War Council gave the most careful consideration to the recent utterances of the German Chancellor and of the Austro-Hungarian Minister of Foreign Affairs, but was unable to find in them any real approximation to the moderate conditions laid down by all the Allied Governments. This conviction was only deepened by . . . the now openly disclosed plans of conquest and spoliation. . . . The Council decided that the only immediate task before them lay in the prosecution with the utmost vigour and in the closest and most effective co-operation of the military efforts of the Allies until such time as the pressure of that effort shall have brought about in the enemy Governments and peoples a change of temper which would justify the hope of the conclusion of peace on terms which would not involve the abandonment, in face of an aggressive and unrepentant militarism, of all the principles of freedom, justice and the respect for the Law of Nations which the Allies are resolved to vindicate.'

CHAPTER LXXII

MAN-POWER AND
AMERICAN ASSISTANCE, 1918

'The Multitude sufficient to confide in for our Security,
is not determined by any certain number, but by comparison with the Enemy we feare; and is then sufficient,
when the odds of the Enemy is not of so visible and conspicuous moment, to determine the event of warre, as to
move him to attempt.' (HOBBES, *Leviathan*, Part II,
c. 17.)

IN essence the man-power problem of 1918 did not differ from previous
phases of the question. The Supreme Command was still confronted
with the inescapable dilemma between the needs of the armies in the
field and those of production and transport. The main difference was
that in the last year of the war the needs of both were greater and our
remaining resources less. The number of men in these islands was no
longer equal to supplying both demands during the whole of the year.
Against this could be set the fact that, by the American intervention, an
almost inexhaustible reservoir of fighting men had been opened up
which could be tapped in increasing volume later in the year, as the
men were enlisted, trained and organized, provided that shipping
transport could be found.

On December 6, 1917, according to a note in my diary, the War
Office gave warning

... that if large numbers of men are not recruited and sent out at once Haig's
army would not be able to hold the line and that the gunners are so tired that
they can scarcely hold the line.

This is inconsistent with Haig's continual reports of bad German morale
and that the German divisions have been put through the mill in Flanders
and knocked out one by one.

On the same day the War Cabinet set up a special committee to consider the question of man-power; it held its first meeting on December
10th. It was composed of the Prime Minister, Curzon, Carson, Barnes
and Smuts with myself as secretary. On December 8th I prepared under
instructions and circulated to the new committee a Memorandum on
the subject in which the issue was thus defined:

From the above notes it will be seen that the Cabinet Committee has to face a situation which differs in two very important particulars from that which has faced previous Cabinet committees on the same subject. These are, first: that the economic crisis, instead of being a danger to be guarded against, is actually present; and second, that the seriousness of the military man-power crisis is not merely that we shall not smash the enemy if the men are not forthcoming, but that the enemy may smash us.

The problem that confronts the Committee, therefore, is to avert a military catastrophe without plunging us into an economic catastrophe equally fatal to the cause of the Allies.

The Flanders offensive had proved very costly. Yet it was indispensable to fill the ranks sufficiently to meet the coming German attack, of which no one had any doubt. The difficulty of replacing the casualties in existing formations was accentuated by the demands for new services such as the Flying Corps, Tank Corps, Heavy Artillery and Poison Gas. In addition large labour corps were required for work behind the front. Put into figures, the requirements of the Fighting Services were:

	The Demand	Numbers available	Deficit
The Navy (Category A men)	90,000	50,000	40,000
The Army and Air Force Category A men[1]	600,000	100,000	500,000
Men of lower categories	320,000	100,000	220,000
Lads of 18 years for Home Defence	240,000	120,000	120,000
TOTAL	1,250,000	370,000	880,000

The Supreme Command were thus faced with a prospective deficit of no less than 880,000 men, of which 500,000 Category A men and 220,000 men of lower categories were, according to the estimates of the Ministry of National Service, due to fall on the Army.

But, if the need for soldiers was great, so were those of industry. Nowhere was this more important than in shipbuilding. The American shipbuilding programme for 1918, which had aimed, over-optimistically, at an output of 6,000,000 tons, was now estimated at 2,000,000 tons. Yet, if the American armies were to be brought over in time for a decisive operation even in 1919, a vast tonnage would be required. Submarine losses, it is true, were now considerably reduced. Neverthe-

---

[1] i.e. after allowing for returning wounded and others who would be made available.

less for the last quarter of 1917 the British war and marine losses (783,000 gross tons) were still more than double the new tonnage brought on to the register (389,000 gross tons). So great, indeed, was the need of the shipyards that the War Cabinet, after a special inquiry, ordered the Army to release 20,000 category A men for shipbuilding. Similarly the time when the Navy was just getting the measure of the submarine was not the one for reducing the output of light cruisers, destroyers, small craft and anti-submarine apparatus of all kinds. No one was prepared to face a reduction in the output of munitions and war material for the Army and Air Force. In 1917, perhaps for the first time in the war, we had had the advantage over the enemy in the weight of artillery fire, but, against that, the enemy was now in a position to bring artillery and ammunition from the Russian Front, so for that reason we dared not reduce output. Tanks and mechanical tractors were the one feature in the land fighting in which we possessed a definite technical superiority over the enemy. There lay our chief hope of victory on land. Neither in mechanical land armaments nor aircraft could we afford to relax our efforts.

In many other respects our requirements for civilian man-power had become greater rather than less. As the number of our merchant ships became smaller, owing to losses, and as the demands on the available tonnage became greater, so did the need become more urgent to turn the ships round in port quicker, so that it was impossible to spare men from the docks. The convoy system also tended to result in the arrival or departure of a large number of ships more or less simultaneously, which put pressure on the dockers in spurts. With the increase of work in shipyards and munition factories the demand for steel became ever more pressing. This again led to a greater demand for more coalminers. It was impossible to take men from any of these national needs for the fighting Services without disastrous reactions on the Services themselves. Again, in order to save tonnage, large agricultural programmes had been put in hand. The requirements of agriculture had been met partly by the temporary release from the colours of a certain number of men at harvest time and for ploughing and sowing, partly by 'land-girls' who were being employed in ever-increasing numbers. But a certain nucleus of fit men was indispensable, and as early as October 1917, the War Cabinet had reluctantly decided that 2,000 skilled ploughmen must be released by the War Office.

A policy of felling timber had been adopted in the spring in connection with the reduction of imports, and had resulted in saving a large

amount of tonnage. The increased demands for coal and for quarries, and the construction of new defence lines in France and Flanders, however, necessitated the production of more timber for pit props, etc., and rendered it impossible to release men from this source.

The results of the Committee's discussion may thus be summarized:

1. The Naval demands were conceded in full owing to the vital importance of maintaining sea communications.

2. To meet the claim of the Army Council that, unless their demand was conceded the Expeditionary Force in France would have to be reduced by fifteen divisions before April 1, 1918, it was decided, after consulting the French Government, to follow the French example—and that of the Germans—by reducing the number of battalions in the division from twelve to nine. The Army chiefs accepted this recommendation with a bad grace.

3. The Army Council were recommended to reduce the five cavalry divisions in France and Flanders, but this was not a hard-and-fast decision.

4. After long and acrimonious consideration by a Committee of the Defence Services the number of divisions retained for home defence was reduced from eight to four. 'The general result', says Robertson, 'was to leave four divisions for home defence and to set free about 40,000 mostly belonging to categories below A1 for employment in France.'[1]

5. The estimates of the War Office for casualties during the defensive campaign of 1918, compared with the offensive battles of 1917, were heavily criticized, especially after hearing French estimates of losses which were much lower, but it was realized that the moment for reducing the estimate could not be calculated exactly.

While this investigation of service requirements was in progress, an equally searching inquiry was made to see if the Ministry of National Service could not release from industry more category A men for active service, the number of whom was calculated to be 950,000 out of a total of 3,500,000 still in civilian service.

Eventually the Committee decided that, in calculating the numbers to be released, the Ministry of National Service must give first priority over all the Services to the Navy and Air Force; second priority for shipbuilding and with, but after, manufacture of aeroplanes and tanks, food production, tree-felling and storage for food. The Committee confirmed the Ministry's calculation that not more than 150,000 of the total of 950,000 in industry could be made available for military service —their original estimate. Even so, risks were being run on the economic

[1] Robertson, II, p. 15.

side of the war effort. This, in effect, was the decision of the Man-Power Committee.

The Ministry of National Service estimated the effect of the Committee's decisions on the strength of the Army to be as follows:

On the assumption of nine months' hard fighting from February 15 to November 15, 1918.

March 31st	Surplus	96,000
June 30th	Deficit	17,500
September 30th	Deficit	102,500
December 30th	Deficit	200,000

On the assumption of six months' hard fighting and six months' light fighting.

March 31st	Surplus	162,000
June 30th	Surplus	114,500
September 30th	Surplus	4,737
December 31st	Deficit	131,500

The War Office did not accept these figures and anticipated nothing but deficits at all stages.

No one pretended that the result of the inquiry was satisfactory. The account had not really been balanced. The prospective deficit of the Army had only been reduced, even in the estimates of the Ministry of National Service which the War Office refused to accept, to figures that were not absolutely staggering, by assuming that defensive warfare was less costly than the offensive and by cutting the strength of divisions from twelve to nine battalions. The War Office rejected the assumption and detested the reduction of divisional strength.

It has to be borne in mind, however, that we were getting very near the bottom of the man-power bag. Our resources had to be doled out with great care, in order to tide us over until the arrival of reinforcements from America on a substantial scale, and to ensure that, when the time came, the seas should be sufficiently safe and the tonnage adequate to ensure their transport. In these circumstances the Supreme Command were right not to run any risks by refusing the Admiralty their full requirements or by curtailing shipbuilding, marine engineering, food production and the other measures designed to maintain the amount of shipping available for this purpose.[1]

[1] It may be noted here that, if the Army's man-power situation was grave from the numerical point of view, it was not wholly satisfactory from that of morale. There was a good deal of war-

All this strengthened the view of the Man-Power Committee and of the War Cabinet that their first aim must be to bring over large numbers of troops from America. After receiving the report, the efforts of the Supreme Command were, therefore, concentrated on increasing the tonnage available for their transport, and all the old ground was gone over again in the hope of scraping up a few thousand tons. In addition, persistent efforts were made to induce the u.s. Government to attach American battalions to British divisions for training purposes pending the time when the American divisions were formed and brought to France; at that time some forty divisions were formed or forming. But, by the end of November 1917, there were only four actually in France and of these only one was actually training in the line. The amount of shipping available was sufficient to transport only one and one-third divisions a month, and it was estimated, on the basis of British experience, that after arrival American divisions would require some months in a quiet part of the line before they were fit for battle.

A proposal was advanced during the November Paris Conference that 150 American battalions should be brought to France as an addition to the divisional programme and that these should be brigaded with British troops. Under this plan they would obtain experience of fighting conditions under experienced staffs speaking their own language. When their own divisional organizations were ready to receive them, they were to be withdrawn from the British brigades.

Some idea of the difficulties which confronted both the Supreme War Council in pressing this proposal and the American Commander-in-Chief in acceding to it may be obtained by reading the following passage from the latter's instructions from the United States Secretary for War:

In military operations against the Imperial German Government you are directed to co-operate with the forces of the other countries employed against that enemy; but in so doing the underlying idea must be kept in view that the forces of the United States are a separate and distinct component of the combined forces, the identity of which must be preserved. This fundamental rule is subject to such minor exceptions in particular circumstances as your judgment may approve. The action is confided to you and you will exercise full

weariness. The men were exhausted by the fighting in Flanders and incessant trench-digging; they needed rest. There was discontent at the high rates paid to men at home whose families were much better off than those of men at the front. There was also discontent at the way men discharged from hospital were drafted into other units which had been depleted—notoriously the Irish Division, owing to lack of volunteers from Southern Ireland where the Cabinet had not felt able to enforce conscription.

discretion in determining the manner of your co-operation. But, until the forces of the United States are in your judgment sufficiently strong to warrant operations as an independent command, it is understood that you will co-operate as a component of whatever army you may be assigned to by the French Government.

These instructions were issued owing to the pressure which the Allies had been exercising on the American Government ever since they entered the war to send them individual recruits or small units such as companies or battalions in order to help them to eke out their man-power; they did not leave Pershing much latitude.

There was also the practical difficulty of finding the additional tonnage required to augment the divisional programme. The United States was prepared to find about half of the shipping required for speeding up the despatch of the additional numbers (though not necessarily to be employed as suggested in the British scheme), but the British Shipping Controller could not see his way to find the balance. The question was not solved either at the Paris Conference or at the Supreme War Council at Versailles, but the pressure was continued. House, before his departure for America on December 6th and after his arrival on December 15th, was the recipient of many messages, pressing for an early and favourable decision.

The proposal had been made before the January decision of the War Cabinet to reduce the number of British battalions in a division from twelve to nine. After that decision the idea of incorporating American battalions in our brigades became more attractive than ever in the eyes of the British Government, and especially of the military authorities, for at a stroke it would restore the number of battalions in the brigade to the original figure. On January 9th and 10th Robertson and Maclay, the Shipping Controller, discussed the matter with Pershing, and, as a sequel Robertson sent the American Commander-in-Chief a Memorandum setting out the gravity of the situation and urging that American troops, instead of being brought to Europe by divisions, should be brought by battalions, which would at first be incorporated in British brigades to get their initial experience, and then combined in American brigades, which, in turn, would be combined into divisions. Robertson was allowed to state that the British Government were even prepared to risk a temporary curtailment of imports of supplies in order to release sufficient shipping to bring over 150 battalions within three or four months, and that this could be done without interfering with the

existing divisional programme for which some twelve thousand American troops were already being brought over in British ships. As no result followed, the subject was further discussed between Haig, Pétain and Pershing at conferences on January 19th and 24th, again without any decision being reached.

General Smuts in 1918

CHAPTER LXXIII

THE ADJUSTMENT OF THE LINE:
THE WESTERN FRONT REVISITED

'In cases of defence, 'tis best to weigh
The enemy more mighty than he seems:
So the proportions of defence are fill'd.'
(SHAKESPEARE, *Henry V*, Act ii, sc. 4).

SHAKESPEARE'S words are applicable to many of the problems that confronted the Supreme Command at different stages of the war, but to none more so than to the vexed question of the extension of the British section of the line, which was one of the most thorny of the difficulties between the British and French Governments and their respective High Commands at the end of 1917 and the beginning of 1918.

The War Cabinet had received long warning that the question was likely to be raised. As early as June 8, 1917, Henry Wilson in warning the Government about the state of the French Army after the failure of the Nivelle offensive, expressed the view that before long the British Government would be approached by the French Government with a request to take over a further section of the line on the Western Front and that a case would be made out which it would be difficult to resist. Information from other sources confirmed the strong feeling in France that we ought to extend our front. In July we learned that the Military Commission of the French Chamber sitting in secret session had adopted a report in favour of an extension of our front by eighty-five miles. It was claimed that the British troops on the ground were double or treble the French in density, and that this was causing much discontent among the *poilus*, who felt that they had borne the hardest part, and that the British Army was not carrying its proper share of the common burden. The extension of the line was treated by the French Government as essential in order to rest their soldiers, so that, in the spring of 1918, they might take the offensive; the alternative would be a disaster and an inconclusive peace. Henry Wilson in July strongly urged that, in order to keep France in good shape, we must treat her with every consideration, and, when she asked us later to take over many miles of her front, we must do so with good grace, bearing in mind that France from the first had been a good comrade. The War Policy Committee had taken cognisance of these warnings, and recog-

nized that before the winter it would be necessary to take over a considerable section of the French line. Further warnings were received in September.

Consequently at the Boulogne conference with Painlevé and Foch (Sept. 25th) Robertson, to whom Lloyd George had allotted the role of spokesman on this military question, was able to announce that the British Government admitted the principle of some extension.[1] He made it clear, however, that the present moment was impossible for carrying it out, as the Flanders offensive was still in full swing, and the divisions not actively engaged in it were resting, refitting and training; the question would be reconsidered in connection with the plans for 1918. If the British Army was to resume the offensive, it would need rest and training. Eventually this important resolution was adopted:

> The British Government having accepted in principle the extension of the line held by the British Army on the Western Front, the two Governments are agreed that the question of the extension and the time at which it should take place should be left for arrangement between the two Commanders-in-Chief.[2]

On arrival later at GHQ, as will be remembered, Lloyd George told Haig of the Boulogne agreement. Haig was immersed in the Flanders offensive which he was personally directing and intended to continue all the autumn. He did not there and then refuse to carry out the Boulogne decision, but he made no secret of his view that it was inconsistent with the plans which he was pursuing, and that no action should be taken until the plans for 1918 had been decided. That point was emphasized by Haig in reporting his views at Lloyd George's request on the military consequences of a Russian collapse.[3]

If the British military authorities were anxious to postpone the implementation of the Boulogne agreement, the French Government and military authorities were equally insistent that the extension of the front should be begun as soon as possible. We now know that, as early as September 22nd, Pétain, in response to a request from the French Government for his views, had suggested that beginning on November 1st the British Army should extend its line as far as Berry-au-Bac, and that the French War Committee had instructed him to ask for this extension.

[1] *War Memoirs*, V, p. 2764.
[2] *Ibid.*, p. 2765.
[3] Haig's letter (dated October 8th) is given in full in *France and Belgium 1918*, I App. I; *vide* also *War Memoirs*, V, p. 2760.

For the moment, however, Pétain held his hand. Perhaps he was aware that sharp tactics were about to be adopted by his superiors such as my diary indicates:

October 9th. . . . Painlevé and Foch are arriving unheralded today. No one knows the reason for their visit.

October 10th. War Cabinet at 11.30 to consider certain proposals made by Painlevé, who is in London, for taking over more of the French line (sixty miles), and for French co-operation in Syria. . . .

Perhaps the French Government's pressure was rather overdone. Whether for this reason, or owing to the determined opposition of Haig, now supported by Robertson, to any extension while the battle of Flanders continued, or because the Boulogne Conference had remitted all details to the two Commanders-in-Chief, the War Cabinet rather resented the attempt of French Ministers to forestall their meeting. It was realized that so long as the Flanders offensive continued, the British divisions engaged and those awaiting their turn could not possibly be spared for extending the line. Those which had been through the mill were so depleted that they were not in a state to do so. It was felt, therefore, that, until the battle was over, there could be no question of the proposed extension, quite apart from the possibility of a resumption of the offensive in 1918 which Haig had in mind. It transpired also that every French soldier by law was entitled to and was getting ten days' leave three times a year which far exceeded that of our own men; transport considerations alone rendered so liberal an allowance impossible for British soldiers, and *a fortiori* even more so for Dominion and Indian soldiers. Why, it was asked, should British soldiers be expected to take over more of the line in order to give the *poilus* longer spells of leave than they received themselves? They had borne the brunt of the fighting all the summer and autumn and were still bearing it. They were not even fighting in their own country as were the French. After the shattering ordeal through which they were passing in Flanders it would be essential to give the troops leave and rest. Until this had been done it would be premature to take over more of the French line. Such was the trend of opinion in British Government circles. They were not in the mood to be rushed. When Franklin Bouillon and Foch returned to the charge on the subject on October 10th and a little later at Chequers (October 13th and 14th) the latter made a formal demand for an extension before November 1st. On this occasion, however, the request was pressed partly on the

economic ground that it was necessary to release from the French Army men of 48 years of age and above for the ploughing and sowing of the fields without which France would starve in 1918. In his reply, Lloyd George, after putting the above and other arguments with tremendous force, made the tentative suggestion that, instead of taking over more of the French line, British divisions should go into camp for training behind the French lines, so that they could reinforce in case of attack. This proposal was very properly rejected on the ground that the communications of the two armies would get intermingled and confused. Lloyd George then suggested that the British Government should make good the wheat supplies which France feared to lose if men could not be released to sow the crops. This proposal was also unacceptable to the French. British prestige in France, they urged, would suffer gravely if, in reply to an appeal to take over more of the French line, all that Britain could offer was commercial assistance.

The net result of all this discussion was that, so far as the extension of the line was concerned, the position in mid-October remained much the same as it was after the Boulogne Conference, i.e. an extension was approved in principle, but the amount of the extension and the time when it was to take place were still left to the two Commanders-in-Chief. Having gained nothing, rather the reverse indeed, by the efforts of their Ministers to rush the British Government, the French now did what they ought to have done earlier and took the question up, as arranged at Calais, through the military channel.

One result of all this political pressure was that the two Commanders-in-Chief did not meet until October 18th, more than three weeks after the Boulogne decision. The story of the meeting which took place at Amiens, and of the subsequent correspondence between them, is told in the Official History. It is sufficient to note here that Pétain rightly assumed that Russia would drop out of the war, and that large German reinforcements which he estimated at thirty, forty or even fifty divisions, would be available for the Western Front. The French Army was losing 40,000 men a month. He was having to scrap divisions, and the strength of those that remained was reduced to 6,000 men. He had to shorten his line if he was to build up a strategical reserve to meet this threatened situation. He asked, therefore, as a beginning that the British Army should take over a front extending as far as the forest of St. Gobain (Barisis), i.e. a front of six divisions. Haig (notwithstanding the Boulogne agreement) avoided accepting the

principle of taking over more of the line, but said he would do his best to meet Pétain's wishes, and would transfer four divisions from the most northerly (coast) sector of the line to carry out the relief. After the conference he asked the War Cabinet to support him in refusing to take over more than a four-division front. In view of the fact that the plans for 1918 had not yet been settled, and were to be considered at a conference in November, the War Cabinet declined to commit themselves as yet to the amount of the extension. For the moment they decided that the proposed relief must be considered in connection with the need for leave, rest and training, and with the plan of future operations when settled. But it could not be begun until the Flanders campaign was at an end. These decisions were communicated by Robertson to Haig on October 24th.

Two days later (October 26th) we received the first news of the Italian disaster at Caporetto. On October 30th, Painlevé came to London to discuss 'the Italian situation and the relief of the French line'.[1] The idea of the establishment of a Supreme War Council, which had been discussed in a preliminary way at Chequers earlier in the month, was now very much to the fore, and Lloyd George took the opportunity of Painlevé's visit to inform him in writing that the question of the extension of the line could not be settled apart from the campaign of 1918. Painlevé agreed that this was a fair stipulation. For the moment, therefore, the question, so far as the Supreme Command was concerned, was temporarily submerged first by the Italian emergency, and afterwards by the Rapallo Conference and the establishment of the Supreme War Council.

In the meantime, however, unknown to the politicians, the two Commanders-in-Chief had made a good deal of progress. In its early stages the question of the extension of the line had always been discussed on the assumption that the battle of Flanders would continue for some time and might be resumed in 1918. When Haig met Pétain at Amiens on October 18th, however, he realized that the battle could not continue very much longer. This impelled him to raise two connected questions: first, whether it was Pétain's intention, on the termination of the battle, to withdraw the French First Army, which had been co-operating in the Flanders offensive on the left of the British Fifth Army, and, second, whether the French wished to take back the coast sector, which had been handed over to the British on June 17th. Pétain's reply was that he intended to withdraw First Army and to take

[1] *vide supra*, p. 718.

back the coast sector. That army consisted of five divisions in the line and three in reserve, but once the battle was over, the line could be held by a much smaller number of divisions. Two divisions were involved in the coast sector. Nevertheless these dispositions constituted a new factor in the situation affecting Haig's calculations and plans for the adjustment of the line.

On November 2nd Haig was able to inform Pétain that:

As I have already told you, I am prepared to prolong my right up to the Oise; I can even fall in with your wishes by relieving a sector, insignificant in extent, south of the river.[1]

That decision was taken by the British Commander-in-Chief in accordance with the discretion allowed him by the Boulogne Conference and without further instructions from the War Cabinet. The actual point for the extension was fixed by the two Commanders-in-Chief at Barisis. Early in November, therefore, the question appeared to have been settled by the generals without the further intervention of the politicians.

The execution of the agreement, however, was rendered extremely difficult by the rapid course of military events. The battle of Flanders came to an end on November 10th. In the last half of November the French began to withdraw their First Army, and by the beginning of December six of its eight divisions had been withdrawn. Two of them, however, relieved the two British divisions in the coast sector. In addition, towards the end of November, two British divisions were detailed to begin the relief of the French divisions on the British right, in other words to make a start with extending the line southwards towards Barisis. Unfortunately Haig found himself compelled to divert these two divisions to meet the German counter-attack at Cambrai. This, however, was by no means the only new factor that affected the prompt carrying out of Haig's agreement to extend his line. Caporetto had necessitated the despatch to Italy during November of five British and six French divisions. If that made the French need for the relief of the line all the greater, it added enormously to Haig's difficulties in carrying it out. By the beginning of December the position had altered materially. Apart from the five British divisions sent to Italy, a sixth (the Fourth Australian Division) had been broken up and converted into a draft-finding unit. The operations at Cambrai had resulted in the allocation of additional divisions to hold that part of the line. In effect, there-

[1] *War Memoirs*, V, p. 2776.

fore, the British Army was, for the purposes of holding the line, reduced by seven divisions; the continuous fighting also had greatly depleted its numbers.

The French Army, too, had been reduced in the number of divisions on the Western Front by events in Italy, but they also had gained partial compensation on the credit side of the account. By a successful minor operation on the Ailette they had been able to reduce their front by the equivalent of two divisions. In addition, from the withdrawal of the French First Army and the taking over of the coast sector, they had gained four divisions. Thus on balance the French, as compared with the position in September at the time of the Boulogne Conference, had gained six divisions to set against the six that had been sent to Italy. Too much, however, must not be made of this, because their calculations had been made on the assumption that the divisions from Flanders would be available towards building up their reserve.

Haig's failure to begin the extension of the line soon produced a protest from the French. On December 1st, the day of the first meeting of the Supreme War Council at Versailles, Clemenceau asked why the promised extension had not begun. Haig, to whom the matter was referred by telegram, replied that he had been obliged to send divisions to Italy and that the two divisions intended to begin the extension of the line had had to be diverted to the Cambrai battle. He pointed out also that the Germans were very much thicker on the ground opposite the British than on the French front. As he was engaged in active operations (at Cambrai) he did not feel justified in making the extension.

On December 14th Pétain again wrote to Haig to press that the relief might be begun. On the same day the British Government learned that Pétain had told the French Cabinet that he must decline responsibility for the holding of the French front unless the British took over a good portion of his line and he received 200,000 more men from civilian sources to prepare fresh lines of defence behind his front. Clemenceau promised to meet this latter requirement, but also presented the British Government with a demand that the British Army should take over the French line as far as Berry-au-Bac. He reinforced his plea by intimating that, if it was not complied with, he would resign. This demand was of course a revival of Pétain's original plan of September 22nd which had never been put forward officially. It was quite impossible for us to accept. It would have involved our taking over thirty-seven miles of trenches beyond Barisis, the farthest point which Haig had been willing

to contemplate. After providing for holding the line we should have had only seven weak divisions in reserve.

Clemenceau, however, was now persuaded to agree to refer the question of the proposed extension to Berry-au-Bac to the Permanent Military Representatives at Versailles. Haig was notified of this on December 15th and on December 17th he met Pétain. Now that the Flanders offensive was over, the latter had become apprehensive that the French Army would be attacked—possibly through Switzerland. He was, therefore, more anxious than ever to build up his reserve. Haig, on the other hand, needed time to rest and replenish his troops. The utmost he could promise was that he would relieve two French divisions on January 10th and try to complete the promised extension to Barisis by the end of that month. Pétain accepted this. In the event Haig was as good as his word. Two French divisions were relieved on January 10th, and by January 30th the whole of the French line had been taken over as far as Barisis. That was the farthest point that ever was taken over. It would be agreeable if the story could be brought to an end at this point on a note of agreement between the two Commanders-in-Chief. Unfortunately, however, Pétain and the French Government did not treat the agreement as more than an instalment and still hoped for a greater take-over of the French line.

The Permanent Military Representatives, who had been left with a great deal of work on their hands after the termination of the December session of the Supreme War Council, did not present their recommendations until January 10th. Their report was in the nature of a compromise. They favoured a point of junction between the two lines on the left bank of the Ailette (a tributary of the Oise) on the Laon–Soissons road, about seventeen miles short of Berry-au-Bac. The exact point of junction was to be settled by the two Commanders-in-Chief. The relief was to take place consecutively from the left as a continuous operation to be arranged between the two Commanders-in-Chief. As part of the plan, the extension of the British line to the right, or of the French line to the left, was to be studied so that, according as the expected German attack fell on the British or French front, the army that was attacked could be relieved of a portion of the line and thus have divisions set free to support the part of the line attacked.

By the time the report of the Permanent Military Representatives reached the hands of the British Supreme Command several new factors had arisen to affect the ultimate decision. Haig, on the very date that the Versailles Report was signed, had begun the relief of two French

divisions, an operation completed by January 14th. The War Cabinet also decided to reduce the number of battalions in the British division from twelve to nine. The proposal for the inclusion of American battalions in British divisions had for a moment taken a more hopeful turn, but the British General Staff always urged that it should not be taken into account as a factor in the question of the extension of the line, as there would not be enough American battalions available to affect the situation before June, and the German attack was believed to be more or less imminent. Yet another factor was that the Permanent Military Representatives at the Supreme War Council had recommended a generally defensive policy on the Western Front. The British Government had accepted the recommendation and, although it still awaited the formal endorsement of the Supreme War Council, it was known that the other Allied and Associated Powers concerned were likely to acquiesce, and all military preparations of the Allies were being made on that basis. Consequently the objection to the extension of the line that our troops were required for a resumption of the offensive early in 1918 no longer held.

In all these circumstances the War Cabinet decided that the question ought to be settled at the coming session of the Supreme War Council, and the Prime Minister and Milner, who were to represent them, were given full powers to make the best arrangement they could. For various reasons, however, the Council was unable to meet until January 30th. In the interval Smuts and I paid a visit to the Western Front, and the visit exercised some indirect effect on the eventual decision in so far as Smuts' report influenced Lloyd George.

The brunt of the detailed work of the Man-Power Committee had fallen on me, and for a long time the ordinary secretarial work of the War Cabinet had been very exacting. Also I had had no leave for many months. Consequently I was delighted when, one day in mid-January, I was given an opportunity to visit the much-discussed British line in France and Flanders in Smuts's delightful company.

January 18th (1918). I lunched with Ll. George, Smuts and Reading. The former in great spirits after his brilliantly successful speech in secret session the previous evening and again to the trade unionists that morning. The conversation drifted on to the subject of our Army leaders and the failure of the War Office to allow any Territorial or new army officers to reach the

BB*

higher commands, a deputation of Liberal Ministers having waited on the P.M. that very morning on this subject. Suddenly Ll. G. said to Smuts, 'I wish you would go out to the Western Front and go right round in order to find out who are the rising men, and to see the new defences they are making to meet the forthcoming German offensive.' Smuts agreed to go at once, and Ll. G. then turned to me and said 'I think you had better go too', which I agreed to do. Ll. G. in subsequent conversation said that if he had his way he would make me Haig's Chief of Staff, but Smuts said, 'No, Hankey has a bigger job as Chief of Staff to the War Cabinet. It needs a wider outlook than c.g.s. of the Expeditionary Force.'

On the next day I took the precaution to see Robertson, who had no sort of objection to the visit. I had for a long time been working very closely with Smuts, who had helped me in some detailed inquiries I had been instructed to conduct on behalf of the Man-Power Committee. The trip we were now about to undertake sealed a friendship which was destined to prove very valuable in after life.

January 21st. Left London at noon with Smuts and arrived at GHQ[1] in time for dinner. I sat between Haig and Lawrence the new c.g.s. I found a considerable amount of peace talk at GHQ.

January 22nd. Before we started out in the morning Haig took me aside and gave me his views about the situation. He said that, if the Government accepted the French proposal that we should take any more of the line, they would have to find a new Commander-in-Chief! It was clear that he had adopted an entirely defensive policy, of which he gave me a sketch. Broadly speaking it consists of a front line to be defended by the armies, but to be given up if heavily attacked; a battle zone, usually in rear of the front line, but occasionally touching it, where important tactical points are situated in the front line; and finally a reserve line. The battle zone is 2–3,000 yards deep and is situated on the most favourable ground for defence. I asked the Field-Marshal if he had any offensive schemes hatching, and he indicated two or three, but showed none of his old enthusiasm for them. In fact that atmosphere of complaisant optimism that formerly pervaded GHQ was conspicuous by its absence. This was true of the whole Army. After this we saw in succession Butler, Deputy Chief of Staff; the O.C. Royal Flying Corps; Heath, the Chief Engineer—who told us that the Army had exhausted nearly all the supplies of barbed wire; and Fowke, the A.G., with whom we lunched. . . . Then we motored on to Cassel, where we stayed with Rawlinson, commanding Fourth Army, who gave us a very interesting appreciation of the position on his front before dinner. We were accompanied throughout

---

[1] GHQ was at Montreuil where I was billeted. Haig lived a mile or two outside the town in a château where Smuts and I had our meals with him.

our trip here and elsewhere by Colonel Armitage, an admirable young officer from GHQ, and by Captain Lane, Smuts's aide—a firm friend of mine.

Many years after, when Armitage had become Commandant of the Army Staff College, Camberley, where I used to lecture, I saw a good deal of him. We often spoke of my visit with Smuts and he told me how delicate his position had been. GHQ and the Army Commanders, well aware that the relations between the Prime Minister and his Commander-in-Chief were not all that they might have been, were naturally suspicious of this visit, amounting to an informal inspection by two people closely associated with Lloyd George. We, of course, realized the position, but at no time did we meet with anything but cordiality, and all our questions were answered readily and without any concealment.

January 23rd. Nice sunny weather. We drove off betimes with Rawlinson to the Flanders Front, through Poperinghe, what remains of Ypres, and across the pitted Flanders battlefield to the ridge behind the Steenbeck stream, where our battle zone is formed. A great deal of work was going on, and the German 'pill-boxes', which run for many miles only a few yards apart, in exactly the right part of the ridge, were being converted to our use. There was a little shelling here and there on both sides, but nothing came our way. The ground was absolutely pitted all over with shell-holes, most of them full of water. An American doctor whom we passed, and who was supervising the draining of these shell-holes, told us they had that morning found five bodies. The normal means of getting about was on duck-boards placed on light trestle pilework. We met my friends Sammy Wilson, Aspinall, Freiberg and Fergusson, temporarily in command of a corps.

With Freiberg, whom I had met several times at 10 Downing Street, in Asquith's time, I discussed his great friend Arthur Asquith, who had just been wounded and was about to have his leg amputated, that very day I think. Freiberg said: 'He is the bravest man I know.' Only a short time before, when lunching with the Asquith's, I had discussed Freiberg with Arthur Asquith. He had made the same remark of Freiberg: 'He is the bravest man I know.' They had served together in the Royal Naval Division and were both good judges. The only other person of whom I ever heard the same remark was Jack Seely to whom the same expression was applied by a comrade in the Imperial Yeomanry in the South African War—Lt.-Col. 'Bobby' Johnson, who was later to become Deputy Master of the Mint.

January 23rd (continued). In the afternoon we motored (inspecting some South African Artillery *en route*) to Ranchicourt, the headquarters of First Army, where we stayed with Horne in a fine château. Before dinner Horne explained to us the situation on the front of his army. Horne and his Chief of Staff, Anderson, both impressed us favourably, though I had a slight feeling in this army that the war had a little lost reality owing to the fact that they had not been fighting so much as some of the armies. At dinner I met Du Cane, Currie (Canadian), Braithwaite and Davies (who was married to a Hankey).

January 24th. We visited the front of First Army, staying for an hour on a coal slag-heap known as Fosse 5, Maroc. Below us, some 1,000 yards away, was Loos, and in the 'Happy Valley' between, one of our batteries was being steadily and persistently shelled, not 800 yards away from us. In front we had a great view towards Hill 70 above Loos and many well-known heights. Away to the west was the Vimy Ridge and Notre Dame de Lorette. Then we went on to a pyramidical coal slag-dump called 'Annequin', a mile or so south of the La Bassée Canal and 2–3,000 yards from the front line. One of our batteries was in action at the foot of the dump. Close by an old man and woman and an old horse were ploughing quietly as though nothing were happening and as though there were no shell-holes. Hard by, in their half-shattered house, lived their married daughter and several children. For miles round every house was shattered, windowless and for the most part roofless in this thickly populated suburban area. Such is war. Luckily no shells came our way. In this army the position is strong and held by very good troops, but the coal-mine district is a tempting mark for the enemy, though they could do much damage by artillery fire alone. The Portuguese in the flat, marshy country north of the La Bassée Canal are also a tempting and easy objective. After lunching with the Army Corps temporarily commanded by Davies . . . , the actual commander, Holland, being away, we motored on to the Vimy Ridge, where the view was unfortunately somewhat obscured by mist hiding Lens, though we could see a good deal. Our guides here were Massey, an artillery general . . . , and a very live Canadian McAvitty. I forgot to mention that during our tour of First Army we had been guided by Atkinson, a sapper and a good hard soldier of mainly Indian experience. After leaving Vimy we motored on for some hours through Arras, the devastated and evacuated territory of the Somme battlefield, to Albert, the headquarters of Third Army, where we stayed with Byng. The latter was suspicious and nervous. . . . He gave us an appreciation of the situation on his front before dinner. . . . Albert was knocked about a good deal, but the inhabitants were beginning to return and rebuild it. The house in which I was billeted was almost the only sound house in the street, but I had a comfortable room with a huge log fire. After all our motoring and walking I was very tired. At dinner I sat next to Byng. . . .

January 25th. Byng took us out to a place called St. Leger in nice open country with rolling downs. Here we made a *rendezvous* with Haldane (old Haldane's cousin) and one of the best and most scientific soldiers out here. To reach it we had to cross again the Somme battlefield and a great tract of territory evacuated by the Germans. Byng considered it dangerous to take us to any point where we could actually see the enemy's positions, but in the distance we could see Bullecourt and other shattered villages in the line. Nevertheless we were spied by a German observation balloon, and suddenly a 4-inch shell burst not forty yards from us, though luckily it fell in soft ground, which threw the bits high and no one was hit. We then moved off in as dignified a manner as we could assume (personally I felt in rather a funk!) down the hill to a sunk lane, whereupon they put about a dozen 5·9-inch shells (some "duds") into the place where we had been. At the next hill the enemy was shelling a brigade headquarters just behind us, the shells whizzing just over our heads, too close to be pleasant. We then had a longish walk to a place whose name I forget, getting no more shells. On this walk I had a long argument with Byng, who was very suspicious of the Prime Minister and (like many officers I have met out here) was firmly convinced that he was responsible for the recent Press campaign against the Higher Command. Then we drove on, stopping for lunch at Mont St. Quentin, an old German observation post overlooking Peronne, the valley of the Somme and part of the Somme battlefield. The sun was shining brightly, but the place and view were desolate and shell-strewn, including, round the post, masses of burst gas-shells. After lunch we drove to a ruined village called Nurlu, where we met Lukin, commanding the South African Brigade. Thence we drove to Villers-Bretonneux, Gough's headquarters. Before dinner Gough gave us the usual appreciation of his situation. He is a terrific fellow; oozing with character and Irish humour. . . . We had a remarkably cheery evening. Congreve dined with us, and was in great form, though I think him too old for his command like a good many others out here. I was billeted out again, quite comfortably.

January 26th. Gough had designed to take us to certain observation posts much nearer to the front than we had been hitherto, but the whole countryside was swathed in thick mist. Hence, at the point adjoining the Bois de Gouzeaucourt and at the much shelled village of Epéhy there was absolute calm, and we scarcely heard a shot all day. Both points were covered with debris of newly fallen shells. We walked round the village of Epéhy, spending an hour inspecting the 'Keep', redoubts, entanglements, communication trenches, dug-outs, and other appurtenances of a modern defended village. The sapper officer who conducted us round showed considerable apprehension particularly at the way Gough and Smuts kept stopping at crossroads, which are always dangerous. He told me that the place was constantly bombarded with high explosive, shrapnel, poison-gas and even machine-guns

day and night. . . . Congreve, who has lost an arm in the war, conducted us round. Then we returned to Amiens and Boulogne, where I wrote a report for Smuts strongly opposing the extension of the British line to the south as desired by the French.[1]

So ended our trip. We had travelled for hundreds of miles for five days through stricken, deserted, despoiled and utterly ruined villages. We had been several times under shellfire and once under aimed shellfire. For a part of every day we had worn steel helmets and gas masks at the 'ready' position. We had watched several air fights and much shelling of aeroplanes. We had seen many German planes but ten times as many British. We carefully studied the whole strategical and tactical situation on maps and on the ground. We have seen a part of the defences both in front and rear. We have conversed with a great number of officers, and seen the men under all sorts of conditions.

My personal view is that the Army is in splendid fettle, though a little tired. I think it will hold against any attack, but I do not think it would be right to expose it to another prolonged attack of the Somme–Flanders type. The defences are well conceived and are being pushed on with vigour. Already strong, they will be extremely powerful in six weeks' time. I do not think the enemy will attack strongly in Flanders or the Somme–Ancre areas, as he will have to re-cross the broken country of the battlefields, and will meet an admirable system of railway communications. I think he might attack from the region of the La Bassée Canal to a point opposite Arras, in order to deprive France of the Bruay coal-mines. I also think he may extend his attack north as far as Armentières across the marshy region. My reason for this belief is that his railway communications in this region are greatly superior to our own, and in the absence of shell-holes, I do not think the ground marshy enough to stop him. He might turn not only the Bruay but also the Flanders position from here. More likely still, I think the enemy may, instead of attacking in force, seek a number of cheap successes—Passchendaele, which is indefensible; Armentières; the territory held by the Portuguese. Bullecourt and the region of Gouzeaucourt are likely points.

My appreciation erred on the side of optimism. The enemy's attacks, which began on March 21st, were delivered on the maximum scale. Our defences were less complete and our resistance less effective than I had anticipated, especially in the southern (Fifth Army) area. Contrary to my anticipations the enemy did attack across the old Somme battle-field; but it proved his undoing. Ludendorff tells us that four days after

---

[1] The Official History records that 'the state of the Army was admirably summed up by General Smuts in a Memorandum prepared for the War Cabinet'. (*France and Belgium 1918*, I, p. 40 *sq.*, where a long extract is given.)

the attack across the Somme battlefield, his Second Army, which was advancing towards Albert, 'was fresher but was already complaining of the old shell-holes',[1] and that a few days later his troops were handi-capped 'by having stuck fast in the western edge of the Somme battle-field'. The region north as well as south of the Scarpe (Arras) was heavily attacked at the end of March and the beginning of April, but the objective was not so much the Bruay coal-mines, as I had anticipated, as to capture the heights east and north of Arras with a view to facilitating future operations in the plain of the Lys. Little progress was made by the Germans in this region, though Ludendorff states that he 'attached the greatest importance to these attacks'.[2] Ludendorff tells us that the marshy region of the Lys, which I had thought a likely point of attack, was proposed by Crown Prince Rupprecht for the main operation, but 'before the middle of April its passability away from roads was doubt-ful'.[3] After the attack on Fifth Army towards Amiens had spent itself, the ground in the Lys valley had dried sufficiently, and the main German attack was transferred to this region (April 9th). At first it was successful, but before the end of the month it had spent itself. The attack was carried far enough, however, to cause us great anxiety about the Bruay coal-mines.

On Sunday, January 27th, Smuts and I returned to London and pro-ceeded at once to Walton Heath to report to the Prime Minister. We could not say much about our conclusions, however, because

. . . we found there a number of journalists—Donald of the *Chronicle* with Perris their correspondent with the French Army. Ll. G. full of Palestine and more suspicious of the soldiers than ever. Very difficult. At 6.30 p.m. Adeline called for me in the car and took me back to Highstead.

He might have been reassured if we had been able to show the report and particularly this most important paragraph:

The point, however, to which I wish to draw attention is that this need of rest is a psychological factor of the utmost importance in relation to the ques-tion of the extension of the line for which the French are pressing. It is my deliberate opinion, as the result of a most careful study of the question, that, if the Army is to be compelled at the present time to take over any further portion of the line beyond that already agreed to, and nearly completed, we shall be running serious risks. We shall be straining the Army too far. Either the defences will not be completed in time, or the essential rest will not be

[1] Ludendorff, II, pp. 599 *sq.*   [2] *Ibid.*, p. 604.   [3] *Ibid.*, pp. 590 and 606.

obtained, and the Army will not be in the state in which it ought to be to resist an attack. Moreover, any further extension of the front will cause great discontent among all ranks.

Lloyd George had to wait for the report until the next day when we were all

. . . off again to Versailles with the Prime Minister and Milner. A huge party as usual, including the First Sea Lord and a number of unfortunate officers on leave from Palestine.

CHAPTER LXXIV

THE SUPREME WAR COUNCIL AT WORK
JANUARY 1918

'... to discover effects even while they are yet in the
wombs of their causes, and consider beforehand whatever may happen on either side, and accordingly what is
to be done when it does happen; that so he may never be
taken unawares, and brought to that lamentable shift of
crying out, "I never once thought of it". These are the
duties, as of a truly courageous and lofty, so of a wise and
judicious mind; ...' (CICERO, *Offices*, c. xxiii.)

WHEN we were very young my mother of blessed memory used every
evening to read to my brothers and myself a chapter or two from one of
the classic novels of the nineteenth century, Scott, Dickens, Thackeray
Harrison Ainsworth, or Charles Reade. I well remember how exasperated we were when, after tracing the threads of one part of the story
and working it up to a most exciting point, the author would suddenly
break off the narrative and start to work up some other part of the tale
in exactly the same manner, always keeping the reader on tenterhooks
until a final chapter in which all the threads would be woven together
and the climax would be reached. It has been found necessary to tell this
part of the tale of the Supreme Command on similar lines, for a number
of the long-drawn issues dealt with earlier converge into the session of
the Supreme War Council which opened at Versailles on January 30,
1918.

The preparations for the session had been thorough, for the Permanent Military Representatives, the Inter-Allied General Staff of the
Supreme War Council, had compiled careful and unanimous reports on
most of the questions to be discussed. In some of these reports fresh
subjects were raised such as the creation of a General Reserve for the
Western and Italian Fronts, the arrangements for the command of this
Reserve, and further developments in the organization of the Supreme
War Council itself. The session forms an important landmark in the
history of the Supreme Command, and points the way towards the
solution of the difficult problem how the issues arising between Allies
can best be settled.

The company that assembled at Versailles was worthy of the occa-

sion. It included the Prime Ministers of France, Italy and the United Kingdom, Milner, the Foreign Ministers of France and Italy, the Commanders-in-Chief of the British, French and United States Armies, the Chiefs of Staff of the British and French War Offices, the Permanent Military Representatives of the Supreme War Council, and a host of staff officers from various theatres of war, experts, secretaries and aides.

The United States was represented on the military side by Pershing and Bliss, the wise Permanent Military Representative at Versailles. On the political side Frazier, First Secretary to their Embassy in Paris, was present as an 'observer'. Like Polonius President Wilson could say:

> And I'll be placed, so please you, in the ear
> Of all their conference.

Clemenceau was wont to allude to Frazier as 'an ear but not a voice', and would speak sardonically of the favourable position in which the American President had placed himself of being able to criticize without ever having to express an opinion. Frazier, a particularly good fellow, took this barbed chaff in good part.

Henry Wilson, the British Permanent Military Representative, had established himself in the Villa Romaine, a comfortable, sunny, well-equipped house at Versailles. Here Lloyd George, Milner and I were always entertained during the Versailles sessions of the Supreme War Council. Not far away were some pleasant woods where one could get a walk on the rare occasions when time permitted.

The Permanent Military Representatives were by this time fully established. The Inter-Allied Secretariat had also come into existence. The British contingent, which was a branch of the War Cabinet Office and under my general supervision, was headed by Storrs and Leo Amery. This secretariat served the needs of the Permanent Military Representatives as well as of the Supreme War Council, when the latter permitted them to do so.

The first business to be taken up, that of the American battalions,[1] was tackled *en petit comité* in Lloyd George's private room in the offices of the Supreme War Council:

January 29th. Conferences in the morning and afternoon with Haig and Pershing at the offices of the Supreme War Council, mainly on the question of the incorporation of American battalions in British brigades. Much misunderstanding because Pershing wanted the troops attached mainly for training, though willing that they should do their share of the fighting, while

[1] *vide supra*, pp. 744 *sq.*

Robertson wanted them mainly for fighting, though willing that they should be trained. Also Pershing wanted to bring the personnel of whole divisions, while Robertson wanted only battalions.

No agreement was reached that afternoon, but on the following day the British representatives accepted a proposal by Pershing, which was in effect a compromise, but which went some way towards meeting our desiderata. The additional sea transport was to be used for bringing over the personnel of entire American divisions as Pershing wished and not merely infantry battalions as proposed by Robertson. But the infantry and auxiliary troops were to be trained with British divisions 'or under such plan as may be agreed on'. The artillery were to be trained under French direction, as was already the case, as they were using French material. The higher commanders and staff were to train with the British Army.

Although the meetings at which this vexed question was settled took place in the offices of the Supreme War Council the agreement was actually concluded behind the scenes and not at a regular meeting of that body.

At the first formal meeting held on January 31st various distinguished persons, staff officers, etc., crowded into the room in such numbers (especially the British contingent, no less than twelve of whom were present) as to hamper the business. At the outset of the second meeting of February 1st, therefore, Lloyd George insisted, as he had done at the Rome Conference a year before, that all except the principals should withdraw. At the second meeting, therefore, there was not even a secretary present. I myself withdrew with the rest—knowing quite well that I should be called in next day to act as British, if not as sole, secretary. To fill in the gap in our records I persuaded the interpreter to produce a *procès-verbal*, 'but Ll. G. repudiated it, and refused to reckon it as a record of the meeting. . . .' After that one secretary was admitted for each ally, and, as usual, it fell to my lot to keep the records of the meetings and to organize the business, though for the last two meetings I smuggled in Storr.

The *pièce de résistance* of the January meeting was the Plan of Campaign for 1918, on which the Permanent Military Representatives had prepared two reports.[1] They favoured a defensive policy on the Western Front during the first part of 1918, and this policy was to be carried out by a reconsideration of the existing defensive lines and the

[1] *France and Belgium 1918*, I, Appendices.

construction of further successive lines to check an advance by the enemy; also by the utmost use of mechanical means in order to set free troops with a view to the creation of the largest possible mobile reserve, as well as for training. Rail and sea communications between the different sections of the Western and Italian Fronts were to be developed as much as possible, and preparations for troop movements between the sections were recommended. This was held to be especially important for the Italian Front, and for the measures to be taken in case of a German attack through Switzerland. The adoption of a generally defensive policy, however, was not intended to exclude either minor forms of active defence for the purpose of maintaining the morale of the troops, or offensive measures in any theatre of war later on when the position in Russia or Italy had become clearer.

In a separate note the Permanent Military Representatives advocated the formation of a General Reserve for the whole of the Western and Italian Fronts. No recommendation was included on the numbers, situation or command of the General Reserve as these were recognized by the Military Representatives to be matters on which the views of the Chiefs of Staffs and Commanders-in-Chief must be paramount.

These recommendations were developed and expanded in a second report, which had been completed in the light of the very latest information just before the opening of the session. Germany, it was calculated, might mount an attack by ninety-six divisions,[1] and against this France would only be safe provided that the French and British forces were maintained at full strength, and American divisions brought over at the rate of two a month; provided also that there was an increase in guns of all calibres, in machine-guns, aeroplanes and tanks; that the defensive lines were strengthened; railway transport improved and co-ordinated; and finally that the whole Allied front in France was treated as a single strategic field of action, and that the disposition of reserves, the periodic readjustment of the line and other arrangements should be dominated by this consideration. Italy was also deemed to be safe provided certain rather obvious conditions were satisfied. If France was safe and Italy was safe, the report continued, then the enemy could not get a favourable decision in 1918. Could the Allies do so? The conclusion of the Permanent Military Representatives was that a decision was unlikely during 1918, apart from such improbable and unforeseeable contingencies as the internal collapse of the Enemy Powers, or the

---

[1] The number of divisions actually assembled for the attack on the British front on March 21st was seventy-four, including eleven position divisions. *vide France and Belgium 1918*, I, p. 152.

revival of Russia as a serious military factor. The final victory, in their opinion, must be looked for in 1919, when America would be able to pull her full weight in the war.

In the meantime what was to be done? Were the Allies to leave the initiative entirely to the enemy? In the Balkan theatre of war any far-reaching decision was considered to be excluded by the strength and comparative homogeneity of the enemy's forces and by the superiority of his lines of communications. In Turkey, however, the Permanent Military Representatives realized that a different state of affairs prevailed. Turkey was defeated and exhausted. Her armies were scattered over three theatres of war separated by vast distances and with very inferior communications between them, and almost without reserves. The forces in Palestine and Mesopotamia, reinforced perhaps from East Africa, where the enemy's resistance was gradually petering out, and from India, should suffice for the job of knocking Turkey out. Later on, when the Greek Army had been equipped and trained, the Permanent Military Representatives thought that perhaps a division or two of British troops might be spared from the Balkans for the Western Front.

The programme of the Permanent Military Representatives, therefore, included a recommendation that the Allies should 'undertake a decisive offensive against Turkey with a view to the annihilation of the Turkish armies and the collapse of Turkish resistance'. Anyone who has followed the course of events will realize how congenial this recommendation was to Lloyd George. Ever since August 1917, when it was first appreciated that the Flanders offensive was not likely to result in the spectacular success hoped for by its authors, and that Cadorna was unwilling to attempt a big offensive against Austria that autumn, the Prime Minister's mind had been turning more and more insistently in the direction of a big offensive against Turkey. In September 1917 he and Milner had discussed the situation and agreed that the Western Front afforded no hope of a complete success and that we ought to turn towards Turkey—the outermost of the 'props' of the Central Powers. Milner shared Lloyd George's view, but had agreed with me that success in the Turkish theatre could only be achieved if the soldiers were wholehearted about it. At the Boulogne Conference, Lloyd George had raised the question of a French expedition to Syria to co-operate with Allenby's advance but had met with a somewhat lukewarm attitude on the part of Foch. The idea of operations against Turkey had continued to haunt the mind of the Prime

Minister, and early in October he persuaded his colleagues to assent to it:

October 9th. . . . A letter from the Prime Minister to Painlevé was approved, urging decisive operations this winter against Turkey. Smuts strongly favours a landing operation at Haifa. He told me after the meeting that he would be willing to assume the command. . . .

It was on this day that Painlevé and Foch arrived in London rather mysteriously[1] and coupled proposals for the extension of the British line with a suggestion for French co-operation in Syria:

October 10th. The latter proposal is for the French to throw in a force on the coast to attack the Turkish communications, but it is only to eventuate in the case of the British having defeated the Turks and drawn in all their reserves.

It was not a very attractive proposal and perhaps was in the nature of an inducement to Lloyd George to support the French views on the question of the extension of the line. If so, it failed in its purpose for nothing came of it. Caporetto and subsequent events had overshadowed these projects for a few weeks, but Allenby's remarkable series of victories, and especially the capture of Jerusalem on December 9th, revived them, and at the end of December Lloyd George asked the Permanent Military Representatives to report on the military and strategical position in the Turkish theatre; it was for this reason that Lloyd George had brought with him the officers on leave from Palestine.

After a discussion which lasted for the whole of two long meetings the programme of the Permanent Military Representatives (including the offensive against Turkey)[2] was adopted, and the Commanders-in-Chief of the various national armies were instructed to prepare their plans on this basis and to forward them to the Supreme War Council in order to ensure their co-ordination.

The decisive offensive against Turkey was only accepted on the understanding that the British Government would not divert forces to that theatre from, or relax its efforts on, the Western Front—a condition to which Lloyd George and Milner felt no difficulty in assenting. Even after this condition had been accepted, however, Robertson thought it necessary to enter a formal protest against the adoption of a decisive offensive against Turkey as part of the plan for 1918, on the ground that it was not a practicable plan, and that to attempt it would

---

[1] *vide supra*, p. 767.   [2] *France and Belgium 1918*, I, p. 75.

be very dangerous and detrimental to our prospects of winning the war.

February 2nd. . . . Robertson afterwards apologized to Lloyd George for this, explaining that he was afraid of being left in the same position as Fisher was over the Dardanelles affair.

We see here the baneful influence of the Dardanelles Inquiry, which led even a man like Robertson to hedge.

The proposals of the Permanent Military Representatives for the creation of a Central Mobile Reserve naturally received close attention. On the principle all the soldiers and statesmen present were agreed, but important points had been left for the decision of the Supreme War Council, including the question of the command. Robertson and Foch proposed that the allocation of the reserves should rest with the Chiefs of Staff of the British and French War Offices, with some special arrangement for Italy (which had no Chief of the General Staff at its War Office) and for the United States. This plan did not commend itself to the Council. Robertson, it was pointed out, would normally be in London, and would probably not be on the spot at the moment when an urgent decision was required. He would only be able to exercise his functions as one of the controllers of the Central Reserve by leaving his post at a possible critical juncture. The Italian representatives also disliked the plan because they could not easily produce a counterpart to the British and French Chiefs of Staff. The proposal was therefore rejected. An alternative suggestion that the control should be vested in the Permanent Military Representatives was not congenial to the French, as Weygand, their representative, was not as yet of sufficiently high status, and they wanted Foch to represent them. The meeting, therefore, adjourned for a new scheme to be drawn up for the command of the reserves.

February 2nd. I brought down to breakfast with me a new scheme for the reserves, which Ll. G., Milner, and Henry Wilson and I discussed at breakfast. Eventually they decided that the reserves should be under the control of a committee consisting of the British, Italian and United States Permanent Military Representatives with Foch in the chair. Having with some difficulty persuaded the Italians to accept it, Ll. G., in a speech of great skill, announced it to the Council, bringing tears to the eyes of Foch, Clemenceau and even Orlando. Foch was so much moved that he could make no reply.

Pershing, in accepting this scheme, expressed regret that Robertson,

for whom he had formed a high regard, could not be included in the new committee.

The new committee for the control of the reserves came to be known as the Executive War Board. It consisted of Foch (chairman), Wilson, Cadorna and Bliss. The resolutions adopted by the Supreme War Council provided for the creation of a General Reserve for the whole of the armies on the Western, Italian and Balkan Fronts. The Executive War Board was made responsible for determining its strength and composition and the contribution to be made to it from each of the national armies; for selecting the localities in which the sections of the reserve were normally to be stationed; for arranging for its transportation and concentration in the different areas; for deciding and issuing orders on the time, place and period of employment of the General Reserve; for determining the time, place and strength of the counter-offensive, and then for handing over to the Commanders-in-Chief concerned the troops required for the operation. The moment the movement of the General Reserve or any part of it should have begun, it was to come under the orders of the Commander-in-Chief to whose assistance it was consigned. Until the movement of the General Reserve began, it was, for purposes of discipline, instruction and administration to be under the orders of the respective Commanders-in-Chief, but no movement could be ordered except by the Executive War Board. In case of irreconcilable differences of opinion any Military Representative had the right of appeal to the Supreme War Council. The Board had the right to visit any theatre of war. The Military Representatives, members of the Executive War Board, had the duty of transmitting its orders to the respective Commanders-in-Chief of the armies of their several countries.

The settlement of the difficult question of the adjustment of the British and French lines on the Western Front was left by the Supreme War Council until the other major questions had been settled, and was facilitated by the nature of the agreements reached and especially by the appointment of Foch as President of the Executive War Board. Lloyd George and the War Council had to choose between the following solutions:

(i) The French proposal to extend the British line thirty miles farther to

Berry-au-Bac: strongly supported by Pétain but strongly opposed by Haig, Smuts—and incidentally myself.

(ii) Haig's proposal to stand fast at Barisis the point already reached: opposed by Pétain and the French Government but in accord with the Smuts Report.

(iii) The proposal of the Military Representatives to extend the line twelve miles farther to the Ailette. This suggestion did not conform to Smuts's advice, but was in the nature of a compromise and was difficult to resist.

To this third proposal Haig, who was present, felt bound to register his objections, which he did with dignity and moderation. He recalled the many occasions on which, on his own responsibility, he had extended his front in order to help the French Army; even during the battle of Flanders he had agreed to extend it as far as Barisis. This he had now done in spite of the fact that his divisions were depleted and needed rest. He emphasized the extraordinarily difficult position of British man-power. Any day, he said, the Germans might attack and he might be faced with 500,000 casualties. This would mean that by October the British Army might be reduced from fifty-seven to thirty-five divisions. The new front he was being asked to take over would require the construction of new railways to link up with his transportation system, and their building would require many men and much time. Lloyd George, developing the argument with remarkable power, emphasized the gravity of overruling the Field-Marshal after he had made the statement that he could not be responsible for holding the extended line. He pointed out that the British Army had borne the brunt of the fighting for many months, with the result *inter alia* that their fortifications were out of repair and needed much labour to put them right. The communications of the British Army, he added, lay parallel to their front, to which they were often so close that a German advance of a few kilometres would endanger them. In one section of the line a German advance of six miles would put out of action coal-mines producing 10,000,000 tons a year. If this happened the British nation would be called upon to make good to France the deficiency of coal, which would involve a large diversion of man-power to the mines, as well as tonnage for transportation.

The French case, however, was also very strong. Their divisions, as we have seen, had been reduced long since to nine battalions. And their battalions were only 600–700 men strong compared with the British nominal establishment of 1,000. In order to prepare defences in rear of

their armies 250,000 men, who had been released from the Army for agriculture where they were urgently needed, or their equivalent, had had to be recalled to the colours. Men up to 50 years of age had been called up for service. With an army perhaps one-third larger than ours they were holding three times the length of front (550 kilometres as compared with our 180 kilometres). Pétain did not deny that, for the reasons given by Lloyd George, our section of the line had to be held twice as densely as the French section, which could be occupied more or less as an outpost line, since in most parts ground could if necessary be given, temporarily at any rate, without much damage. Still, if Haig could say that an extension of the line beyond Barisis would be so dangerous that he could not be responsible for its safety, he, Pétain, could say that he could not be responsible for the safety of the French line unless the British line was extended.

In a search for a solution Lloyd George revived an appeal he had made earlier in the session, when discussing the General Reserve, for a transfer of eleven Italian divisions to the Western Front as a return for the aid given by Britain and France to Italy, thereby providing a safe-guard to Italy against the withdrawal of Anglo-French divisions when the German attack was delivered on the Western Front. Orlando did not refuse—in fact, he commended and at one point supported the proposal—but naturally he declined to commit himself until Diaz had been consulted. The new Executive War Board, which included Cadorna, was asked to study the subject.

Towards the end of the discussion Lloyd George was able to announce[1] that Haig was now prepared to accept in principle the recommendation of the Military Representatives for an extension as far as the Ailette, subject to an agreement between Pétain and himself on the method of giving effect to it. The two Commanders-in-Chief never met again to discuss any further extension, and Barisis, the point agreed to between them, remained the point of contact between the British and French lines until the German attack on March 21st. The controversy and feeling that had been aroused over this long-drawn affair are probably out of proportion to its importance. Blame has been cast on many people for what occurred later, but it has always seemed to me that everyone had a good defence and that, as so often in war, the real culprit was our friend the enemy!

---

[1] According to Lloyd George's account he received, as far as he can recollect from myself, a note stating that Haig had changed his mind and did not now view the proposed extension as altogether unacceptable. *War Memoirs*, V, p. 2778.

February 2nd.... Ll. G. and I left in the afternoon by motor car for Beauvais, where he stayed the night with the Préfet, Fabre, a nice man with a charming wife living in a huge old château. During the day Sylvester fainted. I fear I have worked him too hard.

As we discussed the meeting of the Supreme War Council on our journey it seemed to us both that real progress had been made. This was especially marked in the region of planning. For the first time since the beginning of the war a definite co-ordinated plan had been drawn up by a joint Inter-Allied Staff, and then discussed, in the presence of the Commanders-in-Chief and Chiefs of Staff, by the statesmen who exercised the Supreme Command in Britain, France and Italy. The establishment of a General Reserve under the control of the Executive War Board, if not an ideal arrangement, was at least a step in the right direction. It is true that it never really functioned, but it prepared the way for the unified command. From the moment that Lloyd George proposed Foch as chairman of the Board there was no other man who could have become General-in-Chief of the Allies. The very difficult and politically dangerous question of the extension of the British line had been adjusted on a basis believed to be acceptable to all concerned. Agreement had at last been reached on the question of the attachment of American battalions to British brigades, which at one stroke promised increased efficiency and ensured the arrival of much larger numbers. The new Committees on Aviation, Tanks and Transportation had strengthened the co-ordinating machinery of the Supreme War Council. The Permanent Military Representatives had justified their existence by a number of valuable reports, and, as Orlando put it, 'were beginning to create a tradition of their own'. The whole meeting had been conducted in the best possible spirit of frankness and *camaraderie.* At one moment during some enforced interval Clemenceau, who had always something of the attractiveness of a schoolboy, turned to Lloyd George and said, 'You know you like me. You can't help yourself! You like me!' And it was true.

'*February 3rd* (Sunday). Motored to Boulogne, leaving Beauvais 7.30 a.m. On the way Ll. G. told me his plans for reconstructing the Government. Balfour to come into the War Cabinet. Bob Cecil to the Foreign Office. Derby to Ambassador, Paris. Milner to the War Office. Cave to Master of the Rolls. Walter Long to the Home Office. Or possibly Ll. G. may himself take the F.O. and send Cecil to the Colonial Office.[1] Perfect crossing—the fourth

---

[1] Milner and Derby were the only members of the Government mentioned who were actually transferred to the posts cited.

fine crossing I had had within a fortnight. When nearing Folkestone we heard some heavy explosions in the offing, which, as it transpired, were mines being exploded by our sweepers. I think the Huns must have laid mines on the Calais route, which we usually take. This shows the folly of advertising these conferences. Home about 8 p.m.

CHAPTER LXXV

THE SUPERSESSION OF
SIR WILLIAM ROBERTSON

'It is also a common protection of all monarchies not to make one person too great, or certainly not many; for they will support each other: ... and, if it should seem necessary to deprive anyone of his power, to do it by degrees, and not to reduce him all at once.' (ARISTOTLE, *Politics*, V, c. 11.)

THE powers conferred on Robertson, on which he had insisted when he accepted the post of Chief of the Imperial General Staff, although desirable at the time of his appointment, were very great. To some extent they had weakened the authority of the Secretary of State for War. They had worked well enough so long as the Chief of the Imperial General Staff had seen eye to eye with the Government. When Lloyd George became Secretary of State for War, however, the position had become difficult. When he became Prime Minister, the situation steadily deteriorated, and by February 1918 had become impossible. The difficulties were aggravated by the fact that Robertson's views were shared by Haig, Plumer and other Army commanders, while Lloyd George had the firm support of Milner, the strongest man in his War Cabinet. Nevertheless there was great reluctance on the part of the Government to lose so efficient a public servant, and at one time an effort was made 'not to reduce him all at once'.

Trouble had long been brewing. The fundamental cause was Robertson's firm adherence to the extreme Western Front theory and Lloyd George's mistrust of this plan. This led to their taking different views on many questions on which there seemed to the onlooker less need for them to differ. Robertson's objections to the setting up of the Supreme War Council, for example, and his hostile attitude towards the subsequent developments at Versailles, did much to widen the rift. Their friends did all they could to bring them together. At my suggestion a weekly breakfast was instituted. At first it was proposed that I should be present, but I felt that it would be much better for them to be alone. But it did not work. Many years after I learned from Robertson that this was due to the fact that the Prime Minister liked to remain talking for a long time after his breakfast, a habit to which Robertson's

digestive apparatus could not adapt itself! The growth of the rift was due also in part to the difference between the Celtic and the Anglo-Saxon temperament, which were displayed so strikingly in these two men. The failure of the Flanders offensive and the depressing character of the weekly appreciations by the General Staff at the beginning of 1918 gradually brought Lloyd George to the point of making a change. On January 19th, just before Smuts and I left to visit the Western Front, he was talking of sending Robertson to India as Commander-in-Chief. The outburst at Versailles about the plans for operations against Turkey further incensed him.

On February 9th and the following day (Sunday) I took a much-needed rest at home. When I returned to Town on the 11th I learned that on the 9th, after consultation with Derby, the Prime Minister had offered Robertson the post of British Permanent Military Representative at Versailles.

February 11th. . . . Wilson, who is a good strategist, and gets on well with foreigners, and has been a brilliant success at Versailles, but is distrusted by the Army, is to be Chief of the Imperial General Staff; while Robertson, who is a good administrator, and is popular with the Army, but cannot get on at all with foreigners, is to go to Versailles!

Robertson, however, declined the Versailles appointment and a difficult situation was created.

February 12th. . . . I lunched with Lloyd George and Milner. The latter was very strong for getting rid of Robertson and hinted at resignation. (Later in the afternoon Ormsby Gore, his Parliamentary Private Secretary, came to see me to say that Milner had told him he would not remain in office if Robertson stayed on.) Lloyd George was very seedy with a temperature and very sorry for himself at having to make a speech in Parliament that afternoon. In the afternoon I went down to hear him at the House. Asquith made a hostile speech and asked him a number of very awkward questions, which he refused to answer. He was ill at ease and the House was rather hostile. Altogether he had a bad time. I had to get his references to the Bruay coal mines out of the official and Press reports, as, during my recent visit to France, I had been implored to do all I could to avoid attention being called to this important and essential coal supply, since the Germans could do great damage by artillery fire, and never seemed to have realized their importance. My cold was as bad as Lloyd George's, and I was glad to get home to bed. The combined effect of the failure . . . to refuse to be dictated to by Robertson (whose rather truculent attitude has become known), and the failure to answer questions about the General Reserve, in regard to which I

had from the first urged a public statement, have had a very damaging effect on the Government.

February 13th. . . . After the War Cabinet Lloyd George told me he had come to the conclusion that he could not sack Robertson, who was willing to stay on as C.I.G.S. with reduced powers. Northcliffe's attack on Robertson had, he said, made it impossible for him to get rid of him, as all the world would say that it was done at Northcliffe's dictation. I told him of Milner's attitude, and he asked me to see Milner before 3 p.m., when he was to see Derby and settle the matter up. I hunted out Milner and lunched with him in Great College Street. He was difficult, and was only willing to stand it on condition that there was a clear understanding with Robertson that he should loyally carry out the Versailles policy, and that a public statement was made explaining that Robertson had been offered the choice between the Versailles post and remaining as C.I.G.S. with curtailed powers. I went back to Lloyd George and found him at lunch with Devlin, the Irish M.P. . . . and some general in the R.A.M.C., so I could not get a word in until Milner himself came in. Milner explained his point of view, and Lloyd George asked him and me to draft a statement for publication, which we did. The P.M. then saw Derby, who, as I afterwards learned from Milner, seems to have hardened . . . after a talk with Robertson, and wants to put Wilson at Versailles definitely under Robertson. Milner's draft statement was, as the result of an interview between the P.M. and Milner, sent to Derby, who refused to be a party to it. Later on Milner came to see me and told me these things and said he was going to write and tell Lloyd George he could not stand this. I also saw Henry Wilson, who is behaving very well. The last I heard was that Derby and Robertson are to breakfast with Ll. G.

February 14th. Robertson did not turn up at Lloyd George's breakfast, but Milner's proposed statement was never issued, as Robertson seems definitely to have declined the Versailles post or to remain as C.I.G.S. under the new conditions. After the War Cabinet I lunched alone with Lloyd George, who was extremely seedy. The War Cabinet, which had met in the small drawing-room, had decided that Robertson should again be offered the choice of C.I.G.S. or Military Representative, and Balfour had been commissioned to see him with Derby and invite and persuade him to accept. I felt great doubt whether he had understood that he was to make this offer, so Lloyd George asked me to see him and make sure, and also to tell him that he had decided, if Robertson refused, to offer the post of C.I.G.S. to Plumer and to leave Wilson at Versailles. I eventually ran Balfour to earth lunching somewhere in Mayfair. As I expected, he had not appreciated what his mission was, so I got him into a taxicab and drove him to the War Office and left him there. Balfour and Derby both reported that Robertson had declined—but Lucas, who came to see me, told me that Balfour never properly made the offer. Derby was sent for by the P.M. and was asked to telegraph to Plumer, offer-

ing him c.i.g.s. Later in the afternoon Lloyd George sent for me and came out from the Cabinet Room, where he was interviewing the Ulster members of the Irish Convention, and asked me to see Derby's telegram to Plumer. . . . Derby was away with Curzon, but I got hold of the draft, which was quite calculated to make Plumer refuse. I redrafted it, and eventually, after I had seen Derby, it was sent. In the course of this episode I discovered (1) that Derby as Secretary of State for War had no means of knowing what communications Robertson had sent to Plumer about this affair or anything else, and (2) that Derby could not communicate with the Commander-in-Chief without Robertson's knowledge. A nice position for the Secretary of State! . . .

On the following day (February 15th) rather an awkward question arose. Foch had advised that two of the British divisions on the Italian Front should be brought to the Western Front, and his proposal was supported by Robertson. Milner insisted, on grounds of principle, that the question should be referred to the Permanent Military Representatives at Versailles. In order, however, to avoid a further clash with Robertson, the question was decided in Foch's favour.

February 15th. . . . Ll. G. was still very seedy and insisted on my lunching with him again alone in the small drawing-room. Later he went off to Walton Heath under doctor's orders, leaving me instructions to prepare a Press notice of Robertson's supersession by Plumer, for immediate issue in the event of Plumer's acceptance. Plumer's reply, however, which arrived later, was a refusal couched in terms of general support to Robertson. . . . I was at once sent for by Bonar Law, whom I found with Milner, Henry Wilson joining us later. We told Ll. G. by telephone what had happened, and he insisted on Milner, Wilson and myself coming down after dinner to see him at Walton Heath. The position was very critical for the Government as two great generals[1] had refused the post of c.i.g.s. on the ground of objection to the Government's Versailles policy, and if they could not find a distinguished officer to fill the bill they were faced with resignation or defeat. Bonar Law was gloomy but courageous. I dined with Henry Wilson at his own home. Driving down I remarked that I felt sure we should find Ll. G. rising to the occasion and full of fight. Sure enough it was so. He declared he was better than he had been for months! As the result of our talk he decided that Wilson should become c.i.g.s., and if Derby resigned . . . Milner should become Secretary of State for War. Next morning the Prime Minister reported to the King.

February 16th. The War Cabinet met at 12.30 p.m. and confirmed this. As Robertson's reply was merely a repudiation of the whole system, the Government issued a notice that he had resigned and had been replaced by

[1] i.e. Robertson and Plumer.

Wilson, the notice being on the lines of the one I had drafted on the previous evening. As Curzon had gone away to Kedleston and had not attended the War Cabinet and was suspected of resigning tendencies, I took on myself to send a telegram and Longhurst as special messenger so that Curzon would not have the first notice of Robertson's resignation in Sunday's newspapers.

Curzon was not the only Minister who came near to resignation over the crisis. On the 17th (Sunday) I was again at Walton Heath where I found Haig and Derby who had been summoned to discuss the filling of Henry Wilson's place at Versailles. Derby appeared on the point of resigning, and kept saying: 'Do you see what other course I can take?' My own opinion was that, in all the circumstances, it would be in the public interest for him to leave the War Office. So I was careful not to encourage him to remain and always replied: 'I see your difficulties.' However, Lloyd George took the view that it was better he should remain; eventually Bonar Law saw him and persuaded him to stay.

February 19th. . . . I find I omitted to mention that just before Bonar Law made his statement on Monday (i.e. the 18th) I found Walter Long and him in conversation in his room at the House of Commons. He left me alone with Walter Long, who was on the point of resignation. I then offered to give him an unbiased and unvarnished account of the whole transaction. At the end he said it had greatly influenced him and he thanked me warmly. Batterbee, his Private Secretary, thanked me today for it as it had just made the difference.

On the next day Lloyd George made a statement on the subject of Robertson's resignation in Parliament.

February 19th (continued). I lunched with the P.M. alone. He was in good fettle for his speech, though still seedy. I heard his speech in the House of Commons, where he completely disposed of the whole business. . . . His speech was on the lines of the statement I had written on Sunday and he avoided the pitfalls I had feared he might slip into. I had tea with him afterwards in his room at the House of Commons. He was in great spirits, and walked up and down imitating 'Wully's' heavy walk. This, I hope, ends the Robertson crisis. He is gone, and Henry Wilson reigns in his stead.

The question arises why Lloyd George delayed so long before parting with Robertson. He disagreed fundamentally with his strategy, and their temperaments were incompatible. On the whole Robertson was the embodiment of much which the Prime Minister had come into office to get rid of.

His hesitation must be ascribed, I think, partly to political exigencies and partly to the extraordinary pressure of events, which had not left

cc

him time to tackle this thorny issue. At no previous time during his first year of office was the Prime Minister in a strong enough position to face the consequences of dismissing his popular Chief of the Imperial General Staff. Even the War Cabinet could not be counted on to support him unanimously, and several of his other colleagues in the Government would have resigned. After the failure of the Flanders offensive and the establishment of the Supreme War Council it might have been easier. By that time, however, Lloyd George was beset with innumerable difficulties, any one of which would have amounted to a first-class crisis in normal times—popular uneasiness at the failure of the Army to achieve immediate results on the Western Front commensurate with the colossal losses, which affected so many families; the effects of the submarine campaign, brought home to the masses by the controls of many articles, food restrictions, and food queues; the frequent air-raids, and the depressing lighting restrictions. Then there was the Irish question and the Convention by means of which the Government was seeking a solution of this age-long problem in the hope of setting free the division locked up in that unhappy country and possibly even of inducing the Irish people to accept compulsory service. So difficult was the problem that Carson had resigned from the War Cabinet early in January 1918. There were also immense difficulties with labour. Towards the end of 1917 the Minister of Munitions (Churchill) had increased the wages of certain classes of engineers by $12\frac{1}{2}$ per cent to meet what was a genuine grievance. This resulted in a demand for a similar concession to other classes of labour, involving an enormous toll on the National Exchequer and reacted on the Fighting Services to whom it seemed intolerable that men working safely at home should have their pay increased so far beyond that of men who were risking their lives every day. Another matter greatly preoccupying the Prime Minister was the nursing of the food production programme with its demands for labour, machines and manures. Further, the supersession of Jellicoe by Wemyss on December 26, 1917, had also been a formidable step and the Prime Minister may well have hesitated to make a corresponding change in the sister Service without a decent interval.

The actions of a man in a position of great responsibility must be judged not solely by the merits of the particular issue alone, but also by all the surrounding circumstances, and the whirlwind which revolved round Lloyd George in the last days of 1917 and the early days of 1918 was not conducive to the creation of avoidable difficulties. Added to

this, Lloyd George had a sort of affection for his rugged Chief of Staff. He admired his executive efficiency. He could not fail to be impressed by the high terms in which Clemenceau and Pershing had spoken of him at the Supreme War Council. It was only after tremendous efforts on both sides to work together in the national interest; only after Robertson had made clear that he was fundamentally opposed to the policy of the Government and could not carry it out on the terms that they had laid down, that Lloyd George, urged on by Milner, brought himself to the point of making a change.

A week before the storm burst the Supreme War Council met once more, this time in London. The personnel was the same as at the January meeting, and even the problems were the same, for some of the previous decisions had not been carried out. The General Reserve, the pivot of the Supreme War Council's plans, had not been created. At the previous meeting the Council had not felt it necessary to decide what forces were to be allocated to the General Reserve. As Robertson had said, once the problem of the command of the Reserves had been settled, its composition would settle itself. The question had, therefore, been left to the Executive War Board to determine. Unfortunately the Executive War Board, on which Henry Wilson had been replaced by Rawlinson, and Cadorna by Giardino, had failed to accomplish this part of its task. It had begun by drawing up a scheme for the provision of twenty divisions, including twelve French divisions (eight from France and four from the Italian Front), six Italian, and only two British. The plan had received the approval of the French and Italian Governments, but Haig, notwithstanding that two of the British divisions in Italy had been ordered to rejoin his army, had found it impossible to allot even his small quota. He reported that the Germans had now opposite his army no less than eighty-seven divisions in line and in immediate support with thirty others available in reserve. Against this total of 117 enemy divisions he had only forty British divisions in line and eighteen in reserve, fifty-eight divisions in all. In view of his refusal, Pétain was also unwilling to contribute his quota. Haig and Pétain, however, had agreed between themselves on measures of mutual support in the event of emergency.

It was only on March 13th, the day before the Supreme War Council was due to assemble, that we learned of this difficulty:

March 13th. . . . After lunch I went to see Henry Wilson, who was bothered because Haig won't give up his quota to the Allied General Reserve. In the circumstances he advocates a suspension of the whole scheme, which is tantamount to allowing Haig to flout the Supreme War Council. Today, however, probably on the eve of the enemy's greatest effort in the West, it appears inevitable. Both Milner, whom I saw afterwards, and the Prime Minister take this view, though the latter, whom I saw at 6.30 p.m., vowed he would bring Haig to his bearings presently.

It is difficult to believe that Haig's real reason for refusing to contribute his two divisions to the General Reserve was apprehension lest they would be taken away from him. As Bliss pointed out, even if the two divisions were nominally surrendered to the General Reserve, it was certain, in the circumstances then prevailing, that they would at once be handed back to him, and, while retaining the two divisions, he would have the advantage of the whole of the rest of the General Reserve being available to reinforce him in case of necessity. At that moment the scheme of a General Reserve was already in great danger.

March 17th. . . . Thus the Supreme War Council were faced with the complete breakdown of the scheme they had approved at their last meeting. After some palaver we got over it, as the result of a lunch on Thursday (March 14th) between Lloyd George, Henry Wilson and myself, by putting the whole of the Anglo-French forces in Italy into General Reserve—thus maintaining the principle—and by sending a special committee from Versailles to the Italian Front to investigate how many of these divisions could be spared for the Western Front, and how many Italian divisions could go into General Reserve. I did a masterly draft on this (although I say it who shouldn't). Orlando said to Lloyd George: 'That is very ingenious indeed', and Clemenceau added: 'And if an Italian says that, you may know it is.'

Although the Executive War Board, weakened by the episode of the General Reserve and by the replacement of Wilson and Cadorna, had been set on its legs again, several incidents had occurred to cast doubts on its effectiveness. It became known that Foch had recommended the withdrawal of two divisions from the Italian Front without consulting the Board at all and that the French Government were considering the withdrawal of three out of their six divisions. Further, during the discussions it transpired that the Executive War Board were not being kept informed of the plans of the Commanders-in-Chief. Haig had communicated his plans to Pétain and the latter had told Foch personally of his arrangements, but the other members of the Board were more or less in the dark. The Supreme War Council, on the initiative of

Lloyd George, then decided that the arrangement between Haig and Pétain for mutual support should be communicated formally to the Permanent Military Representatives at Versailles, who were to prepare a plan in concert with them for supporting the Italian Army in the event of an enemy attack on their front. Altogether the Executive War Board had already become rather 'fly-blown'. Apart from this the meeting showed that the Council's machinery was working well as witnessed by the useful reports from the Allied Naval Council, the Allied Maritime Transport Council and the Permanent Military Representatives which resulted in the requisition on March 21st of Dutch shipping in British and American ports. From the point of view of the Supreme Command the interesting thing is that the inter-Allied organizations were functioning as advisers to the Supreme War Council exactly as British Government Departments functioned *vis-à-vis* the War Cabinet.

A question also arose about the desirability of retaliation to German indiscriminating bombing attacks; a similar question arose in the Second World War. The British Government had decided on a policy of reprisals, but the French Government objected to such attacks being undertaken by British air forces from bases on French soil, on the ground that it was resulting in counter-reprisals against French towns. The argument became rather sharp, but it was then found that, in fact, the British air raids always had a military objective, even though announced as reprisals for indiscriminate bombing, and it was agreed that in future both countries, when announcing reprisals, should make clear that our operations had a military objective.

The meeting of the Supreme War Council was followed by a political conference on March 15th and 16th:

March 17th. . . . At the political conference, where I was the sole secretary, the principal subject was Japanese intervention in Siberia, and after a tussle, in which Balfour (hitherto a strong advocate of this policy) pleaded for delay, it was decided to send President Wilson a telegram urging him to encourage Japan to go in. Frazier was present to report what occurred, but without authority to speak. As Clemenceau said: 'President Wilson is listening to what we say, but does not tell us what he thinks—a very favourable position for him.' He said a good many other very shrewd things about Wilson's claim to be a co-belligerent but not an ally, and to run an independent policy all over the world, while protesting if the Allies make any independent announcement, as he did after the last Versailles Conference. I duly recorded his rather witty sallies and have no doubt that Frazier will telegraph

them to the President. Old Clemenceau is a splendid old fellow; short, very broad and solid, with a magnificent head, sturdy, independent, honest, sincere, witty, and with a curious boyish knack of deliberately making regular *'enfant terrible'* observations. I have taken a great liking to him.

Other decisions taken were to invite the Permanent Military Representatives and the Allied Naval Council to report, jointly if possible, on the desirability of despatching a military mission to Archangel in order to prevent the great accumulations of stores at that port from falling into the hands of the enemy; to favour publication of losses from U-boat attack in order to counteract the exaggerated figures published by the enemy, and finally a declaration was issued condemning the 'unprecedented outrage perpetrated under the name of a German peace on the Russian people whose armies spontaneously abandoned the defence of the country'.

Practically the whole of the secretarial work of the heavy meetings of the Council and of the subsequent political conference had fallen upon me and I was not sorry to bid farewell to our guests.

CHAPTER LXXVI

THE 21ST MARCH, 1918

> 'Immediate in a flame,
> But soon obscured with smoke, all heaven appeared,
> From those deep-throated engines belched, whose roar
> Embowelled with outrageous noise the air,
> And all her entrails tore, disgorging foul
> Their devilish glut, chained thunderbolts and hail
> Of iron globes, which on the victor host
> Levelled with such impetuous fury smote,
> That whom they hit, none on their feet might stand,
> Though standing else as rocks; but down they fell
> By thousands, angel on archangel rolled,
> The sooner for their arms; unarmed they might
> Have easily as spirits evaded swift
> By quick contraction or remove: but now
> Foul dissipation followed and forced rout;
> Nor served it to relax their serried files.
> What should they do? if on they rushed, repulse
> Repeated and indecent overthrow
> Doubled, would render them yet more despised,
> And to their foes a laughter: for in view
> Stood ranked of seraphim another row,
> In posture to displode their second tire
> Of thunder: back defeated to return
> They worse abhorred.'
>
> (MILTON, *Paradise Lost*, VI, 584–607.)

THE first part of the story of the German attack of March 21st, as it appeared to the Supreme Command in London, can be told in notes made at the time.

March 21st. Today the long awaited Hun attack began on the very front where we had expected it, and on ground which I had been over with Smuts some seven weeks ago. It is one of the decisive moments of the world's history, but I think our fellows will hold them up. I lunched with Lloyd George, Donald of the *Chronicle* being also present.

March 22nd. War Cabinet 11.30. Although terrific fighting is going on on the Western Front and some bulges have been made in our battle zone, especially on Fifth Army front, there appeared to be no cause for alarm. During the day, however, the news became worse. Fifth Army (Gough) was obviously giving way, and the situation was menacing though Third Army (Byng) was holding splendidly.

March 23rd. News kept coming in all day of the increasing seriousness of the position on Fifth Army front. In fact Fifth Army is retreating to the line of the Somme, and one could not but fear a *débâcle.* Third Army is still holding well, but a hole is said to have been made at Mory, whither I walked some seven weeks ago from St. Leger with Smuts and Byng. The War Cabinet met at 4 p.m. They . . . decided to send the $18\frac{1}{2}$ to 19-year-old men to France. I am rather uncomfortable about the effect of this on home defence.[1] It is a difficult situation, however, as clearly we must have more men for France, as our casualties in this battle are going to be huge. I was late in the office getting out minutes, but got home by 10.15 p.m. Daylight saving tonight, so I get a short night.

March 24th (Sunday). 9.20 train to town. There was nothing doing and little news, so I came home in the afternoon. At 6.30 p.m., while I was singing part-songs with the children in the garden, I received an imperative call from Downing Street that the Prime Minister wanted me. . . . I got Harris, a neighbour, to take me up in his car and arrived about 8.30 p.m. having made my dinner off sandwiches which Adeline had prepared (bless her!). Ll. G. had gone off to dine with Winston Churchill so I pursued them and found Henry Wilson also there. The news was about as bad as it could be for the right of Third Army had been stove in and a breach made between it and Fifth Army. Haig's message concluded: 'the situation is serious'. There was nothing to be done, but Churchill, supported by Wilson, was bombarding the Prime Minister with demands for a *levée en masse.* Eventually the P.M. went off to Walton Heath and the bombardment was transferred to me. The northern part of Third Army which has held so splendidly is under Haldane who made so good an impression on Smuts and myself a few weeks ago.

March 25th. Slept very badly. This has been a really terrible day. Although the gap between Third and Fifth Armies has been filled in, our troops are everywhere being driven back and must be extremely exhausted. The Australians and New Zealanders are due tonight at Albert, and may hold up the enemy until the French forces arrive to cover Amiens. I was with the Prime Minister at 9.30 a.m. and he sent me off to the Admiralty to see Geddes and try and squeeze some Marines out of him as drafts. Geddes had there the Second Sea Lord and the A.A.G. of Marines. I told him we were at the crisis of the nation's fate, and that, to meet the critical emergency, the Navy must do what it can to help out the Army, perhaps even to save the Channel ports. However, they could promise very little, and I think they were right at a moment when we are denuding the home defence forces and the responsibilities of the fleet are greater than ever. The War Cabinet met at 11 a.m., an anxious meeting, at which it was decided to have drafted a Bill extending

---

[1] What I had in mind was the kind of situation that developed in the summer of 1940 when our army in France was driven into the sea, and the danger of invasion became very real, especially as we had no army adequate to deal with any large-scale attack.

compulsory service to Ireland and extending the age limits to cover $17\frac{1}{2}$ to 55. I lunched with Geddes. I wanted to get home for a night in the country, but the Prime Minister insisted on my staying in Town. . . . I had a walk with the Prime Minister before dinner; the news seemed better and we both felt more cheerful—in fact Balfour and Churchill whom I found in company with the Prime Minister were ridiculously optimistic—but on getting back from the usual round of St. James's Park we met Macdonogh, who told us that Courcellettes had fallen. All day I kept thinking of Briand's saying during the drawn-out Verdun attack—'*Nous sommes crucifiés*'.

March 26th. Slept nearly ten hours at Club and woke up enormously refreshed. At the morning Cabinet I learned we had been driven back to the Ancre, but later the news got rather better and on our front there seems to be a lull. I am much puzzled how the enemy have driven us so easily across the Somme battlefield, which is pitted all over with craters and is one vast military obstacle. Our men must have been dead beat. That is the only explanation. After the Cabinet Lloyd George asked French (who is attending regularly), and myself and Winston Churchill to stay behind and discuss the situation. French was most bitter about Haig, who, he said, was no judge of men, had surrounded himself with stupid people and bad commanders. . . . He considered Haig had badly let down the Army in shattering it in the hopeless Flanders offensive. In the evening Lloyd George and I dined with Eric Geddes. His housekeeper, Miss Shepherd, is a wonderful singer and accompanist, and he, to my surprise, a fine singer with a voice like a bull. We had a regular sing-song. The Prime Minister and I came to the conclusion he is prouder of his singing than of his professional attainments! At 11 p.m. we went back to Downing Street, where we were joined by Milner and Henry Wilson, who have come straight from a most important conference at Doullens, not far from the front, with Poincaré, Clemenceau, Foch, Pétain and Haig, Plumer, Byng, etc. They reported that they had agreed to make Foch 'co-ordinating authority' over the whole Western Front, i.e. practically generalissimo. The French are putting in all their reserves and it is hoped to deliver a great counter-stroke, if only they can arrive in time. Milner gave a fine account of the Army commanders, who, he said, were cool as cucumbers and in great heart. Everything behind the front, he said, was orderly, and even some of the remnants of the shattered Fifth Army whom he saw were cheery and in good spirits. Things are a touch brighter. Here is a good story. Henry Wilson, in the midst of our troubles, tells of Clemenceau, who is in great heart. 'Lloyd George,' says Clemenceau, 'goes to Beauvais. He sees plenty of "sheeps" and plenty of "muttons", and he goes back to England and says France has plenty of "breads"! Very shrewd!'[1]

---

[1] Clemenceau's observation referred to remonstrances addressed by Lloyd George to the French Government after our last trip to France when we had stopped on our way home at Beauvais (*supra*, p. 773). There was, in fact, a profusion of foodstuffs in the shops in this agricultural district and on that visit, as well as on a later one, I myself bought and brought home a

CC*

During March 27th and 28th the position on the British front, as
viewed from London, seemed easier. We still had five fresh and several
tired divisions in reserve. There was, however, some anxiety about the
French, who, as we learned on March 28th, had lost their detraining
station at Montdidier, south of Amiens, though they had retorted by a
brilliant local counter-attack near Noyon, advancing three kilometres
and threatening the flank and rear of the enemy at Montdidier.

Meanwhile our Supreme Command was confronted with difficult
problems in finding additional men to fill the Army's depleted ranks,
including that of compulsory service in Ireland.

March 28th. . . . To carry the strong measures in Britain for raising more
men it is essential to announce compulsory service for Ireland. To do this
next Tuesday will be to wreck the Irish Convention which is due to report
next week. If the decision is postponed until Parliament is due to meet on
April 9th, it might be possible, by introducing Home Rule, to soften the
effect of compulsion in Ireland, but every day's delay is dangerous, as the
recruits, whether from England or Ireland, are urgently needed.

March 29th (Good Friday). War Cabinet met at 11.30. Decided to press
President Wilson to send over 100,000 men a month for the next three
months to fight in American battalions in British brigades. Otherwise we
shall be unable to maintain the strength of our Army even after everything
has been done to fill the ranks.

That Good Friday always remains in my memory. We were very
anxious about the situation in front of Amiens, and after the War
Cabinet meeting we telephoned to GHQ in France for news. They too
were anxious and had sent a Staff officer to investigate and report, but
he would not be back until the evening. Lloyd George wrote later:[1]

The only news received by Friday morning about the progress of this
fresh development was not reassuring. We had been forced out of some of
our positions and the battle was still raging. We were barely holding our
own. Sir Maurice Hankey and I sat for hours in the Cabinet Room waiting
anxiously for further reports from the front. We decided at last to go to St.
Anne's, Soho to hear Bach's Passion Music. As we took our seats we heard
the clergyman intone that poignant supplication, 'O God, make speed to
save us'. How fervently we joined in the response, 'O Lord, make haste to
help us'.[2] When we returned to Downing Street we heard that the Germans

quantity of butter, a welcome addition to my wife's larder. This episode had confirmed information picked up in Paris to the effect that they were not nearly so strictly rationed as we were and
had led Lloyd George to make the formal protest to which Clemenceau referred.

[1] *War Memoirs*, V, p. 2914.
[2] I can never forget the glance he gave me at that moment.

had been beaten off by Third Army with heavy losses and that their advance was slowing down opposite Amiens.

We both came back spiritually refreshed—to find the news a little better as reinforcements, British and French, were arriving in the dangerous areas covering Amiens.

March 29th (continued). . . . Churchill, who has all along urged a terrific counter-stroke, telegraphs from Paris that he is satisfied with the preparations the French are making.

March 30th. War Cabinet 11 a.m. Our line all right today, but tonight I hear the French are being driven back by a very heavy attack west of Noyon.

March 31st (Easter Sunday). I have actually had an undisturbed day at home, though I have been in uniform all day with a War Office car ready to take me at the shortest notice to Town or to Walton Heath. The news as telephoned from Town is very much better, both the French and ourselves having gained ground and prisoners. At 10 o'clock tonight Lloyd George rang me up personally at Highstead from Walton Heath to tell me that President Wilson had agreed to send us 100,000[1] men a month not for three months but for four. As the details are left to Pershing and Baker to work out, he thinks either that Baker must come over here, or he and I must go to Paris at once. Of course this is most splendid news, for it prodigiously eases our anxiety in regard to man-power in the future, which is weighing very heavily upon us. This is a good Easter Egg, and means that the prayers I uttered at early Communion this morning are already in a fair way to be answered. Nevertheless I doubt not the future has many terrible things in store for us, and that we shall need stout hearts and firm faith for many a day to come.

April 1st. War Cabinet at 11.30. Prime Minister . . . positively indignant that I had arranged a War Cabinet for Easter Monday although he had given me no instructions to the contrary! After getting rid of his colleagues . . . he held an important conference on the method of transporting troops from U.S.A. In the afternoon Milner sent for me and said he felt the War Cabinet were not being quite kept informed of what was going on. He also lamented the paralysis and inability to discuss anything except the battle on the Western Front at the War Cabinet. Not much news today. I put up a note to the Prime Minister in the evening urging him to delegate some of the accumulating questions of detail to his colleagues and so to keep them busy and happy. In the evening I discussed the question with him and Bonar Law, both being rather 'sniffy' about it. I lunched at the Carlton with Balfour, Eric Drummond and Ian Malcolm, and had to pay 14s for my lunch! I wrote to Storr at Versailles today, to warn him to have ready a plan for getting rid of his papers in case, by some evil chance, a break in the line should bring the Germans even to Versailles.

[1] The correct figure was 120,000 men a month, *vide War Memoirs*, V, p. 3042.

On the next day it was decided at rather short notice that Lloyd George should meet Clemenceau at Beauvais to discuss the situation on the Western Front.

April 2nd. Rather a quiet day dealing with a lot of office business. War Cabinet at 5.30 p.m. At 7 o'clock the Prime Minister, Henry Wilson, Davies, Duncannon (Wilson's A.D.C.), Graeme Thomson and self left for Folkestone where we are to sleep *en route* to Beauvais tomorrow. Arrived about 9.30 and went to bed.

April 3rd. A very long day. Breakfast at 7 a.m. Crossed in a minute 'P' boat, all the destroyers and larger craft being employed to carry reinforcements to France. Luckily it was very calm. 9.30 started from Boulogne to motor to Beauvais, where we arrived at 1 p.m. ravenous. Old Clemenceau came and sat with us as we lunched. The old 'Tiger' as he is called in France, or the 'honey-pot', as he calls himself, looked to me rather worried, as though he was sleeping badly, but he was full of courage and very splendid, I thought. He even managed to joke a little and actually told the 'lots of beefs and lots of muttons' story, which I have already recounted by hearsay.[1] The conference was held at the Hôtel de Ville in a fine room with some good pictures. Clemenceau turned out the French and American secretaries, but turned round and said "Is Hankey here?" and then got to business—which mark of confidence much pleased me. Besides Clemenceau and Lloyd George, Haig, Wilson, Foch, Pétain, Pershing and Bliss were present. The main subject was the co-ordination of Allied strategy, which was eventually put into the sole hands of Foch. It was easy to see that Foch and Pétain did not like each other. The Americans had a big voice in the decision. It was also decided that, if Haig is attacked and Arras is heavily pressed, as he anticipates, the French shall attack. It transpired that Pershing had not heard a word of Wilson's decision to send 480,000 infantry in the next four months to fight as battalions in our brigades, although we heard three days ago. . . . After the conference we motored back to Boulogne, having a picnic dinner off some food which Clemenceau had originally brought for his own lunch, but given to Foch from whom Duncannon pinched it. We got to Boulogne at 9 p.m. and crossed in the 'P' boat again, on a very dark night. Just before leaving Boulogne we had a message that a German submarine was in the neighbourhood, and a bomb was dropped on shore just after we left. However nothing eventful happened. Our ship was a new one, only arrived three days before fresh from the maker's hands. Our skipper, a young lieutenant, had been three years in a battleship and did not know either his ship or the locality, this being his first visit to Boulogne. He had some difficulty in making Folkestone in the dark, but luckily one of the trawlers in the vicinity lit one of the marvellous flares used in lieu of searchlights to try and spot sub-

[1] *vide supra*, p. 787.

marines and the whole harbour and town were illuminated. . . . The whole
sky to the eastward was constantly illuminated by these flares. We got back
to London at 2.15 a.m. after a day of twenty hours, during which we had
motored 200 and steamed fifty miles and attended an important conference. I
slept at the Club. I returned with an impression of confidence on the part of
the French, but our people, especially Lawrence, gave me an uneasy feeling
of lacking confidence. Haig looked well but somehow failed to inspire
confidence. . . . Altogether I am not easy in mind.

One picture remains graven in my memory. As we paced the Quai at
Boulogne we watched a regiment of lads of 18 or 19 for the most part
landing from a Channel steamer. They belonged to some Scottish
regiment and in the glimmer of the dimmed arc lights looked pale and
pathetically young. A few days later they fought gallantly and lost
heavily.

The reason why this conference was necessary after the arrangement
made by Milner at Doullens was that Foch needed a more precise
definition of his powers. The text of that agreement was:

General Foch is charged by the British and French Governments with
co-ordinating the action of the Allied Armies on the Western Front. He will
reach an understanding (*il s'entendra*) to this effect with the Commanders-in-
Chief, who are invited to furnish him with all necessary information.

At Beauvais Foch explained that the situation had now changed. On
March 26th, at Doullens, it was a question of co-ordinating action in
full swing. At Beauvais on April 3rd it was a question of the future
strategy and co-ordinating preparation for future action. For this he
felt his powers to be insufficient—and no wonder when the obstructive-
ness of some of the generals is taken into account. So long as there was
no action either by the French or British armies Doullens gave him no
powers of co-ordination. Now he wanted the power of creating action,
or, as he put it 'powers for the infusion of an idea of action', round
which the preparations should be made in co-ordination. This was the
more important because at the time of the Doullens Conference we
were submitting to battle imposed upon us by the enemy, but at
Beauvais we were thinking of our own action. In a word, Foch wanted
it to be clear that the strategy was in his hands.

Foch was strongly supported by Lloyd George. He emphasized the
confidence which British public opinion felt in the General who, he
insisted, ought to have all the powers he needed. Of course, if Haig felt
that any decision by Foch placed the British Army in danger, he could

appeal to the British Government, and no paper agreement could prevent this. The American generals supported this as did Haig, and the following formula was proposed by Henry Wilson and adopted:

The agreement for the co-ordination of the Higher Command on the Western Front concluded at Doullens on March 26, 1918, should be superseded by the following arrangement:

'General Foch is charged by the British, French and American Governments with the co-ordination of the action of the Allied Armies on the Western Front. To this end all powers necessary to secure effective realization are conferred on him. The British, French and American Governments for this purpose entrust to General Foch the strategic direction of military operations. The Commanders-in-Chief of the British, French and American Armies have full control of the tactical employment of their forces. Each Commander-in-Chief will have the right of appeal to his Government if in his opinion the safety of his Army is compromised by any order received from General Foch.'[1]

The American generals had to reserve this agreement for formal ratification by their Government, which was soon given. The Beauvais Agreement, therefore, extended into the strategical field the powers given to Foch at Doullens. As yet, however, his authority did not extend beyond the Western Front.

By April 5th the first phase of the German attack had come to an end, although I do not think we fully realized that at the time, except for some attacks on the French farther south to improve their position. The enemy had failed to interrupt the main railway line from Calais and Boulogne to Paris or to capture Amiens, although the railway establishments and marshalling yards at that important junction were now under fire from heavy guns at long range. Above all the strategical object of dividing the British and French armies had failed. This failure was due, in part at any rate, to the difficulties of the country resulting from the shell-holes which pitted every inch of the old Somme battlefields.[2] Another contributory cause mentioned in Ludendorff's account was that the German soldiers 'not being always under the firm control of their officers . . . had been checked by finding food depots, and valuable time had thus been lost'. Sea-power and blockade were beginning to produce an effect even in the German Army.

The German High Command then decided to fall back on an alternative plan, which had been put forward by Rupprecht earlier for the

[1] For a full account of the meeting, *vide War Memoirs*, V, p. 2927.
[2] *vide supra*, p. 787.

main operation. This was for an attack in the plain of the Lys between Armentières and La Bassée west of Lille. Smuts and I had spotted this sector as a probable direction of attack.[1] An advance in that region, equal to the maximum advance already accomplished in the Amiens region, would have brought the German Army to Calais and Boulogne and have cut off the whole of the Allied armies to the north. As I had pointed out 'his railway communications in this region are greatly superior to our own, and in the absence of shell-holes I do not think the ground marshy enough to stop him'. Nevertheless this front had been rejected for the original German attack owing to its marshy character. By mid-April, however, it had dried up to a considerable extent, and it was on this section of our front that the Germans decided to renew their offensive.

April 9th. . . . While I was writing this at home I received a message from the office to say that our front had been stove in north of La Bassée and that the Portuguese have been completely overrun. I have always been anxious about this section (see my visit to France in January) but military opinion was opposed to me, because they thought the ground too marshy and that the enemy would get into a sort of *cul-de-sac*, bounded by the river Lys and the La Bassée Canal.

April 10th. The news is very bad. The enemy has attacked with success from La Bassée to the Messines Ridge; has established a bridgehead across the Lys, and has penetrated both sides of Armentières, which we shall have to abandon. Further, our divisions in this area are all divisions used up on the Somme, filled with inexperienced drafts. I fear for the Channel ports.

In order to exploit his initial success the enemy now struck north and south of the gap. This involved attacks on the higher ground to the northward towards Kemmel and south of the La Bassée Canal.

April 13th. The enemy attack beyond Armentières seems for the moment to have spent itself, but they are attacking the Kemmel position, and apparently the long-expected attack opposite Arras and Lens is beginning to develop. Personally I am less pessimistic about the situation than Henry Wilson and some of the War Cabinet. The enemy has knocked us about badly; has gained important ground; and by continuing his attacks threatens to exhaust our man-power and knock out our Army, unless the American battalions arrive in time. On the other hand, on a big map the amount of ground they have gained is not great; the French Army is practically intact; and the enemy must have exhausted nearly half the reserves he had accumulated for this push. Our men are very good stickers, if not very skilful

[1] *vide supra*, p. 760.

fighters or very skilfully led, and they have not been broken up yet. I think the Huns must be a bit bothered at their own losses. Moreover our cause is the right one. But the next month will be a very anxious one.

April 15th. No particular war news except the loss of Neuve Chapelle.

April 16th. The news is again bad, the enemy having made progress towards the vital Kemmel–Mont-des-Cats Ridge, at the foot of which he now stands. He has also captured Bailleul, through which I have so often and so recently motored in peace and security.

April 17th. Slightly better news, as counter-attacks have restored to us Wytschaete and Meteren. . . . Derby told me he is leaving the War Office to go to Paris as Ambassador on Saturday. Bonar Law told me that the Prime Minister is flirting with the idea of taking the War Office himself, but that probably Milner will take it. I gather it is Ll. G.'s intention to add Austen Chamberlain to the War Cabinet as I have long advocated. . . .

April 18th. . . . Today it is settled that Derby goes to Paris; Milner S. of S. for War; and Austen Chamberlain comes into the War Cabinet. At 6 p.m. I attended a conference at 10 Downing Street, with the Prime Minister, C.I.G.S., Q.M.G. (France), Sam Fay and Nash (railway experts) and Shipping Controller in regard to the railway position in France. It was decided to proceed on the assumption that the French supplies of coal from the Pas de Calais would cease; that we must make good the deficit; that the foodstuffs for the French civil population in Northern France should go by sea; and that we would feed the French troops north of the Somme. All this is necessitated by Amiens being under fire. . . .

April 22nd. . . . At 7.30 Milner came to see me. He told me that he had decided to have an Under-Secretary of State, just as Kitchener had Derby, to look after the administration and all matters of detail. He would be a peer. The Prime Minister, he said, had strongly pressed him to take *me*. I at once protested that I was the last person in the world for such a post. My experience was entirely in the field of large questions of policy, and I had no knowledge of or liking for questions of administrative detail. I had no desire to be a peer or to defend the War Office in either House. He agreed with me, but gave as his reason that I was the only person who had any influence over the Prime Minister and that my encyclopædic general knowledge of the war and of all that had happened made me irreplaceable where I was. . . .

April 23rd. . . . Lunched with Balfour and Salisbury. Discussion mainly on Balfour's invitation to the latter to accompany the Duke of Connaught to Japan. After lunch Balfour and I walked to the Admiralty to obtain the latest news of the raid on Zeebrugge.

April 26th. . . . Rather bad news from France as Mont Kemmel has been captured, though Villers-Bretonneux (where I slept three months ago on my visit to Gough) has been recaptured. . . .

April 27th. I went down this morning to Pearson's Works, close to the

Albert Docks, with Ernest Moir of the Ministry of Munitions to see a new 'pill-box' blockhouse, which he is turning out in great quantities for use in France. I drove down with Alanton of the General Staff and Baker a gas expert. The former . . . said that in the recent offensive by the enemy on March 21st our failure was largely due to our neglect to supply nucleus garrisons in the third line, with the result that our forces, shattered in the front line, and shaken in the second line by artillery fire, were rushed over the third line, where there was not even a nucleus force to rally them. Thus between Armentières and La Bassée the great mass of wire protecting the third line remains intact to this day. There were no guards at the points where the roads pass through the wire; it was no one's responsibility to join up the gaps, or destroy the roads, and the Germans in the mist simply marched through in fours, and this immensely strong line was abandoned without a struggle. . . .

April 29th. No War Cabinet. In the morning I wrote a letter to Milner about the above-mentioned causes of our reverses on the Western Front, and suggesting that there ought to be an organization at the front to ascertain the causes of failures or successes and transmit them to all other units. He replied: 'Thanks for your excellent letter and suggestion'. . . .

The capture of Kemmel, which at the time was held by French troops sent to reinforce our Army, turned out to be the last major success achieved by the Germans on our front. The tide had about reached high-water mark and the waters just lapped over this important tactical point, but slightly receded at Villers-Bretonneux. We had, however, no ground for anticipating that this was the case and the fall of Kemmel was naturally treated as an ominous event. It brought to a head various matters that were in everyone's mind such as the need for speeding up the arrival of the American troops, which was hanging fire, the question of the safety of the Channel ports, and other outstanding inter-Allied questions. A meeting of the Supreme War Council was therefore arranged for May 1st. It took place at Abbeville:

May 2nd. Abbeville is swarming with troops—British, French, with some Americans. Before breakfast I had a walk with Lloyd George and we dropped into a church where Low Mass was being celebrated. He seemed fascinated and remarked as we came out, 'If I were going to the trenches, I might be brought to believe in it'. . . . The Council was mainly occupied with interminable discussions about the incorporation of American battalions in British brigades. The U.S. Government accepts our point of view, but leaves a wide discretion to Pershing, who hates the whole scheme as detrimental to the building up of an American Army under his command. He is very obstinate and we had great difficulty in reaching a not very satisfactory agreement.

The agreement was of a very temporary kind, as Pershing did not want to commit himself beyond the month of May. In order to meet his main requirement the Supreme War Council agreed in principle that the American Army should be formed as soon as possible under its own Commander-in-Chief and under its own flag. Pershing agreed that as an emergency arrangement and without losing sight of the necessity of building up an American Army, priority of transport should be given to American infantry and machine-gun units for training and service with the French and British armies. But he accepted this on the under-standing that such infantry and machine-gun units could be withdrawn and united with their own artillery and auxiliary units at the discretion of the American Commander-in-Chief after consultation with Foch. During May this preference to the transportation of infantry and machine-gun units was to be limited to six American divisions. Any excess available tonnage during May was to be allotted to bring over such troops as Pershing might determine. The programme was to be continued into June, but only on the condition that the British Govern-ment should furnish a minimum of 130,000 tons of transport in May and 150,000 in June. In June the first 150,000 men brought over were not to be sent to the French or British armies as in May, but to be allo-cated for training or service as Pershing might decide. But any excess over 150,000 men which the British Government might succeed in bringing over in June was to consist of infantry and machine-gun units. There was to be a fresh review of the situation early in June.

This complicated arrangement, reached only after long haggling, was about as good as could be expected. It established the principle of a separate American Army on which Pershing had so very properly insisted, and it secured for the British and French reinforcements in infantry and machine-guns, of which at that moment they felt in such need, while leaving the matter open for future settlement.

Meantime a more dramatic meeting, technically outside the proceed-ings of the Supreme War Council since it concerned only the British and French Governments, had taken place at the Préfet's private house at 10 a.m., when the question of the threat to the French Channel ports was taken up. Those present were Lloyd George, Haig, Henry Wilson, Wemyss, Lawrence, Clemenceau, Foch, Pétain, Bon with myself as secretary.

May 2nd. The subject was whether in the event of an unavoidable retire-ment we should fall back on the Channel ports, the two Allied Armies

separating, or whether we should let go of the ports with our left hand and retire behind the Somme. Foch said stoutly: *'ni l'un ni l'autre'*, but when pressed and cornered he said that the loss of the ports was not final, and that we should have to cover the battlefield of the Allies. But it would never come to that: *'jamais, jamais, jamais'*.

This phrase was repeated again and again in half-bantering tones with such phrases as: *'ne bougez pas, ne bougez pas: jamais, jamais, jamais'*. It was a remarkable scene, Henry Wilson, Haig and Pétain arguing for withdrawal behind the Seine, Foch half-chaffing, half-contemptuous, rejecting the whole thesis, the statesmen listening for once instead of talking most of the time and vastly intrigued at the experience. But Foch won his way and was proved right.

At later meetings of the whole of the Supreme War Council the extension of Foch's authority to the Italian and Belgian Fronts was discussed, but the representatives of both countries had to ask that decision be deferred owing to constitutional difficulties arising from the fact that in each case the King was head of the fighting forces; it was not until November 8, 1918, that Foch was given strategical direction of all the forces against Germany.

In view of the wide powers conferred on Foch, the Supreme War Council decided on the abolition of the Executive War Board which had now become completely redundant, all its powers having been absorbed by the General-in-Chief. By this time, too, the operation of the Committee of Military Representatives, which was the linch-pin of the Versailles organization, had undergone considerable change. The original idea had been that it should provide an independent tribunal of military advisers to the Supreme War Council, and it had consisted of general officers of the highest rank and authority—Foch, Wilson, Bliss and Cadorna. The personnel had now changed. Foch had been replaced first by Weygand and then by Bélin; Henry Wilson had been replaced first by Rawlinson and at the end of March when the latter replaced Gough in command of Fifth Army, by Sackville-West who was Wilson's 'own man' and virtually took his instructions from him; Cadorna had also been replaced by an officer of lower rank and status and Bliss was the only original member now remaining. Thus the Permanent Military Representatives were now officers distinguished in the second rather than in the first rank who were subordinate—in the case of the French representative to Foch, in that of the British to Wilson. In this modified form, however, which corresponded to my own conception of the ultimate role of the Permanent Military Repre-

sentatives, they continued to do admirable work as the permanent nucleus of the organization.

We returned to London from Abbeville on May 4th and three days later Lloyd George found himself compelled to repel a surprise attack of a most serious character from a wholly unexpected quarter directed against the Government in general and himself in particular:

May 7th. The morning's papers contained a veritable bombshell in the shape of a letter from Maurice accusing the Prime Minister and Bonar Law of false statements in the House of Commons. I was engaged on the matter from 10 a.m. until 11.30 p.m. in frequent conference with the Prime Minister, with whom I lunched alone and dined late together with Kerr. The Cabinet were of course entirely preoccupied with the matter, which threatens the existence of the Government. The Cabinet decided to take disciplinary action against Maurice and to appoint a Court of Honour to examine the matter (two judges), but Parliament wanted a Select Committee. The objection to the latter procedure is that many aspects of the subject are so confidential that their report could not be published during the war and no one will be satisfied. Lloyd George sent for me at 5 p.m. and told me he had decided to resist the proposal for a Select Committee and to make it a question of confidence. He himself would make a great speech, in which he would tell as much as possible, and perhaps more than he would have wished. Immediately after lunch I had luckily put in hand an immense précis of the whole affair. I was working on this with relays of stenographers from 2.30 to 8.30 p.m. and it was brought over to Downing Street at 9.30 p.m. . . . I had to do the whole thing myself because much of it was in the proceedings of international conferences and minutes of the especially secret 'hush' meetings of the War Cabinet and some in this diary even. Of course the issue is immensely wider than the small charges in Maurice's letter.

May 8th. Went to communion service at St. Martin's-in-the-Field. . . . I was working most of the day on material for Lloyd George's speech, looking up past records, etc. At 6 p.m. Lloyd George rehearsed his speech to Milner, Chamberlain, Kerr and self and we cut it about a good deal. Earlier in the afternoon Balfour, who had promised to speak tomorrow, came to the office and cross-examined me for an hour in regard to the facts.

May 9th. . . . I went to 10 Downing Street, and read the notes of the P.M.'s speech and made some alterations. He was walking up and down in the sun on the terrace with Bonar Law. The latter said: 'The case seems so strong that I cannot help feeling that Maurice, who is a clever man, has something up his sleeve.' I have done my best, and only hope there is nothing I have overlooked! I lunched alone with the Prime Minister, as I always do before his big speeches. He was cheerful but in rather a chastened mood. He admitted that speeches dealing with facts and figures were not his strong

point, and that his Celtic temperament made him unable to resist stretching them to their extreme limits. . . . The speech was a superb Parliamentary effort. I was very glad that I got him to insert some passages to give Haig satisfaction, though he might have gone a step farther in this respect. Practically all opposition was crushed. Runciman, who was to have wound up for the Opposition, looked miserable and never rose. Lloyd George's Whips asked him to speak earlier 'because Balfour is to follow' and this finished him. . . . I had many invitations for dinner at the House from the Prime Minister himself, from Eric Geddes, and less important people, but refused them all and mouched off home, where I dined at 9.30 and went to bed to sleep the sleep of the just after my many hours' toil and anxiety.

May 10th. War Cabinet 11.30. General congratulations to the Prime Minister on his speech, and general recognition that it was only rendered possible by my system of records.

The Maurice debate had the effect of clearing the political atmosphere, which had become clouded as the result of the long military crisis created by the German onslaught. The Germans, after a pause of a few weeks for reorganization, next turned their attention to our Allies with a fresh onslaught directed at Paris. The situation continued to be one of anxiety for some months to come, but the sense of immediate apprehension of the separation of the Allied armies and of the threat to the British Army and the Channel ports gradually subsided.

CHAPTER LXXVII

REFLECTIONS ON THE GERMAN OFFENSIVE

'It was an established fact that the enemy's resistance was
beyond our strength.' (LUDENDORFF, II, p. 600.)

THE reasons for our reverses in March–May 1918 have become the subject of formidable controversy which still goes on, and we may pause for a moment to examine what substance there is in the charge that these reverses were due largely to the errors and neglect of the Supreme Command both in England and at Versailles. It may be true that the basic answer is to be found in the quotation at the head of the chapter, and in the final result of the campaign, both proving that our Supreme Command did at least make sufficient provision to avert disaster. It can be argued that there were weaknesses in the arrangements it made, but they were by no means the sole cause of our reverses. We must consider in assessing responsibilities, not only the decisions of the Supreme Command, but the conduct of the campaign by the High Command in France, Pétain and Haig, by their subordinates and their troops; of the last it may be said at once there can be little but praise. Finally there is the 'fortune of war' and factors such as weather and especially fog.

Let us consider first the charges levelled against the Supreme Command, i.e. the Supreme War Council and the War Cabinet, whose responsibility at more than one point was interlocked. Omitting general criticisms against the system, the main charges are as follows:

1. The War Cabinet locked up too many men in home defence.

2. It was wrong in refusing the reinforcements from home to the Army in France demanded by the War Office at the end of 1917.

3. It ought at once to have brought to France some of the divisions in Italy, the Balkans and Egypt.

4. In spite of the refusal of reinforcements it insisted on the extension of the line held by the British.

5. The joint arrangements for a general reserve were inadequate.

To take each charge in turn:

1. The accusation that the War Cabinet was responsible for retaining too many men for home defence is not correct.[1] Throughout the

---

[1] It should be included among the 'legends' about the battle mentioned in the chapter entitled 'Some Reflections' in the official history (*France and Belgium 1918*, II, p. 456). Instead this

war the civilian authorities in the matter of home defence acted on the joint advice of the highest naval and military authorities.

2. The case here is that, though fully apprised by the War Office of the concentration of German forces in France and the grave man-power deficiencies of the British Expeditionary Force, the War Cabinet refused to allot the Army more than about 100,000 category A men of the 615,000 demanded by the War Office, and so endangered the safety of the British Army. But the War Cabinet was under no illusions about the threat arising from the collapse of Russia and the transfer of German divisions from east to west. Lloyd George had been among the first to foresee it. He several times referred to it in his opposition to the Flanders offensive but his warnings fell on deaf ears. The War Cabinet, however, believed that the war could be won only by bringing over American troops. That was the main object and that meant shipping on which our continental Allies had also become increasingly dependent. Although losses from submarine attack had been reduced, they were still heavy—1,273,000 gross tons in the last quarter of 1917—and the arrears were terrible. That was why the War Cabinet put first the protection of shipping, shipbuilding and everything that helped to relieve our dependence on shipping. It was also unwilling to take men from the production of coal and war material the demands for which were insatiable. Risks had to be run somewhere and on a long view it preferred to run them on the Western Front rather than on the shipping front. Who can say the War Cabinet was wrong? It was influenced also by Haig's partiality for the offensive which had shattered our man-power in the Flanders battles. In my diary for December 6, 1917, I find a note that Haig

... only a week or two ago was seriously urging a recommencement of the Flanders offensive in February or March even on the assumption that thirty enemy divisions can be brought from Russia.

He was also sending 'continual reports of bad German morale' and that the German divisions 'have been put through the mill and knocked out one by one'. In these circumstances there was a natural disinclination to take risks elsewhere by giving the War Office all that it asked.

The War Cabinet believed that the War Office estimate of wastage which was nearly double that of the French military authorities, was

quotes without refutation the 'legend' attributed to Hunter Liggett, the distinguished u.s. general, that an army was 'kept in England to repel a mythical invasion'. That is not so.

excessive, particularly for the defensive warfare favoured pending the American concentration, and that a larger proportion of the Army could be made available for front-line service—an old controversy. The main recommendations of the Man-Power Committee, a reduction in the cavalry and of the number of infantry battalions in the division from twelve to nine, were unwelcome to the War Office. The former was ignored and the latter adopted under protest. The criticism of the reduction of battalions in the division was not directed against the principle which was admitted to be sound, but against its inopportuneness since it had to be carried out before the German attack which is stated to have interrupted training and completion of the defences. Actually the reduction process was completed for the whole Army between February 19th (First Army) and March 4th (Fifth Army). Altogether 115 battalions were disbanded which at full establishment would provide about 115,000 men, but thirty-eight were amalgamated to form nineteen units and seven were converted into pioneers instead of being used as drafts. If the military authorities who knew the difficulties of the man-power situation had shown a little more initiative they might have started this obvious reform in November 1917 immediately after the close of the Flanders offensive.[1]

In the event 174,379 men (including 32,384 for Dominions forces and 7,359 labour and non-fighting troops) were sent to France before March 21st in addition to one division from Italy—190,000 men in all compared with the original demand for that period of 350,000 men. Whether the balance of 160,000 men asked for by March 21st would have altered the course of events in the battle is dubious. Their conveyance and absorption would have taken some time. On arrival they would probably have been sent first for training and they would, therefore, have made no very great difference in completing field fortifications; they were, in fact, a reserve in Britain instead of in France. When the events of the battle itself are taken into account, it seems possible that the main result of throwing in these reserves earlier would have been to increase the casualties. As it was, they remained to form part of the big reserve of 544,005 men who were sent to France between March 21st and August 31st making 718,384 in all compared with the original demand of the War Office for 615,000. The whole of these 544,005 men must be considered as an emergency reserve held in this

[1] It should be remembered that at this time the War Cabinet had considerable hope that the Americans might be willing to attach battalions temporarily to British brigades. The reduction from twelve to nine battalions did not increase the numbers of Haig's army; it did make over 100,000 men available for reserves.

country, where many of them were able to continue important war work of various kinds before they were called up. The War Cabinet may have made some miscalculations, e.g. in assuming casualties would be less in defensive than in offensive warfare, but, given Haig's constant depreciation of the Germans when he wanted to attack, this was not unnatural. Criticisms of its action under this head appear exaggerated and in the long run its policy was justified by events.

3. On the alleged failure to bring in reinforcements from the 'side-show' theatres, the total forces eventually brought in from these amounted to the equivalent of five divisions of which one—the 41st from Italy—arrived on March 13th before the battle. The 5th Division also from Italy arrived on April 7th. The 52nd from Egypt arrived at Marseilles on April 19th and the 74th (Yeomanry) in May, as well as forty-four battalions from Egypt and Palestine the whole (omitting the 41st) making a total reinforcement of 100,000 men as well as a little artillery. The only question is whether three divisions, two of which arrived within a month of the opening of the battle, and the additional battalions which would have increased Haig's army by some 6 to 7 per cent, ought to have been sent to France at the beginning of the year. It would have been difficult to send the divisions from Italy any earlier as the Italians were themselves apprehensive of attack. Only a fortnight was required to bring a division from the Italian to the Western Front and the British troops there had already come to be talked of as a conveniently situated reserve for any of the fronts. As one division did arrive a week before the battle began, the other two divisions from Egypt and Palestine and the forty-four battalions would have increased Haig's forces only by a very small percentage.

At the beginning of the year the plans for 1918 were not yet finally decided; Smuts had not yet paid his visit to the Palestine Front and the War Cabinet were not as yet prepared to abandon the projected exploitation of the favourable situation in that theatre which alone presented prospects of some success. Had it been willing to do so, and had Allenby been willing to send the 74th Division without waiting for its relief by an Indian division, two divisions might have been spared for the Western Front, but it is doubtful, for shipping reasons, whether the 74th could have arrived there much before the battle; they both did arrive in time to be useful. The forty-four battalions from the Balkans and Egypt also could not have been sent very promptly as their release was obtained mainly by the reduction of the divisions abroad from a twelve to a three battalion basis which would have taken some time.

4. The decision to take over more of the French front has already been fully dealt with[1] and its necessity demonstrated; it is unreasonable to blame the Supreme Command for the delays when it left all details to the Commanders-in-Chief.

5. The Supreme War Council did decide, on February 2nd, on the creation of a General Reserve for the whole of the armies on the Western, Italian and Balkan Fronts[2] and set up a powerful Executive Board to provide it. The Board drew up a scheme for a reserve of thirty divisions, seven from the British and nine from the French front, and the balance from the Italian front where most of them were to stay until required. The scheme broke down because neither Pétain nor Haig would admit that he had any divisions to spare, and the plan for a General Reserve was superseded by arrangements between the two commanders for mutual support. The responsibility for these rested with them and not with the Supreme Command.

One weakness was the slow arrival of the French reinforcements on the right of the Fifth Army.[3] It seems that Pétain's main apprehensions before the battle were of a German offensive in Champagne—which came later—with perhaps an advance through Switzerland; British GHQ considered this to be 'inherently improbable'. Consequently most of the French reserves were disposed to meet those two eventualities, seventeen divisions for the first and fifteen farther south for the second. The arrangements between Haig and Pétain for mutual support did not provide any undertaking that the French should move up rapidly to support the British in the event of attack and do not appear to have been worked out in detail on the French side. On Fifth Army front all the French divisions except one (the 125th) came up piecemeal, without artillery, ammunition supply or field-kitchens and other transport. Instead of the French forces being placed on arrival under British command where the local situation was known,

... the French generals invariably took charge as they arrived not knowing the ground and—as may be seen from the orders they issued—not having grasped the situation. They did very little to reinforce Fifth Army or stem the German advance westward.[4]

The Official History does not convey the impression that the Haig–Pétain plan of mutual reinforcement was properly co-ordinated in advance or worked satisfactorily, and it is at least possible that the

[1] *vide supra*, c. 73 *passim*   [2] *France and Belgium 1918*, I, p. 77.
[3] *Ibid.*, II, p. 485.   [4] *Ibid.*, p. 486.

Executive War Board, if accepted willingly by the two Commanders-in-Chief, and devoting all its energies to working out the detailed organization for the operation of its reserves, might have produced better results.

Attention, too, is drawn to weaknesses in the British military machine due fundamentally to the fact that it was a gigantic improvisation, e.g. the staff and especially its junior members lacked experience of mobile warfare in any form and particularly of a forced retirement for which the troops also were untrained. Consequently, and inevitably, there were instances of bad staff work and control in the difficult circumstances of this battle was often lost for a time. In the April battles, however, the staff had learned the game and mistakes were fewer.

Another weakness was the system on which Fifth Army fortifications were constructed. These consisted in the main of a series of strongly held posts, supporting one another with flanking fire; they were the best that could be prepared in the time and with the labour available, but it is clear[1] that these 'bird cages' were unpopular with the troops who considered them 'death traps to draw the concentrated fire of the enemy' and would have preferred to fight in continuous trenches. In the heavy fog that prevailed on March 21st and the following days the system broke down badly. How far reinforcements from home and from overseas theatres would have arrived in time to enable these defects to be removed, and the extent to which a continuous line could or would have been constructed in Fifth Army area, are doubtful points. No doubt, however, some improvement would have been made and possibly some of the reserve lines might have been manned.

There were also a number of tactical mistakes such as were bound to occur in a battle of this nature. They include the holding too long of the Flesquières salient in Fifth Army area contrary to the general instructions of the Commander-in-Chief which lost us the equivalent of a division; the 'over-hasty movement' on March 22nd/23rd back to the line of the Crozat Canal and the Somme by one corps and part of another and several failures of French reinforcements to make the most of the situation.

But to the military student it is clear that one of the most adverse influences on the earlier and more disastrous stages of the battle was the dense fog that prevailed on March 21st and the following days, some-

---

[1] *France and Belgium 1918*, II, p. 478.

times lasting until the afternoon, especially on Fifth Army front where the worst break occurred.[1] Here the effects of it were especially severe, partly because the fog persisted until so late in the day and partly owing to the system on which the defences had been devised. As vision was often limited to a few yards the system of flank defence and cross-fire could not operate. The German infantry infiltrated through the gaps unseen and sometimes unheard, so that their presence was not always known to the defenders until they found themselves surrounded. In such conditions machine-guns were of little value. Although in most cases these posts held out gallantly to the last their reduction was only a matter of time. Added to this, heavy and even field artillery lost most of their value as long as fog prevailed, as observation whether from posts in the front line or from the air could not be carried out. Communications by line were cut and even pigeons could not find their way while despatch-riders and runners only too often were killed, wounded, captured or lost their way. The various headquarters experienced the utmost difficulty in keeping abreast of the true state of affairs and effective control of the battle was very difficult. Even aeroplanes were of little value either for reconnaissance or observation of fire so long as the fog lasted; the German advance across the shell-pitted Somme battlefield would have been particularly difficult in weather permitting observation. These were the circumstances in which the worst losses and misfortunes occurred and they must be given a very high place in weighing the true causes of events.

In the battles of March–May 1918 the Supreme Command which had continually to bear in mind the major factors in eventual victory such as American reinforcements, the shipping situation and maintenance of supplies to the armies and to the nations as well as the local factors, took its decisions from a point of view differing from that of the man on the spot; it had good reasons for them. If the number of events that swayed the battle are taken into account, it would be grossly unfair to attribute the misfortunes we suffered to the earlier decisions of the Supreme Command any more than to the mistakes of the local High Command or of our Allies. Indeed the fortune of war and the skill of the enemy were probably more important factors than any of them.

One solid fact stands out prominently: that we did succeed in bringing the German advance to a standstill and in defeating Ludendorff's whole plan.

---

[1] There are no fewer than thirty-four references in the Official History to the effects on the operations of fog and mist.

The real reason for the German failure was the impossible task set to the German troops by Ludendorff misled by his easy successes against Russians ... and under-estimating the fighting qualities of British, French and Belgians.[1]

If this be true, and it undoubtedly is, the case against the Supreme Command falls to the ground. The strength of the forces and the dispositions made by the Supreme War Council and the War Cabinet did in the end prove too much for the German Army and therefore accomplished their purpose. And in war it is success that counts.

[1] *France and Belgium 1918*, II, p. 463.

CHAPTER LXXVIII

THE THREAT TO PARIS

'The cannons have their bowels full of wrath,
And ready mounted are they, to spit forth
Their iron indignation 'gainst your walls.
All preparation for a bloody siege . . .'

(SHAKESPEARE, *King John*, Act ii, sc. i.)

IN the last year of the Great War Providence ordained that each of the Great Powers in turn, as a corrective to their pride, as a warning and as a deterrent to future wars, should sustain disaster. The Russian Empire succumbed to internal strife. Italy incurred a crushing defeat in October–November 1917. We sustained grave set-backs in March–April 1918. And now in May–June 1918 France was smitten by a stroke at the Chemin-des-Dames, threatening Paris itself, which was not relieved until the successes in Champagne and the battles of the Marne in July. Germany's turn was reserved until a few months later.

May 27th. . . . Soon after 11 a.m. the C.I.G.S. came in.[1] He had bad news about the German attack on the Chemin-des-Dames. As usual they seem to have gone through our strong positions like paper. Afterwards we discussed plans for 1919. Wilson thinks we are in for two months of great anxiety; these will be followed by two months of diminishing anxiety; after this, if we survive, we shall have a long interval before we are in a position to strike the tremendous blow which alone can overcome the enemy (no more Passchendaeles!). That interval should be used for striking some blows in the outlying theatres.

May 29th. . . . In the evening Adeline and I drove up with the Prime Minister and Mrs Lloyd George to Arthur Crosfield's house at Highgate for dinner and chamber music by some professionals. Lady Crosfield and her charming sister are two very musical Greek ladies and I talked Greek to them. During the evening we heard that the French had lost Soissons and the Prime Minister was very upset.

May 30th. Very bad news this evening, the Germans having entered Château Thierry. . . .

The bad news from France brought up once again the question of the possible evacuation of the Channel ports. Next day we set forth to Versailles for a meeting of the Supreme War Council.

[1] I was at the time closeted with Lloyd George.

May 31st. Left home at 7.30 a.m. for Versailles. The Prime Minister motored to Folkestone, but the rest of us went by special train. I breakfasted in the train with Balfour, Milner and Henry Wilson. We crossed in a comfortable cross-Channel steamer to Dieppe. It was a five-hour crossing, but luckily very calm, and we had a very pleasant journey. After lunch we had a sort of informal conference on the subject of the proposed evacuation of Dunkirk, the Prime Minister, Eric Geddes, Wemyss, Wilson and myself, but not Balfour. Wilson wants to pull back behind the floods at St. Omer, thereby shortening the line and releasing ten divisions. The Admiralty are strongly opposed, as this would compromise their barrage, give the Germans a new submarine base, and increase their own submarine difficulties. My only contribution to the discussion was that, to give the Germans a new pawn on the vital Channel coast was most undesirable. I would sooner see a readjustment of the line in some other quarter to release the reserves necessary to sustain the battle. . . . Arrived at the Villa Romaine, Versailles, about 7 p.m. After dinner I had a very important conversation with du Cane, head of the British Mission at French headquarters. He expressed considerable misgivings about the future and was particularly anxious at the idea of our having two and a half million hostages on the Continent in the event of a French defeat. He envisages the possibility of the French Army being smashed and cut off from us, the enemy demanding as a condition of peace the handing over of all the ports from Rouen and Havre to Dunkirk, and, in the event of a refusal, the remorseless hammering of our Army by the whole German Army. He does not think we could get our Army away and considers that, if we wanted to go on with the war, we should have to face the prospect of over a million prisoners in France. He evidently thinks that a situation of this kind might develop quite soon. Then we went on to talk about the Americans and he unburdened his mind to me at some length. It appears that Foch has from the first insisted on the importance of maintaining divisions intact, even if our man-power position compels us to reduce their establishment. He points out that the Allies have as many infantry as the Germans, but the latter, having far more divisions, have a more flexible organization. Haig and his advisers, however, have adopted the view that it is better to maintain the larger divisions, and to enable this to be done have been rolling up ten divisions. They insist that in fact the larger division holds more line, so that there is nothing in it. Du Cane says this is untrue and that the German 'makes the boy [i.e. the small division] do the man's work'. The latest development of this controversy, which has continued ever since du Cane joined Foch, relates to the Americans. Foch wants the Americans put in to recreate the ten cadre divisions. Haig wants them to bring the other divisions up to a strength of twelve battalions. According to du Cane, Foch saw Haig a week or two ago and at last persuaded him to take his view and Haig gave the necessary orders. General X, who looks after these matters for Haig, was then in England.

When he returned, according to du Cane, he told Haig 'you really must not decide these matters in my absence', and tore up the whole scheme, though whether with or without Haig's knowledge is not clear. Du Cane said he was in a very difficult position himself, as he was supposed to be loyal both to Haig and Foch, but he made it clear that in his view, as we had made Foch General-in-Chief, we ought to do what he wants. There also seems to be a serious difference of opinion on strategy. Lawrence wants to abandon the Channel ports, and shorten our line by falling back behind the Somme, while it is still possible, shortening the line and creating a big reserve. Foch refuses to give up anything and argues that the enemy would gain more than we should by the shortening of the line, while he would also get the Channel ports without having to fight for them. Foch is probably influenced by the psychology of the French character, which does not like retreats. He also regards the Channel ports as more important than Paris. Finally, says du Cane, Foch wanted to prepare a counter-offensive—by the French in the region of Montdidier, and by the British north of the Somme. When du Cane took it to Lawrence, the latter said it was ridiculous, and, though promising to '*étudier la question*', made it clear that he would do nothing, though the French carried their preparations forward. Lawrence thinks that, if the Germans do not attack, they will have ample reserves to defeat an offensive. If they do attack, they will draw in all our reserves (as is happening at this moment). I did not like to have all this information to myself, so, after imploring du Cane to tell the c.i.g.s., I told the Prime Minister and Milner who were on the balcony. The Prime Minister was very indignant. Du Cane also said that our people are underrating the possible use of the Americans, and that in Foch's opinion (and evidently in his own) the danger was so critical that we ought not to insist on so long a period of training.

I ought perhaps to mention that we were thirteen at dinner (which few observed) and that the Prime Minister got up first. There were two air raids in the night, but I went quietly to sleep nevertheless.

June 1st. A really glorious day. After breakfast I first wrote up this diary and then the Prime Minister, Milner, c.i.g.s., du Cane, Kerr, Bols[1] and I went for a walk in the park. The Prime Minister arranged about the line he was to take at a conference he was to have later this morning with Haig (whom we found at the Villa Romaine on our return at 11 a.m.), namely, that if Haig would not use the Americans, the French should have them. The Prime Minister, Haig, c.i.g.s., Milner and du Cane had a talk on the balcony, but I did not join them as I thought perhaps it might be wiser to leave them to talk quite freely and informally without any notes being taken of their conversations; so I had a quiet morning writing up this diary.

The afternoon was a particularly busy one. I had first to act as sole secretary of a conversation in Clemenceau's room at the Hôtel Trianon on the

---

[1] Chief of Staff to Allenby since September 1917.

subject of American troops and later on the Supreme Council turned out all their experts and secretaries except me in order to discuss the question of the Allied Naval Commander-in-Chief in the Mediterranean.

The origin of this contentious question was the imminent—as we now know, the actual—capture by the German Army of Russian naval bases on the Black Sea opening the possibility that the Russian Fleet, which included two super-dreadnoughts, might be put in commission to reinforce the *Goeben*. With this addition the German Fleet would be far too strong for the small Allied Fleet watching the Dardanelles. The Allied naval authorities, therefore, had decided to reinforce that fleet and three French battleships had been despatched as their share. As this detachment had gravely weakened the French Fleet at the improvised base at Corfu, the French naval authorities had asked the Italians to reinforce them by three battleships from their main fleet at Taranto. The Italians had refused. Neither the efforts of the two Governments nor of the Allied Naval Council had succeeded in finding a solution, so the issue had been brought to the Supreme War Council.

It was too late to reach a decision on Saturday (June 1st). Both sides of the question were heard, and at the very end a suggestion by Eric Geddes for a solution on the lines of the Foch precedent, with Jellicoe as 'admiralissimo', seemed acceptable.

Next day (Sunday) there was no meeting of the Supreme War Council in the morning and after our usual breakfast together Lloyd George spent the morning with Milner, Henry Wilson and Lawrence discussing the line to be taken later in the day with Pershing.

June 2nd (Sunday). At 2 p.m. we met in Clemenceau's room at the Trianon. Gradually about eighteen people assembled in a tiny room with no window open. Pershing was obstinate and would not look at our proposal to make Haig the authority for deciding when American troops were to go into the line, and eventually the question was left to Foch and Pershing. Foch was very rude about our breaking up divisions and kept reiterating that he could not conduct the war unless we maintained our divisions, and Lloyd George repeated the offer accepted by Clemenceau on the previous day to allow a French expert access to all our man-power figures. Eventually they agreed to a declaration to President Wilson by the three Prime Ministers to be accompanied by a technical agreement signed by Milner, Foch and Pershing, who were left to arrange it.

Then we adjourned for tea, and afterwards to the big Conference Chamber to discuss again the question of the Admiralissimo in the Mediterranean. We had thought this to be settled on the previous day, but Sonnino was

DD

extraordinarily obstinate and insisted that the Italians must retain command of the Adriatic. Consequently the Italians brought up a new draft conclusion, which our people would not accept. The discussion went on hour after hour and we tried every sort and kind of draft. I am bound to say that Geddes was just as difficult and uncompromising as the Italians. On the one hand he would concede nothing to Italian *amour propre*, and on the other he would insist on Jellicoe's dispositions being subject to the Allied Naval Council which the Italians would not accept.

Towards the end the meeting fell into disorder, everyone talking at once, at the end of which Lloyd George announced that he was being asked to accept conditions for an 'admiralissimo' which would make the post a sham and that he could not possibly ask a man of Jellicoe's eminence to accept it. He therefore withdrew the original suggestion, and the meeting ended soon afterwards.

It must be admitted that, so far as the naval question was concerned, the meeting was rather a dogfight and at one point it deserved the *bon mot* of a witty American general who, on being asked: 'What is going on in there?' replied: 'I guess they are all at sea except the Italian admiral who won't go there!' Nevertheless soon after the conference the laugh was with the Italians. Throughout the controversy they had claimed stubbornly that their Allies were exaggerating the dangers of the naval situation both at the Dardanelles and in the Adriatic. Actually one of the Russian dreadnoughts was destroyed by its own crew to prevent it falling into the enemy's hands and in the Adriatic an Austrian battle-ship was sunk by a small Italian motor-launch, an act of almost unbelievable gallantry.

That evening we dined at a garden restaurant where we could hear the German guns. Although we were again thirteen at table—for the third night running—I never heard of any evil consequences.

June 3rd. At 7.45 I dictated *procès-verbaux* for a full hour. Breakfast alone with Lloyd George. Afterwards we drove to St. Cloud. Albert Thomas lunched with us at the Villa Romaine and gave a depressing account of the fighting. The French were run over at the start, after a very short bombardment, and by the infiltration of machine-guns through and behind their lines were forced to retreat. They lost heavily, without themselves inflicting heavy casualties. During lunch Henry Wilson took me outside on to the balcony, to tell me that, as he is off to a conference at Pétain's GHQ, I must get the Prime Minister to speak to Clemenceau and insist on Foch shortening his lines in the north, and obtaining his reserves by uncovering Dunkirk and retiring behind the floods. He evidently anticipates a disaster to the French.

The Supreme War Council met again at 3 p.m. and had a comparatively amicable meeting, which calls for no comment.

June 4th. At 8 a.m. we left in motors for Dieppe and I write this on board a cross-Channel packet *en route* to Folkestone. As regards the battle, I return with *une impression peu satisfaisante.* I do not like the outlook. The Germans are fighting better than the Allies and I cannot exclude the possibility of a disaster. I see difficult times ahead.

The question of the evacuation of Dunkirk and a general withdrawal of the Allied line behind the floods had not been settled at the Versailles meeting:

June 5th. . . . After lunch Milner and Wilson came to 10 Downing Street and we discussed the question of the reserves and the proposed evacuation of Ypres and Dunkirk. Decided that Milner and C.I.G.S. should discuss the question with Foch. The latter refuses to budge an inch; Wilson says that, if he does not, there will be a disaster. We also discussed the possibility of withdrawing the whole Army from France if the French crack. It was a very gloomy meeting.

June 6th. . . . Milner and C.I.G.S. are off to France to try and arrange that Haig's reserves shall not be withdrawn. The proposal is that the French troops shall be withdrawn from Flanders to reinforce Foch and that we shall keep the new divisions[1] (which have been filled up with American infantry), to replace them instead of carrying out Foch's proposal to send them to Alsace which involves a very long journey and weeks of delay before the French divisions they are to replace become available for the battle. . . . Milner and C.I.G.S. are also to press for a retirement in the north from Ypres to the St. Omer–Dunkirk line.

The visit of Milner and Henry Wilson to Foch does not seem to have produced any very noteworthy result, for I find no mention of it in my diary. In the end, Pershing succeeded in concentrating his forces in an American Army as he had always desired; Foch stuck firmly to his decision not to retire behind the floods in the northern part of the line, and the success of his operations near Rheims and on the Marne in freeing Paris brought that particular issue to an end.

[1] Actually the divisions which had been reduced to cadres.

CHAPTER LXXIX

HIGH TIDE

'The Tide Rises. The Tide Falls.' (*Sea Music.*)

IN June the Germans had about reached the high tide of their military successes. On the Western Front they still held the initiative, but their attacks were beginning to flag. On June 9th they attacked between Montdidier and Noyon on a front of about twenty miles and penetrated the French lines to a depth of about 6,000 yards, but they were counter-attacked and the situation was still in hand. This was the last big success they were destined to achieve in that region, but we knew it not. All we did know was that they were intending a further onslaught, though when and where no one could foretell. Actually it took place on July 15th in the Champagne from Château Thierry to the Argonne.[1] At sea the British losses from enemy action fell in June to 162,990 gross tons and the world total to 255,587 tons, as compared with 417,925 tons and 687,000 tons for the corresponding month in the year 1917. For the second quarter of 1918 the world output of new shipping (excluding enemy shipping) exceeded world losses, war and marine, by 281,000 tons. Ever-increasing claims were being made for the sinking of enemy submarines. The convoy system was proving a triumphant success. The American troops were pouring into France without loss of a single transport. It was becoming daily clearer that the policy concerted a year before by the War Cabinet under Lloyd George's personal inspiration, and carried out so ably by the Admiralty, Ministry of Shipping, Board of Trade, Ministry of Agriculture and Fisheries, Food Production Department and Ministry of Food, always under the watchful eye of the Prime Minister, was succeeding beyond expectation. Although constant vigilance was still necessary, the submarine peril had ceased to be a main preoccupation.

From June onwards all branches of the Supreme Command were engaged in taking stock of the situation with a view to a decision when and how the hideous business was to be brought to an end. On one point everyone seemed to be agreed—that victory could not be encompassed in 1918. Foch had told the Supreme War Council that 100 American divisions were required in order to defeat the Germans, and

<hr>

[1] *vide infra,* p. 827.

the Council had accepted his view and passed it on to President Wilson. The programme for tanks accepted by the Supreme War Council at the sixth session in early June 1918, envisaged an offensive in 1919. In a brilliant Memorandum on the Munitions Programme, 1919, dated March 5th, Churchill had dealt with 'the fundamental question "How are we going to win the war in 1919?" '[1] Where the forecast was wrong was in not taking into account the tremendous effect which blockade, combined with propaganda, was exercising on Germany, which, in the end, in combination with military successes, not only on the Western Front but also in the so-called 'side-shows', was to bring them to their knees.

Early in June 1918 the Imperial War Cabinet reassembled to co-ordinate the Empire's war effort. The first session in 1917 had been rather tentative in character, as it had taken the Prime Ministers and other representatives all their time to get in touch with the complexities of the war situation. In 1918, however, they were all better informed and did not lose much time in picking up the threads and making themselves felt as a factor in the Supreme Command. Those present included —for Canada, Borden, Meighen, Calder, and Rowell; for Australia, Hughes and Joseph Cook, who did not arrive until June 19th, a week after the opening meeting; for New Zealand, Massey and Joseph Ward; for South Africa, Smuts, who had been regularly attending the War Cabinet since the last session of the Imperial War Cabinet, and Burton; for Newfoundland, Lloyd; for India, Sinha and the Maharaja of Patiala.

Lloyd George in his opening statement on June 11th attributed the situation on the Western Front to the collapse of Russia, delays in the development of America's resources, the exhaustion of our own Army by the events of 1917, and to the advantages derived by the enemy from a single command. He ventured a forecast, which proved right almost to a day, that the situation on the Western Front would continue critical for another two months. He emphasized the importance of the comparative failure of the German submarine campaign, of the British successes in the Turkish theatres, and the accumulating evidence of internal collapse in the enemy countries—all of which would tell increasingly in our favour after the immediate crisis had passed. Short of predicting victory in 1918, this was a prescient forecast.

June 13th. Borden came out with some very plain speaking about the High Command in France. . . . In the afternoon the Prime Minister sent for

---

[1] *World Crisis 1916–1918,* II, p. 394 *sq.*—for discussion of plans for 1919, *vide supra,* pp. 703 *sq.*

me. He is sending the 1917 Report of the Cabinet Committee on War Policy to the Prime Ministers of the Dominions and had that afternoon seen Borden and Currie about the former's indictment of our military methods in France. He asked my advice how he should handle the question tomorrow. I replied that I should, in his place, merely thank Borden for his frankness and say that the question could not be settled until the arrival of Hughes from Australia, but that vital issues were raised, which must be probed *au fond*; that the question could not conveniently be discussed in a 'Duma'; and that the best method would be to deal with it in a Committee of Prime Ministers only. He agreed. He told me that he had ascertained that Smuts had prompted Borden.

Lloyd George followed my advice, and after all the Prime Ministers in turn had taken a line rather similar to Borden, he proposed on June 20th that the whole issue of the Flanders offensive and cognate matters should be referred to a Committee of Prime Ministers, Botha being represented by Smuts, and Milner being added to the Committee as Secretary of State for War, with Henry Wilson in attendance when required.

These meetings of Prime Ministers rather tended to overshadow the Imperial War Cabinet, although both bodies were meeting regularly. Nominally and constitutionally the Prime Ministers were merely a sub-committee of the Imperial War Cabinet appointed to consider and report upon recent failures on the Western Front and the conduct of the war by the High Command. In fact, however, force of circumstances compelled them, every time they met, to take decisions on current matters that would brook no delay, and the specific investigations for which they were appointed proceeded somewhat slowly. The Supreme Command at this period was, to outward appearance at any rate, in rather a jumble and as secretary of all these bodies I had a hard job to keep their business from getting in a tangle. We arranged that the British War Cabinet should meet on the mornings of Monday, Wednesday and Friday; the Imperial War Cabinet on Tuesday and Thursday mornings; and the Prime Ministers when they could manage, which was usually at 6 p.m. In addition the Prime Minister himself was still holding meetings every morning before the official meetings began with Milner and Henry Wilson mainly in order to clear his mind on the subjects likely to be raised. The Imperial War Cabinet was supposed to deal with the wider conduct of the war; the British War Cabinet with the British war effort; and the Prime Ministers with the reference already described. Inevitably, however, with events moving fast there was a good deal of overlap, but the threatened confusion was mitigated

by the fact that Lloyd George presided at all the meetings, that the Empire Prime Ministers were members of the Imperial War Cabinet as well as of the Committee of Prime Ministers; and that the secretary was the same for all these meetings.

The position can best be judged from one or two examples. Towards the end of June the War Office desired as a matter of urgency to withdraw the 54th British Division and Australian troops equivalent to a mounted division from Palestine to France. The man-power situation in France was parlous; the great need was for organized reserves; it was touch-and-go whether we should not lose Amiens, Paris and the Channel ports; Foch was continually calling on us for more divisions; heavy casualties must be expected. Troops had already been drawn from Home Defence, Italy and the Balkans as well as from Palestine itself. Even after the withdrawal of these troops we should possess a numerical superiority over the Turks; if later on the Western Front again became stabilized Palestine could be reinforced. Consequently, unless it could be shown that the position in the Near East would be endangered by the withdrawal, the case was a very strong one. On the other hand there were considerable objections. Most of the Indian battalions sent to Palestine to replace the white battalions already withdrawn had never seen active service and required a good deal of training. Allenby considered that a serious risk would be run, although, if the proposal were sanctioned, he was prepared to do his best to hold his ground. The Suez Canal was such a vital artery of our Imperial communications that no risks ought to be taken. The loss of Jerusalem, so soon after its spectacular capture, would resound throughout the East and damage our prestige, the more so because it was only there that we had achieved any successes at all. Once the troops had been withdrawn it would be doubtful if they would ever be allowed to return, especially when it was remembered that the High Command of the Allies in France was French.

The Prime Minister asked me to advise which of the three bodies was the right one to consider the question. Clearly it was not the War Cabinet, because Australian and Indian as well as British forces were involved. Constitutionally the Imperial War Cabinet appeared to be the proper body, but was rather a large one for discussion of so secret a question, involving the transport of a large number of troops across the submarine-infested waters of the Mediterranean. In those circumstances I had no hesitation in advising that the Committee of Prime Ministers was the proper body and Lloyd George accepted this view.

On June 21st the Prime Ministers agreed, rather reluctantly, that the 54th Division should be brought to France, but that the Australian mounted troops, who were supplied mainly from Australia, should remain in Palestine. On June 26th, however, they reversed this decision. New factors had arisen. The Italians had repulsed an Austrian attack on the Piave, and their morale was reported to have been considerably strengthened. In these circumstances the Prime Ministers felt that one of the three British divisions still remaining in Italy under Cavan's command might safely be earmarked as a reserve for the Western Front. A division could be moved much more safely and rapidly from Italy to France than from Palestine. Unfortunately Henry Wilson had left on the previous day for Italy to discuss with Diaz the possibilities of an offensive on the Italian Front. Although the Deputy Chief of the Imperial General Staff shared the view of the Prime Ministers that the previous decision to withdraw the 54th Division should be reversed, Lloyd George decided that the reversal must remain provisional pending Wilson's return—which shows how careful he was not to flout military opinion if he could avoid it. In fact, however, the new decision stood and the 54th Division took part in the final defeat of the Turks.

The Committee thus took an important decision on its own authority. Sometimes, however, a matter would first come up at the Committee of Prime Ministers and then be passed on to some other authority such as the Supreme War Council. This occurred in the question of Japanese intervention in Siberia, which cropped up out of the general examination of the causes of our recent failures in France and Flanders. The Germans by the end of April had penetrated into Russia as far as Sebastopol and were collecting food, horses, etc., from the Ukraine and elsewhere. Divisions were being employed for this purpose which would otherwise have been available to support Ludendorff's attack in the West. It had long been considered desirable to provide a barrier to further advance and an Allied nucleus round which loyal Russians could gather to form a new front against Germany. At the Supreme War Council on June 1st to 3rd it had been agreed that, if the Japanese were willing to respect the territorial integrity of Russia, to abstain from taking sides in her internal politics, and to advance as far west as possible for the purpose of encountering the Germans, we should make an effort to secure President Wilson's approval for Japanese intervention.

At the end of June the moment was considered by the Imperial War

Cabinet to be particularly favourable to the formation of a barrier against Germany. Allied intelligence reports indicated that the Russians were themselves restive, and that the effects of the Treaty of Brest-Litovsk were now generally realized. On June 24th Lloyd George had seen Kerenski.

June 24th. After lunch the Prime Minister had an interview of one and three-quarter hours with Kerenski. At first he thought of bringing me in but on second thoughts came to the conclusion that the uniform might put him off and took Philip Kerr instead. I caught a glimpse of Kerenski as I was going out.

Lloyd George was more favourably impressed than he had expected by Kerenski who strongly favoured Allied intervention in Siberia and, after at first opposing it, eventually agreed that, provided the Western Allies took some part, a large Japanese expedition might be effective.[1] The Japanese reply to the Allied approaches after the Supreme War Council meeting had been received and were not unfavourable. They were prepared to go as far as Irkutsk, but not to the Urals, and were willing to give the undertakings asked for by the Council. They could, however, do nothing without American assent. We were back, therefore, at the old question how to approach President Wilson.

In spite of previous failures the Prime Minister urged and the Imperial War Cabinet agreed that the Supreme War Council ought to make another effort. A series of resolutions was drawn up for Lloyd George to submit on their behalf to the Supreme War Council in favour of another appeal to the American President; it was pointed out that, without a reconstitution of the Russian Front, there was no reasonable probability of sufficient superiority being concentrated by the Allies on the Western Front to assure victory in 1919. From this it is clear that the Imperial War Cabinet had come round to the view that the climax must be in that year.

The next meeting of the Supreme War Council was arranged for July 2nd. Lloyd George had a happy inspiration and arranged that the Prime Ministers should first visit their respective forces in France and then come on to Versailles in order to meet Clemenceau and Foch and to attend a meeting of the Council.

July 1st. . . . This time we went by Newhaven and Dieppe and had a very smooth crossing in a most disgusting ship. We motored to Versailles from Dieppe. I started with Macdonogh and his staff officer Kisch, but, after 10–20

---

[1] *War Memoirs*, VI, p. 2186.

miles we found the Prime Minister's car broken down. The Prime Minister, Albert Thomas, and Mantoux came in our car, Macdonogh and his staff officer taking the 'lame duck'. We stopped at Forges-les-Eaux for dinner. The idea was to have a 'snack' and a bottle of wine, but, when they discovered who we were, of course they insisted in putting up a great spread. The result was that we were much delayed and did not reach Versailles until after 1 a.m. I had a very hard, uncomfortable seat and was very cramped and enjoyed the trip but little. Thomas, Mantoux and I sang 'Frère Jacques' as a round, and they sang a lot of French songs, including (save the mark!) the 'Internationale', the 'Red Flag' and other ditties of the same order. At Forges Lloyd George had, as usual, an extraordinary welcome, all the officers recognizing him and rising as he entered the hotel. I was dead tired when we arrived in an air raid warning. I was horrified on awakening to find that my boxes of secret papers had not yet arrived. It appeared that Hughes had 'bagged' no less than three cars, with the result that the boxes of papers had gone in a baggage car, which had broken down. The result was that Sylvester had been unable to accompany them, and all the most secret papers of the British Empire, which I would never allow to travel except with a King's Messenger or other responsible person, had been cruising about France in a lost motor car in charge of a French private soldier. I kicked up a fearful hullaballoo with Davies and Sylvester, but after breakfast the car arrived. Still, I must see that this does not happen again. We had no meeting this morning. . . . As a matter of fact the statement went through at the Supreme War Council quite easily, and before the meeting rose I had telegraphed it to President Wilson.[1] The Supreme War Council was comparatively uneventful. There were two Conferences of Prime Ministers, but I did not intrude, thinking it would be better to leave them to discuss without record. It is as important in my job to know when *not* to intrude as when to do so. . . . I had a long talk this evening with Abraham,[2] who tells me that Versailles does not work smoothly. There is much handshaking and outward civility, but they do not really coalesce. The French are too *bourgeois* and the British '*trop gentleman*'. The most distinctive feature of the conference today was a violent outburst by the Prime Minister against Tardieu for interference in the shipment of American troops.[3]

July 3rd. No meeting in the morning. After a talk with Milner and c.i.g.s. we had a conference with the Prime Minister about the future of Versailles. Milner is very keen to avoid continuing the discussion as he thinks it will give rise to all sorts of difficult controversies, and we arranged that at

---

[1] i.e. the appeal to President Wilson on Japanese intervention. *vide War Memoirs*, VI, p. 3192.

[2] One of my staff at Versailles.

[3] Tardieu, head of the French Mission in Washington, had tried to speed up the shipment of American troops without consulting or notifying the British Government which had to find the shipping.

any rate the subject should be preceded by a discussion at the Supreme War Council on the Balkans, where Clemenceau, in defiance of the Council's decisions in favour of a defensive policy, has been ordering an offensive. We are really on the verge of a very serious conflict of British and French policy, which must come to a head by the autumn. Lloyd George and c.i.g.s. want to take the offensive in Palestine in the autumn, which will necessitate the withdrawal of divisions from France. Foch wants himself to undertake certain operations of a secondary character and will protest against any withdrawal of divisions from the Western Front, as he will want to keep them for an offensive next year. The question is whether to take your fight with Clemenceau and Foch now or later. Wilson thinks it is fairer to take it now. The Prime Minister and Milner are inclined to get everything ready in Palestine, and then in the autumn insist on withdrawing them. It is a matter of tactics.

I spent the morning working quietly at the Villa Romaine until about noon, when, just at the very moment I was off for a walk, Hughes turned up unexpectedly, and I had to look after him. He demanded tea (which could not be got) and declined coffee, wine or whisky and grumbled a good deal, but at last I got some tea and he was quite nice.

The Supreme War Council was distinguished only for a terrific, sudden, and extremely violent attack by Lloyd George on the French for appointing Franchet d'Esperey to command at Salonica, and for issuing orders for an offensive there without consulting the Supreme War Council. . . .[1] In regard to the offensive he was quite right, as it was outrageous of the French to order an offensive by the Allied Armies when, only at the previous meeting of the Supreme War Council, it had been decided that the policy in that theatre should be defensive. It is the more mysterious as Clemenceau, as he said at the Supreme War Council, has always been and still professes to be a violent opponent of the Salonica expedition. But there are and always have been subtle influences, possibly of a financial character, behind the French attitude towards the Salonica expedition. Old Clemenceau was put in a most uncomfortable position and Lloyd George handled him very roughly, but perhaps he deserved it, for during the preceding discussion Clemenceau had been very rude to a Belgian general, who had been sent by King Albert to decline a proposal that the Belgian Army should be under Foch, who wants to send three of the Belgian divisions to the Vosges.

July 4th. I accompanied the Prime Minister and Hughes to a review of American and French troops in the Place d'Jèna. Some of the Americans, who had been fighting at Château Thierry, looked tired and disillusioned and depressed, but the others marched well and were as fine a set of ruffians as you would wish to see fighting for you. There were a lot of speeches, that of Pichon, the French Foreign Minister, being by far the best. He has a wonder-

---

[1] *vide Macedonia,* II, p. 166.

ful voice. I have always wondered how so unimpressive a little man had got so far, but now I see. There is always some reason. The French soldiers looked very war-worn but determined. There were a large number of coloured men in their ranks. The contrast between them and the eager, fresh Americans struck a note of pathos. On the way back Lloyd George was much cheered by the crowd.

The final meeting of the session, held this afternoon, was only notable for the fact that the Prime Ministers of the Dominions were present. The proceedings were relatively tame.

Clemenceau, in welcoming the Prime Ministers of the Dominions, told rather a nice anecdote of how, centuries before, the Doge of Venice had come to visit Louis XIV at his new palace at Versailles. After the King had shown his visitor all the glories of the palace—the salons, the chapel, the gardens and so forth, he asked him what surprised him most. The Doge replied that what surprised him most was to be there at all. So, said Clemenceau, what probably most surprised his guests, who had travelled so many thousands of miles to reach Versailles, was to find themselves there at all, assembled together in league against a common foe.

July 4th (continued). So ended the 7th Session of the Supreme War Council. Hardly had I written the above words, in the confident belief that a pleasant and quiet evening was before me, when a telephone message came from Clemenceau to the effect that he was on his way to the Villa with Foch. When they arrived it transpired that Foch objected to a resolution that had been passed at the very end of the meeting in regard to the Versailles organization, defining its position *vis-à-vis* Foch and the other Commanders-in-Chief, and setting them the task of studying the war plans of the future. Foch, it appeared, had not understood the original text, which had been in English, and had been rather rushed through. He now made all sorts of objections, thinking that his own independence as General-in-Chief was compromised, and he had actually threatened to resign. There was a rare old wrangle for a long time between the Prime Minister, Clemenceau, Foch, Weygand, self, and later Henry Wilson. When Clemenceau told Lloyd George of Foch's threatened resignation, Lloyd George replied that generals and admirals were too fond of talking of resignation, and that, if a *'poilu'* talked of resigning, he would be stuck against a wall and shot. Clemenceau's only reply was 'But you know you do not want to shoot him!' I think Foch understood enough English to take in what was said, and he looked very black. Eventually, after much wrangling, it was decided we must have a French translation, and certain officers were turned on to prepare it. . . . During the subsequent discussion Clemenceau, who was taking our side in the matter, got very angry

with the obstinacy of Foch and Weygand and said: '*Ils me font fou*'—and, relapsing into English, 'when I am *fou* I usually try and kill someone—a general, if possible'. Whereat the old boy of 78 began to chase Wilson round the room like a schoolboy. Eventually we got a horrible hybrid draft that satisfied everyone. Before Foch and Weygand left I had to translate it into English; the French, written by Clemenceau, was almost illegible, so it was no joke. I only arrived at dinner at dessert, where Hughes, Lloyd George and Lloyd were wrangling about free trade after the war. At 10 p.m., almost before I had had dinner, I had to go off with Sackville West to see Orlando at the Villa of the Italian general to get his agreement to the new draft conclusion. He boggled a bit about the impropriety of altering a solemn conclusion of the Supreme War Council outside the meeting, but eventually I persuaded him to cede the point of form 'on condition that I, as secretary, took the responsibility', though he pointed out that there was 'no Allied tribunal before which I could be arraigned'. He insisted, however, in deleting words which indicated Foch as 'General-in-Chief of the Allied Armies in France *and Italy*', and, after much argument, agreed to the new draft on condition that 'General-in-Chief Foch' was substituted. This meant getting the consent of all the others. I tackled Lloyd George in bed and got his assent, but no more could be done tonight.

I omitted to mention that, at the moment when Clemenceau was expected at the Villa Romaine, Franklin Bouillon was expected. As he is in opposition Lloyd George is not supposed to see him, and Philip Kerr and Victor Cazalet were sent out to intercept him and keep him 'on ice' until dinner, after Clemenceau had gone. Lloyd George forgot this, and invited Clemenceau and Foch and Weygand to dinner, so I was on tenterhooks. Luckily, however, this French farce had a tame ending, as they declined the invitation and Franklin Bouillon never turned up.

July 5th. I was up at 7 a.m. to try and see Foch about the draft, but he had already left Versailles. So I motored up to Paris through the glorious shady woods, breakfasted with Capel, who is a friend of Clemenceau and our liaison officer, and went on with him to the War Office, where I saw Clemenceau. He was wearing a funny little octagonal smoking cap and was very pleasant, agreeing at once to Orlando's amendment. Then back to Versailles, where I got Foch's agreement by telephone.

We left later in the morning for London.

Other questions of importance were dealt with, e.g. that of Allied intervention in Russia. At the Abbeville meeting (May) it had been decided that Serbian and Czech forces still west of Omsk should be directed to Archangel and Murmansk instead of to Vladivostok. At the sixth session (June) the subject had again been considered. By that time there was evidence that the Germans were contemplating an advance

on these ports; if achieved, this would put an end to the plan for concentrating the Serbs and Czechs; and the probable establishment of a
German submarine base at Murmansk which would bar the approach
to Archangel. At that time there were two British cruisers and one
French cruiser at Archangel, and towards the end of May Poole had
left England on an adventurous mission to organize the Czech and
Serbian forces on arrival at the two ports. The question then arose
whether some force ought not to be sent to Northern Russia as a
nucleus round which the Czechs, Serbs and loyal Russians could rally.
The matter was referred to the Permanent Military Representatives at
Versailles, whose report recommending the despatch of a small expedition of four to six American, British, French or Italian battalions under
a British Commander-in-Chief was submitted to and approved at the
Council's June meeting.

By the time the seventh meeting had assembled, part of one British
battalion had reached Murmansk. The other part was on its way. A
French battalion was also on its way, and two Italian battalions were
ready. Poole, however, had asked for three battalions. Milner, after
consulting Clemenceau and Foch, had sent a telegram asking the
American Government to send these battalions and two batteries of
artillery. The Supreme War Council were given a remarkably entertaining account of his experiences by Eric Geddes, who had just paid a
visit to Murmansk. It was clear that the local Soviet was at loggerheads
with Moscow, and, in spite of protests from the capital, were doing all
they could to facilitate our enterprise, even to the point of making the
local barracks available for our forces. In the end the Council decided
to ask the four Governments concerned to expedite the despatch of
their respective contingents, and to leave the transport arrangements to
the universal provider—the British Government.

Perhaps I should offer an apology for the flippancy of some of the
extracts from my diary. Actually the proceedings at the Council and at
the many conversations and conferences behind the scenes were conducted in very serious vein as befitted the grave matters that were
under discussion. Nevertheless, the fact that a certain amount of amusement could crop up out of these formidable deliberations at such a
dangerous time, is included with intent to show that there was already
some dim presage of the turn of the tide. Perhaps it was partly because
British, American and French statesmen could joke together and
occasionally break into sheer frivolity that we won the war.

CHAPTER LXXX

THE COMMITTEE OF PRIME MINISTERS

'They are autonomous Communities within the British
Empire, equal in status, in no way subordinate one to
another in any aspect of their domestic or external
affairs, though united by a common allegiance to the
Crown, and freely associated as members of the British
Commonwealth of Nations.' (The 'Balfour Formula',
Imperial Conference, 1926.)

AFTER our return from Versailles the Prime Ministers of the Empire
continued their investigations of the causes of recent reverses and pursued the theme into an examination of the policy to be adopted for
bringing the war to a successful termination. Even at the end of August
they failed to realize how near was the end of the war. Yet, when we
left Versailles at the beginning of July, little as it entered any of our
minds, the Supreme War Council was destined at its next meeting
to assemble for the discussion of armistice terms and the final stages
of the war. Here are my general impressions as I wrote them on
July 19th:

... The situation, take it all round, though sufficiently obscure, is, I
think, a little brighter. . . . The submarine warfare, which was giving me
sleepless nights, has, for the moment at any rate, passed into a less acute
phase. So long as we can maintain our general command of the sea, so long as
we can build ships as fast as we lose them, I for one will remain confident of
ultimate victory. Moreover, given undiminished actual and relative sea-
power I care not if we sink to third place among our Allies as a military
power. . . . Russia, since these pages opened, has gone through every phase
of degeneracy and degradation, but there are not lacking signs that President
Wilson, even though grudgingly, may allow the Japanese sun to rise in the
Far East and bring its vitalizing rays to revivify what remains of life in the
frozen steppes of Russia, recreating for Germany an eastern front. Should
this happen Germany, with her failing man-power, with her dying allies, will
be hard put to it to hold her position against the ever-growing volume of
fresh American troops in the west. Meanwhile the blockade, the dreadful
weapon of our sea-power, is accomplishing gradually and unseen its inevitable purpose; gnawing the vitals and relentlessly sapping the strength of our
foes. Germany is hungry; part of Austria starving! We have great difficulties
of our own, but nothing to compare with these, thank God.

Meantime the question of the allocation of American divisions to Haig's army had come up once more in an acute form:

July 12th. . . . At 4 p.m. I was summoned to a conference at 10 Downing Street, between the Prime Minister and Haig, Milner and c.i.g.s. also being present. As a result I was commissioned to draft a letter for the Prime Minister to send to Clemenceau, c.i.g.s. sending at the same time a letter to Foch, urging that five more American divisions be put for training behind our lines, available to reinforce in case of necessity. Esher had tea with me and I spent the rest of the evening drafting the letter.

July 13th. The Prime Minister tried to catch me for breakfast, but failed, as I was at Limpsfield. After getting agreement of c.i.g.s. to the letter to Clemenceau I spent most of the morning with the Prime Minister tuning it up. It was a very strong letter in the end. . . . In the afternoon motored home to pick up Adeline *en route* to Danny Park, where Riddell is entertaining Lloyd George. Arrived just before dinner and found Ll. G. very rampageous still about getting more Americans.

July 14th (Sunday). Very wet. Loafed about until noon when the Prime Minister came down. He had arranged last night and this morning for Borden and Smuts to come this afternoon. He also urgently needed Milner, who was at his home in the country with no telephone. While we were discussing the matter in came news that Foch, convinced that the big attack was coming immediately between Château Thierry and the Argonne, had ordered four British divisions as well as the French reserves to this region. The Prime Minister was frightfully fussed, as Henry Wilson had led him to believe that the main attack is coming on the British. He was more determined than ever to get Milner and started to write a letter and asked that my car might take it. Partly from a sense of duty I volunteered to go and bring Milner back, starting immediately. I motored eighty miles to Sturry Court, Milner's home near Canterbury. After a short talk with Milner . . . . a short row on the Stour, and a look at Milner's charming old church and beautiful garden, I motored back with him to Danny, arriving about dinner-time. Borden and Smuts had already arrived and Wilson and Radcliffe arrived a few minutes later. After dinner we had an informal conference of about two hours' duration. The Prime Minister was very strong (almost violent) about the withdrawal of divisions. He evidently suspected Clemenceau of using unfair political influence on Foch to save the French Army and Paris at all costs. He was willing to trust Foch, but regarded Clemenceau's personality and his daily visits to Foch as a great danger, tending to bias the Allied Commander-in-Chief unduly. Whether the great attack was to come off in the Champagne or not we must have more American divisions to train in our lines. They had come in our ships and we were entitled to them. Such was his line. Smuts supported him actively, Borden supported him on the whole. Smuts thought

two attacks were coming—one in Champagne, the other in the north. Milner, Wilson and Radcliffe were inclined to support Foch as we had appointed him Allied Commander-in-Chief. Eventually it was decided to send a telegram to Haig reminding him of the Beauvais agreement which authorized him to appeal against Foch if he thought the safety of the British Army endangered; it was also decided to send Smuts over. About midnight I drafted a telegram to Haig. Wilson, Radcliffe and Smuts motored back, Borden and Milner staying the night.

July 15th. The storm has burst. The Germans have attacked from Château Thierry to the Argonne, exactly where Foch had expected. Clive,[1] who came to see me in the afternoon, said the French were completely prepared with all reserves on the spot, and knew the very date of the attack. There was no surprise. Prisoners, deserters, agents, aircraft, 'dumps' had all agreed.

July 16th. . . . Smuts made rather a reassuring statement of his visit to GHQ. Haig and Lawrence now say that the 123 German divisions *in line* are 'cooked' and useless for offensive purposes and that the enemy relies entirely on his reserve divisions for the offensive, so that Rupprecht cannot now put up a very great attack against us. . . . The Prime Minister kept me until about 7.45 talking on the terrace. He told me that Eric Geddes had informed him that the Scotland–Norway anti-submarine mine barrage is now complete; that a German order to submarines has been captured saying that they must go out through Norwegian territorial waters; that this neutral passage is to be watched, and if submarines are seen in it the Norwegians are to be told that, if they do not close it, we shall.

July 18th. . . . Slept at Club—badly; the reaction of joy at Foch's counter-offensive seemed to disturb me more than the grim days of defeat.

The French repulse of the German attack in the Champagne and its immediate sequel, Mangin's counter-attack on July 18th by eighteen French and two American divisions which had been concentrated in the forests of Villars Cotteret, at once changed the whole military situation, and, as one result, relieved the unfortunate difficulties that had threatened between the British and French Governments. At Monchy, where Haig met Foch on July 15th, the Field-Marshal consented to send the four British divisions to the south. Smuts, returning from GHQ, reported that he had learned from Haig that Foch was well disposed towards the idea of strengthening the American troops behind our line, and had expressed a willingness to despatch thither the artillery of those

---

[1] The head of our Mission at French Headquarters.

American divisions whose infantry and machine-gunners were already training there; Clemenceau gave a favourable reply to Lloyd George's letter on the same subject.

In the meantime the Prime Ministers of the Empire, before their visit to Versailles, had made contact with their own contingents in France and had discussed the military situation with the respective commanders. On resuming the discussions in London one after the other expressed the view that our reverses in the spring had been a reaction from the Flanders offensive. They made allowances for the bad luck experienced in the weather, both in Flanders in the autumn and in Picardy in the spring, but no attempt was made to palliate what was felt to have been a first-class mistake in launching the Flanders campaign. No doubt the Report of the Committee on War Policy, 1917, which had been circulated and studied, with its prophetic forecasts by Lloyd George about what eventually occurred, was not without effect in forming their opinion.

Occasionally in committee, and frequently in private, doubts were expressed about the Higher Command of the British Expeditionary Force. Criticisms were not confined to strategy. The selection of corps and divisional commanders also came under review. Why, it was asked, had no Territorial or New Army men been promoted to command corps or divisions, and so few to brigades? The Prime Ministers pointed out that the highest officers of the Dominions contingents included only a small proportion of professional soldiers, and this had not prevented their forces from achieving a high standard of organization and efficiency. How was it, they asked, that the same opportunities had not been extended to Territorial soldiers in the British Army? To limit the opportunities for promotion of civilian officers to the rank of brigadier-general was to deprive the higher ranks of the Army of the best brains of the nation.

These discussions led Lloyd George to be very insistent with Milner about the High Command in France.

July 23rd. At 10.30 Cavan who has been called home from Italy, nominally to tell the Committee of Prime Ministers about the Italian Front, but really in order to enable the Prime Minister to 'vet' him with a view to his replacing Haig, called on me. He amused me by beginning with a remark: 'Well, Hankey, I am not accustomed to Prime Ministers and War Cabinets. Will you tell me how far I can talk freely to them? I do not want what I say to leak back to Diaz.' Of course I told him that he could talk as freely to the Prime Ministers as to the c.i.g.s.

Later in the day I found myself closeted with the Prime Minister and Smuts to compare impressions about Cavan.

Smuts expressed himself as favourably impressed. I thought he was good and alert . . . he had begun by strongly pressing for an offensive on the Italian Front with the idea of dealing the Austrians a severe blow. He would not agree to an attack across the Piave, which he rightly characterized as bad strategy, even though the Prime Minister suggested that a much bigger disaster could be inflicted on the Austrians in the plains than in the mountains. But when pressed to say what they could do in the mountains he admitted that the Italians could not go far owing to the difficulty of the communications. His ideas boiled down to an attack on the Asiago to extend the distance between the Italians on the edge of the plateau, combined with an attack on Trent. This is not the crushing success that the Prime Minister has in mind, or that Cavan had given the impression of, when he began.

This episode is mentioned mainly to bring out these points, first, how serious the Prime Minister was in his desire to replace Haig, and second, that his mind was reverting to his old love, the smashing up of the Austrian Army, which in fact was destined to take place within a few months and to become an essential factor in 'knocking away the props' of the enemy's strength.

However, all thoughts of a change in the Higher Command in France were soon dismissed, for on August 8th Haig turned fiercely on the Germans from opposite Amiens to Montdidier and won such a success as to free that section of the railway communications from the harassing fire of the enemy. The plan of attack was kept a profound secret. The first hint of a coming attack reached the Committee of Prime Ministers on August 1st, when Borden told them that on the previous evening he had learned in the greatest secrecy that the Canadian Corps was being moved from the Arras region to another part of the line with a view to a coming offensive. Even Henry Wilson did not admit to knowing anything of what was intended. The Prime Ministers were rather perturbed at this intelligence. They did not want to interfere with strategical or tactical matters, but they felt that, at that stage of the war, they, as representing the Governments of the Empire, had a right to know what was the scope of the intended operation. It was they who controlled the dwindling resources of the Empire nations. If they felt that these resources were being reduced too low, they had the right and duty to exercise restraint. The withdrawal of even a few men from shipbuilding might produce the most serious results; the withdrawal of a few thousand engineers to the Army had lately caused

the tank programme to fall by half. What they dreaded was a repetition of the Flanders operation. The Chief of the Imperial General Staff was instructed to ascertain what was the scope of the operation. It then transpired that this was limited to a series of attacks intended to rectify the line, which Henry Wilson had already advocated and which Foch had decided to undertake; no further objection was raised.

The decision was justified by success. Foch had entrusted the enterprise, which involved French as well as British troops, to Haig, who commanded in person. About ten divisions (Australian, Canadian and British), with three British divisions and the Cavalry Corps in reserve, and eight French divisions took part, supported effectively by large air forces. The method, at any rate so far as the British divisions were concerned, was the one which the designers of the tanks had always advocated, a surprise attack by some 420 tanks without any preliminary bombardment. The result was a complete rupture of the German line. The effects, both material and moral, were tremendous. Two days later, when the French armies attacked, they found the position in front of them abandoned. The Prime Ministers sent their congratulations to the Field-Marshal, and to the troops under his command on their brilliant success. There was henceforward no question of replacing him, for which I myself was glad, as I never discovered any other officer of the same calibre as Haig.

Meanwhile the Committee of Prime Ministers was continuing its inquiry. Having completed their review of the past, they started to block in the main lines of grand strategy for the future in order that Lloyd George might be aware of their views before they dispersed to their several Dominions. The foundation of this part of their inquiry was a Memorandum prepared for them at the end of July by Henry Wilson. In it Wilson planked strongly for the Western Front theory and the Prime Minister, needless to say, was furious about this performance.[1]

July 30th. . . . After the meeting I had a talk with the Prime Minister about Wilson's important Memo. on future military policy. He was bitterly disappointed with its purely 'Western Front' attitude and described it as simply 'Wully *redivivus*'.

The reaction of most of the Prime Ministers was much the same.

July 31st. . . . A very strong anti-Western Front bias was shown by all, but especially by Milner, Smuts and the Prime Minister. The strong feeling

[1] *War Memoirs*, VI, pp. 3108 *sq.*

was that we were running the risk of shattering the American Army next year, as we shattered our own Army in 1916 and 1917, without achieving a decision.

August 2nd. .... After lunch I saw the c.i.g.s. (about 4.45 p.m.), as the Prime Minister had requested me to do, in regard to the war policy. I told him the Prime Minister found him too much 'Western Front' in his ideas, and too much like Robertson. 'It is Irish instead of Scotch, but it is still whisky.' He admitted he was dominated by the idea of not quarrelling with our Allies and more especially with Foch, but explained a scheme he had for concentrating twelve divisions this winter on the Italian Front. On the whole my interview was satisfactory. Afterwards I saw the Prime Minister to tell him the result, but only had a minute's conversation, as he was about to have his hair cut. During this operation I induced him to sign a photograph for me to keep.[1]

Being by this time familiar with the ways of Prime Ministers I had begun to sketch in the main lines of the Report of the Committee of Prime Ministers as early as August 5th, and was therefore not too taken aback when the Prime Minister, at the end of a meeting on the afternoon of August 12th, told me that Borden was leaving in a few days' time and demanded the early production of a Report.

August 13th. Locked myself up with shorthand writers all the afternoon and until late in the evening, drafting the Report for the Prime Ministers.

August 14th. Spent morning tuning up and completing the draft Report. ... In the evening I had to go off with the Prime Minister to Danny Park, to spend the evening going through my draft Report. Our party was small but select—the Prime Minister, Smuts, Reading, and myself. My draft Report was acclaimed as a huge success, but they made a good many alterations, and I sat up until after midnight inserting them.

August 15th. Up at 6 a.m. after a very good, if short, sleep, and off with Smuts by car to London. In office at 8.30 to get the Report cyclostyled in part and circulated to give the Prime Ministers time to read it before the afternoon. The reason for this colossal hustle is that Borden is due to leave tomorrow. ... In the afternoon, as I anticipated, the Prime Ministers had not read my draft Report and adjourned their meeting until 9 a.m. tomorrow.[2]

August 16th. 9 a.m. Breakfast at 10 Downing Street, with the Prime Ministers Committee followed by a two hours' discussion of the draft Report. We only discussed the conclusions. It was really the first time we got to grips at all and the discussion was quite excellent. War Cabinet at 11.30. I had a terrible rush in the afternoon owing to the fact that the Prime Minister

---

[1] I have it to this day.
[2] They had spent the whole morning at the Imperial War Cabinet.

is leaving for Criccieth tonight or tomorrow, and many things had to be cleared up. I spent an hour and a half or so with Milner going through the draft Report of the Prime Ministers. At 6.30 I had a long talk with the Prime Minister, who gave me a mass of instructions. On my way to London Bridge my car ran into a boy on a bicycle. We ought to have killed him, but to my intense relief he picked himself up. Nevertheless I had a very bad night of it, fearing lest he might come to some harm.

That was what might be called 'the end of a perfect day'. Luckily the boy, about whom I inquired next morning, was quite unhurt.

August 17th. Rest of the day was working on the Prime Ministers' Report.

August 19th. Worked all day at home on the revise of the Report, Sylvester coming down in the car. Nine hours' solid work, which left me very weary.

August 21st. In the afternoon I called on Massey at the Savoy to say goodbye. . . . I got his definite agreement to the Report.

These details are inserted in order to show the immense pressure at which we were all working. I did eventually get the agreement to the Report of all the Prime Ministers except Hughes, who sent me rather an enigmatic letter on the subject. The result was that I could never get Lloyd George to sign it, or to allow me to circulate it, so that to this day it remains an unsigned draft, in spite of all the hard work that was put into it. The fact was that it had become rather out of date owing to the rapid course of events, although it remains an historical document of considerable interest. The next day (August 22nd) I left with Milner, Amery and Bertram Dawson to join Lloyd George at Criccieth.

While the Committee of Prime Ministers had been hatching out their report on past operations and future military policy, the Imperial War Cabinet had been working away at a number of other matters including the munitions programme, and the important subject of communications between the Governments of the Empire. On this Borden wrote a letter to Lloyd George. I have not the text of it, but he seems to have voiced the general opinion of the Dominion Prime Ministers that, with the establishment of the Imperial War Cabinet and the important share taken by the Dominions in the war effort and by the Prime Ministers in its direction, the time had come to send communications direct from Prime Minister to Prime Minister instead of through the Colonial Secretary; as yet, of course, the Dominions Office had not yet come into existence. This was not very convenient

to us because the Prime Minister's office had always consisted only of a few private secretaries who changed with every new Prime Minister, and the War Cabinet Secretariat was treated as a war expedient likely eventually to disappear. As an office the Secretariat was still viewed with suspicion by some of the older civil servants, although it was recognized that we were useful in war, and individually the staff was rather popular.

July 8th. . . . In the afternoon I had a long talk with Batterbee, Walter Long's secretary, about the Dominions Department of the Colonial Office, and the relation thereto of Borden's letter to the Prime Minister asking that in future communications should pass through the Prime Minister and not through the Colonial Secretary.

July 10th. . . . At 4 p.m. I had an hour's conversation at the Colonial Office with Walter Long and Fiddes (Permanent Under-Secretary) about Borden's letter. I brought them to the same view as I had brought Kerr the previous evening, that the proper step now is to allow direct communications between the Prime Minister of the United Kingdom and the Prime Ministers of the Dominions, on the understanding that it is confined to business of Cabinet importance of an intimately secret nature, all other business continuing as at present through the Colonial Office. The analogy is the direct communications that pass between the Prime Minister and his colleagues as distinct from the business done through official channels—or the communications between the Prime Minister and Clemenceau, for example.

July 18th. . . . Then Kerr and Christie (Borden's Private Secretary) came in to talk over Borden's proposals for more direct communication between the Dominions Prime Ministers and our Prime Minister and I gave Christie my proposals, with which he agreed. I dined alone with Smuts tonight to discuss the same question. He was not quite satisfied with my proposals and obviously wants more, particularly the elimination of the Governor-General as a channel of communication with the Home Government, but accepts my ideas as an immediate step—my idea being the establishment of direct communication between the Dominions Prime Ministers and our Prime Minister on Cabinet questions, each Dominion Prime Minister being at liberty to nominate an assistant secretary to my office.

July 25th. . . . Most important discussion on the constitutional question of relations between the Mother Country and the Dominions. My scheme, drafted two or three weeks ago, for direct communication between the Prime Ministers of the Dominions and the Mother Country was read out and accepted. In addition the Prime Minister proposed that each Dominion should establish a Resident Minister, and that a committee should be set up to consider the future machinery of communication after the war.

July 26th. . . . Saw Prime Minister about 6.30 p.m. and secured his agreement to a short note summarizing his own proposals as regards channels of Imperial communication.

July 30th. Imperial War Cabinet at 11.30. Very important decision giving the Prime Ministers of the Dominions the right of direct communication with our Prime Minister and the right of nominating a Minister to remain in London to attend meetings of the Imperial War Cabinet held between the regular sessions. I drafted both these decisions (one of them four weeks ago) and, in spite of the constitutional difficulties involved, they were accepted without alteration. They refused altogether, however, to accept a proposal for an informal committee to examine future relations.

That success was the result of the very careful preparation that had been undertaken, in which Leo Amery gave me very great assistance.

August 2nd. Started from home at 7.15 a.m. in my office car and motored to the Savoy, where I breakfasted alone with Borden. We discussed the detailed arrangements about the future communications between the Dominions Prime Ministers and our Prime Minister. He undertook to leave a private secretary with the Canadian representative, who should have a seat in my office and eventually be available as an assistant secretary.

August 21st. In the afternoon I called on Massey at the Savoy to say goodbye. . . . He told me that, while he attached the greatest importance in principle to the right lately extended to the Dominions to nominate a representative of the Imperial War Cabinet in London, he did not intend to take advantage of it for the moment. First, he wished to return home and discuss the matter with his colleagues and in Parliament. Further, he thought that the larger Dominions ought to give New Zealand a lead in the matter. We parted with the most friendly sentiments on both sides. Borden has not yet definitely nominated a member of the Imperial War Cabinet, though Kemp is available to attend when required. I have had a very friendly letter from Borden speaking of my personal services in the very highest terms.

These developments were in line with the conclusions of 1911 and 1912 which led Borden in 1914 to send Perley to London as his representative on the Committee of Imperial Defence and Massey to send Allen to attend meetings of that Committee in 1913,[1] and they prepared the way for the remarkable development of the British Empire delegation and its joint secretariat at the Peace Conference.

One other subject which the Imperial War Cabinet discussed before they separated was war aims. This throws some light on their rather cautious attitude on the future of the war. Does it not perhaps betoken

[1] *vide supra*, p. 134.

that in their heart of hearts they were beginning to realize that the war might be over in 1918? If that was their real belief, why did they not say so? The answer is that their technical advisers gave them no reasons to justify the assumption of an early termination of the war; indeed, up to within a week of the armistice, some leading British and French military authorities were unable to say that the German Army on the Western Front was incapable of holding on the short line to which they were retiring. If, therefore, the Committee of Prime Ministers failed to read the signs of the times aright, they failed in good company.

CHAPTER LXXXI

KNOCKING AWAY THE PROPS

'The Supreme Command insists on its demand of
Sunday, September 29th, that a peace offer to our enemies
be issued at once. As a result of the collapse of the
Macedonian front and the weakening of our Western
reserves which this has brought about, and now that it is
impossible to make good the very considerable losses
which have been incurred in the battles of the last few
days, there is, so far as can be foreseen, no longer a prospect of forcing peace on the enemy.' (From Hindenburg's
letter of October 3, 1918, quoted in Max of Baden,
Memoirs, II, p. 19.)

WHEN the Supreme War Council separated in July the question of a
Balkan offensive was remitted for consideration to the Permanent
Military Representatives in consultation with diplomatic representatives of the Powers concerned. Pending these consultations the
independent orders issued to Franchet d'Esperey by Clemenceau were
held in abeyance.[1] Robert Cecil and Derby were nominated by the
Imperial War Cabinet to represent Britain at the proposed meeting at
Versailles. The Bulgarian people were now notoriously discontented at
the prolongation of the war. The Germans were unpopular; the
country was being denuded through the export of foodstuffs to the
Central Powers. There was constant friction on the Turco-Bulgarian
frontier. The Sofia Government was unwilling to break off relations
with the United States which had not declared war upon Bulgaria. But
diplomatic action on our part to induce her to make peace was difficult
owing to the war aims or expectations of Greece and Serbia. Moreover
it was unlikely that her Government would discuss a separate peace
until they knew the issue of the German offensive on the Western
Front. Hence the British Government was not averse to an offensive
provided the results were likely to increase the desire of the Bulgarian
people for peace. The general conclusion of the Versailles Conference
had been that an offensive was not desirable unless it would lead to a
victory of more than local importance.[2] The Military Representatives
had studied the matter and on August 3rd recommended, subject to the
needs of the Western Front and the availability of shipping, prepara-

[1] *Macedonia*, II, p. 105; and *vide supra*, p. 821.　　　　　[2] *Ibid.*, p. 106.

tions for an offensive in the Balkan theatre before October 1st, the precise date being left to the Allied Commander-in-Chief.[1] The French Government then took the initiative and on September 4th Guillaumat, who had taken Sarrail's place on December 22, 1917, and on his recall on June 6, 1918, to be Governor of Paris, had been succeeded as Commander-in-Chief by Franchet d'Esperey, arrived in London with the mission of persuading the British Government to agree to an offensive against Bulgaria. He gave a glowing account of the military position. The Allied Army was represented as good and well found. There had been only three Greek divisions at the end of 1917; there were now nine and, including auxiliaries, the Greeks were reported to have 180,000 men in the field with 300,000 to 350,000 available as drafts. They were not too well equipped with artillery but the Bulgarian lines were not very strong and, provided that the mountain artillery which had been promised was sent, there was good prospect of success. The attack could be begun within a week or two by the Serbians who were practically ready. Supported by French divisions they were to advance into old Serbia and then into the Yugoslav districts of Austria. If this operation was successful, it would be followed by a Greek attack in the Struma valley supported by the British Army with the recapture of the Greek districts of Seres, Drama and Kavalla as their object.

After withdrawing for a short time to consult Henry Wilson and Robert Cecil, Lloyd George decided to accept the advice of the French general with his local knowledge, and to overrule Henry Wilson who, in his Memorandum of July 25th and as a convinced 'Western Fronter', was still very lukewarm about a Balkan offensive.[2] The Prime Minister gave the British Government's consent to the plan so far as the use of British troops was concerned, but insisted strongly on the importance of a concerted attack by the Italians with the object of containing the Austrian forces which otherwise could be released to reinforce the Bulgarians. He disclaimed any intention to delay the attack until Italian co-operation was assured. As Foch was known to be pressing Diaz to take the offensive, it was proposed that Henry Wilson should accompany Guillaumat to Paris where it was hoped to arrange for him to meet Foch and Diaz.

This was one of the rare cases in which Lloyd George actually overruled his own military adviser; his flair turned out to be correct. The importance of his prompt decision will be appreciated when it is realized that Franchet d'Esperey proposed to launch the first attack by the

<hr />

[1] *Macedonia*, II, p. 110.   [2] *Ibid.*, p. 111; and *vide supra*, p. 830.

Serbians in eleven days' time, i.e. on September 15th, and Allenby was to open a fresh offensive in Palestine on September 18th. If, therefore, Diaz could be induced to attack within the next two or three weeks, all the 'props' would be assailed at once, which would be most disconcerting to an enemy already finding it difficult to hold the assault of the British, French and American forces in the main theatre. Henry Wilson, however, never started for Paris. All reports agreed that Diaz was not yet ready to take the offensive and it was even said that it was too late for him to do so. Indeed, the Italians were actually considering the despatch of further divisions to the Western Front which they actually did send a little later.

Shortly after Guillaumat's visit the indefatigable Prime Minister went off to make a series of political speeches. In those days, when Parliament was not sitting, the most important method of keeping popular opinion straight about the war was by speechmaking. For this reason any further session of the Supreme War Council was postponed for the moment. At Manchester he fell seriously ill with influenza and was laid up for some time. This enabled me to take a much-needed rest of a fortnight with my family at Totland Bay in the Isle of Wight, where I remained for just over a fortnight—the longest spell I had during the war; every day, however, I received a big despatch-case from the office and watched the situation carefully. The news was entirely satisfactory and called for no decisions by the Supreme Command. The successes by the British and French armies, which had begun with Haig's attack on August 8th, continued. There were no signs of a new Passchendaele. The War Cabinet, naturally suspicious owing to the repeated disillusionments of past years, were ever on the watch for anything of the kind, but Henry Wilson was always able to reassure them with irrefutable evidence of diminished casualties and an ever-increasing tale of captures of prisoners and war material. On September 12th–13th the American Army, which at long last had been concentrated under Pershing's command, bit off the St. Mihiel Salient, to the great relief of the French at Verdun, and were preparing their big attack in the Argonne. In France people were beginning to say that Germany would soon be suing for peace.

The most spectacular successes, however, were occurring against Bulgaria and Turkey. Franchet d'Esperey opened his attack on September 15th, on a wide front west of the Vardar. In the centre of this attack, against what appeared an impregnable position, the resistance of the Bulgarian Army at once collapsed, and the Serbian Army, to whom

the principal role had been assigned, pushing forward with great élan, was reported on September 18th to have already advanced twenty-five miles across the mountains. On that date British and Greek forces (who fought well) began their advance on either side of Lake Doiran, and, although their role was a more modest one, inflicted heavy casualties and contained considerable enemy forces on their front. On the 24th we learned that the Serbian Army had cut the main line of communications of the Bulgarian forces confronting the British and Greek armies, and Prilep to the south-west had been occupied by the French. On the 25th the Serbians occupied Ishtip and Veles on the Vardar. Our air forces supported the ground forces with brilliant success and in the subsequent pursuit by bombing and machine-gunning the retreating army in the mountain ravines played a decisive part in the rout and complete demoralization of the Bulgarian Army.

Meanwhile Allenby had opened his attack in Palestine on September 19th, routed the Turks at Megiddo, and was in full pursuit with cavalry and aircraft, which, as in Macedonia, were wreaking frightful havoc. On the 23rd Haifa and Acre and Es Salt were occupied and on the 25th the Hejaz railway was cut by British cavalry at Amman. The plight of the Turkish Army was obviously desperate. Such was the position developing when I returned from leave on September 22nd.

September 23rd. . . . I think the Palestine victory is largely due to the action of the Committee of Prime Ministers last July in refusing to allow the transport of the 54th Division from Palestine to the Western Front. As c.i.g.s. said to me in the afternoon, the victories in Palestine and Salonica are most glaring examples of 'amateur strategy'—but he is very pleased all the same.

September 27th. When I reached the office I found there a telegram to the effect that Bulgaria had asked for an armistice with a view to peace. They had sent the *parlementaire* to the British and not to the French or Serbian lines. I at once saw Bonar Law and we rang up the Prime Minister at Danny and ascertained his views. Then we got Balfour and Wilson over for a discussion before the Cabinet. The action approved by the War Cabinet was to send the message on to the French advising that we should not grant an armistice, but should hear what the Bulgarians have to say. The whole thing became public more or less during the day. . . .

September 23th. . . . The situation is one of quite extraordinary interest. On the Western Front the big Franco-American attack has been launched, and yesterday we put in a big attack at Cambrai. A number of other attacks are to come. The Germans, therefore, are very busy and can hardly spare troops for elsewhere, since they are rather on their beam's ends. Meanwhile

the Bulgars have been so badly hammered that they are asking for a separate peace, so that there is a good chance of cutting communications with Turkey. The Turks have lost practically their whole Palestine army with all its material. They cannot hope to replenish this material if Bulgaria goes out and they can hardly send troops, if they are likely to be threatened by an Allied Army marching on Constantinople from Bulgaria. . . .

September 30th. . . . I saw Bonar Law about tomorrow's War Cabinet and found him very elated after a most successful War Loan speech in the City. *Bulgaria has accepted an armistice with all the conditions we insisted on.*[1]

THE FIRST OF THE PROPS HAD FALLEN.

October 1st. . . . I left with Wemyss for Danny to spend the night. Wilson and French were also there. The topic we were summoned to discuss was the exploitation of the Bulgarian truce. The Prime Minister wanted to switch the whole of Milne's army towards Constantinople, placing it, as well as the Palestine force, under Allenby's command. He had sent up a draft telegram from himself to Clemenceau that morning and I had attended a conference with Balfour, Milner and C.I.G.S. on the subject after lunch, at which it had been agreed we must ask the Prime Minister to reconsider it. This was mainly due to the military danger of attack on Bulgaria from north of the Danube. After much discussion the Prime Minister agreed, and at 11.30 p.m. I drafted a telegram to the effect that C.I.G.S. was coming to Paris immediately and that Lloyd George would follow him on Friday, and that Orlando should be asked to come, in order that we might press on him the importance of an Italian offensive, if only to prevent Austria from sending divisions to the Balkans. It was the first time I had seen the Prime Minister since his serious illness at Manchester and he was looking fit and well.

A few days later, however, we were somewhat reassured as to the probability of an offensive by the Italian Army:

October 4th (at Versailles). Started at 8.25 from Victoria with Lloyd George for Paris. Cavan was the only especially distinguished passenger in our special train, apart from the Prime Minister. He has had to break his leave, having been recalled to Italy, which looks like an offensive on that front.

October 5th. . . . In the morning we received a number of memoranda, etc., from Clemenceau giving the views of Berthelot, Guillaumat and Foch on the proper way to exploit the situation in the Balkans. The two former wish to push up the Danube and join hands with the Roumanians, organizing thereafter an advance into Austria. In fact Berthelot has already started

---

[1] Italics not in the original; the armistice had been signed on September 29th.

for the Balkans with some mad scheme of flying in an aeroplane to Roumania and organizing a rising there, notwithstanding that Roumania is still in German occupation. Foch thinks they are trying to do too much at once, and wants to cut the Constantinople railway at Nish and on the Maritza, and to occupy all the strategic points in Bulgaria, before tackling Roumania. Broadly speaking the French want to deal with Turkey by isolating her; to cut her off from the Black Sea, they have an absurd scheme for transporting submarines by rail to Varna and Braila. We, on the contrary, want to deal with Turkey by an immediate advance on Constantinople, either direct or first opening the Dardanelles. After a preliminary discussion among ourselves at the Villa Romaine, Wilson, Hope and I accompanied the Prime Minister about noon to the Ministry of War, where the Prime Minister held a private conversation with Clemenceau and Orlando. None of our experts were present, but the Prime Minister told me afterwards that Clemenceau was much put out at our proposal, and more particularly at the suggestion that Allenby should command the operations against Constantinople, which he considered, if undertaken, should be Franchet d'Esperey's affair, as it is part of the fruits of his victory. There is a good deal really to be said for this point of view, as it will be distinctly awkward to have two Commanders-in-Chief in the same theatre with two armies, both served by one port, Salonica the only efficient base in this region. The upshot of the conversation was that a conference was arranged to take place at the Villa Romaine this afternoon at 5 o'clock. Personally I regret the desire of Ll. George, Wilson and others to take this command from Franchet d'Esperey. They, and others such as Sackville-West, all think the French are claiming too much credit for Franchet d'Esperey's success. This is a French foible that does not trouble me in the least. They have lost so much in the early part of the war, and are so subject to fits of depression and elation that they require the kudos of the splendid feats of Foch and Franchet d'Esperey to enable them to hold their heads up and to maintain the great place in the world which their genius entitles them to. I put this to Lloyd George when driving up to Paris. . . . At 5 p.m. we had a conference at the Villa Romaine between the Prime Minister, Clemenceau, Orlando, Foch, Wilson, Hope and self. Clemenceau sprung upon us the announcement that the Central Powers had asked for an armistice.[1] Most of the discussion, however, related to the operations in the Balkans and Foch delighted the Prime Minister, and annoyed Clemenceau, by planking for our project for an attack on Constantinople.

October 6th (Sunday). . . . Lunch with Derby at the Paris Embassy, the Serbian Minister and several other people being present. . . . Conference at the Quai d'Orsay at 3 p.m. Aldrovandi informed me that I am to receive an Italian decoration. The conference was devoted partly to considering the

---

[1] The German Note was sent to President Wilson on October 3rd; the Austrian Note on October 4th.

terms of an armistice with Turkey, if asked for, and the terms of an armistice with the Central Powers. We had already prepared a draft of the former, which was remitted to a naval and military conference—Albi the French C.G.S., Wilson, Bon, Hope, Grassi and myself. As I had been at the conference of the 'Frocks' and knew their views, I informally took the chair, and very rapidly secured agreement. Then I went off to the Embassy to tea and to get the results typed, which took them preposterously long. Then I had to go round in a car distributing the copies to those who had to take part in a new conference to clew the matter up. French Government offices are rum places. No one would undertake to give the note without delay to Albi and eventually I forced my way through many cold, dark and dreary passages into the room of one of his staff officers. After this I went to Clemenceau's room at the Ministry of War. I had actually been delegated by Lloyd George, still rather weak after his illness, to represent him at the resumed conference, although I was accompanied by Wilson and Hope. Before long I found myself entangled in an argument with Sonnino, who wanted to wedge in some Italian claims (not fully recognized yet) in the armistice conditions. By declining to approve the agreement if this were inserted I got the matter dropped. I accepted and rejected some amendments to the conditions of an armistice with Turkey, both at the political conference, and at a military drafting committee held afterwards and was supported by Lloyd George in all that I had done. . . .

October 7th. . . . We had a conference at the Villa Romaine at 10.30 with Foch and Weygand on the subject of British man-power. Foch, who was very friendly to me personally, made a strong appeal to us not to reduce our divisions. . . . I had a very busy morning getting out my *procès-verbaux* for last night's conference, and of the conference this morning; as well as the Memorandum of Conditions for an Armistice with Turkey agreed to yesterday. After lunch I drove with the Prime Minister and J. T. Davies to the Ministry of War, as, before the afternoon conference, Lloyd George had arranged to see Clemenceau about a plan received from Franchet d'Esperey. This plan provided for the British Army, which has for two years been lying in the malarious district of the Struma on the eastern flank·of the Allied Army, to march into Bulgaria, while an army of three Greek, one French and one British division marches on Constantinople. The Prime Minister was absolutely furious and went to tell Clemenceau that Milne would be taken away from the command of Franchet d'Esperey and ordered to march on Constantinople. I was not in the room at the interview, which was very short, but they agreed to adjourn it to the conference which was about to meet at the Quai d'Orsay. . . . Here Clemenceau completely piped down, but Lloyd George volunteered to drop the scheme for placing Milne's army under Allenby and allowed it to remain 'under Franchet d'Esperey', provided Milne commanded the section ordered to march on Constantinople.

While they wrangled I drafted the formula on the above lines, which was accepted, and Clemenceau there and then dictated to Pichon (whom he treated like a stenographer rather than a Foreign Minister) a very sharp telegram, rapping Franchet d'Esperey on the knuckles for dividing the armies, for taking the British from the eastern front of his army, and for launching two separate columns of French troops into Albania—one towards Elbasan and Durazzo, the other towards Alessio and Scutari. . . . As Lloyd George said at the conference, 'It is a political and not a military plan'. Clemenceau as usual took the big line and behaved very well. . . . After this a discussion took place on the terms of an armistice with Germany and the question was referred to the Military Representative at Versailles with whom naval representatives were to be associated. We then returned to Versailles and dined. I had, of course, to get out the *procès-verbaux*, which I did before dinner. I received today my order as 'Commendatore' of the Crown of Italy.

The two following days were devoted to discussions on the German armistice, and on October 10th we returned home. Throughout this series of conferences I had been contending with a desperately bad cold, which I had picked up from Balfour at lunch the day before we started, so I was not sorry to leave Paris. On the journey I made some jottings of various impressions:

October 10th. Started from the Villa Romaine and came by train from Paris to Boulogne. Very interesting to travel once more by Amiens. It is a good deal knocked about by long-range gunfire, especially round about the railway, but the Cathedral appears from the railway to be untouched. Very interesting also is the huge system of defences on the Paris side of Amiens for many miles along the railway. Barbed wire, trenches, deep dug-outs in the railway embankment, etc. In many places the railway has been heavily shelled and bombed. Paris . . . is a changed city. The feeling of strained endurance which pervaded it during our last visit during the era of 'Bertha' and bomb-raids has disappeared and great hope and confidence has taken its place. . . . We are at the zenith of a well-earned popularity.

After our return to London I went through a particularly difficult time. The War Cabinet was in almost constant session and there were innumerable questions to be settled. The Agenda papers had constantly to be upset by the arrival of urgent telegrams from America about the German request for an armistice, or from one or other of the theatres of war. This would necessitate the sudden cancellation at the last moment of the arrangements already made for a meeting, to the great incon-

EE

venience of Ministers not members of the War Cabinet who had been summoned for particular business. The Prime Minister also was much preoccupied with the tremendous questions that kept arising and often found it difficult to come up from Walton Heath, where he was spending the nights, to attend the meetings. He was still suffering from the after effects of his bad attack of influenza and his health had not been improved by the exhausting series of meetings in Paris. Difficulties arose also, for the first and only time during Lloyd George's régime, about the limited distribution of certain very secret papers, though only two Ministers were concerned in them. I had to bear the brunt of all this, and to devote much time to the task of explaining to the Ministers concerned the peculiar circumstance of each cause of complaint as it arose. On one occasion I was forced to write a very outspoken letter to Lloyd George on the subject, but I am bound to say that he did not in the least resent it and continued to treat me with the greatest kindness and good humour. However, these troubles were short lived, for on October 28th we left once more for Paris for the armistice discussions, and remained there until November 4th.

Bulgaria had fallen out of the war on September 30th. At noon on October 21st, while the War Cabinet was in session, there arrived a telegram announcing that Townshend, who had been a prisoner of war in Turkey ever since the surrender of Kut-el-Amara on April 29, 1916, had been released, and, accompanied by the A.D.C. of the Turkish Minister of Marine, had arrived via Mytilene at Lemnos with definite overtures for peace from Turkey. After a good deal of palaver, instructions were sent to Calthorpe the same day to the effect that the British Government were prepared to discuss with properly accredited Turkish representatives the measures necessary for throwing off the German yoke. Peace could not be discussed without consulting our Allies, which would take time, but we would consider an armistice, the conditions of which would be communicated on the next day and which had already been settled in Paris. The Admiral was accordingly instructed on October 22nd to try to secure the Paris conditions, but, if he could not get the whole, to close the Straits to free passage. The French and Italian Governments were informed of these instructions.

Calthorpe was much hampered in his negotiations by the attitude of his French and Italian colleagues; Admiral Amet, for example, declined to agree that the command of any Allied fleet proceeding up the Dardanelles should be British. He also wished, not unnaturally, to take part in the armistice negotiations, but, as the credentials of the Turkish

delegates entitled them to negotiate only with the British Admiral, he had to forgo this privilege. The Turks also made a great point that the forts of the Dardanelles should be occupied only by British and French troops and not by Italians. As the Italians had taken no effective part in the various campaigns against Turkey, Lloyd George felt justified in authorizing Calthorpe to accept this stipulation, and a telegram to that effect was despatched from Folkestone on our journey to Paris on October 28th.

All this time operations against Turkey had been proceeding apace. Following the capture of Damascus on October 1st, Sidon was occupied on October 6th; the Allies occupied Tripoli on the 13th and Homs on the 15th; Aleppo was taken on October 26th, British cavalry playing a great part in this drive. Practically the whole of Syria was now in the hands of the Allies. In Mesopotamia Marshall, in command of the Mesopotamia Expeditionary Force since November 18, 1917, began his advance on Mosul on October 23rd and secured the surrender of the Turkish force at Shargat on the 30th, continuing his advance on the next day; Mosul itself was not occupied until November 4th, after the armistice. By this time also we had obtained command of the Caspian Sea in order to block the road to India.

The discussions in Paris were mainly concerned with the German armistice but I find the following note about the Turkish affair:

October 30th (Paris). A row between the French and ourselves because Calthorpe conducted the armistice negotiations with Turkey without calling in the French Admiral at Lemnos (Amet) to represent Gauchet the French naval Commander-in-Chief. Lloyd George quoted Franchet d'Esperey's conduct of the Bulgarian negotiations and gave more than he got. In the end the French accepted the *fait accompli* as we heard during the meeting that the armistice is to be signed today. The whole thing was artificial and probably connected with the French Parliamentary Commission.

Sure enough the Turkish armistice was signed on October 30th and came into force next day.

THE SECOND PROP HAD CRASHED!

For some time Diaz had resisted the pressure of Foch and of the British and French Governments to undertake an offensive on his front. He does not seem to have decided to attack until after the Bulgarian armistice on September 30th, and it was not until October 24th that he began the final Italian advance, which culminated a few days later in the

decisive victory of Vittorio Veneto. Cavan received the honour of command of an Italian army. On October 30th Orlando, who had just arrived in Paris from Italy, brought the news that, while passing through Turin on the previous day, he had been called to the telephone to speak to Diaz, who had informed him that he had that day received from the Austrian Commander-in-Chief, under flag of truce, a request for an armistice. The Austrian Government had sent a separate note to President Wilson asking for an armistice on October 4th. On October 27th they had sent a further note to the President asking for an armistice, 'without awaiting the result of other negotiations'. We had been expecting this request and Lloyd George at once put forward the heads of military terms which had been drafted for him by Henry Wilson. They were adopted in principle and remitted to the Allied military experts to elaborate in detail. The Allied Naval Council, which happened to be meeting in Paris, had already worked out a draft of the Naval Terms:

October 30th. . . . During the discussion of naval terms of armistice with Austria Clemenceau commented on the Allied Naval Council's propositions as follows: 'They have not asked for the Emperor's trousers, but that is about all.'

October 31st. . . . One very interesting thing occurred today. . . . I was not present at the important meeting held at House's residence in the morning. Neither was any other secretary. Eric Geddes had acted as secretary to the extent of correcting the various documents discussed, viz. the military terms of an armistice with Austria, and the naval terms. In correcting the military terms Geddes missed out one very important addition *re* the surrender of artillery and put in another addition in the wrong place. After the meeting he handed me the corrected document, and I had it reproduced and placed on the table at the Supreme War Council. The French had entrusted their interests to Mantoux, the admirable interpreter . . . and, of course, he had reproduced nothing, and had, as French text, only a lot of untidy rough notes, not stitched together properly. The result of his uncertain French text, which was not read out, and of my inaccurate version communicated by Geddes was inextricable confusion. So the conference had to appoint a drafting committee to get it right, and a nice job it was! The naval terms went off better, because, after the meeting of Prime Ministers, Geddes and Wemyss assembled the Allied Naval Council and straightened it out. Even here, however, there were difficulties, because of course the French . . . had not got out a French text and every word had to be translated. Henry Wilson told everyone that the trouble was all due to my not being present at the meeting. 'If you once lose hold of Hanky-Panky you are done, absolutely done!' I

heard him saying. I pointed the moral to Auchincloss and to Aldrovandi, and they faithfully promised it should not occur again, if they could influence their chiefs.

Of course any experienced secretary could have done the job as well as I could, and some better. It is always a mistake, however, for delegates to meet without a secretary, especially where it is a case of discussing a draft. This requires the whole attention of one man, particularly when there are two languages. A delegate trying to do the job is at the disadvantage that he is doing two things at once—criticizing the draft from his own point of view, and trying to catch the amendments and counter-amendments suggested by others in a rapid criss-cross of conversation. An interpreter is equally at a disadvantage in reproducing after the meeting a good summary of the discussion. His notes are made very hastily, and suffice only for immediate translation, many of them being practically illegible afterwards. In fact he has not time to make notes of very short remarks, such as are made in the discussion of a draft, so that his record is bound to be incomplete and depends upon whether or not he can remember what he had no time to note. For this reason the great interpreters, like Mantoux and his successors, have always declined to be responsible for drafting, though, of course, they are of the greatest assistance to secretaries in checking doubtful points.

October 31st (continued). . . . During the day we heard that the armistice with Turkey was signed, and hastily telephoned a communiqué to London to be read out in the House of Commons, explaining that the *British* Admiral had made the armistice. After the Supreme War Council Lloyd George, Bonar Law, Geddes, Wemyss, Duncannon, Philip Kerr and I motored up to Paris, dined at the Meurice and went on to 'La Fille de Madame Angot'. Bonar Law made the characteristic remark—'it would be less intolerable if only they would not sing!' Thus we celebrated the exit of Turkey from the war. In the Meurice we met Orlando, who told us that one of the Austrian delegates, who are waiting at Diaz's GHQ, had a '*crise de douleur*' in the course of which he said that the condition of the Austrian Army was such that they would accept any terms. I telegraphed the whole of the Austrian terms to London for the War Cabinet.

The only remaining point in the Austrian armistice that cropped up at Paris was in connection with the surrender of the Austrian Fleet. This had been handed over on October 31st to the Jugo-Slav National Council, who were themselves anxious to surrender to the Allies. The Italians were apprehensive lest the Jugo-Slavs should be allowed to

keep the ships, which might become the nucleus of a fleet to be used against Italy. Eventually it was arranged that the fleet should be brought to Corfu and surrendered to the Allies there. On the afternoon of Sunday, November 3rd, the Prime Minister, Clemenceau, Orlando, Hymans, House and I, with perhaps one or two more, were assembled at House's residence, discussing some detail of the German armistice terms.

November 3rd. . . . Just as we were breaking up Orlando received a telegram to say that the armistice with Austria had been signed. I shall not easily forget the scene of enthusiasm. All stood up and shook hands and the utmost cordiality and jubilation prevailed. I drove back from the Embassy to Versailles with the Prime Minister, Philip Kerr having been sent on with a press message to telephone to London about the Austrian armistice. The Prime Minister was curiously piano. He said that as a Celt he was superstitious about so much success. However, he determined to get back tomorrow night, so as to be able to read the Austrian terms of armistice in the House of Commons on Tuesday afternoon.

Yet for him it was a moment of supreme triumph.

THE LAST OF THE PROPS HAD FALLEN!

On the Western Front, day after day, resounding blows were being struck at the front gate of the German Empire. The French had begun the process in July. The British Expeditionary Force had dealt its first hammer stroke on August 8th. On August 17th came the second battle of Noyon, followed by the battles on the Somme between August 21st and September 3rd. On August 26th another front of attack was opened at Arras. On September 12th and 13th came the brilliant American affair at St. Mihiel, and on the same date Haig began the long-drawn out battles of the Hindenburg line. And so the campaign continued until the end, first one army then another taking up the sequence with an ever-increasing tale of prisoners, guns and war material. To those of us who had been concerned in the evolution of the tank, their success was especially gratifying.[1]

To the importance of tanks in the Allied successes must be added that of aircraft, which had played a decisive part in the victories in Palestine and Macedonia, and on the Western Front their operations were equally important. In addition to their co-operation with the Army, an Independent Air Force had been formed in France under Trenchard's

[1] *vide* Ludendorff's tribute to the tanks in II, p. 692; *vide* also Max of Baden, *Memoirs*, II, p. 3 *sq.*

command which had been conducting strategical bombing with great activity against a variety of targets in Western Germany; about 360 industrial targets were attacked during the last thirteen months of the war. Just before its end, on October 26th after difficult discussions between the French and British Governments, Trenchard was appointed as Commander-in-Chief of the Inter-Allied Independent Air Force.[1]

In spite of the many signs of the enemy's discomfiture, his continual defeats, the state of his man-power, the huge captures of prisoners and war material, and even his demand for an armistice, the Supreme Command of the Allies was not encouraged by its military advisers to believe that the war would necessarily end this year. On October 7th Lloyd George and Bonar Law, accompanied by Henry Wilson, Macready and other experts, conferred with Foch in order to point out our man-power difficulties. The Marshal, while admitting that the military problem of 1918 was solved, kept harping on the necessity for the maintenance of our divisions for a supreme effort in April 1919. As late as October 16th Henry Wilson held that there was nothing to justify the assumption that the present military situation warranted the Germans giving in; he thought it possible that the enemy might be able to winter on a line from behind the Scheldt to Valenciennes on the uplands as far as the Aire. On October 17th Ludendorff reported:[2]

I regard a break-through as possible, but not probable. If you ask me on my conscience I can only answer that I do not expect it.

Again, on October 25th, Haig advised that the German Army was by no means broken. Whenever they were attacked, they hit back and inflicted heavy casualties. They showed none of the symptoms of a disorganized army. Their retirement was effected in good order and conducted with the greatest skill. Although in the earlier fighting we had made great captures of guns, we were now only picking up a few here and there, mostly damaged by our own artillery. Haig considered that the German Army would retreat from their present line 250 miles long to one of 155 miles and that nothing the Allies could do would prevent it. On the shorter line they would save seventy divisions and be able to

[1] On April 1st the long controversy between the supporters of separate Navy and Air Forces had been decided by the amalgamation of the Royal Flying Corps and the Royal Naval Air Service into the Royal Air Force, the Air Council having already been formed on January 2nd. All this had been done on the advice of Smuts to whom this long controversy had been remitted by Lloyd George in August 1917. I myself was frequently consulted by Smuts but can add little to the full account in the Official History.

[2] Ludendorff, II, p. 753.

hold on. At one of the meetings connected with the armistice discussions on November 1st, Lloyd George confronted Foch with Haig's views. Foch replied that Haig had taken the same line at a meeting of the Commanders-in-Chief of the British, French and American armies on the subject of armistice terms. He himself agreed that the German Army was neither disorganized nor beaten, that it would undoubtedly take up a new position and that the Allies could not prevent it. He held, however, that he could continue to drive the Germans back during the winter.

There is ample evidence in the enemy memoirs to show the importance attached to the fall of the 'props'. After describing the difficult situation of the German Army in the West, Ludendorff begins his exposition of the situation thus:[1]

The Austro-Hungarian line held in Italy. There were no indications of an Italian offensive. Thus matters stood when Bulgaria forced us to grave decisions.

He then goes on to describe the Allied advance and the collapse of the Bulgarians, who, according to his account, did not put up a fight, with the result that after September 15th their army was disintegrating; the German troops in Bulgaria were insufficient to stop the gap.

There were no illusions about the seriousness of the situation created by the collapse of Bulgaria.

Turkey, too, was now in great difficulties. Her Palestine front was broken beyond repair. Here, again, the German officers and men had done their duty, and had fought like heroes on the Jordan. They were, however, limited in numbers, and could only keep the Turkish Army together for a time.

Ludendorff then turns to the threat to Turkey from Syria, and to Constantinople from the Allied forces on the Maritza, where there were only very weak Turkish forces. A few German battalions, all that the limited shipping resources of the Black Sea would permit, were moved from the Ukraine to Constantinople, but that was not enough to restore the situation.

It was too late, however, to do anything decisive. Constantinople was bound to fall, and whether it fell in November or December made very little difference to the situation as a whole. Once the city fell, it was to be expected

---

[1] The quotations are all from Ludendorff, II, pp. 712 *sq.*; compare, in Max of Baden, II, pp. 3 *sq.*, the report made by a representative of the High Command to the German Government: 'The collapse of the Bulgarian front has upset all calculations.'

that the Entente Fleets would establish communication with Roumania
through the Black Sea, and send troops through Bulgaria to the Danube. We
could not hope to keep Roumania neutral. Sooner or later her hostile attitude
would become unmistakable. . . .

If the Bulgarian Army fell out altogether, then it would certainly be time
for Germany and Austria to send substantial forces to the Balkans.

In our situation it was vital to do everything to secure our position in the
Balkan Peninsula in order to prevent the Entente moving into Hungary and
making a flank attack on Germany and Austria.

He describes how he managed to scrape up about a dozen divisions
(including seven from the West) to send to Bulgaria but transport was
so bad that the concentration could not be completed before the middle
of October and before that Bulgaria had signed an armistice and with
an attack sure to come in Italy and uncertainty how the Austrian troops
there would fight:

The general military position could only become definitely worse;
whether it would move slowly or with terrifying speed could not be foreseen.
It was probable that it would be all over in a relatively short time, as actually
happened in the Balkans and on the Austro-Hungarian front in Italy.

In these circumstances I felt compelled to take on myself the heavy
responsibility of hastening the end of the war, and for the purpose to move
the Government to decisive action. . . .

Equally the letter from Hindenburg to the German Chancellor
quoted at the head of this chapter provides convincing vindication of
Lloyd George's plan of 'knocking away the props' in order to confront
Germany with the prospect of having to meet an advance from every
side. It is clear that Ludendorff was not over-anxious about the
Western Front. He did not expect a break-through. He was even taking
the risk of sending away reinforcements from that front to the Balkans.
What got him down, what brought him to the point of insistence on
his Government's making terms, was the impossibility of securing the
eastern and southern approaches to Germany after the collapse of
Bulgaria and Turkey (whose fall would release a large Allied army) and
the prospective collapse of Austria, in other words, 'the fall of the
props'. That Ludendorff's apprehensions were in no way exaggerated
is proved by what happened on November 4th in Paris. On that morning the heads of the various delegations met at House's residence at
11 a.m. to discuss the future strategy of the Allies. Foch unfolded a vast
scheme for the utilization of the Italian Army, reinforced by British

EE*

and French troops and eventually from the armies of the Balkans and Palestine for an invasion of Germany through Bavaria. The production of this plan of the Allied General-in-Chief was the climax of the triumph of Lloyd George's theories. Some such plan had been the ultimate aim of his policy from first to last. He had never under-estimated the importance of the Western Front, but he had never believed that Germany could be conquered on that front alone. It was first necessary to clear a flank on which to develop a turning move-ment, and the whole of his grand strategy for 'knocking away the props' was conceived with this object. As events turned out the mere threat, as soon as its feasibility became clear, was sufficient to bring Germany to her knees.

CHAPTER LXXXII

THE GERMAN ARMISTICE

'Four lagging winters and four wanton springs end in a
word.'
(SHAKESPEARE, *Richard II*, Act i, sc. 3.)

WITHIN the compass of a history of the Supreme Command it
is not possible to tell the whole story of the coming of peace and
the armistice negotiations.[1] All that is attempted here is to give
a glimpse of some of the aspects that came under my immediate
view.

I have already told how about 5 p.m. on October 5th the first news
that the Central Powers had asked for an armistice had been sprung by
Clemenceau on a small conference at the Villa Romaine. My diary contains no information to prompt my memory on how the news was
received. My recollection is that all stood up and that we joined hands
and circled round the room; that Henry Wilson began to chaff Foch
about a pair of new bright yellow gaiters he was wearing which did not
match his boots, asking him if he was preparing for a long, long war
and, generally, that for a few minutes hilarity prevailed after which we
returned to business.

Next day (Sunday, October 6th) it was decided that work should be
started on the German armistice terms in case anything came of it. The
position was rather an awkward one for the Allies. The German appeal
had been addressed not to them but direct to President Wilson and
forwarded through the Swiss Government. It urged him to invite the
belligerents to enter into peace negotiations on the basis of the fourteen
points and to conclude an armistice at once. The terms of the German
Note had been published, but day followed day and no request for the
views of the Allied statesmen assembled in Paris was received from the
President. Woodrow Wilson was rather an inscrutable person, inclined
to keep his own counsel. Situated as he was, far from the scene of
action, without any intimate contact with the armies, no one could tell
how he would react to the German overture which so vitally concerned
us all; as late as 3 p.m. on October 8th, when the conference met, there
was still no reply from him.

[1] In his memoirs Lloyd George devotes a hundred pages to them and House's editor more
than 150.

October 8th. . . . . At 3 p.m. the conference reassembled, but did little business, as we are still waiting for a communication from President Wilson about the Central Powers' request for an armistice. We had before us the views of Foch as well as of the Military Representatives at Versailles. They were both in my opinion much too extreme, as they involved complete disarmament and many most humiliating conditions such as surrender of several fortresses, of bridgeheads across the Rhine, etc. The general view was that we were not in a position to impose such severe conditions, and the question was adjourned for further consideration.

Next day (October 9th) we became acquainted with the terms of the note which the President had despatched on the previous day to Germany without consulting the Allies. In this note before replying to the German appeal he asked for certain explanations. He wished to know whether the German Government accepted the fourteen points and the terms laid down by the President in subsequent addresses, and whether their 'object in entering into discussions would be only to agree upon the practical details of their application'. He 'would not feel at liberty to propose a cessation of arms to the Governments with which the Government of the United States is associated against the Central Powers so long as the armies of those Powers are upon their soil. The good faith of any discussion would manifestly depend upon the consent of the Central Powers immediately to withdraw their forces everywhere from invaded territory.' The President concluded by asking 'whether the Imperial Chancellor is speaking merely for the constituted authorities of the Empire who have so far conducted the war. He deems the answer to those questions vital from every point of view.'

October 9th (Versailles and Paris). . . . After lunch the Prime Minister, Bonar Law, Cecil and I had a conference on what action should be taken on Wilson's reply to the enemy's application for an armistice. Lloyd George is irritated with Wilson for replying without consulting us. Not only because, in asking if the Germans accept his fourteen points, he almost seems to assume that we do accept them (although as a matter of fact we totally reject the doctrine of freedom of the seas), but still more owing to the statement that withdrawal from the occupied territories is an indispensable condition of an armistice. Lloyd George agrees it is an indispensable condition, but, of course, many other conditions are indispensable and he fears that the Huns will try to assume that it is the only condition, and, when we insist on other conditions, will say that we intervened and upset a promising negotiation for peace. We then motored up to Paris to the Quai d'Orsay. I shared a car with Cecil and drafted a message to be sent by the Allies to Wilson. Writing in a train, as I am doing at this moment, is child's play to drafting a despatch in a

motor car travelling fast over bumpy roads. The conference was in great spirits on the receipt of news of Haig's great victory and break-through between Cambrai and St. Quentin. Midway, the conference adjourned for the three Foreign Ministers to draft a secret and confidential despatch to Washington, and reassembled at 6 p.m. I had to stay to help the three Foreign Ministers, and so was hard at work from 3 p.m. to 7 p.m. continuously. After dinner at Versailles I had to dictate the Minutes, which took a couple of hours. Nevertheless the marvellous Sylvester got them typed that night.

The answer to the President was dominated mainly by the views of Foch and the Military Representatives. Opinion had considerably hardened since the preliminary discussion on October 8th. It was assumed that the President had been informed by Bliss of the general tenor of these views, which had at first sight seemed rather stiff, and that he probably supposed that his note was in accordance with them. Nevertheless it was felt in all the circumstances to be essential to notify the present views of the three Allies to him. In the Note sent on the evening of October 9th, therefore, the President was informed that the conditions for an armistice suggested in his note to the enemy Powers were insufficient, since they would not prevent the enemy from taking advantage of an armistice, which did not result in peace, to improve their military position. They would be able to withdraw from their present critical positions, save their war material, re-form their units, shorten their front, and form up on new positions, which they would have time to fortify.[1] The conditions of an armistice, it was urged, ought to be fixed only after consultation between the military experts who were actually at work on the subject.

Political subjects were not touched on in this communication, but a separate message was sent pointing out that the time had come when important decisions would have to be taken at very short notice, and the President was asked to send an American representative enjoying the full confidence of his Government to Europe to confer with the Associated Governments; in response to this request the President sent House. No steps were taken at this time to complete in detail the armistice conditions, as Foch insisted that they would vary according to the circumstances of the moment.

The German Government's reply to the President's note of October

---

[1] German sources amply confirm the wisdom of this attitude, e.g. Max of Baden (II, p. 9) talks of Ludendorff being 'possessed by a conviction that the enemy would grant the respite he asked for; then he hoped to be able to fight on again and avert the worst'.

8th was sent on the 12th. They accepted the three conditions prescribed by the President, but asked for a mixed commission to negotiate the process of evacuation. This was exactly the sort of reply that we had feared, namely, one calculated to gain as much time as possible for the renovation of the German Army. Lloyd George took prompt action.

October 13th (Sunday). On my way home from church I was met by Adeline with a message that the Prime Minister wanted me at Danny, so I started off immediately after lunch, arriving about 2.30. I found there, already in conference over their cigars, the Prime Minister, Bonar Law, Balfour, Churchill, Reading, First Sea Lord, c.i.g.s., with Philip Kerr. We conferred for three hours on the subject of the German acceptance of Wilson's conditions. The Germans have assumed, as we expected they would, that in his message the President intended the evacuation of occupied territories to be the sole condition of an armistice. After much . . . palaver it was decided to ask the President to disillusion the Germans even before he consults us about the conditions of an armistice. Another difficult point is that the fourteen points are by no means clear; that we do not accept them all, e.g. 'Freedom of the Seas', and that they are by no means comprehensive, omitting as they do all reference to the sea. A telegram giving him a hint of this was also sent. . . .

President Wilson's next communication to the Germans was a very stiff one. Although sent once more without prior consultation with the Allies it showed that the communication drafted at Danny had not been overlooked. He laid down that 'it must be clearly understood that the process of evacuation and the conditions of armistice are matters which must be left to the judgment and advice of the military advisers of the United States Government and Allied Governments, and the President feels it his duty to say that no arrangement can be accepted by the United States Government which does not provide absolutely satisfactory safeguards and guarantees of the maintenance of the present military supremacy of the armies of the United States and the Allies in the field. He feels confident that he can safely assume this will also be the judgment and decision of the Allied Governments'. The President also harped at some length on the impossibility of making peace with a Power that continued submarine warfare against merchant ships, and whose armies were guilty of wanton destruction in their retirement. The note also contained a diatribe against the form of the German Government as one that can 'separately, secretly, and of its own choice disturb the peace of the world'.

This stiff note speedily brought the German Government to terms,

and on October 20th they accepted all the President's conditions. The terms of the armistice were to be left to the military advisers of the Allied and Associated Powers; German U-boats were to be ordered to spare passenger liners; the armies in retreat were to respect private property; arbitrary power was to be abolished in Germany and the Government was to be freed from military influence. It was only on October 23rd that the President communicated officially to the Allies his correspondence with Germany, which was completed by a final telegram to Germany summarizing the terms he was about to communicate to the Allies; making clear that the only armistice he would accept was one which 'would leave the Allied and Associated Powers in a position to enforce the arrangements made, and to make the renewal of hostilities on the part of Germany impossible'. It concluded with a lecture on the monarchical régime of Germany, the retention of which would compel the United States to demand 'not peace negotiations but surrender'. That was the nearest point reached to 'unconditional surrender' in the armistice negotiations.

Such was the position when on October 29th the Allied Governments met again in Paris, where they were joined by House. President Wilson up to this point had not, in theory at any rate, committed the Allies at all. His negotiations with the enemy had been virtually bilateral. On the question of the military conditions of an armistice the position was entirely satisfactory, for the President had cleverly manœuvred the enemy into a position where they had to accept practically whatever the Allied and Associated naval and military advisers should prescribe. On the political side, however, the position was less satisfactory. The President had laid down certain bases for the eventual Peace Treaty which he himself would be prepared to accept and to propose to the Allies if they were accepted by the enemy. This the enemy had done, and the President's next step had been to propose them formally to the Allies. However much the latter might appear free in form, in fact it would have been very difficult for them to reject these preliminaries of peace even if they wished to do so, and the discussions at Paris were largely dominated by this consideration.

The Paris Conference had been preceded by the usual discussions at the War Cabinet, and Lloyd George left London with instructions to get 'a good peace' if he could, rather than to continue the war with the object of punishing Germany. Freedom of the seas was to be repudiated before the Peace Conference.

We had not been long in Paris before the latter point arose, the only

one in the fourteen points which was really embarrassing to the British Government. It read as follows:

Absolute freedom of navigation upon the seas, outside territorial waters alike in peace and war, except as the seas may be closed in whole or in part by international action, for the enforcement of international covenants.

On the face of it this formula appeared to mean that, if we ever became involved in war again, we should not be able to apply a blockade or exert effective economic pressure on our enemy unless we could persuade the nations that the war was being fought for the enforcement of international covenants. It is true that the project of a League of Nations also was included in the fourteen points. But at the time of the armistice discussions no one could foretell what shape it was to take, or whether it would ever become so important a factor in world politics as to exclude all possibility of wars except for the enforcement of international covenants. Personally I was profoundly sceptical. Moreover, the moment at which we were asked to subscribe to this rule was precisely the one at which the blockade had come to its own.

In a Memorandum[1] on the Freedom of the Seas which at his request I had submitted to Asquith on June 23, 1915, I had written that the effect of the blockade is:

. . . cumulative and the process inevitably slow. It may be that years must elapse before its effect is decisive. But when the psychological moment arrives and the cumulative effects reach their maximum and are perhaps combined with crushing defeats of the enemy, the results may be not merely material, but decisive.

The psychological moment had now arrived. The cumulative effects of the blockade had reached their maximum, and their effect had become one of the decisive factors in the victory of the Allied and Associated Powers. In combination with 'crushing defeats of the enemy' the blockade had overwhelmed the Central Powers with depression and despair. Its hardships had broken the enemy's home front. Even the soldiers were affected in spite of the iron discipline of the German system.

Ample as was our information on all these points, it has since been more than confirmed by German writers:

The misery in the towns about the middle of October was indescribable. No coal, no adequate clothing, a ceaseless hunger. The influenza epidemic

---

[1] *vide supra*, p. 375.

was striding over Europe. In Berlin alone on October 15th its victims numbered 1,722.

Ludendorff, at the meeting of the German War Cabinet on October 17th, is recorded in the published Minutes as follows:

The division which had broken down on August 8th had had influenza, and had no potatoes. The morale of the drafts which came from home was not good either. The transports arrived in a condition which no longer fulfilled the requirements of discipline and order.

Scheidemann is recorded as reporting:

There is a question of potatoes. We have no more meat. Potatoes cannot be delivered, because we have 4,000 trucks a day too few. Fat is absolutely unobtainable. The want is so great that it is to me just a riddle what North Berlin and what East Berlin live on. Until this riddle is solved, any improvement of morale is out of the question. . . .[1]

Economic pressure at this moment had thus become, if not 'the decisive factor', at least 'one of the decisive factors' in the victory of the Allied and Associated Powers. And it was at this very moment that we were asked to break this weapon in half and to throw away the pieces for all time. No wonder that Lloyd George was unwilling to make such a sacrifice, or that the War Cabinet had given him a decisive instruction not to do so.

Lloyd George, however, with his usual prescience, had fortified himself with a knowledge that enabled him to withstand the heavy pressure to which he was about to be subjected. Eric Geddes had just paid a visit to the United States, where he had discussed with President Wilson this very matter. He had reported to the Prime Minister that the President was very vague on the subject and his views unformed. It was known, too, to some of us that this theory was a pet fad of House, which he had been pressing in season and out of season ever since the early stages of the war. In Paris he at once started propaganda on the subject. Certain British officials in close touch with him warned us that the matter was most serious and that the second of the fourteen points was one to which we must agree, or else risk of the United States making a separate peace. Lloyd George was quite unmoved. Convinced that this was more House's point than the President's, he steeled himself to call the Colonel's bluff which he did in a masterly and effective manner.[2]

[1] All these quotations come from Max of Baden (II, pp. 92, 111, 117).
[2] Cf. House, IV, p. 165 sq.

The clash came first on the afternoon of October 29th at the Quai d'Orsay, where Lloyd George, Balfour, Clemenceau, Pichon, Sonnino and House with myself as secretary, were assembled for a preliminary discussion on the fourteen points. As soon as the second point was reached Lloyd George made clear that in no conditions could he accept it. The suggestion was to hand over power to the League of Nations, but, if Britain were fighting for her life no League of Nations could prevent her from enforcing a blockade. Before he could discuss the point he must see the League thoroughly established and proved. After this weapon had been used with so much success by the Allied fleets, including that of the United States, to hand it over to a League not yet in existence would be to give up a most powerful weapon. To this House replied that neutrals had only stood the blockade because Germany had perpetrated so many atrocities. In some future war, when perhaps similar atrocities had not been committed, the neutrals would not stand it. Clemenceau interjected caustically that it was not the business of the Allies to say whether belligerents in a future war would behave well or badly. His general line was that war would not be war if there were freedom of the seas. Sonnino was equally caustic. Nations, like animals, he maintained, had different weapons. One animal had teeth, another tusks, a third claws. So it was with nations. The proper answer to President Wilson was that we could not see our way out on this question and should deal only with the armistice.

Under this overwhelming fire of opposition, barbed as it was with irony, House, never a good debater and accustomed to work behind the scenes rather than on the stage, was rapidly losing his self-control. At this point he played his big bluff. It was coming to this, he said, that all the negotiations with Germany and Austria up to this point would have to be cleaned off the slate. The question would then arise whether America would have to take up these questions direct with Germany and Austria. Clemenceau, old realist as he was, then put the direct question whether he meant a separate peace between America and the enemy. House said it might come to that. It would depend on whether the United States could agree to the conditions of its associates. This was the moment for which Lloyd George had been waiting. The expected bluff had been uttered. The moment had come for the counter-stroke. It was, he said, impossible for the British Government to agree. If the United States were to make a separate peace, we should greatly regret it, but nevertheless should be prepared to go on fighting. (Clemenceau here interjected 'Yes'.) We could not, Lloyd George

continued, give up the power which had enabled the American troops to be brought to Europe. That was a thing we were prepared to fight through. Britain was not really a military nation. Her main defence was her Fleet. To give up the right to use her Fleet was a thing to which no one in England would consent. Eventually it was decided that the British, French and Italian Governments should get together and formulate their exceptions to the fourteen points.

October 29th. . . . Then back to Versailles to dictate my notes of the meeting, which I completed before dinner. Quiet dinner with Lloyd George, Milner and Amery. . . . I forgot to mention that on our way back we ran into an aeroplane chassis being towed by a motor lorry at St. Cloud in the little place beyond the bridge. We badly smashed the aeroplane and broke our lamps and tyres and were a little shaken, but no one was hurt. The Prime Minister took it very calmly and showed no signs of being shaken. To bed early.

October 30th. Another glorious day and another walk in the woods early. At 11 a.m. I motored with the Prime Minister and Kerr to the French War Office, where he had a meeting with Clemenceau and House. . . . These three in twenty minutes agreed to our comments on the fourteen points.

During the morning Lloyd George prepared the draft of a note to President Wilson embodying these decisions, and this was accepted at another meeting held at the Quai d'Orsay that afternoon. Subject to two qualifications, the fourteen points were accepted by the Allied Governments as the basis of peace negotiations. The first reservation, which dealt with freedom of the seas, stated that the term 'is open to various interpretations, some of which they (the Allies) could not accept. They must therefore reserve to themselves complete freedom on the subject when they enter the Peace Conference.' It should be noted that France and Italy associated themselves with this point of view. The second reservation provided that compensation must be paid by Germany for all damage caused to the civilian population of the Allies and their property by land, by sea and in the air. The note transmitting these decisions was sent on November 1st.

The subject of freedom of the seas came up once more on Sunday, November 3rd, when President Wilson's reply was available. On that afternoon[1] Lloyd George joined Clemenceau, Orlando, and Hymans at House's residence in the Rue de l'Université. As we had anticipated, the Allied reply had not produced the effect on President Wilson that House had suggested as the reply shows:

[1] *vide supra*, p. 848.

The President says that he freely and sympathetically recognizes the necessities of the British, and their strong position with regard to the seas both at home and throughout the Empire. Freedom of the seas, he realizes, is a question upon which there should be the freest discussion and the most liberal exchange of views. The President is not sure, however, that the Allies have definitely accepted the principle of freedom of the seas; and that they are reserving only the limitations and free discussion of the subject.

The President insists that the terms 1, 2, 3 and 4 are essentially American terms in the programme and he cannot recede from them. The question of the freedom of the seas need not be discussed with the German Government, provided we have agreed amongst ourselves beforehand.

Blockade is one of the questions which has been altered by the developments in this war, and the law governing it will certainly have to be altered. There is no danger, however, that it will be abolished.

Here there was no threat of a separate peace, but an admission of the importance of the question to ourselves, a realization that the freest discussion was needed, accompanied by a natural insistence that the subject could not be dropped. After Lloyd George had emphasized once more the great importance of blockade to all the Allied and Associated Powers and had pointed out that the Austrian nation had surrendered to it before their army was defeated, House made a final appeal—as he was bound to do in view of the above message—for acceptance of the principle of freedom of the seas. This Lloyd George, in accordance with his instructions from the War Cabinet, categorically declined. The principle of freedom of the seas, he pointed out, had come to be associated with the abandonment of blockade. If he were to accept it, it would only mean that in a week's time a new Prime Minister would be here who would say that he could not accept the principle. The British people would not look at it. On this point the nation was absolutely solid. Consequently it was no use for him to say he could accept, when he knew he was not speaking for the British nation. After some further conversation, however, he consented to express willingness to discuss the freedom of the seas in the light of the new conditions that had arisen in the course of the present war. After adjourning the matter to enable him to discuss it with Balfour, he ended the controversy by sending House the following letter (dated November 3rd):

I write to confirm the statement I made in the course of our talk this afternoon at your house, when I told you that 'we were quite willing to discuss the freedom of the seas in the light of the new conditions which have arisen in the course of the present war'. In our judgment this most important

subject can only be dealt with satisfactorily through the freest debate and the most liberal exchange of views.

I send this letter after having had an opportunity of talking the matter over with the Foreign Secretary, who quite agrees.

Never in my long association with Lloyd George did I see him rise to greater heights, nor express the national sentiments with greater vigour, dignity and authority than in those quiet conversations at the Quai d'Orsay and the Rue de l'Université.

The remainder of the armistice discussions need not detain us. Between October 28th, when we arrived in Versailles, and November 4th when Lloyd George and I left for London, there were no fewer than ten recorded meetings attended by the heads of Governments and House, as well as many meetings of a less formal character. The machinery of the Supreme War Council was working throughout at the highest pressure. The naval, military and air conditions of the armistice were being dealt with by the Supreme War Council, assisted by its subordinate bodies, the Permanent Military Representatives and the Allied Naval Council, which were in a state of continuous activity. The Foreign Ministers of the Allies were in constant communication with one another. But all matters were under the overall supervision of the heads of Governments—Clemenceau, Lloyd George and Orlando —with whom House was associated.

When Lloyd George left Paris the work was substantially finished. The agreed bases of peace had been transmitted to President Wilson and by him to the German Government. The armistice with Austria had been signed. The technical terms of the armistice with Germany had been approved for communication to the enemy as soon as the technical formalities had been concluded. The general lines of the military policy to be adopted if Germany should at the last moment reject the terms had been blocked in.

CHAPTER LXXXIII

THE JOURNEY HOME

'What of my dross thou findest there, be bold
To throw away; but yet preserve the gold.
What if my gold be wrapped up in ore?
None throws away the apple for the core.
But if thou shalt cast all away as vain,
I know not but 'twill make me dream again.'
(BUNYAN, *Pilgrim's Progress*, conclusion to Part I.)

November 4th. . . . Had to rush off in the middle of lunch at the Embassy to the train, as we are off this afternoon leaving Balfour, Milner and Geddes to represent Britain at the final meeting of the Supreme War Council this afternoon. I write in the train *en route* to Boulogne. Our party—the Prime Minister, Reading, Amery, Kerr, Sylvester and self. A car meets me at Folkestone 9 p.m. to take me home. It has been an amazing week. Turkey and Bulgaria and Austria are out of the war. Germany is isolated and suing for peace. British prestige is higher than it has ever been before. So is Lloyd George's. . . .

Later—Fearful passage in the destroyer *Termagant*. So rough at Dover that we could not go alongside the wall, and had to land in a picket boat. This was no joke for Lloyd George, getting from the destroyer to the picket boat in black darkness and a heavy sea, while even landing was difficult. It took an hour and a half to get ourselves and baggage ashore. No special train and only motors. Lloyd George motored to Sandwich. I motored home, arriving 2.30 a.m., having one puncture and one minor breakdown in a Rolls Royce car driven by Asquith's former chauffeur.

THROUGHOUT that long and lonely night drive without headlights, for we were still under war conditions, I pondered over the events of the last four years. I saw in my mind a panorama of all that long sequence—the weary years of failure and defeat; the many frustrated hopes; the dramatic change in August 1918; the delirium of victory. What had brought it about? What nation and what individual had made the greatest contribution? What were the fundamental causes? Who was the man who had won the war?

I saw in retrospect many mistakes. That was inevitable after a century of freedom from unlimited war. Our preparations had not been on a scale commensurate with the vast territories, trade and other interests which we had to defend nor in any way sufficient for the universal

cataclysm that had developed. We had only been able at the outset of the war to throw up a screen that was barely sufficient to cover the slow process of mobilizing our resources. I recalled, however, that our policy had been to avert that cataclysm, a policy of peace. It followed logically that our military policy must be defensive in character, non-aggressive in conception. I felt grateful that our preparations had been sufficient, although only barely sufficient for their purpose. I recalled that our territory, with very minor exceptions, had remained inviolate; that our trade under divine protection had not suffered any severe losses until, long after the outbreak of war, the unforeseen submarine campaign had developed to formidable dimensions. And even then we had suffered almost as much from the diversion of shipping for the military effort of our Allies and ourselves, from the drain on our man-power and its effect on shipbuilding and the rate of turning round ships in our ports, as from enemy action. We were at fault, of course, in not preparing a plan for the mobilization of our man-power and for the expansion of war industry. But even in this respect we were in company with land Powers with great conscript armies, which had also neglected this part of their war preparation. The worst fault I found in our preparation or lack of preparation was the adoption of rules of naval warfare that could not possibly stand the test of war conditions; they could have no effect in maintaining peace, since they bore with especial severity on the efficacy of sea-power, on which we, the Power with the greatest influence for peace, depended, and the Declaration of Paris and the Declaration of London, I recalled, had hampered our exercise of sea-power for half the war.

Next my thoughts turned to the early stages of the war. Given the long peace that had preceded the war, the essentially peaceful, and in some cases pacifist, temperament of nearly all our political leaders, the bewildering and kaleidoscopic novelty of events, the gigantic scale of the conflict, the tremendous problems that had to be solved often on the spur of the moment, the complexity of the administrative difficulties confronting us, the lack of human experience in the conditions of modern warfare, the scale of the casualties, and the incredible expenditure of ammunition compared with that of any previous war—given all this, it seemed to me that, in spite of many mistakes, our Supreme Command had done well. We owed a good deal in those early days to the courage and inspiration of Winston Churchill, who, undaunted by difficulties and losses, set an infectious example to those of his colleagues who had given less thought than he, if indeed any thought

at all, to war problems. He may have been rash at times, but he was a tower of strength and I hope his fellow-countrymen will never forget it, in spite of the tremendous addition he has since made to his claims to an outstanding place in history.

Waking from a doze owing to the puncture of a tyre my mind turned to the first two years when the main burden of the war had fallen upon Asquith's broad shoulders. That had been a period of improvisation. He had sown. Others had fertilized and had eventually reaped. But I could never forget that it was Asquith who had brought the nation to face the rigours of war, and by the dauntless courage and unfailing and far-sighted confidence of his public pronouncements during the dark days had done much to sustain the spirit and confidence of the nation and the Empire. It was Asquith who, on Kitchener's advice, had taken the supreme decision to improvise an army on the continental scale. It was under his leadership that Lloyd George had founded and brought to fruition the Ministry of Munitions, one of the principal factors in winning the war. It was under his leadership too that Kitchener had carried out that amazing feat of recruitment by voluntary means, which had produced more troops and better troops than were ever raised by compulsion. Yet when the voluntary system failed to produce the numbers required, it was Asquith who, however reluctantly, had brought himself to introduce compulsion. I recalled also that Asquith had stood firm, when some of his colleagues were weakening, before House's blandishments and subtle arguments in the matter of the freedom of the seas, which, if adopted, must have lengthened and perhaps have lost us the war. During those anxious years Asquith, like everyone else, was groping for the proper system of exercising the Supreme Command, always advancing, if somewhat slowly. Each of his devices was an improvement on its predecessor, the War Council, the Dardanelles Committee (even if wrong in its conception), and finally the War Committee. Similarly in the inter-Allied field he had done all he could to extend the system of conference by which our relations with our Allies became steadily closer. If he did not complete the process in either field it was due largely to circumstances over which he had no control, such as the lack of unity in a Cabinet that was essentially a Coalition, rather than a National, Government. Even though he had failed to stay the course to the end, I felt that Asquith had earned a very high place in the history of our war-time Prime Ministers.

Then as my Rolls Royce sped through the fields and woods to a

more familiar countryside my thoughts turned to the last two years and memory lit up first one incident and then another until, after midnight, as the side lights flickered on mists rising at the roadside, I seemed to see the familiar figure of Lloyd George, towering like a giant above every other figure in the war. I recalled that he had inherited a good foundation on which to build—an overwhelmingly powerful Navy, carefully conserved so as to ensure a great preponderance of strength over the German High Sea Fleet: an Army already built up to the continental scale: an organization of his own creation for the supply of munitions of war on an ever-increasing scale: a naval staff which, if it sometimes seemed to lack imagination, had always refused willingly to dissipate our naval strength on 'side shows': a General Staff of the Army which, although directed by a man more conspicuous for character than imagination, included men with brains and inspiration: first-rate intelligence departments for the Navy and Army: and Government Departments staffed by the finest Civil Service in the world, reinforced by some of the best brains of the nation: and a central Secretariat, which did not lack experience. In the Imperial field no great progress had been made in Asquith's time in the direction of close co-ordination of Governments, but all parts of the Empire had sent their best to co-operate with the British forces in one or other theatre of war. In the inter-Allied field, even before Lloyd George became Prime Minister, the habit of conference was already rapidly developing to supplement the older and slower methods of diplomacy. He had therefore inherited all the elements of a great National, Imperial and inter-Allied administrative machine. All that was required was decision and drive and imagination to weld it together. I saw that it was just those qualities that Lloyd George had brought to the task. He had, of course, had his difficulties with some of his military advisers. But in Haig and Robertson he had had to deal with men who were antipathetic to him. Well grounded in principle, with their minds soaked in military tradition, try as they would they could not adapt themselves to the versatile and nimble-minded Welshman, nor he to them. Eventually therefore Robertson had to go. Lloyd George was in political danger from this situation more than once, at the time of the Nivelle affair for instance, and of the Flanders offensive. Haig was sometimes in danger, but the Prime Minister could not discover a Commander-in-Chief who would be easier for him to work with and at the same time equally reliable. These temperamental differences, however, sank into insignificance in comparison with Lloyd George's achievements. Perhaps the greatest

work he accomplished was in the sphere of organization. Co-ordination was accomplished in one great field of war effort after another, first, in that of home administration by the creation of the War Cabinet and its Secretariat; then in that of the Empire by calling into existence the Imperial War Cabinet; and finally in the vast arena of inter-Allied war effort by the establishment of the Supreme War Council. In neither case did he act on a mere impulse or 'brainwave'. In all these matters he had matured his plans long before. Day and night, month in, month out he was looking ahead and planning his schemes of organization. But when the psychological moment came he invariably acted with lightning rapidity. The War Cabinet was in operation all day on December 9, 1916, although he had only begun to form his new Government on the night of the 7th. The Imperial War Cabinet was summoned within a week or two of his coming into office, before the new machinery of Government had had time to settle down. The opportunity of the Italian disaster was seized upon for the visit to Rapallo and for the decision, which he insisted on in the teeth of opposition from his own principal military adviser, to establish the Supreme War Council in accordance with long matured and carefully considered plans. So it was with the unified command. Undeterred by the Nivelle failure he never abandoned his intention to bring about this great reform. I have a vivid recollection of being summoned out of the Cabinet room at Downing Street, where an international conference was in progress, to interpret for Lloyd George and Foch over a cup of tea. After comparing notes with the French General over the desirability of a unified command, and after establishing complete agreement, the Prime Minister concluded by affirming his intention to bring it about when the opportunity offered and added 'and I know the man for the job', looking hard at Foch. It fell to Milner, whose mind ran with his chief's on the subject, to seize the psychological moment at Doullens, but Lloyd George followed up the original step by a work of extension and consolidation at Beauvais and Abbeville. A noteworthy feature of many of his greatest innovations was the way in which he would seize the opportunity of some terrible disaster to bring his plans to fruition. This was true of the three cases mentioned. It was true of the foundation of the Ministry of Munitions, when he flung himself into the breach at the moment of crisis, and equally true of the adoption of the convoy system. In the latter case he took advantage of the moment when shipping losses had reached their maximum to put the Admiralty into a position where they were forced themselves to propose a reform which up to that time they

had opposed. His political courage had always been tremendous and inspired by the public interest.

Of course no man could have accomplished all that Lloyd George did single-handed. Part of his genius lay in his choice of men. He determined from the first that his Government should be a true National Government, not a coalition like that from which Asquith had suffered before him. Of course it contained a political element—Bonar Law, Balfour, Curzon, Robert Cecil, Walter Long, Austen Chamberlain, Arthur Henderson and George Barnes, to mention only a few. But several of his key men were without any political following to speak of and some of them were at the time of their appointment almost unknown to the country as a whole—the brothers Geddes, Joseph Maclay, H. A. L. Fisher and Robert Horne. Moreover, he did not by any means limit his consultations to the official circle. Every moment of the day that was not devoted to the War Cabinet, the Imperial War Cabinet, some international negotiation or some other of the multifarious duties of a Prime Minister, including, of course, his Parliamentary duties and speeches in the country, was occupied by interviews with men and women of high or low degree, who, he thought, could give him useful information, or stimulate his mind. Breakfast, lunch, tea and dinner were almost entirely given up to this process of increasing his stock of knowledge and ideas. When he left London for the country, whether at his home at Walton Heath or during his rare visits to his beloved Criccieth, there was a constant stream of motor cars or of travellers by train and an endless succession of more or less informal conferences. Whenever I had the good fortune to accompany him on these excursions, which was usually the case, my time was as fully occupied with taking and writing up notes as though I had been in the office of the War Cabinet at 2 Whitehall Gardens—with the difference that I lacked the facilities of a Government office and I must often have failed but for my indefatigable stenographer, Sylvester, whose energy was inexhaustible. And it was just the same—only more so—when we visited Paris, Versailles, or Rome, or St. Jean de Maurienne, or Rapallo, or Calais, or Beauvais, or Abbeville, or Boulogne or any other foreign place for purposes of inter-Allied business. There was a constant stream of callers, an endless succession of conferences and visits, most of which required some kind of official or semi-official record. Here also the visitors were by no means confined to the official circle but would include politicians in Opposition, well-informed journalists of many nationalities and anyone whose information

or ideas might be useful. The fact that he was never content to rely entirely on the ideas of his own fertile mind and of his immediate entourage adds lustre to Lloyd George's extraordinary achievements.

As I neared my home on that night of storm and drenching rain I perceived clearly how the war had been won and by whom. Belgium, by holding for a short time at Liège, had made an invaluable contribution when hours counted. Russia, by her altruistic diversion in East Prussia, had saved France from disaster and made possible the miracle of the Marne. France for the first half of the war had borne the brunt of the assaults on the Western Front, while Great Britain and the Dominions were improvising their military effort. Serbia had played a part out of proportion to her resources. Italy had intervened at a moment when her aid was invaluable to the Allied cause. Japan, Roumania, Greece and Portugal had made their contribution. The United States did not come into the war until April 6, 1917, and were very slow starters, being totally unprepared for war. Nevertheless they worked with a will and were good comrades. The very fact of their intervention gave the Allies a moral uplift of immeasurable value, and in the last few months of the war their material contribution, both actual and prospective, was sufficient to place the ultimate result beyond all doubt. To me, however, it seemed that night as it seems today, that the British Empire had borne the heat and the burden of the day. Throughout the war the British Navy had been the main factor in keeping open the seas to the Allies, and in denying them to the enemy. This was the indispensable foundation of victory. It had secured the whole of the territories of the Allies at home and abroad against seaborne attack other than sporadic raids by insignificant forces. It had enabled them to draw supplies of every sort and kind from all parts of the world. At the same time it had deprived the enemy from all overseas resources, except what they could manage to smuggle in through neutral countries. This had compelled them to 'live on their own fat' until it was all consumed, and thereafter to plunge recklessly into foreign adventures in order to plunder their neighbours, ever increasing their military commitments and the numbers of troops required to hold down the subject populations and adding to the hatred and mistrust already created throughout the world by their original unprovoked but premeditated aggression. Eventually, however, these ill-gotten gains had failed to meet their needs and they had succumbed. As Tirpitz put it some years later—'In the last war England defeated us first of all

economically. . . .'[1] Perhaps that was the British Empire's most important contribution to the victory of the Allies.

Second to the Royal Navy came the Mercantile Marine which carried across the seas the greater part of the armies of ourselves and our Allies, including those of the United States of America, as well as of their supplies, to the various theatres of war, undaunted by the terrifying dangers from submarine, torpedo, mine and surface craft.

The contribution of the improvised land armies of the Empire was also of decisive importance. At first they were little more than a token force, an earnest of what was to come. During the last year or two, however, even on the Western Front they were taking the lion's share of fighting activity, e.g. in Flanders in 1917, in 1918 first in defence on the Somme and afterwards in attack on all sections of their front. Again and again they were tried to the limit of human endurance, if not beyond, but in the end the unique characteristics of the British soldier carried us through to victory.

It was British ingenuity that contributed the most important factor on land—the tank. It was the forces of Great Britain, the Dominions and India that deprived the Germans of all their colonies in succession, conquered Turkey and bore a large share of the operations in the Balkans. The Royal Air Force also had throughout the war made an ever-increasing contribution to the common cause, which reached its zenith in 1918 after the creation of the Air Ministry and the Independent Air Force under Trenchard. Although in these early days it could not attain the transcendent heights of the Second World War, its achievements in the naval campaign, the anti-submarine campaign and the later stages of the land campaigns in France and Flanders, Macedonia and Palestine were of decisive importance; they were a presage of what was to happen in that later war. The courage of our airmen in accomplishing so much with the inferior aircraft of these days will live for evermore. Nor let us forget that, in addition, Great Britain was to a great extent the banker, the dockyard and the arsenal of the Alliance, at any rate during the first three years of the war.

Just as many nations contributed, so did many individuals to our war effort: every sailor, soldier and airman, petty officer or NCO who gave up life or limb or endured a burden of misery, suffering and self-sacrifice: every officer and man in the Mercantile Marine: every staff or regimental officer: every commander of our fleets, squadrons, brigades,

[1] The quotation is from Tirpitz's article in the Berlin *Boersenzeitung* of January 14, 1920.

divisions, corps or armies; the whole hierarchy of the Royal Air Force: my own grand old corps, the Royal Marines: every Commander-in-Chief by sea, land and air, who bore a much heavier responsibility than is generally realized: and above all Foch, the greatest military genius whom the war produced. Going up the scale it is necessary to mention the great contribution of the leading members of the Governments of both Asquith and Lloyd George, and at the very top our beloved monarch, King George V, who set a shining example to the whole nation and Empire by his steadfast faith, his ceaseless devotion to duty and his inspiring leadership.

To no single one of these leaders, and to no foreign leader could our victory be ascribed. The war was won primarily by a tremendous combined system of co-ordination and goodwill, which focused all the efforts of all the Allies on the supreme task of defeating the enemy, but which only reached its maximum in the last year of the war. The man who made by far the greatest contribution towards the creation and direction of that system was unquestionably Lloyd George. So, as the storm-swept car drew in at the gates of my modest country home and roused a household anxious at my non-arrival, I said to myself— LLOYD GEORGE WAS THE MAN WHO WON THE WAR.

November 5th. Went up to Town, viz. by 9.50. I am afraid I must have looked very haggard after my trying experiences. Even my lady shorthand writer inquired in tones of real anxiety after my health. The War Cabinet, on Chamberlain's suggestion, passed a formal Minute thanking me for the way I had kept them posted on all that happened in Paris. The Prime Minister said very nice things and remarked that it was a great physical feat on my part; at the end of a meeting he himself was dog-tired, but my work was only begun. This was gratifying. I heard the Prime Minister read the terms of the Austrian armistice in the House of Commons in the afternoon. . . . Was 'punctured' a second time against influenza on my way home.

This was the last occasion on which I was destined to meet the War Cabinet until after the German Armistice was signed, for on the very next day, November 6th, I fell a victim to the scourge of influenza that was spreading all over the world and is said to have exacted a greater toll of human life than the war itself. Every member of my household but one suffered the same misfortune within a day or two, and my wife, hiding the fact that she too was a victim, nursed

us all until, herself brought to death's door, she too had to take
to her bed.

November 17th. On Monday, November 11th, at 11 a.m. the armistice
came into operation. They telephoned it from the office a few minutes before.
Adeline threw open the windows for a few minutes so that, lying in bed, I
might hear the joy bells.

INDEX

FF

*

RETURN TO LIBRARY

DAILY EXPRESS,

On his eightieth birthday Lord Hankey received the following letter from the Prime Minister, which appeared in the press on the following morning:

'I am writing on my own behalf and on behalf of my colleagues in the Cabinet to send you a message of congratulation and good wishes on your eightieth birthday.

'In fashioning the machinery of the Cabinet Secretariat you made a notable contribution to the development of our system of Cabinet Government; and the instrument you created has proved over the years to be a most valuable aid to Ministers in the discharge of their collective business. It must give you great satisfaction that the system which you introduced forty years ago is still in force today.'

That letter describes what Lord Hankey did. This book tells how it was done and the development during the First World War which made it possible. Lord Hankey has not written another history of that war, but the history of the Supreme Command which is, so to speak, its inner history. These pages abound with sidelights on the conduct of the war, the development of the Supreme Command from Balfour to Lloyd George, and the emergence of the Cabinet Secretariat from the Secretariat of the War Cabinet and contains intimate glimpses of the statesmen, sailors and soldiers who guided our affairs to the great victory of 1918. It will remain for long a necessity of all students of war and of government and for the general reader a unique picture of how a great war is conducted, the war which so many still remember.

Some of the tributes that have been paid to the author appear on the back flap.